Oxford excellence for the Caribbean

BOOK 2

STP
Caribbean
Mathematics

FOURTH EDITION

S Chandler
E Smith
K Chan-Tack
W R Griffith
K D Holder
L Bostock
A Shepherd

OXFORD

UNIVERSITY PRESS

Great Clarendon Street, Oxford, OX2 6DP, United Kingdom

Oxford University Press is a department of the University of Oxford. It furthers the University's objective of excellence in research, scholarship, and education by publishing worldwide. Oxford is a registered trade mark of Oxford University Press in the UK and in certain other countries

The Publisher would like to acknowledge the contributions of Karyl Chan-Tack, Wendy Griffith and Kenneth Holder to this series.

First published in 1987

Second edition published by Stanley Thornes (Publishers) Ltd in 1997

Third edition published by Nelson Thornes Ltd in 2005

This edition published by Oxford University Press in 2019

British Library Cataloguing in Publication Data
Data available

978-0-19-842652-3

9 10

Paper used in the production of this book is a natural, recyclable product made from wood grown in sustainable forests. The manufacturing process conforms to the environmental regulations of the country of origin.

Printed in China by Shanghai Offset Printing Products Ltd

Acknowledgements
The publishers would like to thank the following for permissions to use copyright material:

Cover image: Cover image: Radachynskyi/iStock

p160: Jiradelta/iStock; **p160**: tuu sitt/Shutterstock; **p160**: tOOn_in/ Shutterstock; **p162**: Emilio100/Shutterstock; **p162**: MattGrant/iStock; **p162**: Mile Atanasov/Shutterstock

Artwork by Thomson Digital

Although we have made every effort to trace and contact all copyright holders before publication this has not been possible in all cases. If notified, the publisher will rectify any errors or omissions at the earliest opportunity.

The manufacturer's authorised representative in the EU for product safety is Oxford University Press España S.A. of El Parque Empresarial San Fernando de Henares, Avenida de Castilla, 2 – 28830 Madrid (www.oup.es/en or product.safety@oup.com).OUP España S.A. also acts as importer into Spain of products made by the manufacturer.

Contents

Introduction

To the student

This new edition of *STP Caribbean Mathematics Student Book 2* attempts to meet your needs as you begin your study of Mathematics at the Secondary school level. Your learning experiences at this stage lay the foundation for future achievement in CSEC Mathematics and beyond. We are very conscious of your need for success and enjoyment in doing Mathematics, which comes from solving problems correctly. With this in mind, we have divided most of the exercises into three types of question:

Type 1 questions

These are identified by numbers written in bold print, e.g. **12**. They help you to see if you understand the topic being discussed and should be attempted in every chapter you study.

Type 2 questions

These are identified by a single underline under the bold print, e.g. **<u>12</u>**. They are extra questions for you to do and are not more difficult. They should be attempted if you need extra practice or want to do revision at a later time.

Type 3 questions

These are identified by a double underline under the bold print, e.g. **<u>12</u>**. They are for those of you who completed Type 1 questions fairly easily and want to attempt questions that are more challenging.

Multiple choice questions

Multiple choice questions have been used throughout the book to help you become more familiar with the format of your assessments at CSEC.

Mixed exercises

Most chapters end with Mixed exercises to help you advance your critical thinking, problem-solving and computational skills. These exercises will also help you revise what you have done, either when you have finished the chapter or as you prepare for examinations.

Use of calculator

You should be able to use a calculator accurately before you leave school. We suggest that you use a calculator mainly to check your answers. Whether you use a calculator or do the computations yourself, always estimate your answer first and always ask the question, 'Does my answer make sense?'

Suggestions for use of student book

- Break up the material in a chapter into manageable parts.

- Have paper and a pencil with you always when you are studying mathematics.

- Write down and look up the meaning of all new vocabulary you encounter.

- Read all questions carefully and rephrase them in your own words.

- Remember that each question contains all the information you need to solve the problem. Do not look only at the numbers that are given.

- Practise your mathematics. This will ensure your success!

You are therefore advised to try to solve as many problems as you can.
Above all, don't be afraid to make mistakes as you are learning. The greatest mathematicians all made many mistakes as they tried to solve problems.

You are now on your way to success in mathematics – GOOD LUCK!

To the teacher

In writing this series, the authors attempted to present the topics in such a way that students will understand the connections among topics in mathematics, and be encouraged to see and use mathematics as a means to make sense of the real world. The exercises have been carefully graded to make the content more accessible to students.

This new edition is designed to:

1   Assist you in helping students to

- attain important mathematical skills

- connect mathematics to their everyday lives and understand its role in the development of our contemporary society

- see the importance of critical thinking skills in everyday problems

- discover the fun of doing mathematics both individually and collaboratively

- develop a positive attitude towards doing mathematics.

2   Encourage you to include historical information about mathematics in your teaching.

Topics from the history of mathematics have been incorporated to ensure that mathematics is not dissociated from its past. This should lead to an increase in the level of enthusiasm, interest and fascination among students, thus enriching the teaching and learning experiences in the mathematics lessons.

Investigations

'Investigation' is included in this revised STP Caribbean Mathematics series. This is in keeping with the requirements of the latest Lower and Secondary and CSEC syllabuses in the region.

Investigations are used to provide students with the opportunity to explore hands-on and minds-on mathematics. At the same time, teachers are presented with open-ended explorations to enhance their mathematical instruction.

It is expected that the tasks will

- encourage problem solving and reasoning
- develop communication skills and the ability to work collaboratively
- connect various mathematical concepts and theories.

Suggestions

1   At the start of each lesson, give a brief outline of the topic to be covered in the lesson. As examples are given, refer back to the outline to show how the example fits into it.

2   List terms that you consider new to the students and solicit additional words from them. Encourage students to read from the text and make their own vocabulary list. Remember that mathematics is a foreign language. The ability to communicate mathematically must involve the careful use of the correct terminology.

3   Have students construct different ways to phrase questions. This helps students to see mathematics as a language. Students, especially in the junior classes, tend to concentrate on the numerical or 'maths' part of the question and pay little attention to the information that is required to solve the problem.

4   When solving problems, have students identify their own problem-solving strategies and listen to the strategies of others. This practice should create an atmosphere of discussion in the class centred on different approaches to solving the same problem.

As the students try to solve problems on their own they will make mistakes. This is expected, as this was the experience of the inventors of mathematics: they tried, guessed, made many mistakes and worked for hours, days and sometimes years before reaching a solution.

There are enough problems in the exercises to allow the students to try and try again. The excitement, disappointment and struggle with a problem until a solution is found will create rewarding mathematical experiences.

1 Working with numbers

Did you know?

The googol (10^{100}) is said to have been so named by Milton Sirotta, the 9-year-old nephew of the American mathematician Edward Kasner.

You need to know...

✔ the meaning of place value in numbers
✔ how to work with fractions, decimals and percentages.

Key words

approximation, associative, closure, commutative, decimal place, distributive, identity element, index (plural indices), integer, inverse element, rough estimate, scientific notation, significant figures, standard form

Working with integers

Integers are all the positive and negative whole numbers including zero.

The number line is a useful tool in representing integers.

The list below summarises the rules for working with integers that you met in Book 1.

The rules for multiplying integers are:

- when two positive numbers are multiplied the answer is positive (e.g. $3 \times 4 = 12$)

- when two negative numbers are multiplied the answer is positive (e.g. $-3 \times -4 = 12$)

- when a positive number and a negative number are multiplied the answer is negative (e.g. $-3 \times 4 = -12$ and $3 \times -4 = -12$).

The rules for dividing integers are:

- when a negative number is divided by a positive number and when a positive number is divided by a negative number the answer is negative (e.g. $-12 \div 3 = -4$ and $12 \div -3 = -4$)

- when a negative number is divided by a negative number the answer is positive (e.g. $-12 \div -3 = 4$).

The rules for a calculation that involves a mixture of brackets, multiplication, division, addition and subtraction are:

- work out calculations inside brackets first

- then do multiplication and division

- finally do addition and subtraction.

For example, $10 + 3 \times (6 - 8) = 10 + 3 \times -2 = 10 - 6 = 4$

The mnemonic **B**less **M**y **D**ear **A**unt **S**ally may help you remember this order.

Exercise 1a

Calculate:

1 $2 \times (-3)$

2 $2 - (-4)$

3 $(-50) \div (-10)$

4 $(-6) \div (-12)$

5 $4(5 + 1) \times (-3)(3 - 2)$

6 $8 - 2(15 - 12)$

7 $12 \times 4 - 3(6 - 18)$

8 $2 - 4 \div 3(6 - 7)$

9 $\dfrac{2 - 8}{3 - 5}$

10 $\dfrac{2 \times (16 - 5)}{(12 + 10) \times (-3)}$

11 $(-8)(5 - 10) \div 2(4 - 16)$

12 $3 \times 3 + 16 \times 6 - 2 \div (-8)$

Laws of numbers

From previous work you know that

$$8 + 17 = 17 + 8 \quad \text{and that} \quad 8 \times 17 = 17 \times 8$$

i.e. for addition and multiplication the order of the numbers does not matter. We say that numbers are *commutative* under addition and multiplication.

On the other hand $8 - 17$ and $17 - 8$ do not give the same answer; neither do $8 \div 17$ and $17 \div 8$.

In this case numbers are *non-commutative* under subtraction and division.

You have also seen that

$$5 + (6 + 7) = (5 + 6) + 7 = 5 + 6 + 7$$

and that
$$4 \times (6 \times 8) = (4 \times 6) \times 8 = 4 \times 6 \times 8$$

i.e. the brackets can be removed without changing the answer, so there is no ambiguity in writing $5 + 6 + 7$ or $4 \times 6 \times 8$.
This illustrates the *associative* law for the addition and multiplication of numbers.

On the other hand, for $7 - (5 + 6)$ and $(6 + 9) \div 3$ the answers will be different if the brackets are removed. Subtraction and division of numbers **do not** satisfy the associative law.

In other calculations you know that $5(10 + 9) = 5 \times 10 + 5 \times 9$.

Here multiplication is distributing itself over addition. This is the *distributive* law and is the only law expressing a relation between two basic operations.

Exercise 1b

In questions **1** to **10**, which law, if any (associative, commutative or distributive), does each of the statements illustrate?

1. $3 \times (4 \times 3) = (3 \times 4) \times 3$
2. $10 + (5 + 7) = (10 + 5) + 7$
3. $9 + 12 = 12 + 9$
4. $7 \times (3 + 5) = 7 \times 3 + 7 \times 5$
5. $7 + 3 + 2 = 2 + 7 + 3$
6. $(4 \times 6) \times 2 = 4 \times (6 \times 2)$
7. $8 \times (4 - 1) = 8 \times 4 + 8 \times (-1)$
8. $3 \times (3 + 2) = 3 \times 3 + 3 \times 2$
9. $5 \times 4 = 4 \times 5$
10. $6 \times (6 - 2) = 6 \times 6 - 6 \times 2$

The identity element

In a set of numbers when 0 (zero) is added to any number it preserves the identity of that number, i.e. it does not change its value, e.g. $5 + 0 = 5$ and $0 + 7 = 7$ so 0 is the *identity element* for addition.

The identity element for multiplication is 1. Multiplying a number by 1 does not change its value, e.g. $6 \times 1 = 6$ and $1 \times 10 = 10$.

The inverse element

For every number, another number can be found so that the result of adding it to the original number is the identity element. The second number is called the *inverse* of the first number.

For addition the identity element is 0 so the inverse of 8 under addition is -8 and the inverse of -4 is 4.

For every number, except 0, another number can be found such that when it multiplies the given number, it produces the identity for multiplication, namely 1. For example, for multiplication, the inverse of 3 is $\frac{1}{3}$, because $3 \times \frac{1}{3} = 1$.

Closure

You will also have noticed that if you start with a number from the set $\{\ldots, -2, -1, 0, 1, 2, \ldots\}$ and perform any of the operations $+$, $-$ or $\times$ the result is still a member of the set. However, if you divide one member of the set by another you may get a number that is not in the set, e.g. $17 \div 8$.

We say that the numbers in the set $\{\ldots, -2, -1, 0, 1, 2, \ldots\}$ are closed under $+$, $-$ and $\times$ but not under $\div$.

Exercise 1c

1   In the statement $10 + 0 = 0 + 10$ how would you describe the zero (0)?

2   In the statement $1 \times 8 = 8 \times 1$ how would you describe the 1?

3   In the statement $10 + (-10) = 0$ how would you describe the -10?

4   What is the inverse of 9 under addition?

5   What is the inverse of 9 under multiplication?

6   What is the inverse of -5 under addition?

In questions **7** to **14**, write down the letter that goes with the correct answer.

7   The inverse of 4 under addition is

    A -4 **B** 0   **C** $\frac{1}{4}$ **D** 4

8 The inverse of 4 under multiplication is

    A 4   **B** -4 **C** $\dfrac{1}{4}$ **D** 0

9 $6 + 0 = 6$ so 0 is

    A not a member of the set of integers

    B the identity element under addition

    C the inverse under addition

    D the inverse under multiplication.

10 a and b are integers and $a + b = c$. c is

    A an integer

    B the identity element

    C the inverse under addition

    D the inverse under multiplication.

11 x and y are even numbers and $x + y = z$. z is

    A an even number

    B an odd number

    C a fraction less than 1

    D the identity element under addition.

12 p and q are odd numbers and $p + q = r$. r is

    A a fraction smaller than 1

    B the inverse of p under addition

    C an odd number

    D an even number.

13 a is an odd number, b is an even number, and $a + b = c$. c is

    A the identity element under addition

    B the inverse of b under addition

    C an odd number

    D an even number.

14 a is an odd number, b is twice the value of a, and $a + b = c$. c is

    A an odd number

    B an even number

    C the inverse of b under addition

    D the identity element under addition.

15 a, b and c are integers. Which of the following statements are always true?

    A $a + b = b + a$ **E** $a \div b$ is an integer

    B $a - b = b - a$ **F** $a + b \times c = a \times c + b$

    C $a + b - c = a - c + b$ **G** $a \div b \times c = a \times c \div b$

    D $a \times b$ is an integer

Changing between fractions, decimals and percentages

- To change a fraction to a decimal, divide the numerator by the denominator.

  The fraction $\frac{3}{8}$ means $3 \div 8$.

  You can calculate $3 \div 8$:

  $$\begin{array}{r} 0.375 \\ 8\overline{)3.000} \end{array}$$

  So $\frac{3}{8} = 0.375$

  Any fraction can be treated like this.

- To change a decimal to a fraction express it as a number of tenths or hundredths, etc. and, if possible, simplify.

  The decimal 0.6 can be written $\frac{6}{10}$, which simplifies to $\frac{3}{5}$,

  and the decimal 1.85 can be written $1\frac{85}{100}$, which simplifies to $1\frac{17}{20}$.

- To change a percentage to a decimal divide the percentage by 100.

  To express a percentage as a decimal, start by expressing it as a fraction, but *do not simplify,* because dividing by 100, or by a multiple of 100, is easy.

  For example $44\% = \frac{44}{100} = 44 \div 100 = 0.44$ and $12.5\% = \frac{12.5}{100} = 12.5 \div 100 = 0.125$

- To change a decimal to a percentage simply multiply by 100.

  For example $0.34 = 34\%$ and $1.55 = 155\%$.

- To change a percentage to a fraction divide by 100 and simplify.

  We know that 20% of the cars in a car park means $\frac{20}{100}$ of the cars there.

  Now $\frac{20}{100}$ can be simplified to the equivalent fraction $\frac{1}{5}$, i.e. $20\% = \frac{1}{5}$.

  Similarly, 45% of the sweets in a bag means the same as $\frac{45}{100}$ of them

  and $\frac{45}{100} = \frac{9}{20}$, i.e. $45\% = \frac{9}{20}$.

- To change a fraction to a percentage change it to a decimal, then multiply by 100.

  You can write a fraction as a percentage in two steps.

  First write the fraction as a decimal. For example, $\frac{4}{5} = 4 \div 5 = 0.8$

  Then change the decimal to a percentage: $0.8 \times 100\% = 80\%$.

Exercise 1d

1   Work out each fraction as a decimal.

    a $\dfrac{3}{4}$ **b** $\dfrac{3}{5}$ **c** $\dfrac{3}{10}$ **d** $\dfrac{3}{20}$ **e** $\dfrac{7}{8}$ **f** $\dfrac{6}{25}$

2   Work out $\dfrac{9}{20}$ as a decimal.

    Now decide which is larger, $\dfrac{9}{20}$ or 0.47?

3   Write each decimal as a fraction in its lowest terms, using mixed numbers where necessary.

    a 0.06   **b** 0.004   **c** 15.5   **d** 2.01   **e** 3.25

In questions **4** and **5** write each decimal as a fraction in its lowest terms.

4   It is estimated that 0.86 of the families in Northgate Street own a car.

5   There were 360 seats on the aircraft and only 0.05 of them were vacant.

6   Write these decimals as percentages.

    a 0.3   **b** 0.2   **c** 0.7   **d** 0.035   **e** 0.925

7   Write these decimals as percentages.

    a 1.32   **c** 2.4   **e** 2.555

    b 1.5   **d** 1.05

Remember that 1 is 100%, so 1.66 = 100% + 66% = 166%.

8   Write these percentages as decimals.

    a 45%   **b** 60%   **c** 95%   **d** 5.5%   **e** 12.5%

9   Express each percentage as a fraction in its lowest terms.

    a 40%   **b** 65%   **c** 54%   **d** 25%

10   Express each fraction as a percentage.

    a $\dfrac{2}{5}$ **b** $\dfrac{3}{20}$ **c** $\dfrac{21}{50}$ **d** $\dfrac{15}{40}$

In questions **11** to **14** express the given percentage as a fraction in its lowest terms.

11   Last summer 60% of the pupils in my class went on holiday.

12   At my youth club only 35% of the members are boys.

13   The postal service claims that 95% of the letters posted arrive the following day.

14   A survey showed that 32% of the pupils in a year group needed to wear glasses.

In each question from **15** to **18** express the fraction as a percentage.

15   At a youth club $\frac{17}{20}$ of those present took part in at least one sporting activity.

16   About $\frac{17}{50}$ of first-year pupils watch more than 20 hours of television a week.

17   Approximately $\frac{3}{5}$ of sixteen-year-olds have a Saturday job.

18   Recently, at the local garage, $\frac{1}{8}$ of the cars tested failed to get a test certificate.

19   Copy and complete the following table.

Fraction	Percentage	Decimal
$\frac{3}{5}$	60%	0.6
$\frac{4}{5}$		
	75%	
		0.7
$\frac{11}{20}$		
	44%	

20   The registers showed that only 0.05 of the pupils in the first year had 100% attendance last term.

    a   What fraction is this?

    b   What percentage of the first-year pupils had a 100% attendance last term?

21   Marion spends $\frac{21}{50}$ of her income on food and lodgings.

    a   What percentage is this?

    b   As a decimal, what part of her total income does she spend on food and lodging?

22   Marmalade consists of 28% fruit, $\frac{3}{5}$ sugar and the remainder water.

    a   What fraction of the marmalade is fruit?

    b   What percentage of the marmalade is sugar?

    c   What percentage is water?

23   An alloy is 60% copper, $\frac{7}{20}$ nickel and the remainder is tin.

    a   What fraction is copper?

    b   What percentage is **i** nickel **ii** either nickel or copper?

    c   Express the part that is tin as a decimal.

Positive indices

We have seen that 3^2 means 3×3

and that $2 \times 2 \times 2$ can be written as 2^3

The small number at the top is called the *index* or *power*. (The plural of index is indices.)

It follows that 2 can be written as 2^1, although we would not normally do so.

> 5^1 means 5

Exercise 1e

Find:

1	3^2		**7**	2^7
2	4^1		**8**	10^1
3	10^2		**9**	4^3
4	5^3		**10**	10^4
5	10^3		**11**	10^6
6	3^4		**12**	3^3

> $2^7 = 2 \times 2 \times 2 \times 2 \times 2 \times 2 \times 2$

Find the value of:

13	7.2×10^3	**17**	2.75×10^1			
14	8.93×10^2	**18**	5.37×10^5			
15	6.5×10^4	**19**	4.63×10^1	**21**	7.09×10^2
16	3.82×10^3	**20**	5.032×10^2	**22**	6.978×10^1

> $10^3 = 10 \times 10 \times 10$

Multiplying numbers written in index form

We can write $2^2 \times 2^3$ as a single number in index form because

$$2^2 \times 2^3 = (2 \times 2) \times (2 \times 2 \times 2)$$

$$= 2 \times 2 \times 2 \times 2 \times 2$$

$$= 2^5$$

$$\therefore \qquad 2^2 \times 2^3 = 2^{2+3} = 2^5$$

But we cannot do the same with $2^2 \times 5^3$ because the numbers multiplied together are not all 2s (nor are they all 5s).

We can multiply together different powers of the *same* number by adding the indices but we cannot multiply together powers of different numbers in this way.

Exercise 1f

Write as a single expression in index form:

1 $3^5 \times 3^2$ 5 $b^3 \times b^2$

2 $7^5 \times 7^3$ 6 $5^4 \times 5^4$

3 $9^2 \times 9^8$ 7 $12^4 \times 12^5$ 9 $4^7 \times 4^9$

4 $2^4 \times 2^7$ 8 $p^6 \times p^8$ 10 $r^5 \times r^3$

$3^5 \times 3^2 = 3^{5+2}$

Dividing numbers written in index form

If we want to write $2^5 \div 2^2$ as a single number in index form then

$$2^5 \div 2^2 = \frac{2^5}{2^2} = \frac{\cancel{2} \times \cancel{2} \times 2 \times 2 \times 2}{\cancel{2} \times \cancel{2}} = \frac{2^3}{1}$$

i.e. $$\frac{2^5}{2^2} = 2^{5-2} = 2^3$$

We can divide different powers of the *same* number by subtracting the indices.

Exercise 1g

Write each as a single expression in index form:

1 $4^4 \div 4^2$ 6 $15^8 \div 15^4$ 11 $6^4 \times 6^7$ 16 $2^2 \times 2^4 \times 2^3$

2 $7^9 \div 7^3$ 7 $6^{12} \div 6^7$ 12 $3^9 \div 3^6$ 17 $4^2 \times 4^3 \div 4^4$

3 $5^6 \div 5^5$ 8 $b^7 \div b^5$ 13 $2^8 \div 2^7$ 18 $a^2 \times a^2 \div a^3$

4 $10^8 \div 10^3$ 9 $9^{15} \div 9^{14}$ 14 $a^9 \times a^3$ 19 $3^6 \div 3^2 \times 3^4$

5 $q^9 \div q^5$ 10 $p^4 \div p^3$ 15 $c^6 \div c^3$ 20 $b^2 \times b^3 \times b^4$

Investigation

1   Everyone has two biological parents.

Going back one generation, each of your parents has two biological parents.

Copy and complete the tree – fill in the number of ancestors for five generations back.

Do not fill in names!

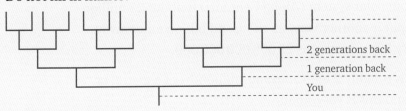

2 generations back
1 generation back
You

2   Giving your answers as a power of 2, how many ancestors does this table suggest you have

   a   five generations back

   b   six generations back

   c   ten generations back?

3   If we assume that each generation spans 25 years, how many generations are needed to go back 1000 years?

4   Find the number of ancestors the table suggests that you would expect to have 6000 years back. Give your answer as a power of 2.
    What assumptions are made to get this answer?

5   About 6000 years ago, according to the Bible, Adam and Eve were the only people on Earth. This contradicts the answer from part **4**.
    Suggest some reasons for this contradiction.

Mixed questions on indices

Exercise 1h

Find the value of:

1   2^2

2   4^3

3   5^3

4   3^4

5   4^1

6   2.41×10^3

7   4.971×10^2

8   5.92×10^4

9   7.834×10^2

10   3.05×10^4

Write each as a single number in index form:

11 $2^3 \times 2^4$

12 $4^6 \div 4^3$

13 $3^2 \times 3^4$

14 $a^4 \times a^3$

15 $a^7 \div a^3$

Standard form

The nearest star beyond our solar system (Alpha Centauri) is about 25 million million miles away, or to put it another way, 25 thousand billion miles away. Written in figures this very large number is 25 000 000 000 000.

The diameter of an atom is roughly 2 ten-thousand-millionths of a metre, or 0.000 000 000 2 metres, and this is very small.

These numbers are cumbersome to write down and, until we have counted the zeros, we cannot tell their size. We need a way of writing such numbers in a shorter form from which it is easier to judge their size: the form that we use is called *standard form*. It is also called *scientific notation*.

Written in standard form 25 000 000 000 000 is 2.5×10^{13}.

> Standard form is a number between 1 and 10
> multiplied by a power of 10.

So 1.3×10^2 and 2.86×10^4 are in standard form, but 13×10^3 is not in standard form because the first number is not between 1 and 10.

Exercise 1i

Each of the following numbers is written in standard form. Write them as ordinary numbers.

1 3.78×10^3

2 1.26×10^3

3 5.3×10^6

4 7.4×10^{14}

5 1.3×10^4

6 3.67×10^6

7 3.04×10^4

8 8.503×10^4

9 4.25×10^{12}

10 6.43×10^8

Changing numbers into standard form

To change 6800 into standard form, the decimal point has to be placed between the 6 and the 8 to give a number between 1 and 10.

Counting then tells us that, to change 6.8 to 6800, we need to move the decimal point three places to the right (i.e. to multiply by 10^3)

i.e. $6800 = 6.8 \times 1000 = 6.8 \times 10 \times 10 \times 10 = 6.8 \times 10^3$

Exercise 1j

Change the following numbers into standard form:

1	2500	**12**	547 000	**23**	40.5
2	630	**13**	30 600	**24**	503 000 000
3	15 300	**14**	4 060 000	**25**	99 000 000
4	260 000	**15**	704	**26**	84
5	9900	**16**	79.3	**27**	351
6	39 070	**17**	80 600	**28**	36
7	4 500 000	**18**	60.5	**29**	5090
8	530 000 000	**19**	7 080 000	**30**	268 000
9	40 000	**20**	560 800	**31**	30.7
10	80 000 000 000	**21**	5 300 000 000 000		
11	26 030	**22**	708 000		

Investigation

If you read about computers, you will notice specifications such as '4 GB RAM' or '1 TB hard disk'. GB stands for gigabytes and TB stand for terabytes.

'Giga' and 'tera' are prefixes used to describe very large numbers.

There are other prefixes used to describe very small numbers.

Find out what giga and tera mean.

Find out what other prefixes are used to describe very large and very small numbers and what they mean.

Approximations: whole numbers

We saw in Book 1 that it is sometimes necessary to approximate given numbers by rounding them off to the nearest 10, 100, ... For example, if you measured your height in millimetres as 1678 mm, it would be reasonable to say that you were 1680 mm tall to the nearest 10 mm.

The rule is that if you are rounding off to the nearest 10 you look at the units. If there are 5 or more units you add one on to the tens. If there are fewer than 5 units you leave the tens alone.

For example, 67 is closer to 70 than to 60, as you can see on the number line. So 67 = 70 to the nearest ten.

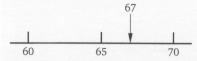

Similar rules apply to rounding off to the nearest 100 (look at the tens); to the nearest 1000 (look at the hundreds); and so on.

For example, 435 is closer to 400 than to 500, so 453 = 400 to the nearest hundred.

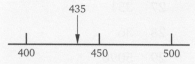

Round off 1853 to

a   the nearest ten

b   the nearest hundred

c   the nearest thousand.

a   185⋮3 = 1850 to the nearest 10 (put a cut-off line (⋮) after the 10s)

b   18⋮53 = 1900 to the nearest 100 (put a cut-off line (⋮) after the 100s)

c   1⋮853 = 2000 to the nearest 1000 (put a cut-off line (⋮) after the 1000s)

Round off each of the following numbers to

a   the nearest ten   **b**   the nearest hundred   **c**   the nearest thousand.

1	1547	**3**	2750	**5**	68414	**7**	4066	**9**	53804	**11**	4981
2	8739	**4**	36835	**6**	5729	**8**	7507	**10**	6007	**12**	8699

A building firm stated that, to the nearest 100, it built 2600 homes last year. What is the greatest number of homes that it could have built and what is the least number of homes that it could have built?

Look at this number line.

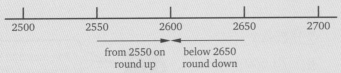

The smallest whole number that can be rounded up to 2600 is 2550.

The biggest whole number that can be rounded down to 2600 is 2649.

So the firm built at most 2649 homes and at least 2550 homes.

13 A bag of marbles is said to contain 50 marbles to the nearest 10. What is the greatest number of marbles that could be in the bag and what is the least number of marbles that could be in the bag?

14 To the nearest thousand, the attendance at a particular international football match was 45 000. What is the largest number that could have been there and what is the smallest number that could have attended?

15 1500 people came to the school bazaar. If this number is correct to the nearest hundred, give the maximum and the minimum number of people that could have come.

16 The annual accounts of Scrub plc (soap manufacturers) gave the company's profit as $3 000 000 to the nearest million. What is the least amount of profit that the company could have made?

17 The chairman of A. Brick (Builders) plc said that they employ 2000 people. If this number is correct to the nearest 100, what is the least number of employees that the company can have?

Approximations: decimals

If you measure your height in centimetres as 167.8 cm, it would be reasonable to say that, to the nearest centimetre, you are 168 cm tall.

We write 167.8 = 168 correct to the nearest unit.

If you measure your height in metres as 1.678 m, it would be reasonable to say that, to the nearest $\frac{1}{100}$ m. you are 1.68 m tall.

Hundredths are represented in the second decimal place so we say that 1.678 = 1.68 correct to 2 *decimal places* (abbreviated to 2 d.p.).

Exercise 1I

Give each of the following numbers correct to

a	2 decimal places	**b**	1 decimal place	**c**	the nearest unit:

1	2.758	**6**	3.896
2	7.371	**7**	8.936
3	16.987	**8**	73.649
4	23.758	**9**	6.896
5	9.858	**10**	55.575

You may find it helpful to draw a cut-off line.

Give the following numbers correct to the number of decimal places given in brackets:

11	5.07	(1)	**16**	0.9752	(3)
12	0.0087	(3)	**17**	5.5508	(3)
13	7.897	(2)	**18**	285.59	(1)
14	34.82	(1)	**19**	6.749	(1)
15	0.007831	(4)	**20**	9.999	(2)

 Puzzle

What is the largest number you can make with two nines?

Significant figures

In the previous two sections we used a height of 1678 mm as an example. This height was measured in three different units and then rounded off:

in the first case to   1680 mm   correct to the nearest 10 mm,

in the second case to   168 cm   correct to the nearest centimetre,

in the third case to   1.68 m   correct to 2 d.p.

We could also give this measurement in kilometres, to the same degree of accuracy, as 0.00168 km correct to 5 d.p.

Notice that the three figures 1, 6 and 8 occur in all four numbers and that it is the 8 that is the corrected figure.

The figures 1, 6 and 8 are called the *significant figures* and in all four cases the numbers are given correct to 3 significant figures. Note that significant figure is abbreviated to s.f.

Using significant figures rather than place values (i.e. tens, units, first d.p., second d.p., ...) has advantages. For example, if you are asked to measure your height and give the answer correct to 3 significant figures, then you can choose any convenient unit. You do not need to be told which unit to use and which place value in that unit to correct your answer to.

The first significant figure is the **non-zero** digit with the highest place value. For example, for the number 170.6, the digit with the highest place value is 1.

So l is the first significant figure in 170.6.
The second significant figure is the next digit to the right (7 in this case).
The third significant figure is the next digit to the right again (0 in this case), and so on.

In 0.0305, the first non-zero digit is 3, so this is the first significant figure. The first significant figure can never be zero, but zeros after the first significant figure are significant figures. The next figure to the right of 3 in 0.0305 is 0, so 0 is the second significant figure.

Exercise 1m

For the number 0.001 503, write

a   the first significant figure

b   the third significant figure.

a   The highest non-zero place value digit in 0.001 503 is 1 so the first s.f. is 1.

b   The third s.f. is 0.   Note that zeros after the first significant figure *are* included.

For each of the following numbers write the significant figure specified in the bracket:

1	36.2	(1st)	**6**	5.083	(3rd)
2	378.5	(3rd)	**7**	34.807	(4th)
3	0.0867	(2nd)	**8**	0.076 03	(3rd)
4	3.786	(3rd)	**9**	54.06	(3rd)
5	47 632	(2nd)	**10**	5.7087	(4th)

Exercise 1n

Give 32 685 correct to 1 s.f.

The highest non-zero place value digit is 3, so 3 is the first significant figure.

(As before, to correct to 1 s.f. we look at the second s.f.: if it is 5 or more we add one to the first s.f.; if it is less than 5 we leave the first s.f. alone.)

So $\qquad$ 3̣2685 = 30 000 to 1 s.f.

Give the following numbers correct to 1 s.f.:

1	59 727	4	586 359	7	51 488	10	908
2	4164	5	80 755	8	4099	11	26
3	4 396 185	6	476	9	667 505	12	980

Give the following numbers correct to 2 s.f.:

13	4673	16	892 759	19	72 601	22	53 908
14	57 341	17	6992	20	444	23	476
15	59 700	18	9973	21	50 047	24	597

Give 0.021 94 correct to 3 s.f.

2 is the first s.f. so 9 is the third s.f.

(The fourth s.f. is 4 so we leave the third s.f. alone.)
So $\qquad$ 0.0219̣4 = 0.0219 to 3 s.f.

Give the following numbers correct to 3 s.f.:

25	0.008 463	28	78.49	31	7.5078	34	53.978
26	0.825 716	29	46.8451	32	369.649		
27	5.8374	30	0.007 854 7	33	0.989 624		

Give each of the following numbers correct to the number of significant figures indicated in the brackets.

35	46.931 06	(2)	40	4537	(1)
36	0.006 845 03	(4)	41	37.856 72	(3)
37	576 335	(1)	42	6973	(2)
38	497	(2)	43	0.070 865	(3)
39	7.824 38	(3)	44	0.067 34	(1)

Find $50 \div 8$ correct to 2 s.f.

(To give an answer correct to 2 s.f. we first work to 3 s.f.)

$$\begin{array}{r} 6.2\vdots5 \\ 8\overline{)\,50.00} \end{array}$$

So $\qquad\qquad\qquad 50 \div 8 = 6.3$ to 2 s.f.

Give, correct to 2 s.f.:

45	$20 \div 6$	**47**	$25 \div 2$	**49**	$125 \div 9$	**<u>51</u>**	$73 \div 3$	**<u>53</u>**	$0.23 \div 9$
46	$10 \div 6$	**48**	$53 \div 4$	**<u>50</u>**	$143 \div 5$	**<u>52</u>**	$0.7 \div 3$	**<u>54</u>**	$0.0013 \div 3$

? **Puzzle**

Everton Giles stands on the middle rung of a ladder. He climbs 3 rungs higher but has forgotten something so descends 7 rungs to get it. He now goes up 16 rungs and reaches the top of the ladder. How many rungs are there to the ladder?

Rough estimates

If you were asked to find 1.397×62.54 you could do it by long multiplication or you could use a calculator. Whichever method you choose, it is essential first to make a rough estimate of the answer. You will then know whether the actual answer you get is reasonable or not.

One way of estimating the answer to a calculation is to write each number correct to 1 significant figure.

So $\qquad\qquad 1\vdots397 \times 6\vdots2.57 \approx 1 \times 60 = 60$

Exercise 1p

Correct each number to 1 s.f. and hence give a rough answer to:

a 9.524×0.0837 $\qquad\qquad$ **b** $\quad 54.72 \div 0.761$

a $\quad 9\vdots524 \times 0.08\vdots37 \approx 10 \times 0.08 = 0.8$

b $\quad \dfrac{5\vdots4.72}{0.7\vdots61} \approx \dfrac{50}{0.8} = \dfrac{500}{8} = 62.5$

$\qquad\qquad\qquad = 60$ $\quad$ (giving $500 \div 8$ to 1 s.f.)

Correct each number to 1 s.f. and hence give a rough answer to each of the following calculations:

1	4.78×23.7	**6**	$82.8 \div 146$	**11**	34.7×21	**16**	$0.0326 \div 12.4$
2	56.3×0.573	**7**	0.632×0.845	**12**	8.63×0.523	**17**	$0.007\,24 \times 0.783$
3	$0.0674 \div 5.24$	**8**	0.0062×574	**13**	$34.9 \div 15.8$	**18**	$3581 \div 45$
4	354.6×0.0475	**9**	$7.835 \div 6.493$	**14**	$0.47 \div 0.714$	**19**	1097×94
5	576×256	**10**	4736×729	**15**	$985 \div 57.2$	**20**	45.07×0.0327

Correct each number to 1 s.f. and hence estimate $\dfrac{0.048 \times 3.275}{0.367}$ to 1 s.f.

$$\frac{0.048 \times 3.275}{0.367} \approx \frac{0.05 \times 3}{0.4} = \frac{0.15}{0.4} = \frac{1.5}{4}$$

$$= 0.4 \text{ (to 1 s.f.)}$$

21	$\dfrac{3.87 \times 5.24}{2.13}$	**25**	$\dfrac{43.8 \times 3.62}{4.72}$	**29**	$\dfrac{0.527}{6.41 \times 0.738}$
22	$\dfrac{0.636 \times 2.63}{5.47}$	**26**	$\dfrac{89.03 \times 0.07937}{5.92}$	**30**	$\dfrac{57.8}{0.057 \times 6.93}$
23	$\dfrac{21.78 \times 4.278}{7.96}$	**27**	$\dfrac{975 \times 0.636}{40.78}$		
24	$\dfrac{6.38 \times 0.185}{0.628}$	**28**	$\dfrac{8.735}{5.72 \times 5.94}$		

Calculations: multiplication and division

display

When you key in a number on your calculator it appears on the display. Check that the number on display is the number that you intended to enter.

Also check that you press the correct operator, i.e. press × to multiply and ÷ to divide.

To find 38.4×0.67, first estimate:

$$38.4 \times 0.67 \approx 40 \times 0.7 = 28$$

On your calculator, press [3] [8] [.] [4] [×] [0] [.] [6] [7] [=]

The display shows 25.728, so $38.4 \times 0.67 = 25.7$ correct to 3 s.f.

Exercise 1q

First make a rough estimate of the answer. Then use your calculator to give the
answer correct to 3 significant figures.

1   2.16×3.28

2   2.63×2.87

3   1.48×4.74

4   4.035×2.116

5   3.142×2.925

6   6.053×1.274

7   2.304×3.251

8   8.426×1.086

9   $5.839 \div 3.618$

10 $6.834 \div 4.382$

11 $9.571 \div 2.518$

12 $5.393 \div 3.593$

13 $7.384 \div 2.51$

14 $4.931 \div 3.204$

15 $8.362 \div 5.823$

16 23.4×56.7

17 384×21.8

18 45.8×143.7

19 $537.8 \div 34.6$

20 $45.35 \div 6.82$

21 63.8×2.701

22 $40.3 \div 2.74$

23 $400 \div 35.7$

24 $(34.2)^2$

25 5007×2.51

26 $5703 \div 154.8$

27 39.03×49.94

28 $2000 \div 52.66$

29 $(36.8)^2$

30 $29\,006 \div 2.015$

31 0.366×7.37

32 0.0526×0.372

33 $6.924 \times 0.007\,93$

34 0.638×825

35 52×0.0895

36 0.0826×0.582

37 24.78×0.0724

38 0.00835×0.617

39 0.5824×6.813

40 $(0.74)^2$

41 $0.583 \div 4.82$

42 $0.628 \div 7.61$

43 $0.493 \div 1.253$

44 $0.518 \div 5.047$

45 $82.7 \div 593$

46 $89.5 \div 0.724$

47 $38.07 \div 0.682$

48 $5.71 \div 0.0623$

49 $7.045 \div 0.0378$

50 $6.888 \div 0.0072$

51 $45.37 \div 0.925$

52 $8.41 \div 0.000\,748$

53 $6.934 \div 0.0829$

54 $0.824 \div 0.362$

55 $0.572 \div 0.851$

56 $0.528 \div 0.0537$

57 $0.571 \div 0.824$

58 $0.0455 \div 0.0613$

59 $0.006 \div 0.04\,703$

60 $0.824 \div 0.000\,08$

61 $5000 \div 0.789$

62 $(0.078)^2$

63 0.0608×573

64 $(78.5)^3$

65 $\dfrac{3.782 \times 0.467}{4.89}$

66 $4.88 \times 0.004\,17$

67 $0.9467 \div 7683$

68 $0.0467 \div 0.000\,074$

69 $(0.00031)^2$

70 $\dfrac{54.9 \times 36.6}{0.406}$

71 $68.41 \div 392.9$

72 $0.0482 \div 0.002\,89$

73 $(0.0527)^3$

74 $\dfrac{0.857 \times 8.109}{0.5188}$

Mixed exercises

Exercise 1r

1   Find the value of 4^3.

2   Simplify $b^5 \div b^2$.

3   Find the value of $\dfrac{3^2 \times 3^3}{3^5}$.

4   Write 36 400 in standard form.

5   Give 57 934 correct to 1 s.f.

6   Give 0.061 374 correct to 3 s.f.

7   Find 0.582 × 6.382, giving your answer correct to 3 s.f.

8   Find 45.823 ÷ 15.89, giving your answer correct to 3 s.f.

Exercise 1s

1   Find the value of 6^3.

2   Write $\dfrac{2^4 \times 2^2}{2^3}$ as a single number in index form.

3   Find the value of $5^6 \div 5^3$.

4   Simplify $a^2 \times a^4 \times a$.

5   Write 650 000 000 in standard form.

6   Give 45 823 correct to 2 s.f.

7   The organisers of a calypso show hope that, to the nearest thousand, 8000 people will buy tickets. What is the minimum number of tickets that they hope to sell?

8   Find the value of 12.07 ÷ 0.008 97 giving your answer correct to 3 s.f.

9   Find the value of $(0.836)^2$ giving your answer correct to 3 s.f.

10 Change 35% into

    a   a fraction in its lowest terms   **b**   a decimal.

Exercise 1t

1   Find the value of $5^2 \times 5^3$.

2   Simplify $\dfrac{a^8}{a^3 \times a^2}$.

3   Find the value of $3^2 \times 3^4 \div 3^6$.

4   Write 78 260 in standard form.

5   Give 9764 correct to 1 s.f.

6   Give 0.050 806 correct to 3 s.f.

7   Correct to 1 significant figure, there are 70 matches in a box. What is the difference between the maximum and the minimum number of matches that could be in the box?

8   Find $0.0468 \div 0.004\,73$ giving your answer correct to 3 s.f.

9   Find $\dfrac{56.82 \times 0.714}{8.625}$ giving your answer correct to 3 s.f.

10 Change $\dfrac{5}{8}$ into

    a a percentage   **b** a decimal.

Exercise 1u

Select the letter that gives the correct answer.

1   $\dfrac{7}{20}$ as a decimal is

    A 0.33   **B** 0.35   **C** 0.36   **D** 0.37

2   30% as a fraction in its lowest terms is

    A $\dfrac{3}{10}$ **B** $\dfrac{1}{3}$ **C** $\dfrac{3}{8}$ **D** $\dfrac{2}{5}$

3   $\dfrac{9}{40}$ as a percentage is

    A 20%   **B** 22.5%   **C** 24.5%   **D** 25%

4   0.006 as a fraction in its lowest terms is

    A $\dfrac{1}{600}$ **B** $\dfrac{1}{300}$ **C** $\dfrac{3}{500}$ **D** $\dfrac{1}{125}$

5   The value of 4.36×10^5 is

    A 4360   **B** 43 600   **C** 436 000   **D** 4 360 000

6   As a single expression in index form $3^{10} \div 3^6$ is

    A 3^4 **B** 3^5 **C** 3^6 **D** 3^{16}

7 8.743×10^2 is

    A 8.743   **B** 87.43   **C** 874.3   **D** 8743

8 Expressed in standard form, 60 800 is

    A 6.08×10^1 **B** 6.08×10^2 **C** 6.08×10^3 **D** 6.08×10^4

9 Correct to the nearest 100, the number 8507 is

    A 8400   **B** 8500   **C** 8600   **D** 8700

10 Correct to two decimal places, 63.549 is

    A 63.00   **B** 63.54   **C** 63.55   **D** 63.56

11 Correct to two significant figures, 4.5707 is

    A 4.5   **B** 4.6   **C** 4.7   **D** 4.71

12 Correct to 3 s.f., 279.540 is

    A 279   **B** 279.5   **C** 279.55   **D** 280

13 A rough estimate for the value of $0.005\,27 \times 0.717$ is

    A 0.0035   **B** 0.035   **C** 0.055   **D** 0.35

14 47% as a decimal is

    A 0.047   **B** 0.47   **C** 4.7   **D** 47

Did you know?

Did you know these facts?

1 1729 is the smallest positive integer that can be represented in two ways as the sum of two cubes:

$$9^3 + 10^3 \quad \text{or} \quad 1^3 + 12^3$$

2 The total number of gifts given in the song 'The Twelve Days of Christmas' is 364. That is one gift for each day of the year except Christmas Day. Check it.

3 $2592 = 2^5 \times 9^2$.

In this chapter you have seen that...

✔ the associative and commutative laws are true for the addition and multiplication of whole numbers but not for subtraction and division,
 e.g. $7 + 8 = 8 + 7$ and $7 \times 8 = 8 \times 7$
 but $7 - 8$ is not equal to $8 - 7$
 and $7 \div 8$ is not equal to $8 \div 7$

✔ the identity element is 0 for addition and 1 for multiplication

✔ the inverse element for any whole number under addition is minus it, and for multiplication it is the reciprocal, e.g. the inverse of 4 under multiplication is $1 \div 4 \left(\text{or} \times \dfrac{1}{4} \right)$

✔ you can interchange fractions, percentages and decimals using these rules

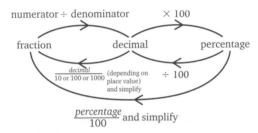

✔ you can multiply different powers of the same number by adding the indices, e.g. $3^4 \times 3^3 = 3^{4+3} = 3^7$

✔ you can divide different powers of the same number by subtracting the indices, e.g. $5^7 \div 5^2 = 5^{7-2} = 5^5$

✔ a number in standard form or scientific notation is a number between 1 and 10 multiplied by a power of 10, e.g. 1.2×10^5 is in standard form

✔ the first significant figure is the first non-zero digit in a number. The next digit (zero or otherwise) is the second significant figure, and so on

✔ to correct a number to a given degree of accuracy, place a cut-off line after the place value required and look at the next digit – if it is 5 or more, round up, otherwise round down

✔ you can make a rough estimate of a calculation by first writing each number correct to one significant figure

✔ you need to be careful when you use a calculator to work out accurate answers.

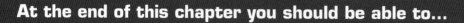

2 Number bases

At the end of this chapter you should be able to...

1 use markers to represent groups of fives or powers of fives for a given number
2 write in figures the numbers represented by markers under the headings of five and powers of five
3 write, in headed columns, numbers to a given base
4 write, in base ten, numbers given in other bases
5 write a number given in base ten as a number to another given base
6 perform operations of addition, subtraction and multiplication in bases other than ten
7 determine the base in which given calculations have been done.

Did you know?

Computers work using different number systems from the one based on powers of 10 that we use in daily life. One of these is the hexadecimal system.

Find out what you can about hexadecimal numbers and why they are important.

You need to know...

✔ your multiplication tables — and this means instant recall.

Key words

base, binary, denary system, number base

Denary system (base ten)

We have ten fingers. This is probably why we started to count in tens and developed a system based on ten for recording large numbers. For example

$$3125 = 3 \text{ thousands} + 1 \text{ hundred} + 2 \text{ tens} + 5 \text{ units}$$

$$= 3 \times 10^3 + 1 \times 10^2 + 2 \times 10^1 + 5 \times 10^0$$

Each place value is ten times the value of its right-hand neighbour. The base of this number system is ten and it is called the *denary system.*

Base five

If man had started to count using just one hand, we would probably have a system based on five.

Suppose we had eleven stones. Using one hand to count with, we could arrange them like this:

•	•	•	•	
	•		•	
•	•	•	•	•

i.e.   two handfuls + one ⎫
or   2   fives   + 1 ⎭

The next logical step is to use a single marker to represent each group of five. We also need to place these markers so that they are not confused with the marker representing the one unit. We do this by having separate columns for the fives and the units, with the column for the fives to the left of the units.

Fives	Units
•	
•	•

We can write this number as 21_5 and we call it 'two one to the base five'. We do *not* call it 'twenty-one to the base five', because the word 'twenty' means 'two tens'.

To cope with larger numbers, we can extend this system by adding further columns to the left such that each column is five times the value of its right-hand neighbour. Thus, in the column to the left of the fives column, each marker is worth twenty-five, or 5^2.

For example

Twenty-fives	Fives	Units
	•	
	•	•
•	•	•

The markers here represent 132_5 and it means

$$(1 \times 5^2) + (3 \times 5) + 2$$

Exercise 2a

Write in figures the numbers represented by the markers:

5³	5²	5	Units
•	• • •		• •

1	3	0	2

The number is 1302₅

(The '5' column is empty, so we write zero in this column.)

Write in figures the numbers represented by the markers in questions **1** to **4**:

	5⁴	5³	5²	5	Units
1			• •	•	• • •
2		• •		•	• • • •
3	• • • •	•	• •	• • • •	
4	• • •		• •		•

Write 120₅ in headed columns.

5²	5	Units
1	2	0

Write the following numbers in headed columns:

5	31₅	**7**	410₅	**9**	34₅	**11**	204₅
6	42₅	**8**	231₅	**10**	10₅	**12**	400₅

Write 203_5 as a number to the base 10

5^2	5	Units
• •		• • •
2	0	3

$$203_5 = (2 \times 5^2) + (0 \times 5) + 3$$
$$= 50_{10} + 0 + 3_{10}$$
$$= 53_{10}$$

(Although we do not normally write fifty-three as 53_{10}, it is sensible to do so when dealing with other bases as well.)

Write the following numbers as denary numbers, i.e. to base 10:

13 31_5 **16** 121_5 **19** 32_5 **22** 400_5

14 24_5 **17** 204_5 **20** 20_5 **23** 240_5

15 40_5 **18** 43_5 **21** 4_5 **24** 300_5

Write 38_{10} as a number to the base 5.

(To write a number to the base 5 we have to find how many ... 125s, 25s, 5s and units the number contains.)

(Starting with the highest value column.)

38 contains no 125s.

$$38 \div 25 = 1 \text{ remainder } 13 \quad \text{i.e. } 38 = 1 \times 5^2 + 13$$
$$13 \div 5 = 2 \text{ remainder } 3 \quad \text{i.e. } 13 = 2 \times 5 + 3$$
$$\therefore \quad 38 = 1 \times 5^2 + 2 \times 5 + 3$$
$$= 123_5$$

Write the following numbers in base 5:

25 8_{10} **28** 39_{10} **31** 7_{10} **34** 128_{10}

26 13_{10} **29** 43_{10} **32** 21_{10} **35** 82_{10}

27 10_{10} **30** 150_{10} **33** 30_{10} **36** 100_{10}

Other bases

Any number can be used as a base for a number system.

If the base is 6, we write the number in columns such that each column is 6 times the value of its right-hand neighbour. For example, writing 253_6 in headed columns gives:

6^2	6	Units
2	5	3

We see that 253_6 means $(2 \times 6^2) + (5 \times 6) + 3$

Similarly for 1011_2, we can write this in headed columns.

2^3	2^2	2	Units
•		•	•

Therefore 1011_2 means $(1 \times 2^3) + (0 \times 2^2) + (1 \times 2) + 1$.

Exercise 2b

Write 425_7 in headed columns and then write it as a denary number.

7^2	7	Units
4	2	5

$$\therefore \quad 425_7 = (4 \times 7^2) + (2 \times 7) + 5$$
$$= 196_{10} + 14_{10} + 5_{10}$$
$$= 215_{10}$$

Write the following numbers

a   in headed columns   b   as denary numbers.

1	23_4	5	57_8	**9**	21_3	**13**	303_4
2	15_7	6	204_5	**10**	18_9	**14**	1001_2
3	131_4	7	210_3	**11**	24_6	**15**	1211_3
4	101_2	8	574_9	**12**	175_8	**16**	1000_6

Write 29_{10} as a number

a   to the base 9

b   to the base 2.

a $29 \div 9 = 3$ remainder 2

so $29_{10} = 3 \times 9 + 2$

$\therefore \qquad 29_{10} = 32_9$

b
$$2\overline{)29}$$
$$2\overline{)14} \quad \text{remainder} \quad 1 \text{ (unit)}$$
$$2\underline{)\ 7} \quad \text{remainder} \quad 0 \text{ (twos)}$$
$$2\underline{)\ 3} \quad \text{remainder} \quad 1 \ (2^2)$$
$$2\underline{)\ 1} \quad \text{remainder} \quad 1 \ (2^3)$$
$$\ 0 \quad \text{remainder} \quad 1 \ (2^4)$$

$$\therefore \quad 29_{10} = 11101_2$$

Write the following denary numbers to the base indicated in brackets:

17	9	(4)	**25**	8	(3)	**33**	163	(8)
18	12	(5)	**26**	15	(6)	**34**	640	(4)
19	24	(7)	**27**	34	(9)	**35**	142	(2)
20	7	(2)	**28**	28	(3)	**36**	158	(6)
21	13	(5)	**29**	56	(7)	**37**	43	(6)
22	32	(6)	**30**	89	(9)	**38**	55	(5)
23	53	(8)	**31**	45	(2)	**39**	99	(2)
24	49	(7)	**32**	333	(3)	**40**	394	(7)

Express each of the following numbers as a number to the base indicated in brackets:

41	45_6	(4)	**44**	432_5	(3)	**47**	11011_2 (8)
42	23_4	(6)	**45**	562_8	(4)	**48**	378_9	(3)
43	17_8	(2)	**46**	2120_3	(5)	**49**	3020_4	(8)

Addition, subtraction and multiplication

Numbers with a base other than 10 do not need to be converted to base 10; provided that they have the same base they can be added, subtracted and multiplied in the usual way, as long as we remember which base we are working with.

For example, to find $132_5 + 44_5$ we work in fives, not tens. To aid memory, the numbers can be written in headed columns:

Twenty-fives	Fives	Units	
1	3	2	
	4 ①	4	+
①			
2	3	1	
	⑧	⑥	

Adding the units gives 6 units:

$$6 \text{ (units)} = 1 \text{ (five)} + 1 \text{ (unit)}$$

We put 1 in the units column and carry the single five to the fives column.

Adding the fives gives 8 fives:

$$8 \text{ (fives)} = 5 \text{ (fives)} \qquad + 3 \text{ (fives)}$$
$$= 1 \text{ (twenty-five)} \quad + 3 \text{ (fives)}$$

We put 3 in the fives column and carry the 1 to the next column.

Adding the numbers in the last column gives 2,

i.e. $\qquad 132_5 + 44_5 = 231_5$

If the numbers are not to the same base we cannot add them in this way.

For example, 432_7 and 621_8 cannot be added directly.

Exercise 2c

Find $174_8 + 654_8$

8^3	8^2	8	Units	
	1	7	4	
①	6 ①	5 ①	4	+
1	0	5	0	
	⑧	⑬	⑧	

$\therefore 174_8 + 654_8 = 1050_8$

Find:

1 $12_5 + 31_5$

2 $11_3 + 2_3$

3 $11_4 + 13_4$

4 $10_2 + 1_2$

5 $24_6 + 35_6$

6 $21_3 + 11_3$

7 $43_8 + 52_6$

8 $101_2 + 11_2$

9 $43_5 + 24_5$

10 $132_4 + 201_4$

11 $345_6 + 402_6$

12 $1101_2 + 111_2$

13 $122_3 + 101_3$

14 $231_4 + 103_4$

15 $635_7 + 62_7$

16 $10010_2 + 1111_2$

Make sure that you are clear about which base you are working in. Use headed columns if necessary.

Find $132_4 - 13_4$

(There are two methods of doing subtraction and we show both of them here.)

First method

4^2	4	Units
1	$\cancel{3}$ ②	$\cancel{2}$ ⑥
	1	3	–
1	1	3

(We cannot take 3 from 2 so we take one 4 from the fours column, change it to 4 units and add it to the 2 units.)

Second method

If you use the 'pay back' method of subtraction, the calculation looks like this:

4^2	4	Units
1	3	$\cancel{2}$ ⑥
	1 ①	3	–
1	1	3

In either case $132_4 - 13_4 = 113_4$

Find:

17	$153_6 - 24_6$	**21**	$210_3 - 1_3$	**25**	$231_4 - 32_4$	**29**	$144_6 - 53_6$
18	$110_3 - 2_3$	**22**	$30_5 - 14_5$	**26**	$153_7 - 64_7$	**30**	$1010_2 - 101_2$
19	$32_4 - 23_4$	**23**	$253_8 - 25_8$	**27**	$205_6 - 132_6$	**31**	$724_8 - 56_8$
20	$52_7 - 14_7$	**24**	$10_2 - 1_2$	**28**	$100_2 - 10_2$	**32**	$120_3 - 12_3$

Find $352_6 \times 4_6$

6^3	6^2	6	Units	
	3	5	2	
②	③	①	4	×
2	3	3	2	

$15 = 2 \times 6 + 3$ $21 = 3 \times 6 + 3$ $8 = 6 + 2$

$352_6 \times 4_6 = 2332_6$

Find:

33 $4_5 \times 3_5$

34 $2_4 \times 3_4$

35 $12_3 \times 2_3$

36 $20_4 \times 3_4$

37 $5_6 \times 4_6$

38 $13_5 \times 2_5$

39 $24_7 \times 3_7$

40 $56_9 \times 3_9$

41 $132_4 \times 2_4$

42 $501_6 \times 5_5$

43 $202_3 \times 2_3$

44 $241_5 \times 2_5$

Find:

45 $261_7 + 123_7$

46 $32_4 \times 2_4$

47 $434_5 - 142_5$

48 $36_7 \times 2_7$

49 $451_6 + 124_6$

50 $232_4 - 103_4$

51 $22_5 \times 4_5$

52 $365_8 + 173_8$

53 $121_3 - 112_3$

54 $34_8 \times 5_8$

Harder examples

Exercise 2d

Calculate $133_4 \times 32_4$

First place the number in headed columns, then use long multiplication, i.e. multiply by 2_4 and then by 30_4:

4^4	$4^3 (=64)$	$4^2 (=16)$	4	Units
		1	3	3
			3	2
$\times 2$		3	3	2
		$2+1=3$	$6+1=7=4+3$	$6=4+2$
$\times 30$	1	1	3	1	0
	$3+2=5=4+1$	$9+2=11=2\times4+3$	$9=2\times4+1$	
+	1	2	3	0	2

$133_4 \times 32_4 = 12302_4$

Find:

1 $123_4 \times 23_4$

2 $413_5 \times 24_5$

3 $1001_2 \times 1101_2$

4 $73_8 \times 26_8$

5 $2120_3 \times 212_3$

6 $46_8 \times 35_8$

7 $234_5 \times 423_5$

8 $452_7 \times 324_7$

9   **a**   Find $64_8 \times 27_8$ as a number to the base 8.

    b   Express 64_8 and 27_8 as denary numbers.

    c   Multiply together your two answers for **b**.

    d   Change your answer to **c** into a number to the base 8. Does this answer agree with your answer to **a**?

10   **a**   Find $476_9 \times 57_9$ as a number to the base 9.

    b   Express 476_9 and 57_9 as denary numbers.

    c   Multiply together your two answers for **b**.

    d   Change your answer to **c** into a number to the base 9 . Does this answer agree with your answer to **a**?

11   Find $55_8 \times 43_8$ and use the process described in questions **9** and **10** as a check on your working.

12   Choose a base and make up a long multiplication question of your own. Check your calculation using the process above.

Binary numbers

Numbers with a base of two are called *binary numbers*. We have singled binary numbers out for special attention because of the wide application that they have, especially in the world of computers.

Exercise 2e

1   If you have access to a computer and have done some programming using machine code, or have copied program listings from magazines, you will have seen instructions such as

        BIN 1101, 1011, 11001, 100, 1100, 11101

    'BIN' means 'binary'.

    Convert the binary numbers given above to denary numbers.

2   Basically, computers are very simple; their fundamental computing parts can only be off (0) or on (1), i.e. computers count in binary numbers.

+	0	1
0		
1		

    a   Complete the adjacent addition table for binary numbers.

    b   Find $1011011_2 + 110101_2$.

3 **a** Subtract 23_{10} as many times as you can from 138_{10}. Hence find the value of $138_{10} \div 23_{10}$.

b Subtract 11_2 from 1111_2 as many times as you can. Hence find $1111_2 \div 11_2$.

4 Complete the following multiplication table for binary numbers.

×	0	1
0		
1		

Investigation

1 Convert 7_{10}, 5_{10}, 10_{10}, 16_{10}, 19_{10}, 24_{10}, into binary numbers.

2 How many symbols are needed to represent all binary numbers?

3 Write each of the denary numbers 1 to 20 as binary numbers.

4 How can you see when a binary number is even?

5 How can you see when a binary number is odd?

6 Find some machine code and see if you can interpret it.

Mixed exercises

Exercise 2f

1 Convert the following denary numbers to base 3 numbers:

    a 5   **b** 8   **c** 12   **d** 31

2 How many different symbols are needed to represent all numbers in base three?

3 Make up a multiplication table for base three numbers.

4 Use repeated subtraction to find the value of $1111_3 \div 101_3$.

5 Convert the following denary numbers to base 5 numbers:

    a 27   **b** 18   **c** 153

6 What do you think 31.2_5 could mean?

7 If a number to the base 10 ends in 0, what does the same number to the base 5 end in?

8 Is it possible to write a number in base one? Give a reason for your answer.

9 How many digits are there in 5^3 written in base 5?

10 How many digits are there in 3^7 written in base 3?

11 **a** Convert $10_2, 10_3, 10_4, 10_5, 10_6, 10_7, 10_8$ into denary numbers.

  b Find **i** $1101_2 \times 10_2$ **ii** $121_3 \times 10_3$ **iii** $175_8 \times 10_8$

  c What is the effect of multiplying a number by the base number?

Find the base in which the following calculation has been done:

$13 + 5 = 22$

$$
\begin{array}{r}
13 \\
①5\, + \\
\hline
22 \\
\hline
\end{array}
$$
⑧

From the addition, $5 + 3 = 8$. To leave 2 in the units column, 6 units have been carried to the next column. The total in the next column is 2, so the 6 units have been carried as 1 to the next column.

∴ the base is 6

Find the bases in which the following calculations have been done.

12 $15 + 23 = 42$

13 $12 + 13 = 31$

14 $110 + 121 = 1001$

15 $134 + 213 = 350$

16 $13 - 4 = 4$

17 $21 - 2 = 17$

18 $13 \times 2 = 31$

19 $21 \times 3 = 103$

20 Is the following statement true or false? Give a reason for your answer.
A number written to any base is even if it ends in zero.

Exercise 2g

1 Write the following numbers as denary numbers:
  a 12_4 **b** 101_2 **c** 403_6

2 Write the denary number 20 as a number to the given base:
  a 5 **b** 3 **c** 8

3 Find:
  a $204_5 + 132_5$ **b** $110_3 - 2_3$ **c** $212_8 \times 3_8$

4 There are four possible answers given below to the calculation $213_4 \times 2_4$.
Only one answer is correct. Which one is it?
  A 426_4 **B** 2130_4 **C** 1032_4 **D** 221_4

Exercise 2h

Select the letter that gives the correct answer.

1   Expressed as a denary number 34_5 is

 A 15   **B** 19   **C** 21   **D** 24

2   Written to the base 5, the number 31_{10} is

 A 100_5 **B** 101_5 **C** 110_5 **D** 111_5

3   The denary number 54, written as a number to the base 8, is

 A 52_8 **B** 57_8 **C** 66_8 **D** 67_8

4   Working to the base 2, the value of $1011_2 + 10111_2$ is

 A 100010_2 **B** 100110_2 **C** 110110_2 **D** 111010_2

5   $254_8 - 24_8$ equals

 A 222_8 **B** 224_8 **C** 230_8 **D** 234_8

6   $33_5 + 4_5$ equals

 A 32_5 **B** 42_5 **C** 52_5 **D** 342_5

7   $31_5 \times 20_5$ equals

 A 112_5 **B** 160_5 **C** 1120_5 **D** 1122_5

8   Expressed as a denary number $54_8 + 27_8$ equals

 A 11   **B** 21   **C** 67   **D** 81

9   $165_8 - 20_8$ equals

 A 45_8 **B** 145_8 **C** 187_8 **D** 205_8

10   In what base has the calculation $23 - 4 = 13$ been made?

 A 3   **B** 4   **C** 6   **D** 8

Did you know?

The Jivaro Indians of the Amazon rain forest express the number 'five' by the phrase 'wehe amukei', meaning 'I have finished one hand', and the number 'ten' by 'mai wehe amukahei', meaning 'I have finished both hands'.

In this chapter you have seen that...

✔ numbers can be expressed in any base

✔ if a number is in base a, the first column from the right is units, the second column gives the number of a's, the next column gives the number of a^2's and so on. For example, 165_8 means
$1 \times 8^2 + 6 \times 8^1 + 5$

✔ you can add, subtract and multiply numbers in a base other than ten in the usual way, but it is sensible to write them in headed columns so that you can keep track of your working.

3 Algebra

At the end of this chapter you should be able to...

1 solve simple equations
2 form simple equations and use them to solve problems
3 construct formulae from given information
4 substitute numerical values in a formula.

Did you know?

The German mathematician Carl Friedrich Gauss (1777–1855) was the leading algebraist and theoretical astronomer of the day. He was born of poor parents but, because of his prodigious talent, his education was paid for by the Duke of Brunswick. Nearly all his fundamental mathematical discoveries were made before he was 22.

You need to know...

✔ how to simplify expressions containing brackets
✔ how to collect like terms
✔ the order in which to do multiplication, division, addition and subtraction
✔ how to multiply directed numbers
✔ what the lowest common multiple means
✔ how to convert units to smaller or larger units.

Key words

area, breadth, directed number, eliminate, equation, equilateral triangle, equivalent, expression, formula (plural formulae), like terms, negative number, perimeter, rectangle

Equations

On the left-hand side there are two bags each containing the same (but unknown) number of apples and three loose apples.

Imagine a balance.

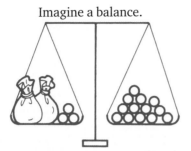

On the right-hand side there are thirteen apples.

Using the letter x to stand for the unknown number of apples in each bag we can write this as an *equation*:

$$2x + 3 = 13$$

We can solve this equation (i.e. find the number that x represents) as follows:

take three apples off each pan $2x + 3 - 3 = 13 - 3$

$$2x = 10$$

halve the contents of each pan $x = 5$

Remember that we want to isolate x and that we can do anything as long as we do it to both sides of the equation.

Exercise 3a

Solve the equation $5x - 4 = 6$

$$5x - 4 = 6$$

Add 4 to each side $5x - 4 + 4 = 6 + 4$

$$5x = 10$$

Divide each side by 5 $x = 2$

Check: LHS $= 5 \times 2 - 4 = 6$ RHS $= 6$

Solve the following equations:

1	$2x = 8$	**6**	$3x - 2 = 10$
2	$x - 3 = 1$	**7**	$5 + 2x = 7$
3	$x + 4 = 16$	**8**	$5x - 4 = 11$
4	$2x + 3 = 7$	**9**	$3 + 6x = 15$
5	$3x + 5 = 14$	**10**	$7x - 6 = 15$

Equations with letter terms on both sides

Some equations have letter terms on both sides. Consider the equation

$$5x + 1 = 2x + 9$$

We want to have a letter term on one side only so we need to take $2x$ from both sides. This gives

$$3x + 1 = 9$$

and we can go on to solve the equation as before.

Notice that we want the letter term on the side which has the greater number of x's to start with.

If we look at the equation

$$9 - 4x = 2x + 4$$

we can see that there are fewer x's on the left-hand side, so there are more x's on the right-hand side. Add $4x$ to both sides and then the equation becomes

$$9 = 6x + 4$$

and we can go on as before.

Exercise 3b

Solve $5x + 2 = 2x + 9$

Deal with the letters first, then the numbers.

$$5x + 2 = 2x + 9$$

$2x < 5x$ so take $2x$ from both sides $\qquad 3x + 2 = 9$
(< means 'less than')

Take 2 from both sides $\qquad\qquad\qquad 3x = 7$

Divide both sides by 3 $\qquad\qquad\qquad x = \dfrac{7}{3} = 2\dfrac{1}{3}$

Solve the following equations:

1 $3x + 4 = 2x + 8$

2 $x + 7 = 4x + 4$

3 $2x + 5 = 5x - 4$

4 $3x - 1 = 5x - 11$

5 $7x + 3 = 3x + 31$

6 $6z + 4 = 2z + 1$

7 $7x - 25 = 3x - 1$

8 $11x - 6 = 8x + 9$

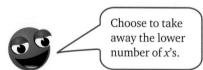

Choose to take away the lower number of x's.

9	$2x + 5 = x + 9$	<u>14</u>	$x + 4 = 4x + 1$
10	$3x + 2 = 2x + 7$	<u>15</u>	$3x - 2 = 2x + 1$
11	$x - 4 = 2 - x$	<u>16</u>	$1 - 3x = 9 - 4x$
12	$3 - 2x = 7 - 3x$	<u>17</u>	$2 - 5x = 6 - 3x$
13	$2x + 1 = 4 - x$	<u>18</u>	$5 - 3x = 1 + x$

Equations containing like terms

If there are a lot of terms in an equation, first collect the *like terms* on each side separately.

Exercise 3c

Solve the equation $2x + 3 - x + 5 = 3x + 4x - 6$

$$2x + 3 - x + 5 = 3x + 4x - 6$$

Simplify each side $\qquad\qquad x + 8 = 7x - 6$

Take x from both sides $\qquad\qquad 8 = 6x - 6$

Add 6 to both sides $\qquad\qquad 14 = 6x$

Divide both sides by 6 $\qquad\qquad \dfrac{14}{6} = x$

$$x = \dfrac{7}{3} = 2\dfrac{1}{3}$$

Solve the following equations:

1	$3x + 2 + 2x = 7$	9	$5x + 6 + 3x = 10$	17	$4x - 2 + 6x - 4 = 64$
2	$7 + 3x - 6 = 4$	10	$8 = 7 - 11 + 6x$	18	$2x + 7 - x + 3 = 6x$
3	$6 = 5x + 2 - 4x$	11	$7 + 2x = 12x - 7x + 2$	19	$6 - 2x - 4 + 5x = 17$
4	$9 + 4 = 3x + 4x$	<u>12</u>	$1 + 4 - 3 + 2x = 3x$	20	$9x - 6 - x - 2 = 0$
5	$3x + 2x - 4x = 6$	<u>13</u>	$3x + 4x - x = x + 6$	<u>21</u>	$x - 3 + 7x + 9 = 10$
<u>6</u>	$7 = 2 - 3 + 4x$	<u>14</u>	$2 + 4x - x = x + 8$	<u>22</u>	$15x + 2x - 6x - 9x = 20$
<u>7</u>	$5x + x - 6x + 2x = 9$	15	$4 - x - 2 + x = x$		
<u>8</u>	$5 + x + x = 1 + 4x$	16	$3x + 1 + 2x = 6$		

Solve the equation $4x + 2 - x = 7 + x - 3$

$$4x + 2 - x = 7 + x - 3$$

Collect like terms	$3x + 2 = 4 + x$
Take x from each side	$2x + 2 = 4$
Take 2 from each side	$2x = 2$
Divide each side by 2	$x = 1$

Solve the following equations:

23 $x + 2 + 2x = 8$

24 $x - 4 = 3 - x + 1$

25 $3x + 1 - x = 5$

26 $4 + 3x - 1 = 6$

27 $7 + 4x = 2 - x + 10$

28 $3 + x - 1 = 3x$

29 $x - 4 + 2x = 5 + x - 1$

30 $x + 5 - 2x = 3 + x$

31 $x + 17 - 4x = 2 - x + 6$

32 $8 - 3x - 3 = x - 4 + 2x$

33 $5x - 8 = 2$

34 $4 - x = 3x$

35 $5 - x = 7 + 2x - 4$

36 $4 - 2x = 8 - 4x$

37 $15 = 21 - 2x$

38 $x + 4 - 3x = 2 - x$

39 $3x - 7 = 9 - x + 6$

40 $x + 4 = 6x$

41 $8 - 3x = 5x$

42 $5 - 4x + 7 = 2x$

Brackets

Reminder: If we want to multiply both x and 3 by 4, we group x and 3 together in a bracket and write $4(x + 3)$.

So $4(x + 3)$ means that both x and 3 are to be multiplied by 4. (Note that the multiplication sign is invisible, as it is in $5a$.)

So $4(x + 3) = 4x + 12$

($4x$ and 12 are unlike terms so $4x + 12$ cannot be simplified.)

When we multiply out brackets, this is called expanding the brackets.

Exercise 3d

Expand the following brackets:

1	$6(x+4)$	**3**	$4(x-3)$	**5**	$4(3-2x)$	**7**	$3(2-3x)$	**9**	$2(5x-7)$
2	$3(2x+1)$	**4**	$2(3x-5)$	**6**	$5(4x+2)$	**8**	$7(5-4x)$	**10**	$6(7+2x)$

Simplify:

11 $2(3+x)+3(2x+4)$

12 $7(2x+3)+4(3x-2)$

13 $4(6x+3)+5(2x-5)$

14 $2(2x-4)+4(x+3)$

First expand the brackets, then collect like terms.

15 $5(3x-2)+3(2x+5)$ **23** $3(x-4)+7(2x-3)$

16 $3(3x+1)+4(x+4)$ **24** $2(2x+1)+4(3-2x)$

17 $5(2x+3)+6(3x+2)$ **25** $6(2-x)+2(1-2x)$

18 $6(2x-5)+2(3x-7)$ **26** $5(4+3x)+3(2+7x)$

19 $8(2-x)+3(3+4x)$ **27** $4(3+2x)+5(4-3x)$

20 $5(7-2x)+4(3-5x)$ **28** $8(x+1)+7(2-x)$

21 $3(2x-1)+4(x+2)$ **29** $3(2x+7)+5(3x-8)$

22 $5(2-x)+2(2x+1)$ **30** $9(x-2)+5(4-3x)$

Solve the following equations:

31 $2(x+2)=8$

32 $4(2-x)=2$

33 $5(3x+1)=20$

34 $2(2x-1)=6$

Start by expanding the brackets.

35 $3(2x+5)=18$

36 $3(3-2x)=3$

37 $2(x+4)=3(2x+1)$ **42** $3(1-4x)=11$

38 $4(2x-3)=2(3x-5)$ **43** $5(3-2x)=3(4-3x)$

39 $6(3x+5)=12$ **44** $7(1+2x)=21$

40 $6(x+3)=2(2x+5)$ **45** $7(2x-1)=5(3x-2)$

41 $8(x-1)=4$ **46** $4(3x+2)=14$

Directed numbers

Reminder: $(+2) \times (+3) = +6$ $(+2) \times (-3) = -6$

$(-2) \times (+3) = -6$ $(-2) \times (-3) = +6$

Another way to remember these rules when multiplying directed numbers is like signs give positive, unlike signs give negative.

Division is the reverse of multiplication, e.g. $4 \div 4 = 1$, so $-4 \div (-4) = 1$

This means that dividing a negative number by a negative number gives a positive number,

e.g. $-8 \div (-2) = +4$

In the same way $(+8) \div (-2) = -4$

and $(-8) \div (+2) = -4$

Hence we can use the rules of multiplication of directed numbers for the division of directed numbers.

Exercise 3e

Evaluate:

1 $(+2) \times (-4)$

2 $(-3) \times (-5)$

3 $(-6) \times (+4)$

4 $\left(-\dfrac{1}{2}\right) \times (+6)$

5 $(-16) \div (-8)$

6 $(-4) \times (-7)$

7 $(+12) \div (-3)$

8 $\left(+\dfrac{1}{2}\right) \times \left(+\dfrac{2}{3}\right)$

9 $(-6) \div (-2)$

Simplify $4(x - 3) - 3(2 - 3x)$

Remember that the positive sign is often omitted, i.e. 6 means +6.
Multiply out the brackets. Remember that $-3(2 - 3x) = -3 \times 2 - 3 \times (-3x)$

$$4(x - 3) - 3(2 - 3x) = 4x - 12 - 6 + 9x$$

Collect like terms $= 13x - 18$

Simplify:

10 $7 - 2(x - 5)$

11 $2x + 5(3x - 4)$

12 $3x - 6(3x + 5)$

13 $4 - 7(2x - 3)$

14 $3x - 4(5 - 3x)$

15 $3(x - 4) + 6(3 - 2x)$

16 $2(3x + 5) - 2(4 + 3x)$

17 $5(2x - 8) - 3(2 - 5x)$

18 $7(x - 2) - (2x + 3)$

Solve the following equations:

19 $4x - 2(x - 3) = 8$

20 $7 - 3(5 - 2x) = 10$

21 $4x + 2(2x - 5) = 6$

22 $3(x - 4) - 7 = 2(x - 3)$

23 $4 - 3x = 3 + 4(2x - 3)$

24 $3x - 2(4 - 5x) = 5 - 3x$

Start by multiplying out brackets, then collect like terms.

? Puzzle

My dog weighs nine-tenths of its weight plus nine-tenths of a kilogram.

What does it weigh?

Formulae

For all rectangles it is true that the area is equal to the length multiplied by the breadth, provided that the length and breadth are measured in the same units.

If we use letters for the variable quantities (*A* for area, *l* for length, *b* for breadth) we can write the first sentence more briefly as a formula: $A = l \times b$.

The multiplication sign is usually left out giving

$A = lb$

Exercise 3f

The letters in the diagrams all stand for a number of centimetres.

The perimeter of the square below is P cm. Write a formula for P.

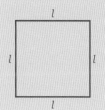

Start by writing the perimeter in terms of the letters in the diagram: this is $l+l+l+l$ (cm). As we are told that P cm is the perimeter we can write

$$P = l+l+l+l$$

Collect like terms

$$P = 4l$$

In each of the following figures the perimeter is P cm. Write a formula for P starting with $P =$

1

3

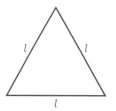

5

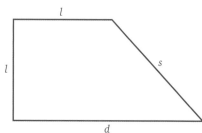

2

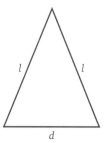

4

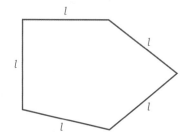

G is the number of girls and B is the number of boys in a class.

Given that T is the total number of students in the class, write a formula for T in terms of G and B.

Start by writing an expression for the total number of students.

The total number of students in the class is the sum of G and B, i.e. $G+B$.

As T is equal to the total number of students,

$$T = G+B$$

6   I buy x lb of apples and y lb of pears. Write a formula for W if W lb is the mass of fruit that I have bought.

Read each question carefully.

7   If l m is the length of a rectangle and b m is the breadth, write a formula for P if the perimeter of the rectangle is P m.

8   I start a game with N marbles and win another M marbles. Write a formula for the number, T, of marbles that I finish the game with.

9   I start a game with N marbles and lose L marbles. Write a formula for the number, T, of marbles that I finish with.

10   The side of a square is l m long. Write a formula for A if the area of the square is A m².

11   Peaches cost n cents each. Write a formula for N if the cost of 10 peaches is N cents.

12   Oranges cost x cents each and I buy n of these oranges. Write a formula for C where C cents is the total cost of the oranges.

13   I have a piece of string which is l cm long. I cut off a piece which is d cm long. Write a formula for L if the length of string which is left is L cm.

14   A rectangle is $2l$ m long and l m wide. Write a formula for P where P m is the perimeter of the rectangle.

15   Write a formula for A where A m² is the area of the rectangle described in question **14**.

16   I had a bag of sweets with S sweets in it; I then ate T of them. Write a formula for the number, N, of sweets left in the bag.

17   A lorry has mass T tonnes when empty. Steel girders with a total mass of S tonnes are then loaded on to the lorry. Write a formula for W where W tonnes is the mass of the loaded lorry.

18   I started the term with a new packet of N felt-tipped pens. During the term I lost L of them and R of them were recycled. Write a formula for the number, S, that I had at the end of the term.

19   A truck travels p km in one direction and then it comes back q km in the opposite direction. If it is then r km from its starting point, write a formula for r.

20   One box of tinned fruit has mass K kg. The mass of n such boxes is W kg. Write a formula for W.

21   A letter costs x cents to post. The cost of posting 20 such letters is $\$q$.
Write a formula for q.

Be careful – look at the units given.

22 One grapefruit costs y cents. The cost of n such grapefruit is $\$L$. Write a formula for L.

Look carefully at the units.

23 A rectangle is l m long and b cm wide. The area is A cm². Write a formula for A.

24 On my way to work this morning the bus I was travelling on broke down. I spend t hours on the bus and s minutes walking. Write a formula for T if the total time that my journey took was T hours.

Substituting numerical values into a formula

The formula for the area of a rectangle is $A = lb$.

If a rectangle is 3 cm long and 2 cm wide, we can substitute the number 3 for l and the number 2 for b to give $A = 3 \times 2 = 6$.

So the area of that rectangle is 6 cm².

When you substitute numerical values into a formula you may have a mixture of operations, i.e. ( ), $\times$, $\div$, $+$, $-$, to perform. Remember the order from the capital letters of 'Bless My Dear Aunt Sally'.

Exercise 3g

If $v = u + at$, find v when $u = 2$, $a = \dfrac{1}{2}$ and $t = 4$.

$$v = u + at$$

When $u = 2$, $a = \dfrac{1}{2}$, $t = 4$, $v = 2 + \dfrac{1}{2} \times 4$ (Do multiplication first)

$$= 2 + 2$$

$$= 4$$

1 If $N = T + G$, find N when $T = 4$ and $G = 6$.

2 If $T = np$, find T when $n = 20$ and $p = 5$.

3 If $P = 2(l + b)$, find P when $l = 6$ and $b = 9$.

4 If $L = x - y$, find L when $x = 8$ and $y = 6$.

5 If $N = 4(l - s)$, find N when $l = 7$ and $s = 2$.

6 If $S = n(a + b)$, find S when $n = 20$, $a = 2$ and $b = 8$.

7 If $V = lbw$, find V when $l = 4$, $b = 3$ and $w = 2$.

8 If $A = \dfrac{PRT}{100}$, find A when $P = 100$, $R = 3$ and $T = 5$.

9   If $w = u(v - t)$, find w when $u = 5$, $v = 7$ and $t = 2$.

10   If $s = \dfrac{1}{2}(a + b + c)$, find s when $a = 5$, $b = 7$ and $c = 3$.

If $v = u - at$, find v when $u = 5$, $a = -2$ and $t = -3$.

$$v = u - at$$

When $u = 5$, $a = -2$, $t = -3$: $v = 5 - (-2) \times (-3)$

$$= 5 - (+6)$$

$$= 5 - 6$$

$$= -1$$

(Notice that where negative numbers are substituted for letters they have been put in brackets. This makes sure that only one operation at a time is carried out.)

---

11   If $N = p + q$, find N when $p = 4$ and $q = -5$.

12   If $C = RT$, find C when $R = 4$ and $T = -3$.

13   If $z = w + x - y$, find z when $w = 4$, $x = -3$ and $y = -4$.

14   If $r = u(v - w)$, find r when $u = -3$, $v = -6$ and $w = 5$.

15   Given that $X = 5(T - R)$, find X when $T = 4$ and $R = -6$.

16   Given that $P = d - rt$, find P when $d = 3$, $r = -8$ and $t = 2$.

17   Given that $v = l(a + n)$, find v when $l = -8$, $a = 4$ and $n = -6$.

18   If $D = \dfrac{a - b}{c}$, find D when $a = -4$, $b = -8$ and $c = 2$.

19   If $Q = abc$, find Q when $a = 3$, $b = -7$ and $c = -5$.

20   If $l = \dfrac{2}{3}(x + y - z)$, find l when $x = 4$, $y = -5$ and $z = -6$.

Put negative numbers in brackets.

Given that $2S = d(a + l)$, find a when $S = 20$, $d = 2$ and $l = 16$.

$$2S = d(a + l)$$

Substituting $S = 20$, $d = 2$, $l = 16$ gives

$$40 = 2(a + 16)$$

We can now solve this equation for a.

Multiply out the brackets $40 = 2a + 32$

Take 32 from each side $8 = 2a$

Divide by 2 $4 = a$ or $a = 4$

21   Given that $N = G + B$, find B when $N = 40$ and $G = 25$.

22   If $R = t \div c$, find t when $R = 10$ and $c = 20$.

23   Given that $d = st$, find t when $d = 50$ and $s = 15$.

24   If $N = 2(p + q)$, find q when $N = 24$, and $p = 5$.

25   Given that $L = P(2 - a)$, find a when $L = 10$ and $P = 40$.

26   Given that $v = u + at$, find u when $v = 32$, $a = 8$ and $t = 4$.

27   If $v^2 = u^2 + 2as$, find a when $v = 3$, $u = 2$ and $s = 12$.

28   If $H = P(Q - R)$, find Q when $H = 12$, $P = 4$ and $R = -6$.

Problems

Exercise 3h

1   Given that $v = at$, find the value of

    a v when $a = 4$ and $t = 12$ **c** t when $v = 18$ and $a = 3$

    b v when $a = -3$ and $t = 6$ **d** a when $v = 25$ and $t = 5$.

2   Given that $N = 2(n - m)$, find the value of

    a N when $n = 6$ and $m = 4$ **c** n when $N = 12$ and $m = 2$

    b N when $n = 7$ and $m = -3$ **d** m when $N = 16$ and $n = -4$.

3   If $A = P + QT$, find the value of

    a A when $P = 50$, $Q = \dfrac{1}{2}$ and $T = 4$

    b A when $P = 70$, $Q = 5$ and $T = -10$

    c P when $A = 100$, $Q = \dfrac{1}{4}$ and $T = 16$

    d T when $A = 25$, $P = -15$ and $Q = -10$.

4   If $P = 100r - t$, find the value of

    a P when $r = 0.25$ and $t = 10$

    b P when $r = 0.145$ and $t = 15.6$

    c t when $P = 18.5$ and $r = 0.026$

    d r when $P = 50$ and $t = -12$.

A rectangle is $3l$ cm long and l cm wide. If the area of the rectangle is A cm², write a formula for A.

Use your formula to find the area of this rectangle if it is 5 cm wide.

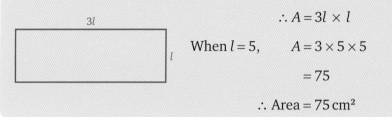

$$\text{Area} = \text{length} \times \text{width}$$
$$\therefore A = 3l \times l$$

When $l = 5$, $\quad A = 3 \times 5 \times 5$

$$= 75$$

$$\therefore \text{Area} = 75 \text{ cm}^2$$

5 Oranges cost n c each. If the cost of a box of 50 of these oranges is C cents, write a formula for C. Use your formula to find the cost of a box of oranges if each orange costs 12 c.

6 Lemons cost n c each. The cost of a box of 50 lemons is $\$L$. Write a formula for L. Use your formula to find the cost of a box of these lemons when they cost 10 c each.

Be careful with the units.

7 A rectangle is a cm long and b cm wide. Write a formula for P if P cm is the perimeter of the rectangle. Use your formula to find the perimeter of a rectangle measuring 20 cm by 15 cm.

8 The length of a rectangle is twice its width. If the rectangle is x cm wide, write a formula for P if its perimeter is P cm. Use your formula to find the width of a rectangle that has a perimeter of 36 cm.

9 A roll of paper is L m long. N pieces each of length r m are cut off the roll. If the length of paper left is P m, write a formula for P. Use your formula to find the length of paper left from a roll that was 20 m long after 10 pieces, each of length 1.5 m, are cut off.

10 An equilateral triangle has sides each of length a cm. If the perimeter of the triangle is P cm, write a formula for P. Use your formula to find the lengths of the sides of an equilateral triangle whose perimeter is 72 cm.

11 Tins of baked beans weigh a g each. N of these tins are packed into a box. The empty box weighs p g. Write a formula for W where W g is the weight of the full box. Use your formula to find the number of tins that are in a full box if the full box weighs 10 kg, the empty box weighs 1 kg and each tin weighs 200 g.

12 The rectangular box in the diagram is l cm long, w cm wide and h cm high. Write a formula for A if A cm² is the total surface area of the box (i.e. the area of all six faces). Use your formula to find the surface area of a rectangular box measuring 50 cm by 30 cm by 20 cm.

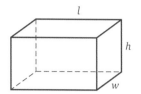

13 A person whose weight on Earth is W finds his weight on certain planets from these formulae:

   a weight on Venus 0.85 W

   b weight on Mars 0.38 W

   c weight on Jupiter 2.64 W.

Calculate your weight on each of the above planets.

Expressions, equations and formulae

In this chapter you have worked with expressions, equations and formulae.

Remember that:

- An *expression* is a collection of one or more algebraic terms, for example $2x$, $5x + 2y$, $a^2 - 4b$ and $6(2x - 3)$ are expressions.

- An *equation* is an equality between two expressions, for example $2x = 4$ and $y + 2 = 3x + 1$ are equations.

- A *formula* is a general rule for finding one quantity in terms of other quantities, for example the formula for finding the area, A cm², of a rectangle measuring l cm by b cm is $A = l \times b$.
  ($A = l \times b$ is also an equation.)

Exercise 3i

For each question write whether what is given is an expression, an equation or a formula.

1 $P = 2(l + b)$ **5** $y = \dfrac{1}{2}(3x + 3z)$ **9** $3x + 2y = 6$

2 $5x - 1 = 4x + 2$ **6** $3(x - 2) + 8$ **10** $A = \pi r^2$

3 $5x - 9 - \dfrac{1}{2}x = 0$ **7** $5a + 2b - 3(a - b)$ **11** $r = \dfrac{C}{2\pi}$

4 $4(a - 3) + 2(b + 4)$ **8** $\dfrac{1}{3}(x + 3) = 4$ **12** $4(7a + 4)$

Mixed exercises

Exercise 3j

1   Solve the equation $8 = 3 + 2x$.

2   Solve the equation $x - 4 = 5 - 2x + 1$.

3   Multiply out $3(2x - 8)$.

4   Simplify the expression $3x - 2(4 - x)$.

5   Write a formula for P if P cm is the perimeter of the figure in the diagram. (Each letter stands for a number of centimetres.)

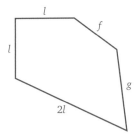

6   If $P = a - b$, find the value of P when $a = 2$ and $b = 5$.

Exercise 3k

1   Solve the equation $3 - x = 2 + 2x$.

2   Solve the equation $3(2x + 2) = 10$.

3   Simplify $6(3 - 2x) - 4(2 - x)$.

4   If $z = x - 2y$, find z when $x = 3$ and $y = -6$.

5   There are three classes in the first year of Appletown School. There are a children in one class, b children in another class and c children in the third class. Write a formula for the number, N, of children in the first year.

6   Given that $n = N - ab$, find the value of N when $n = 6$, $a = -1$ and $b = 2$.

Exercise 3l

1   Solve the equation $5(3 - 4x) = x - 2(3x - 5)$.

2   I think of a number and double it, then I add on 3 and double the result: this gives 14. If x stands for the number I first thought of, form an equation for x and then solve it.

3   Given that $r = s - vt$, find the value of r when $s = 4$, $v = 3$ and $t = -2$.

4   A rectangle is twice as long as it is wide. If it is a cm wide, write a formula for P where P cm is the perimeter of the rectangle.

5   Simplify $3(a - 5) - (4 - 3a) + 6a - 2$

6   Given $L = 3pq$, find the value of p when $L = 18$ and $q = 2$.

Exercise 3m

Select the letter that gives the correct answer.

1   The value of x that satisfies the equation $7x - 6 = 15$ is
    A 1   **B** 2   **C** 3   **D** 4

2   The value of x that satisfies the equation $2x + 3 = 5x - 9$ is
    A 2   **B** 3   **C** 4   **D** 5

3   The value of x that satisfies the equation $3x - 2 + 7x - 4 = 24$ is
    A 3   **B** 4   **C** 5   **D** 6

4   $2(x - 2) + 3(x + 5)$ simplifies to
    A $x + 2$ **B** $3x + 11$ **C** $4x - 1$ **D** $5x + 11$

5   $(+20) \div (-4)$ is equal to
    A -16 **B** -5 **C** 5   **D** 16

6   If $3x - 2(x - 5) = 14$ then $x =$
    A 3   **B** 4   **C** 5   **D** 6

7   Given that $P = q + r$, the value of P when $q = 3$ and $r = -4$ is
    A -2 **B** -1 **C** 1   **D** 2

8   Given that $R = 3(s + t)$, the value of s when $R = 48$ and $t = 11$ is
    A 2   **B** 3   **C** 4   **D** 5

9   I think of a number, treble it and add 3. The result is 18.
The number I first thought of was
    A 2   **B** 3   **C** 4   **D** 5

10 I think of a number, halve it and subtract 4. The result is 2.
The number I first thought of was
    A 6   **B** 8   **C** 10   **D** 12

Did you know?

The Italian scholar Jerome Cardan (1501–1576) was one of the greatest 16th century mathematicians. He was also considered to be a very strange man. Cardan 'read the stars', and claimed that he could, through them, tell the exact day of his death.

In this chapter you have seen that...

✔ to solve an equation where the unknown quantity is on both sides of the equals sign, collect the terms containing the unknown on the side where there are more of them

✔ when an equation contains brackets, multiply these out first

✔ when you substitute numerical values into a formula, place negative numbers in brackets.

4 Inequalities

At the end of this chapter you should be able to...

1 solve inequalities algebraically

2 represent inequalities on a diagram

3 use set builder notation to describe an inequality.

Did you know?

You know that there are an infinite number of counting numbers: 1 is the 1st, 2 is the 2nd, 3 is the third, 4 is the 4th, and so on.

Did you know that there are exactly the same number of positive even numbers? 2 is the 1st, 4 is the 2nd, 6 is the 3rd, 8 is the 4th, and so on.

You need to know...

✔ the meaning of the symbols <, ≤, > and ≥

✔ how to draw a number line

✔ the meaning of a set.

Key words

inequality, range, set builder notation, symbols <, ≤, > and ≥

Inequality notation

Consider the statement

'More than 1000 people came to see a firework display.'

This is an example of an inequality.

We do not know how many people were at the firework display, but if we use x as the variable number of people, we can write this statement as

$$x > 1000$$

where the symbol > means 'is greater than'.

Now consider the statement

'At least 50 students belong to the chess club.'

This is also an inequality but it is slightly different from the first example because it means 50 or more students belong to the chess club. Using n for the number of students we can write this statement as

$$n \geqslant 50$$

where the symbol $\geqslant$ means 'is greater than or equal to'.

Other inequalities involve quantities that are less than, or less than or equal to, a given quantity. For example, 'The cost of oil is now less than $60 a barrel' or 'Ten or fewer people came to the meeting'.

The symbols used in these cases are $<$ which means 'is less than' and $\leqslant$ which means 'is less than or equal to'.

Exercise 4a

Form an inequality from the statement 'more than 100 guests attended the wedding'.

$n > 100$ where n is the number of guests who attended the wedding.

Form an inequality from the following statements. For each question choose a letter to represent the variable and state what your letter stands for.

1 A school library can afford to buy fewer than 20 new books.

2 Fewer than 100 people attended a rally.

> Read the questions **very** carefully to make sure you understand whether the inequality includes the number given or does not.

3 More than 20 albums were sold on the first day.

4 Fifty or more cars passed the school between 9 and 10 a.m.

5 The perimeter of a rectangle is not more than 50 cm.

6 The cost of making a widget is less than $5.

7 Ceejay owns at least 3 goats.

8 There are more than 50 one dollar coins in a bag.

9 It takes at least 250 days to build a bungalow.

10 Victoria has more than 5 pens in her school bag.

11 Jesse has fewer than 5 rubbers in his school bag.

12 A box of fireworks contains at least 50 fireworks.

13   A bus journey takes 10 minutes or less to get to school.

14   There are at most twenty $5 bills in a cash box.

15   Anna is at least two years older than her sister Charelle, who is 4 years old.

Using a number line to illustrate inequalities

Consider the statement

$$x > 5$$

This is an *inequality* (as opposed to $x = 5$ which is an equality or equation).

This inequality is true when x stands for any number that is greater than 5. Thus there is a range of numbers that x can stand for and we can illustrate this range on a number line.

The circle at the left-hand end of the range is 'open', because 5 is not included in the range.

Exercise 4b

Use a number line to illustrate the range of values of x for which $x < -1$

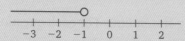

(The open circle means that −1 is not included. All values smaller than −1 are to the left of it on the number line.)

Use a number line to illustrate the range of values of x for which each of the following inequalities is true:

1    $x > 7$ 4 $x > 0$ <u>7</u> $x < 5$

2    $x < 4$ 5 $x < -2$ <u>8</u> $x < 0$

3    $x > -2$ 6 $x > \dfrac{1}{2}$ <u>9</u> $x < 1.5$

10   State which of the inequalities given in questions **1** to **9** are satisfied by a value of x equal to

     a   2   b   −3   c   0   d   1.5   e   0.0005

11   For each of the questions **1** to **9** give a number that satisfies the inequality and is

     a   a whole number   b   not a whole number.

12 Consider the true inequality $3 > 1$.

    a Add 2 to each side.   **c** Take 5 from each side.

    b Add −2 to each side.   **d** Take −4 from each side.

    In each case state whether or not the inequality remains true.

13 Repeat question **12** with the inequality $-2 > -3$.

14 Repeat question **12** with the inequality $-1 < 4$.

15 Try adding and subtracting different numbers on both sides of a true inequality of your own choice.

Solving inequalities

From the last exercise we can see that:

> An inequality remains true when the *same* number is added to, or subtracted from, *both* sides.

Now consider the inequality $x - 2 < 3$.

Solving this inequality means finding the range of values of x for which it is true.

Adding 2 to each side gives $x < 5$.

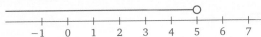

We have now solved the inequality.

Exercise 4c

Solve the following inequalities and illustrate your solutions on a number line:

1 $x - 4 < 8$ 5 $x + 4 < 2$

2 $x + 2 < 4$ 6 $x - 5 < -2$

3 $x - 2 > 3$ 7 $x - 3 < -6$

4 $x - 3 > -1$ 8 $x + 7 < 0$

Add 4 to each side first.

9 $x + 2 < -3$

Solve the inequality $4 - x < 3$.

$4 - x < 3$

(Aim to get the x term on one side of the inequality and the number term in the other.)

Add x to each side $\qquad\qquad 4 < 3 + x$

Take 3 from each side
If 1 is less than x then $\qquad 1 < x \quad$ or $\quad x > 1$
x must be greater than 1.

An inequality remains true if the sides are reversed but you must remember to reverse the inequality sign.

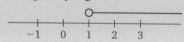

Solve the following inequalities and illustrate your solutions on a number line:

10 $4 - x > 6$	**16** $3 - x > 2$	**22** $3 - x < 3$
11 $2 < 3 + x$	**17** $6 < x + 8$	**23** $5 < x - 2$
12 $7 - x > 4$	**18** $2 + x < -3$	**24** $7 > 2 - x$
13 $5 < x + 5$	**19** $2 > x - 3$	**25** $3 > -x$
14 $5 - x < 8$	**20** $4 < 5 - x$	**26** $4 - x > -9$
15 $2 > 5 + x$	**21** $1 < -x$	**27** $5 - x < -7$

28 Consider the true inequality $12 < 36$.

    a Multiply each side by 2.   **d** Divide each side by 6.

    b Divide each side by 4.   **e** Multiply each side by −2.

    c Multiply each side by 0.5.   **f** Divide each side by −3.

    In each case state whether or not the inequality remains true.

29 Repeat question **28** with the true inequality $36 > -12$.

30 Repeat question **28** with the true inequality $-18 < -6$.

31 Repeat question **28** with a true inequality of your own choice.

32 Can you multiply both sides of an inequality by any one number and be confident that the inequality remains true?

An inequality remains true when both sides are multiplied or divided by the same *positive* number.

Multiplication or division of an inequality by a negative number should be avoided, because it destroys the truth of the inequality.

Exercise **4d**

Solve the inequality $2x - 4 > 5$ and illustrate the solution on a number line.

$$2x - 4 > 5$$

Add 4 to both sides $\qquad 2x > 9$

Divide both sides by 2 $\qquad x > 4\frac{1}{2}$

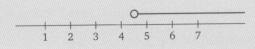

Solve the inequalities and illustrate the solutions on a number line:

1 $\quad 3x - 2 < 7$ $\qquad$ **3** $\quad 4x - 1 > 7$ $\qquad$ **5** $\quad 5 + 2x < 6$ $\qquad$ **7** $\quad 4x - 5 < 4$

2 $\quad 1 + 2x > 3$ $\qquad$ **4** $\quad 3 + 5x < 8$ $\qquad$ **6** $\quad 3x + 1 > 5$ $\qquad$ **8** $\quad 6x + 2 > 11$

Solve the inequality $3 - 2x \leqslant 5$ and illustrate the solution on a number line.
($\leqslant$ means 'less than or equal to'.)

(As with equations, we collect the letter term on the side with the greater number to start with. In this case we collect on the right.)

$$3 - 2x \leqslant 5$$

Add $2x$ to each side $\qquad 3 \leqslant 5 + 2x$

Take 5 from each side $\qquad -2 \leqslant 2x$

Divide each side by 2 $\qquad -1 \leqslant x \qquad$ i.e. which in reverse is $x \geqslant -1$

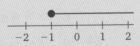

(A solid circle is used for the end of the range because -1 *is* included.)

Solve the inequalities and illustrate each solution on a number line:

9 $\quad 3 \leqslant 5 - 2x$ $\qquad$ **12** $\quad 4 \geqslant 9 - 5x$ $\qquad$ **15** $\quad x - 1 > 2 - 2x$ $\qquad$ **18** $\quad 2x + 1 \leqslant 7 - 4x$

10 $\quad 5 \geqslant 2x - 3$ $\qquad$ **13** $\quad 10 < 3 - 7x$ $\qquad$ **16** $\quad 2x + 1 \geqslant 5 - x$ $\qquad$ **19** $\quad 1 - x > 2x - 2$

11 $\quad 4 - 3x \leqslant 10$ $\qquad$ **14** $\quad 8 - 3x \geqslant 2$ $\qquad$ **17** $\quad 3x + 2 \leqslant 5x + 2$ $\qquad$ **20** $\quad 2x - 5 > 3x - 2$

Find, where possible, the range of values of x which satisfy both of the inequalities:

a $x \geqslant 2$ and $x > -1$ **b** $x \leqslant 2$ and $x > -1$ **c** $x \geqslant 2$ and $x < -1$

a

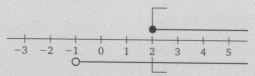

(Illustrating the ranges on a number line, we can see that both inequalities are satisfied for values on the number line where the ranges overlap.)

∴ $x \geqslant 2$ and $x > -1$ are both satisfied for $x \geqslant 2$.

b

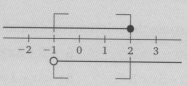

$x \leqslant 2$ and $x > -1$ are both satisfied for $-1 < x \leqslant 2$.

c

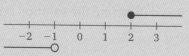

There are no values of x for which $x \geqslant 2$ and $x < -1$ are both satisfied. (The lines do not overlap.)

Find, where possible, the range of values of x for which the two inequalities are both true:

21 **a** $x > 2$ and $x > 3$

    b $x \geqslant 2$ and $x \leqslant 3$

    c $x < 2$ and $x > 3$

22 **a** $x \geqslant 0$ and $x \leqslant 1$

    b $x \leqslant 0$ and $x \leqslant 1$

    c $x < 0$ and $x > 1$

23 **a** $x \leqslant 4$ and $x > -2$

    b $x \geqslant 4$ and $x < -2$

    c $x \leqslant 4$ and $x < -2$

24 **a** $x < -1$ and $x > -3$

    b $x < -1$ and $x < -3$

    c $x > -1$ and $x < -3$

Solve each of the following pairs of inequalities and then find the range of values of x which satisfy both of them:

25 $x - 4 < 8$ and $x + 3 > 2$

26 $3 + x \leqslant 2$ and $4 - x \leqslant 1$

27 $x - 3 \leqslant 4$ and $x + 5 \geqslant 3$

28 $2x + 1 > 3$ and $3x - 4 < 2$

29 $5x - 6 > 4$ and $3x - 2 < 7$

30 $3 - x > 1$ and $2 + x > 1$

31 $1 - 2x \leqslant 3$ and $3 + 4x < 11$

32 $0 > 1 - 2x$ and $2x - 5 \leqslant 1$

Find the values of x for which $x - 2 < 2x + 1 < 3$.

$(x - 2 < 2x + 1 < 3$ represents two inequalities,

i.e. $x - 2 < 2x + 1$ and $2x + 1 < 3$, so solve each one separately.)

Some people call this a double-sided inequality.

$x - 2 < 2x + 1$	$2x + 1 < 3$
$-2 < x + 1$	$2x < 2$
$-3 < x$ i.e. $x > -3$	$x < 1$

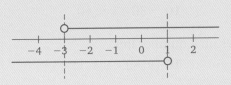

So $-3 < x < 1$

Find the range of values of x for which the following inequalities are true:

33 $x + 4 > 2x - 1 > 3$

34 $x - 3 \leqslant 2x \leqslant 4$

35 $3x + 1 < x + 4 < 2$

36 $2 - x < 3x + 2 < 8$

37 $2 - 3x \leqslant 4 - x \leqslant 3$

<u>38</u> $x - 3 < 2x + 1 < 5$

<u>39</u> $2x < x - 3 < 4$

<u>40</u> $4x - 1 < x - 4 < 2$

<u>41</u> $4 - 3x < 2x - 5 < 1$

<u>42</u> $x < 3x - 1 < x + 1$

 Puzzle

Find two numbers, one of which is twice the other, such that the sum of their squares is equal to the cube of one of the numbers.

Using set builder notation

The inequality $x > 5$ can also be described in words as 'the set of values of x such that x is greater than 5'. This can be written in symbols as $\{x \,|\, x > 5\}$, where the vertical line is short for 'such that'.

This is called *set builder notation*.

Similarly, $\{x \,|\, x \leqslant -1\}$ means 'the set of values of x such that x is less than or equal to -1',

and $\{x \,|\, 2 < x < 12\}$ means 'the set of values of x such that x is greater than 2 and less than 12'.

Exercise 4e

Write the following inequalities in set builder notation.

1 $x > 12$

2 $x < 2$

3 $x \geqslant -2$

4 $x \leqslant 10$

5 $2 < x < 6$

6 $-2 < x < 1$

7 $3 \leqslant x < 5$

8 $5 < x \leqslant 8$

9 $-3 \leqslant x \leqslant 0$

10 $30 < x \leqslant 40$

Illustrate the following inequalities on a number line.

11 $\{x \mid x > 5\}$

12 $\{x \mid x \leqslant -1\}$

13 $\{x \mid x \leqslant 4\}$

14 $\{x \mid x \geqslant 3\}$

15 $\{x \mid x \geqslant -1\}$

16 $\{x \mid -2 < x \leqslant 1\}$

17 $\{x \mid 0 \leqslant x \leqslant 3\}$

18 $\{x \mid -1 \leqslant x < 0\}$

19 $\{x \mid -2 < x \leqslant 2\}$

20 $\{x \mid -2 < x \leqslant -1\}$

Exercise 4f

Select the letter that gives the correct answer.

1 Which two of the numbers 3, 4, 6 and 7 satisfy the inequality $x > 5$?

  A 3 and 7   **B** 4 and 6   **C** 4 and 7   **D** 6 and 7

2 The solution of the inequality $5 - x > 4$ is

  A $x < 1$ **B** $x < 2$ **C** $x < 3$ **D** $x < 5$

3 If $4 \leqslant 7 - 3x$ then

  A $x < -1$ **B** $x \leqslant -1$ **C** $x < 1$ **D** $x \leqslant 1$

4 If $x > 3$ and $x \leqslant 4$ then

  A $2 < x \leqslant 4$ **B** $3 < x < 4$ **C** $3 < x \leqslant 4$ **D** $3 \leqslant x \leqslant 4$

5 Given that $x - 5 < 7$ and $x + 2 > 1$, then

  A $-1 < x < 12$ **B** $-1 < x \leqslant 10$ **C** $1 < x < 10$ **D** $1 < x < 12$

6 Written in set builder notation, $x > -3$ is

  A $\{x \mid x > -3\}$ **B** $\{x \mid x > -2\}$ **C** $\{x \mid x > 0\}$ **D** $\{x \mid x > 3\}$

7 One element on a number line that is **not** defined by $\{x \mid x \leqslant 2\}$ is

  A -2 **B** 0   **C** 1   **D** 3

8 One element on a number line defined by $\{x \mid -1 < x \leqslant 0\}$ is

  A -2 **B** -1 **C** 0   **D** 1

Did you know?

Optical illusions use patterns, shapes or colours to create images that are misleading.

Estimate which distance is the greater – from A to B or from B to C.

Now check your answer by measuring.

Investigate other optical illusions.

In this chapter you have seen that...

✔ an inequality remains true when the same number is added to, or subtracted from, both sides

✔ an inequality remains true when both sides are multiplied or divided by the same **positive** number. Do not multiply or divide an inequality by a negative number. It changes the direction of the inequality.

5 Sets

Did you know?

Venn diagrams are named after John Venn (1834–1923), an Englishman born in Yorkshire who studied logic at Cambridge University.

Key words

disjoint sets, element, empty set, equal set, finite set, infinite set, intersection of sets, member, null set, proper subset, set, subset, union of sets, universal set, Venn diagram, the symbols $\in$, $\notin$, $\subset$, $\subseteq$, $\cup$, $\cap$, $\emptyset$ and { }

Set notation

A *set* is a collection of things having something in common.

Things that belong to a set are called *members* or *elements*. When written down, these members or elements are usually separated by commas and enclosed by curly brackets or braces.

Instead of writing 'the set of Jamaican reggae artists', we write {Jamaican reggae artists}.

The symbol ∈ means 'is a member of' so that 'History is a member of the set of school subjects' may be written History ∈ {school subjects}.

Similarly the symbol ∉ means 'is not a member of'.

'Elm is not a breed of dog' may be written Elm ∉ {breeds of dogs}.

Exercise 5a

1 Use the correct set notation to write the following sets:

    a the set of teachers in my school   **b** the set of books I have read.

2 Write two members from each of the sets given in question **1**.

Describe in words the set {2, 4, 6, 8, 10, 12}.

{2, 4, 6, 8, 10, 12} = {even numbers from 2 to 12 inclusive}

3 Describe in words the given sets:

    a {1, 3, 5, 7, 9}

    b {Monday, Tuesday, Wednesday, Thursday, Friday}

Note that these descriptions must be very precise, e.g. it is correct to say
{1, 2, 3, 4, 5} = {first five natural numbers}
but it is incorrect to say
{alsation, boxer} = {breeds of dogs}
because there are many more breeds than the two that are given.

4 Describe a set that includes the given members of the following sets and state another member of each.

    a Hungary, Poland, Slovakia, Bulgaria   **b** 10, 20, 30, 40, 50

Write each of the following statements in set notation.

5 John is a member of the set of boys' names.

6 English is a member of the set of school subjects.

7 June is not a day of the week.

8 Monday is not a member of the set of domestic furniture.

State whether the following statements are true or false.

9 32 ∈ {odd numbers}

10 Washington ∈ {American states}

11 Washington ∈ {capital cities}

12 1 ∉ {prime numbers}

Finite, infinite, equal and empty sets

When we can write down all the members of a set, the set is called a *finite set*,
e.g. A = {days of the week} is a finite set because there are seven days in a week.
If we denote the number of members in the set A by $n(A)$, then $n(A) = 7$.

Similarly if B = {5, 10, 15, 20, 25, 30}, $n(B) = 6$
and if C = {letters in the alphabet}, $n(C) = 26$.

If there is no limit to the number of members in a set, the set is called an *infinite set*,
e.g. {even numbers} is an infinite set because we can go on adding 2 time and time
again.

Two sets are *equal* if they contain exactly the same elements, not necessarily in
the same order,

e.g. if A = {prime numbers greater than 2 but less than 9}

and B = {odd numbers between 2 and 8}

then $A = B$, i.e. they are equal sets.

A set that has no members is called an *empty* or *null* set. It is denoted by $\varnothing$ or { }.

Exercise 5b

Are the following sets finite or infinite sets?
1 {odd numbers}
2 {the number of leaves on a particular tree}
3 {trees more than 60 m tall}
4 {the decimal numbers between 0 and 1}

Find the number of elements in each of the following sets.
5 A = {vowels}
6 C = {prime numbers less than 20}

If $n(A)$ is the number of elements in set A, find $n(A)$ for each of the
following sets.
7 A = {5, 10, 15, 20, 25, 30}
8 A = {the consonants}
9 A = {players in a soccer team}

State whether or not the following sets are equal.
10 A = {8, 4, 2, 12}, B = {2, 4, 6, 8}

11   C = {letters of the alphabet except consonants}, D = {i, o, u, a, e}

12   X = {integers between 2 and 14 that are exactly divisible by 3 or 4},

   Y = {3, 4, 6, 8, 9, 12}

Determine whether or not the following sets are null sets.

13   {animals that have travelled in space}   15   {prime numbers less than 2}

14   {multiples of 11 between 12 and 20}   16   {consonants}

Universal sets

Think of the set {pupils in my class}.

With this group of pupils in mind we might well think of several other sets,

i.e. A = {pupils wearing spectacles}

   B = {pupils wearing brown shoes}

   C = {pupils with long hair}

   D = {pupils more than 150 cm tall}

We call the set {pupils in my class} a *universal set* for the sets A, B, C and D.

All the members of A, B, C and D must be found in a universal set, but a universal set may contain other members as well.

We denote a universal set by U or $\mathscr{E}$.

{pupils in my year at school} or {pupils in my school} would also be suitable universal sets for the sets A, B, C and D given above.

Exercise 5c

Suggest a universal set for {5, 10, 15, 20} and {6, 18, 24}.
U = {integers}

In questions **1** to **3** suggest a universal set for:

1   {knife, teaspoon}, {fork, spoon}

2   {10, 20, 30, 40}, {15, 25, 35}

3   {8, 12, 16, 20, 24}, {9, 12, 15, 18, 21, 24}

4 $U = \{$integers from 1 to 20 inclusive$\}$

$A = \{$prime numbers$\}$ $B = \{$multiples of 3$\}$

Find $n(A)$ and $n(B)$.

5 $U = \{$positive integers less than 16$\}$

$A = \{$factors of 12$\}$ $B = \{$prime numbers$\}$

$C = \{$integers that are exactly divisible by 2 and by 3$\}$

List the sets A, B and C.

6 $U = \{x,$ a whole number, such that $4 \leqslant x \leqslant 20\}$

$A = \{$multiples of 5$\}$ $B = \{$multiples of 7$\}$ $C = \{$multiples of 4$\}$

Find $n(A), n(B)$ and $n(C)$.

Subsets

If all the members of a set B are also members of a set A, then the set B is called a *subset* of the set A. This is written $B \subseteq A$. We use the symbol $\subseteq$ rather than $\subset$ if we don't know whether B could be equal to A.

Subsets that do not contain all the members of A are called *proper subsets*. If B is such a subset we write $B \subset A$.

Exercise 5d

If $A = \{$David, Edward, Fritz, Harry$\}$, write down all the subsets of A with exactly three members.

The subsets of A with exactly three members are

$\{$David, Edward, Fritz$\}$

$\{$David, Edward, Harry$\}$

$\{$David, Fritz, Harry$\}$

$\{$Edward, Fritz, Harry$\}$

1 If $A = \{$John, Joy, Peter, Anora, Tissha$\}$, write down all the subsets of A with exactly two female members.

2   If N = {positive integers from 1 to 15 inclusive}, list the following
    subsets of N:

   A = {odd numbers from 1 to 15 inclusive}

   B = {prime numbers less than 15}

   C = {multiples of 3 that are less than or equal to 15}

   Do sets A and B have any element in common?

3   If A = {even numbers from 2 to 20 inclusive}, list the following
    subsets of A:

   B = {multiples of 3}

   C = {prime numbers}

   D = {numbers greater than 12}

 Puzzle

During the day, because of the heat, the pendulum of a clock lengthens,
causing it to gain half a minute during daylight hours. During the night
the pendulum cools, causing it to lose one-third of a minute. The clock
shows the correct time at dawn on the first of August. When will it be five
minutes fast?

Venn diagrams

In the *Venn diagram* the universal set (U) is usually represented by a rectangle
and the subsets of the universal set by circles within the rectangle.

If U = {families}, A = {families with one car} and
B = {families with more than one car} the Venn diagram would be
as shown.

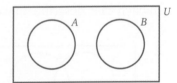

No family can have just one car and, at the same time, more than
one car,

i.e. A and B have no members in common.

Two such sets are called *disjoint sets*.

Exercise 5e

1

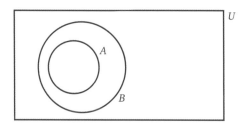

You are given the following information:

U = {pupils in my year}

A = {pupils in my class who are my friends}

B = {pupils in my class}

a Copy the Venn diagram and shade the region that shows the pupils in my class that are not my friends.

b Are all my friends in my class?

For each of questions **2** to **5** draw the diagram given below.

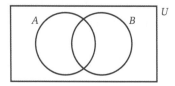

In questions **2** to **5**:

U = {pupils who attend my school}

A = {pupils who like coming to my school}

B = {pupils who are my friends}

In each case describe, in words, the shaded area.

2

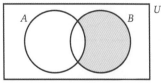

4

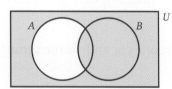

3

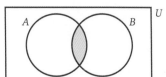

5

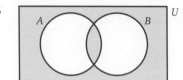

Union and intersection of two sets

If we write down the set of all the members that are in either set A or set B we have what we call the *union* of the sets A and B.

The union of A and B is written $A \cup B$.

The set of all the members that are members both of set A and of set B is called the *intersection* of A and B, and is written $A \cap B$.

$U = \{1, 2, 3, 4, 5, 6, 7, 8\}$

If $A = \{2, 4, 6, 8\}$ and $B = \{1, 2, 3, 4, 5\}$ find $A \cup B$ illustrating these sets on a Venn diagram.

$A \cup B = \{1, 2, 3, 4, 5, 6, 8\}$

We could show this on a Venn diagram as follows.

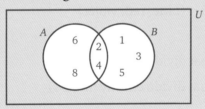

The white area represents the set $A \cup B$.

In questions **1** to **3** find the union of the two given sets, illustrating your answer on a Venn diagram.

1 $U = \{$girls' names beginning with the letter J$\}$

   $A = \{$Janet, Jill, Jamila$\}$ $B = \{$Judith, Janet, Jacky$\}$

2 $U = \{$positive integers from 1 to 16 inclusive$\}$

   $X = \{4, 8, 12, 16\}$ $Y = \{2, 6, 10, 14, 16\}$

3 $U = \{$letters of the alphabet$\}$

   $P = \{$letters in the word GEOMETRY$\}$

   $Q = \{$letters in the word TRIGONOMETRY$\}$

4 Draw suitable Venn diagrams to show the unions of the following sets, and describe these unions in words as simply as possible.

   a $U = \{$quadrilaterals$\}$ $A = \{$parallelograms$\}$ $B = \{$trapeziums$\}$

   b $U = \{$angles$\}$ $P = \{$obtuse angles$\}$ $Q = \{$reflex angles$\}$

$U = \{$integers from 1 to 12 inclusive$\}$

If $A = \{1, 2, 3, 4, 5, 6, 7, 8\}$ and $B = \{1, 2, 3, 5, 7, 11\}$ find $A \cap B$ and show it on a Venn diagram.

$A \cap B = \{1, 2, 3, 5, 7\}$

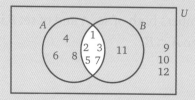

The white area represents the set $A \cap B$.

Draw suitable Venn diagrams to show the intersections of the following sets. In each case write the intersection in set notation.

5　$U = \{$integers from 4 to 12 inclusive$\}$

　　$X = \{4, 5, 6, 7, 10\}$　　　$Y = \{5, 7, 11\}$

6　$U = \{$colours of the rainbow$\}$

　　$A = \{$red, orange, yellow$\}$　　　$B = \{$blue, red, violet$\}$

7　$U = \{$positive whole numbers$\}$

　　$C = \{$positive whole numbers that divide exactly into 24$\}$

　　$D = \{$positive whole numbers that divide exactly into 28$\}$

8　$U = \{$integers less than 25$\}$

　　$A = \{$multiples of 3 between 7 and 23$\}$

　　$B = \{$multiples of 4 between 7 and 23$\}$

Simple problems involving Venn diagrams

Exercise 5g

If $U = \{$girls in my class$\}$

$A = \{$girls who play netball$\} = \{$Helen, Bina, Natori, Sara, Lana$\}$ and
$B = \{$girls who play tennis$\} = \{$Kath, Sara, Helen, Maria$\}$

Illustrate A and B on a Venn diagram. Use this diagram to write the following sets:

a　$\{$girls who play both netball and tennis$\}$

b　$\{$girls who play netball but not tennis$\}$

c If $n(U) = 30$ find the number of girls who play neither netball nor tennis.

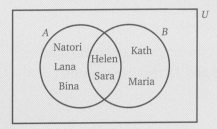

From the Venn diagram

a {girls who play both netball and tennis} = {Helen, Sara}

b {girls who play netball but not tennis} = {Natori, Lana, Bina}

c n(girls who play neither netball nor tennis) = 30 − 7 = 23

1 U = {the pupils in a class}

X = {pupils who like history}

Y = {pupils who like geography}

List the set of pupils who

  a like history but not geography

  b like geography but not history

  c like both subjects.

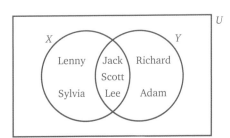

2 U = {boys in my class}

A = {boys who play soccer}

B = {boys who play rugby}

Write the sets of boys who

  a play soccer

  b play both games

  c play rugby but not soccer.

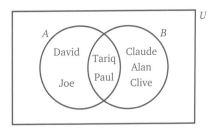

3 U = {my friends}

P = {friends who wear glasses}

Q = {friends who wear brown shoes}

List all my friends who

  a wear glasses

  b wear glasses but not brown shoes

  c wear both glasses and brown shoes.

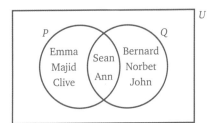

4   U = {whole numbers from 1 to 14 inclusive}

   A = {even numbers between 3 and 13}

   B = {multiples of 3 between 1 and 14}

   Illustrate this information on a Venn diagram and hence find
   a   the even numbers between 3 and 13 that are multiples of 3
   b $n(A)$ and $n(B)$.

5   U = {letters of the alphabet}

   P = {different letters in the word SCHOOL}

   Q = {different letters in the word SQUASH}

   Show these on a Venn diagram and hence find
   a $n(P)$
   b $n(P \cup Q)$
   c $n(P \cap Q)$

U = {months of the year}

A = {months of the year beginning with the letter J}

B = {months of the year ending with the letter Y}

a   Find $n(U)$, $n(A)$ and $n(B)$

Hence find

b $n(A \cap B)$
c $n(A \cup B)$

a $n(U) = 12$ (there are 12 months in a year)
   A = {January, June, July} so $n(A) = 3$
   B = {January, February, May, July} so $n(B) = 4$
b   We can illustrate these sets with a Venn diagram using the numbers in
   each region, rather than the members.

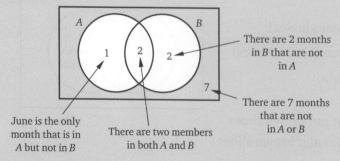

This shows that $n(A \cap B) = 2$.

c $n(A \cup B) = 5$

Alternatively, we know that $A \cup B$ is the set of months in both A and B. However two months, January and July, are in both A and B. This means that we cannot find $n(A \cup B)$ just by adding $n(A)$ and $n(B)$, because that includes the two months in $(A \cap B)$ twice.

Hence $n(A \cup B) = n(A) + n(B) - n(A \cap B)$

$$= 3 + 4 - 2 = 5$$

For any two sets, A and B, $n(A \cup B) = n(A) + n(B) - n(A \cap B)$

6   U = {letters of the alphabet}

  P = {letters used in the word LIBERAL}

  Q = {letters used in the word LABOUR}

  a   Find $n(U)$, $n(P)$ and $n(Q)$.

  b   Show these on a Venn diagram.

  c   Hence find **i** $n(P \cap Q)$ **ii** $n(P \cup Q)$ describing each of these sets.

7   U = {counting numbers less than 12}

  C = {prime numbers}

  D = {odd numbers}

  a   Find $n(U)$, $n(C)$ and $n(D)$.

  b   Show these on a Venn diagram.

  Hence find **i** $n(C \cap D)$ **ii** $n(C \cup D)$.

8   U = {whole numbers from 1 to 35 inclusive}

  R = {multiples of 4}

  S = {multiples of 6}

  a   Find $n(U)$, $n(R)$ and $n(S)$.

  b   Find **i** $n(R \cap S)$ **ii** $n(R \cup S)$.

9   A and B are two sets such that $n(A) = 8$, $n(B) = 5$ and $n(A \cap B) = 3$.
  Find $n(A \cup B)$.

Complement of a set

If U = {pupils in my school}

and A = {pupils who represent the school at games}

then the *complement* of A is the set of all the members of U that are not members of A.

In this case, the complement of A is

{pupils in my school who do not represent my school at games}

The complement of A is denoted by A'.

Similarly if U = {the whole numbers from 1 to 10 inclusive}

and A = {1, 3, 5, 7, 9}

the complement of A, i.e. A' = {2, 4, 6, 8, 10}.

Exercise 5h

Give the complement of P where

P = {Thursday, Friday} if U = {days of the week}

P' = {Monday, Tuesday, Wednesday, Saturday, Sunday}

Give the complement of each of the following sets.

1   A = {5, 15, 25} if U = {5, 10, 15, 20, 25}

2   B = {7, 8, 9, 10} if U = {5, 6, 7, 8, 9, 10, 11}

3   V = {a, e, i, o, u} if U = {letters of the alphabet}

4   P = {consonants} if U = {letters of the alphabet}

5   A = {Monday. Wednesday, Friday} if U = {days of the week}

6   X = {children} if U = {human beings}

7   M = {British motor cars} if U = {motor cars}

8   S = {male tennis players} if U = {tennis players}

9   C = {Jamaican towns} if U = {Caribbean towns}

10   D = {squares} if U = {quadrilaterals}

11   E = {adults over 80 years old} if U = {adults}

12   F = {male doctors} if U = {doctors}

If A = {men} and A' = {women}, what is U?

$U = A + A'$ = {adults}

13   If A = {homes with television sets}
and A' = {homes without television sets}, what is U?

14   If A = {vowels} and A' = {consonants}
     a   find $n(A)$ and $n(A')$
     b   what is $n(U)$?

15   X = {a, b, c, d, e} and X' = {f, g, h, i, j}.
     a   Write down $n(X)$ and $n(X')$. What is U?
     b   Hence write down $n(U)$.

16

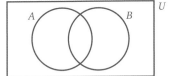

     a   Copy the Venn diagram and shade the region representing A'.
     b   Copy the Venn diagram and shade the region representing B'.

17

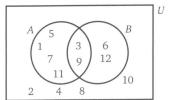

   Use this Venn diagram to find:
     a $n(A')$
     b $n(B')$
     c $n(A \cup B)$
     d $n(A \cup B)'$
     e $n(A \cup B) + n(A \cup B)'$
     f   Find $n(U)$ and compare your answer to your answer for part **e**.

18   U = {1, 2, 3, 4, 5, 6, 7, 8, 9, 10, 11, 12, 13, 14, 15}
     A = {factors of 12}   and B = {odd numbers}
     Show U, A and B on a Venn diagram.
     Hence find
     a $n(A' \cap B')$
     b $n(A \cup B)$
     c $n(A \cap B)'$
     d $n(A \cup B)'$
     e $n(A \cup B) + n(A \cup B)'$.
     f   Compare your answer for part **e** with the value of $n(U)$.

Using algebra and Venn diagrams to solve problems

In both questions **17** and **18** in the last exercise, part **f** showed that
$n(U) = n(A \cup B) + n(A \cup B)'$.

These Venn diagrams show that this result is true for any two sets.

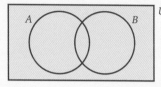 = 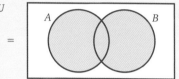 +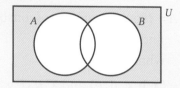

Therefore $n(U) = n(A \cup B) + n(A \cup B)'$

Now consider this example:

The Venn diagram illustrates the number of students

in A = {students who play soccer} and

in B = {students who play baseball}

from a group of 36 students.

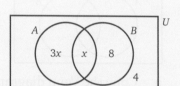

From the information in the diagram,

$n(A \cup B) = 3x + x + 8$ and $n(A \cup B)' = 4$

We know there are 36 students in the group, so $n(U) = 36$.

Using the result above we can form the equation

$36 = 3x + x + 8 + 4$

We can now solve this equation to find x:

Simplifying the equation gives $\quad 36 = 4x + 12$

Taking 12 from each side gives $\quad 24 = 4x$

Therefore $\quad x = 6$

Now we know the value of x we can find the value of $n(A)$ and of $n(B)$,

i.e. $\quad n(A) = 4x = 24$ and $n(B) = x + 8 = 14$

Exercise 5i

1   This Venn diagram shows the number of students in the chess
club (C) and the number of students in the athletics club (A)
in a class of 33.
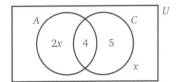
   a   Use the information to form an equation in x.
   b   Solve the equation and hence find the number of students
who are not in either club.

2   The Venn diagram shows the number of people in a drama
club who will sing (S) and the number of people who will
dance (D).
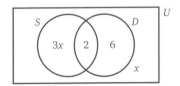
   a   Given $n(S) = 11$, form an equation in x.
   b   Solve the equation and hence find $n(U)$.

3   a   Use the information in the Venn diagram to find
expressions in terms of x for $n(A \cup B)$ and $n(A \cup B)'$.
   b   Given that $n(U) = 40$, form an equation in x.
   c   Solve the equation and hence find $n(A \cap B)$.

4   In the Venn diagram, P is a subset of A, and Q is a subset of B.

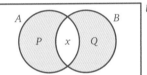

   a   Given that $n(A) = 10$ and $n(B) = 8$, write expressions for $n(P)$ and
$n(Q)$ in terms of x.
   b   If $n(A \cup B) = 24$, form an equation in x and solve it.
   c   Given that $n(A \cup B)' = 30$, find $n(U)$.

5   A and B are two sets and B is a subset of A.
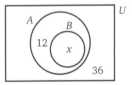
   a   Form an expression for $n(U)$ in terms of x.
   b   Form an equation in x given that $n(U) = 60$.
   c   Solve the equation and hence find $n(B)$.

6   A and B are two sets where $n(U) = 21$ and $n(A) = 8$.
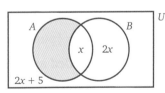
   a   Form an equation in x and solve it.
   b   Hence find $n(B)$ and $n(A \cap B')$.

Exercise 5j

Select the letter that gives the correct answer.

1 Which of the following are finite sets?

   i   vowels in the alphabet

   ii   trees less than 30 m tall

   iii decimal numbers between 1 and 2

   iv the number of leaves on a particular tree

   A i and ii   **B** i, ii and iii   **C** i, ii and iv   **D** i, iii and iv

2 If $P = \{2, 4, 6, 8, 10, 12, 14\}$, $n(P) =$

   A 5   **B** 6   **C** 7   **D** 8

3 Which of these three sets are null sets?

   $P = \{$multiples of 7 between 8 and 16$\}$

   $Q = \{$prime numbers less than 2$\}$

   $R = \{$multiples of 9 between 10 and 17$\}$

   A P and Q **B** P and R **C** P, Q and R **D** Q and R

4 $U = \{x,$ a whole number such that $5 \leqslant x \leqslant 20\}$.

   If $A = \{$multiples of 5$\}$ then $n(A)$ is

   A 1   **B** 2   **C** 3   **D** 4

5 If $U = \{$pupils who attend my school$\}$

       $X = \{$pupils who walk to school$\}$

       $Y = \{$pupils who are my friends$\}$

the shaded area in this Venn diagram represents

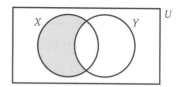

   A pupils who are my friends who walk to school

   B pupils who are my friends who do not walk to school

   C pupils who are not my friends who walk to school

   D pupils who are not my friends who do not walk to school.

6 If $U = \{$pupils who attend my school$\}$

       $X = \{$pupils who walk to school$\}$

       $Y = \{$pupils who are my friends$\}$

the shaded area in this Venn diagram represents

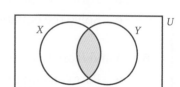

   A pupils who are my friends who walk to school

   B pupils who are my friends who do not walk to school

   C pupils who are not my friends who walk to school

   D pupils who are not my friends who do not walk to school.

7 $U = \{1, 2, 3, 4, 5, 6, 7, 8, 9, 10\}$

The set $\{2, 3, 4, 6, 8, 9, 10\}$ are the members in the set

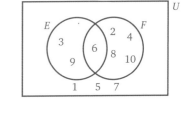

A E

B $E \cup F$

C $E \cap F$

D F

8 Using the same data as in question **7**, the members 3, 6, 9 are the only elements in the set

A E **B** $E \cup F$ **C** $E \cap F$ **D** F

Use this Venn diagram for questions **9** and **10**.

$U = \{\text{pupils in my class}\}$

$P = \{\text{pupils in my class who like maths}\}$

$Q = \{\text{pupils in my class who like science}\}$

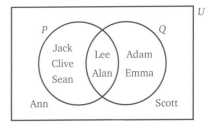

9 The pupils who like both maths and science are

A Adam and Emma

B Alan and Lee

C Ann and Scott

D Clive, Jack and Sean

10 The pupils who like maths but not science are

A Adam and Emma

B Alan and Lee

C Ann and Scott

D Clive, Jack and Sean

Investigation

Ask any 12 members of your class these questions:

Do you swim?   Do you play cricket?   Do you play football?

Now write the following sets:
A = {pupils in my class who swim}
B = {pupils in my class who play cricket}
C = {pupils in my class who play football}

Now write each name in the correct place in this Venn diagram.

For example a classmate who swims and plays cricket but does not play football goes in the region that is inside circle A, inside circle B but outside circle C. This is marked with a ×.

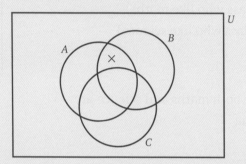

Write down a possible universal set.

Are there any empty sets? If there are, write a sentence to explain what each one means.

In this chapter you have seen that...

✔ an infinite set has no limit on the number of members in it

✔ in a finite set, all the members can be counted or listed

✔ the intersection of two sets contains the elements that are in both sets

✔ a proper subset of a set A contains some, but not all, of the members of A

✔ the union of two sets contains all the members of the first set together with the members of the second set that have not already been included

✔ when two sets have exactly the same members, they are said to be equal

✔ a set that has no members is called an empty or null set and is written { } or $\varnothing$

✔ $n(A \cup B) = n(A) + n(B) - n(A \cap B)$ and $n(U) = n(A \cup B) + n(A \cup B)'$.

6 Relations

Relations

Look at the pairs of numbers in the set $\{(1, 2), (2, 4), (6, 12)\}$.

There is the same relation between the numbers in each pair: the second number in each pair is twice the first number.

The pairs (1, 2), (2, 4) and (6, 12) are called *ordered pairs* because the order of the numbers in them is important. This is because if, for example, we change (1, 2) to (2, 1), it is no longer true that the second number is twice the first.

The set {(1, 2), (2, 4), (6, 12)} is an example of a relation.

A *relation* is a set of ordered pairs with a rule that connects the two objects in each pair.

The objects do not have to be numbers, and the relation does not have to be mathematical.

For example, John, David and Mary are friends.

John is taller than David and David is taller than Mary; each of these is a relation between two children.

We can write this information as a set of pairs: (David, John), (Mary, David).

John must also be taller than Mary, so we can add another pair with the same relation: (Mary, John).

Again, the order of the two names in each pair is important. For example, for the pair (John, David), the relation is not true because David is not taller than John.

We can describe the relation as 'the second child in each pair is taller than the first child'. We can write this relation as the set of ordered pairs

{(David, John), (Mary, David), (Mary, John)}

Exercise 6a

1   Describe the relation between the second and the first number in each pair in this set.

$$\{(1, 2), (2, 3), (5, 6), (10, 11)\}$$

2   Describe the relation between the second and the first number in each pair in this relation.

$$\{(1, 3), (2, 4), (6, 8), (10, 12)\}$$

3   Describe the relation between the second and the first number in each pair in this relation.

$$\{(2, 4), (3, 9), (4, 16), (5, 25)\}$$

4   This table shows the subject and number of pages in three school books.

Title	Number of pages
Maths	160
Spanish	210
Science	140

Write the set of ordered pairs in the relation described as 'The second book in each pair has more pages than the first book.'

5   This is a set of shapes {□, ⌂, ▲}.

Write the relation described as the set of ordered pairs where the first object is the number of sides and the second object is the shape.

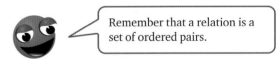

Remember that a relation is a set of ordered pairs.

6   This table lists some countries and their populations.

Country	Population
Jamaica	2 500 000
Trinidad	1 300 000
Barbados	300 000
St Lucia	150 000

Give the relation described as 'the second country has a larger population than the first country'.

7   The second number in each pair in this relation is the square of the first number. Fill in the missing numbers.

$$\{(2, 4), (5, \quad), (\quad , 64)\}$$

8 The second number in each pair in this relation is the next prime number that is larger than the first number. Fill in the missing numbers.

$$\{(8, 11), (6, \quad), (1, \quad), (14, \quad)\}$$

Domain and range

The *domain* of a relation is the set of the first objects in the ordered pairs.

For example, the domain of the relation {(1, 2), (2, 4), (6, 12)} is the set {1, 2, 6} and the domain of the relation {(David, John), (Mary, David), (Mary, John)} is the set {David, Mary}.

Notice that we do not include Mary twice as it is the same person.

The *range* of a relation is the set of the second objects in each ordered pair.

For example, the range of the relation {(1, 2), (2, 4), (6, 12)} is the set {2, 4, 12} and the range of the relation {(David, John), (Mary, David), (Mary, John)} is the set {John, David}.

Exercise 6b

1 Write the domain and the range of the relation {(1, 2), (2, 3), (5, 6), (10, 11)}.

2 Write the domain and range of each relation.
    a {(a, b), (a, c), (b, c)}   **b** {(□, □), (△, △), (▱, □)}

3 The set {2, 4, 6} is the domain of a relation. The second number in each ordered pair is the square of the first number. What is the range?

4 Fred, Dwayne and Scott are three boys. Fred is older than Dwayne and Dwayne is older than Scott.
    a Write the relation described as 'the second boy in each pair is older than the first boy.'
    b Give the domain and range.

5 Write the domain and range of each relation.
    a {(10°, acute), (150°, obtuse), (45°, acute), (175°, obtuse)}
    b {(t, t), (t, u), (s, t), (s, w)}

Mapping diagrams

We can represent a relation with a mapping diagram.

This mapping diagram represents the relation {(1, 2), (2, 4), (6, 12)}

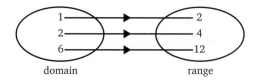

domain   range

The members of the domain are placed in one oval and the members in the range are placed in a second oval. The arrows show the association between the members in the domain and the members in the range.

We say that 1 maps to 2, 2 maps to 4 and 6 maps to 12.

This mapping diagram represents the relation {(David, David), (Mary, David), (Mary, John)}.

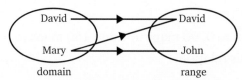

domain   range

This shows clearly that David maps to David and that Mary maps to John and David. This mapping diagram represents another relation.

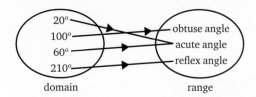

domain   range

We can use this diagram to write down the relation as a set of ordered pairs:

{(20°, acute angle), (100°, obtuse angle), (60°, acute angle), (210°, reflex angle)}

Exercise 6c

1   Draw a mapping diagram to represent these relations.
    a   {(1, 2), (2, 3), (5, 6), (10, 11)}
    b   {(a, b), (a, c), (b, c)}
    c   {(2, 4), (3, 9), (4, 16), (5, 25)}
    d   {(a, 2a), (b, 2b), (c, 2c)}

Start by writing down the domain and the range. Remember that these are sets so only list the different members of the set.

2   Each diagram represents a relation. Write the relation as a set of ordered pairs.

a

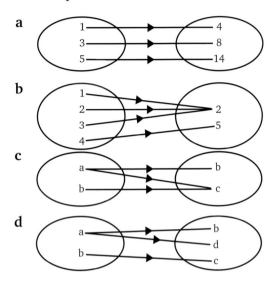

b

c

d

3   A relation is described as 0 maps to 0, 90 maps to 1 and 180 maps to 0. Draw a diagram to represent this relation.

Types of relation

Look again at the relation $\{(1, 2), (2, 4), (6, 12)\}$.

No two ordered pairs have the same first number, and no two ordered pairs have the same second number.

We can see this clearly from the mapping diagram:

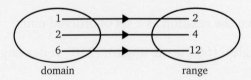

domain   range

There is only one arrow from every member of the domain. There is only one arrow to every member of the range. Every member of the domain maps to only one member of the range, and every member of the range comes from only one member of the domain.

Any relation where this is true is called a 'one to one' relation.
This is written as $1 : 1$ or 1–1.

There are other types of relation.

One type is where more than one member of the domain maps to one member of the range.

This is the case with this relation.

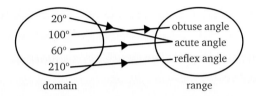

This type is called a 'many to one' relation, which we write as $n:1$.

Another type is where a member of the domain maps to more than one member of the range.

This is the case with this relation.

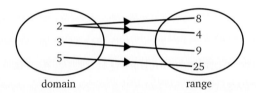

This is an example of a 'one to many' relation, written as $1:n$.

The last type of relation is where a member of the domain maps to more than one member of the range *and* more than one member of the domain maps to one member of the range.

This is the case with the relation {(David, John), (Mary, David), (Mary, John)}.

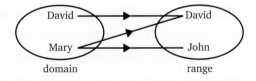

This type is called a 'many to many' relation. We write this as $n:n$.

This diagram summarises the different types of relation.

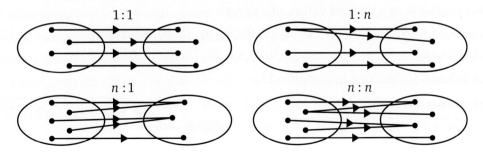

Exercise 6d

Describe the type of relation in each question in Exercise 6c.

Investigation

Kim, David, Jenny and Clare are Emma's family. They are Emma's mother, father, younger brother and younger sister.

1 David is older than Emma.

2 Clare is not Emma's younger brother.

3 Jenny is not Emma's father. She is also not Emma's younger sister.

Who is the mother, father, younger brother and younger sister?

Using tables

When the ordered pairs in a relation are numbers, such as {(1, 2), (2, 4), (6, 12)}, we can represent them in a *table of values*.

We use x to stand for the values of the first number in each pair and y to stand for the values of the second number in each pair.

So the relation {(1, 2), (2, 4), (6, 12)} can be represented by the table

x	1	2	6
y	2	4	12

The values of x give the members of the domain and the values of y give the members of the range.

Exercise 6e

1 Represent each relation as a table of values of x and y.

    a {(1, 2), (2, 4), (3, 6), (4, 8)}
    c {(10, 0), (7, 3), (5, 5), (0, 10)}

    b {(2, 1), (4, 2), (6, 3), (9, 4.5)}
    d {(0, 0), (1, 4), (2, 6), (3, 8), (4, 6)}

2 What type of relation is each one in question **1**?

3 The table represents a relation.

x	1	4	4	8	8
y	1	0	2	0	6

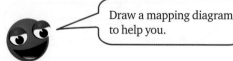

Draw a mapping diagram to help you.

What type of relation is this? Give a reason for your answer.

4   Repeat question **3** for these tables.

a

x	1	1	4	4	9
y	−1	1	−2	2	−3

b

x	1	2	2	4	3
y	1	1	2	2	−3

c

x	1	2	3	4	5
y	1	2	3	4	5

Equations

We have already seen that we can describe the connection between the two numbers in each ordered pair in the relation $\{(1, 2), (2, 4), (6, 12)\}$ as 'the second number in each pair is twice the first number'.

Using x to stand for the first number and y to stand for the second number, we can describe the connection more briefly as the equation $y = 2x$.

If we also give the values that x can have, we can use the equation to define the relation as

$$\{(x, y)\} \quad \text{where} \quad y = 2x \quad \text{for } x = 1, 2, 6$$

Now consider the relation $\{(x, y)\}$ where $y = 2x - 1$ for $x = 2, 4, 6, 8$.

This means that the value of x in the first ordered pair is 2 and we use the equation $y = 2x - 1$ to find the value of y by substituting 2 for x.

Remember that $2x$ means $2 \times x$, so when $x = 2$,

$$y = 2 \times 2 - 1$$

$$= 4 - 1 \text{ (do multiplication before subtraction)}$$

$$= 3$$

We can find the other ordered pairs in the same way and represent the relation in a table.

x	2	4	6	8
y	3	7	11	15

Exercise 6f

1 A relation is given by $\{(x, y)\}$ where
$y = 3x$ for $x = 1, 2, 3$.

Copy and complete this table of values.

x	1	2	3
y		6	

Remember that $3x$ means $3 \times x$.
To find y when $x = 1$, use the equation $y = 3x$ and substitute 1 for x, i.e. when $x = 1$, $y = 3 \times 1$.

2 A relation is given by $\{(x, y)\}$
where $y = 4x - 1$ for $x = 1, 2, 3$.

Copy and complete this table of values.

x	1	2	3
y		7	

Remember that multiplication and division must be done before addition and subtraction.

3 A relation is given by $\{(x, y)\}$ where $y = 10 - x$ for $x = 2, 4, 6, 8$.

Copy and complete this table of values.

x	2	4	6	8
y		6		

4 A relation is given by $\{(x, y)\}$ where $y = 12 - 2x$ for $x = 1, 2, 5, 6$.

Copy and complete this table of values.

x	1	2	5	6
y			2	

5 A relation is given by $\{(x, y)\}$ where
$y = x^2 + 1$ for $x = 1, 2, 3, 4$.

Copy and complete this table of values.

x	1	2	3	4
y			10	

Remember that x^2 means $x \times x$, so when $x = 2$, $x^2 + 1 = 2 \times 2 + 1$.

6 A relation is given by $\{(x, y)\}$ where
$y = 2x^2 - 1$ for $x = 1, 2, 3, 4$.

Copy and complete this table
of values.

x	1	2	3	4
y			17	

$2x^2$ means $2 \times x \times x$, so when $x = 4$,
$2x^2 - 1 = 2 \times (4 \times 4) - 1$.

7   A relation is given by $\{(x, y)\}$ where $y = x^2 - 3x + 4$ for $x = 1, 2, 3, 4$.

Copy and complete this table of values.

x	1	2	3	4
y		2		

8   A relation is given by $\{(x, y)$ where
$y = x^2 - x$ for $x = 1, 2, 3, 4$.

a   Copy and complete this table of values.

x	1	2	3	4
y		2		

b   Write the domain and range.

c   Represent the relation with an arrow diagram.

 d   What type of relation is this?

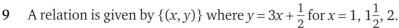

This means, is it a
1 : 1 relation or is
it one of the other
types?

9   A relation is given by $\{(x, y)\}$ where $y = 3x + \frac{1}{2}$ for $x = 1, 1\frac{1}{2}, 2$.

a   Copy and complete this table of values.

x	1	$1\frac{1}{2}$	2
y	$3\frac{1}{2}$		

b   Write the domain and range.

c   Represent the relation with an arrow diagram.

d   What type of relation is this?

10   A relation is given by $\{(x, y)\}$ where $y = x^2 - 5x + 6$ for $x = 1, 2, 3, 4$.

a   Copy and complete this table of values.

x	1	2	3	4
y		0	0	

b   Write the domain and range.

c   Represent the relation with an arrow diagram.

d   What type of relation is this?

11   A relation is given by $\{(x, y)\}$ where $y = x^3 - 8x^2 + 15x$ for $x = 0, 2, 3, 5$.

a   Copy and complete this table of values.

x	0	2	3	5
y			0	

b   Write the domain and range.

c   Represent the relation with an arrow diagram.

d   What type of relation is this?

Exercise 6g

Select the letter that gives the correct answer.

1   The relation between the first number and the second number in each
    of the pairs in the set {(2, 3), (3, 5), (4, 7), (5, 9), (6, 11)} is
    A   double the first number and subtract 1
    B   double the first number and add 1
    C   treble the first number
    D   treble the first number and subtract 3.

2   The second number in each pair in the following relation is double the
    first plus 3:
    {(3, 9), (6,), (8, 19)}
    The missing number is
    A   12   B   14   C   15   D   18

3   The domain of the relation {(3, 5), (4, 7), (5, 9), (6, 11)} is the set
    A   {3, 4, 5}   B   {3, 4, 5, 6}
    C   {4, 5, 6}   D   {5, 7, 9, 11}

4   The range of the relation {(3, 9), (4, 12), (5, 15), (6, 18)} is the set
    A   {3, 4, 5, 6}   B   {4, 5, 6}
    C   {9, 12, 15}   D   {9, 12, 15, 18}

5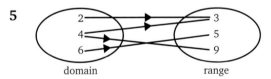

    Which type of relation is this?
    A   1 : 1   B   1 : n   C   n : 1   D   n : n

6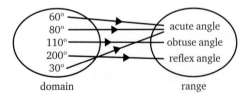

    Which type of relation is this?
    A   1 : 1   B   1 : n   C   n : 1   D   n : n

7 What type of relation is represented by the set {(a, b), (a , c), (b ,c), (c , b)}?

    A 1:1   **B** 1:n **C** n:1   **D** n:n

8 The table represents a relation.

x	2	5	4	5	7
y	1	0	3	2	5

What type of relation is this?

    A 1:1   **B** 1:n **C** n:1   **D** n:n

9 A relation is given by {(x, y)} where $y = 8 - 2x$ for $x = 1, 2, 4, 6$

x	1	2	4	6
y	6	4		−4

The missing number from this table is

    A −2   **B** 0   **C** 2   **D** 4

10 A relation is given by {(x, y)} where $y = x^2 - 3x + 4$ and x takes the values 1, 2, 3, 4.

x	1	2	3	4
y	2		4	8

The missing number from this table is

    A 0   **B** 1   **C** 2   **D** 4

Did you know?

One of the most important relations in physics is the relation between the position of a subatomic particle and its momentum. It is called the 'uncertainty relation' and was stated by the German theoretical physicist Werner Heisenberg in 1927 as:

> 'The more precisely the position is determined, the less precisely the momentum is known in this instant, and vice versa.'

In this chapter you have seen that...

✔ a relation is a set of ordered pairs

✔ the set of the first objects in each pair is the domain and the set of the second objects in each pair is the range

✔ a relation can be represented by a mapping diagram, e.g.

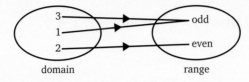

✔ a relation where a number maps to a number can be represented by an equation, e.g. $y = 2x$, together with the values that x can take

✔ there are four types of relation: $1:1$, $n:1$, $1:n$ and $n:n$.

REVIEW TEST 1: CHAPTERS 1–6

In questions **1** to **10**, choose the letter for the correct answer.

1 To two significant figures, 6.7483 =
   A   6.7   B   6.74   C   6.75   D   6.8

2 When simplified, $8 - 3(x - 2) =$
   A $5x - 10$ B $14 - 3x$ C $6 - 3x$ D $5x - 2$

3 Given that $p = q - 3r$, if $q = 5$, $r = -2$, then $p =$
   A   11   B   9   C   1   D   –4

4 The inverse of 3 under addition is
   A   3   B   –3   C $\frac{1}{3}$ D   0

5 p is an even number, q is an odd number and $r = p + q$.
   r is
   A   the identity element under addition
   B   the inverse of q under addition
   C   an odd number
   D   an even number.

6 64% as a fraction in its lowest terms is
   A $\frac{64}{100}$ B $\frac{32}{50}$ C $\frac{16}{25}$ D $\frac{16}{100}$

7 The value of 0.005 473 correct to 3 significant figures is
   A   0.005 47   B   0.0055   C   0.005   D   0.010

8 $\frac{3}{8}$ written as a decimal is
   A   0.3   B   0.375   C   0.8   D   0.875

9 $0.1 \div 0.001 =$
   A   10   B   100   C   1000   D   10 000

10 What type is the relation {(0, 0), (1, 5), (2, 6), (3, 5), (4, 6)}?
    A $1:1$ B $1:n$ C $n:1$ D $n:n$

11 Write in standard form
    a   243.2   b   57 300   c   426 000

12 Simplify   a $a^7 \div a^5$ b $\dfrac{a^5 \times a^7}{a^4}$

13 Give
    a 43 542 correct to 1 s.f.   **b** 4 260 000 correct to 2 s.f.

14 Change 55% into
    a a fraction in its lowest terms   **b** a decimal.

15 A book contains four short stories. The first is $\frac{1}{6}$ of the whole, the second $\frac{1}{8}$ of the whole, the third 126 pages, and the fourth $\frac{1}{3}$ of the whole. How many pages are there in the book?

16 Write
    a 27_{10} in base 5   **b** 34_5 in base 10.

17 Find
    a $12_4 + 231_4$ **b** $31_5 - 14_5$ **c** $23_5 \times 3_5$

18 Solve the equations
    a $x + 15 = 4x + 3$ **b** $2(3x - 3) = 9$

19 Simplify
    a $3(1 - 2x) + 9x - 2$ **b** $4(3x - 5) - 2(3 - 4x)$

20 **a** Solve the inequalities and illustrate each solution on a number line:
      i $5 > 7 + x$ **ii** $3x - 1 > 5$
    b Solve the inequalities $x - 3 < 7$ and $x + 2 > 4$.
      Now find the range of values of x which satisfy both inequalities.

21 $U = \{$letters of the alphabet$\}$
    $P = \{$letters used in the word ARITHMETIC$\}$
    $Q = \{$letters used in the word CARIBBEAN$\}$
    a Find $n(U)$, $n(P)$ and $n(Q)$.   **b** Show these sets on a Venn diagram.

22 If $N = \{$the positive integers 1 to 12 inclusive$\}$, list the following subsets of N:
    $A = \{$even numbers from 1 to 12 inclusive$\}$
    $B = \{$prime numbers $< 12\}$
    $C = \{$multiples of 3 that are less than or equal to 12$\}$.
    Do sets A and B have any element in common?

23 **a** Write down the domain and range of {(1, 4), (2, 5), (4, 7), (10, 13)}.

    b Draw a mapping diagram to represent the relation

       {(2, 5), (3, 10), (4, 17), (5, 26)}.

       What type of relation does this diagram represent?

24 A relation is given by {(x, y)} where $y = 5 + 2x$ for $x = 2, 4, 6, 8$.

    Copy and complete this table of values:

x	2	4	6	8
y		13		

25 A relation is given by {(x, y)} where $y = x^2$ for $x = -2, -1, 0, 1, 2, 3$.

    a Copy and complete this table of values:

x	-2	-1	0	1	2	3
y		1				

    b Write the domain and range.

    c Represent the relation with an arrow diagram.

    d What type of relation is this?

7 Coordinate geometry

At the end of this chapter you should be able to...

1 describe the position of a point with reference to a pair of perpendicular axes
2 plot points on a rectangular grid given the coordinates
3 write the coordinates of given points on a rectangular grid
4 know the meaning of the equation of a straight line and plot its graph
5 find the gradient of a straight line
6 find the equation of a straight line parallel to the *x*- or *y*-axis
7 illustrate a simple inequality as a region of the *xy*-plane.

Did you know?

The ideas used in this chapter are part of Descartes' *Geometry*. He thought of these ideas as he watched a fly crawling along a ceiling.

You will learn more about Descartes later.

You need to know...

✔ how to work with directed numbers

✔ what a relation is

✔ how to solve an inequality

✔ how to represent an inequality on a number line.

Key words

axis, Cartesian coordinate system, Cartesian plane, coordinates, domain, gradient, inequalities, range, region, relation, *y*-intercept

Plotting points using positive coordinates

There are many occasions when you need to describe the position of an object. For example, telling a friend how to find your house, finding a square in the game of battleships or describing the position of an aeroplane showing up on a radar screen. In mathematics we need a quick way to describe the position of a point.

We do this by using squared paper and marking a point O at the corner of one square. We then draw a line through O across the page. This line is called Ox. Next we draw a line through O up the page. This line is called Oy. Starting from O we then mark numbered scales on each line.

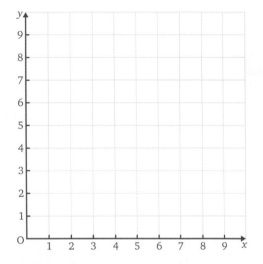

O is called the origin

Ox is called the x-axis

Oy is called the y-axis

We can now describe the position of a point A as follows:

start from O and move 3 units along Ox, then move 5 units up from Ox parallel to Oy.

We always use the same method to describe the position of a point:

start from O, *first* move *along* and *then up*.

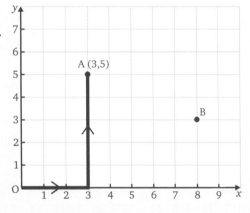

We can now shorten the description of the position of the point A to the number pair (3, 5).

The number pair (3, 5) is referred to as the *coordinates* of A.

The first number, 3, is called the x-coordinate of A.

The second number, 5, is called the y-coordinate of A.

Now consider another point B

whose x-coordinate is 8

and whose y-coordinate is 3.

If we simply refer to the point B(8, 3) this tells us all that we need to know about the position of B.

The origin is the point (0, 0).

The coordinates of a point are another example of an ordered pair.

The x-coordinate always comes first and the y-coordinate is always second.

This way of specifying the position of a point is called the *Cartesian coordinate system.*

Exercise 7a

1 Write the coordinates of the points A, B, C, D, E, F, G and H.

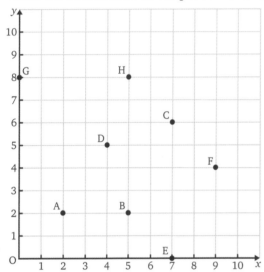

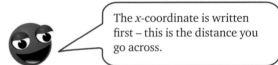

The x-coordinate is written first – this is the distance you go across.

2 Draw a set of axes of your own. Along each axis mark points 0, 1, 2, ..., 10 units from O. Mark the following points and label each point with its own letter:

A(2, 8) B(4, 9) C(7, 9) D(8, 7) E(8, 6) F(9, 4) G(8, 4)
H(7, 3) I(5, 3) J(7, 2) K(7, 1) L(4, 2) M(2, 0) N(0, 2)

Now join your points together in alphabetical order and join A to N.

3 Draw a set of axes and give them scales from 0 to 10.
Mark the following points:

A(2, 5) B(7, 5) C(7, 4) D(8, 4) E(8, 3)
F(9, 3) G(9, 2) H(6, 3) I(6, 1) J(7, 1)
K(7, 0) L(5, 0) M(5, 2) N(4, 2) P(4, 0)
Q(2, 0) R(2, 1) S(3, 1) T(3, 2) U(0, 2)
V(0, 3) W(1, 3) X(1, 4) Y(2, 4)

Remember, the first number is the distance you go across and the second number is the distance you go up.

Now join your points together in alphabetical order and join A to Y.

4 Mark the following points on your own set of axes:

A(2, 7)   B(8, 7)   C(8, 1)   D(2, 1)

Join A to B, B to C, C to D and D to A. What is the name of the figure ABCD?

5 Mark the following points on your own set of axes:

A(2, 2)   B(8, 2)   C(5, 5)

Join A to B, B to C and C to A. Describe fully the triangle ABC.

<u>6</u> Mark the following points on your own set of axes:

A(4, 0)   B(6, 0)   C(6, 4)   D(4, 4)

Join A to B, B to C, C to D and D to A. What is the name of the figure ABCD?

7 Mark the following points on your own set of axes:

A(5, 2)   B(8, 5)   C(5, 8)   D(2, 5)

Join the points to make the figure ABCD. What is ABCD?

<u>8</u> On your own set of axes mark the points A(8, 4), B(8, 8) and C(14, 6). Join A to B, B to C and C to A.

Describe fully the figure ABC.

For each of questions **9** to **14** you will need to draw your own set of axes.

9 The points A(2, 1), B(6, 1) and C(6, 5) are three corners of a square ABCD. Mark the points A, B and C. Find the point D and write the coordinates of D.

10 The points A(2, 1), B(2, 3) and C(7, 3) are three vertices of a rectangle ABCD. Mark the points and find the point D. Write the coordinates of D.

11 The points A(1, 4), B(4, 7) and C(7, 4) are three vertices of a square ABCD. Mark the points A, B and C and find D. Write the coordinates of D.

12 Mark the points A(2, 4) and B(8, 4). Join A to B and find the point C which is the midpoint (the exact middle) of the line AB. Write the coordinates of C.

13 Mark the points P(3, 5) and Q(3, 9). Join P and Q and mark the point R which is the midpoint of PQ. Write the coordinates of R.

14 Mark the points A(0, 5) and B(4, 1). Find the coordinates of the midpoint of AB.

Negative coordinates

If A(2, 0), B(4, 2) and C(6, 0) are three corners of a square ABCD, we can see that the fourth corner, D, is two squares below the x-axis.

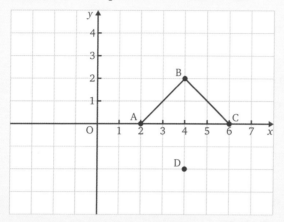

To describe the position of D we need to extend the scale on the y-axis below zero. To do this we use the negative numbers

$$-1, -2, -3, -4, \ldots$$

In the same way we can use the negative numbers $-1, -2, -3, \ldots$ to extend the scale on the x-axis to the left of zero.

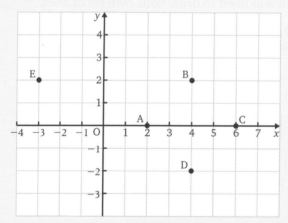

The set of the perpendicular x- and y-axes defines what is called the *Cartesian plane*.

The y-coordinate of the point D is written -2 and is called 'negative 2'.

The x-coordinate of the point E is written -3 and is called 'negative 3'.

The numbers 1, 2, 3, 4, ... are called positive numbers. They could be written as $+1, +2, +3, +4, \ldots$ but we do not usually put the $+$ sign in.

Now D is   4 squares to the right of O so its *x*-coordinate is 4

and   2 squares below the *x*-axis so its *y*-coordinate is –2,

D is the point (4, –2)

E is   3 squares to the left of O so its *x*-coordinate is –3

and   2 squares up from O so its *y*-coordinate is 2,

E is the point (–3, 2)

Exercise 7b

Use this diagram for questions **1** and **2**.

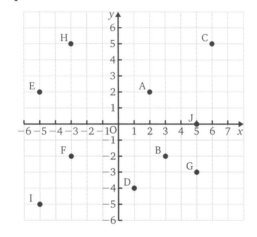

1 Write down the *x*-coordinate of each of the points A, B, C, D, E, F, G, H, I, J and O (the origin).

2 Write the *y*-coordinate of each of the points A, B, C, D, E, H, I and J.

In questions **3** to **8** draw your own set of axes and scale each one from –5 to 5.

3 Mark the points A(–3, 4), B(–1, 4), C(1, 3), D(1, 2), E(–1, 1), F(1, 0), G(1, –1), H(–1, –2), I(–3, –2).

Join the points in alphabetical order and join I to A.

4 Mark the points A(4, –1), B(4, 2), C(3, 3), D(2, 3), E(2, 4), F(1, 4), G(1, 3), H(–2. 3), I(–3, 2), J(–3, –1).

Join the points in alphabetical order and join J to A.

5 Mark the points A(2, 1), B(–1, 3), C(–3, 0), D(0, –2).

Join the points to make the figure ABCD. What is the name of the figure?

6 Mark the points A(1, 3), B(−1, −1), C(3, −1).
Join the points to make the figure ABC and describe ABC.

7 Mark the points A(−2, −1), B(5, −1), C(5, 2), D(−2, 2).
Join the points to make the figure ABCD and describe ABCD.

8 Mark the points A(−3, 0), B(1, 3), C(0, −4).
What kind of triangle is ABC?

In questions **9** to **18**, the points A, B and C are three corners of a square ABCD.
Mark the points and find the point D. Give the coordinates of D.

9   A(1, 1)   B(1, −1)   C(−1, −1)   **14**   A(−3, −1)   B(−3, 2)   C(0, 2)

10 A(1, 3)   B(6, 3)   C(6, −2)   **15**   A(0, 4)   B(−2, 1)   C(1, −1)

11 A(3, 3)   B(3, −1)   C(−1, −1)   **16**   A(1, 0)   B(3, 2)   C(1, 4)

12 A(−2, −1) B(−2, 3)   C(−6, 3)   **17**   A(−2, −1)   B(2, −2)   C(3, 2)

13 A(−5, −3) B(−1, −3) C(−1, 1)   **18**   A(−3, −2)   B(−5, 2)   C(−1, 4)

In questions **19** to **28**, mark the points A and B and the point C, the midpoint of
the line AB. Give the coordinates of C.

19 A(2, 2)   B(6, 2)   **24** A(2, 1)   B(6, 2)

20 A(2, 3)   B(2, −5)   **25** A(2, 1)   B(−4, 5)

21 A(−1, 3)   B(−6, 3)   **26** A(−7, −3) B(5, 3)

22 A(−3, 5)   B(−3, −7)   **27** A(−3, 3)   B(3, −3)

23 A(−1, −2) B(−9, −2)   **28** A(−7, −3) B(5, 3)

Straight lines

When the ordered pairs in a relation are numbers, as in {(1, 2), (2, 4), (6, 12)},
we can think of them as sets of coordinates.

This means we can represent them in a table and plot them as points, (x, y), on
a plane.

We use x to stand for the values of the first number in each pair and y to stand
for the second number in each pair.

So the relation {(1, 2), (2, 4), (6, 12)} can be represented by the table

x	1	2	6
y	2	4	12

The values of x give the members of the domain and the values of y give the
members of the range.

We can then represent these ordered pairs as points on a graph.

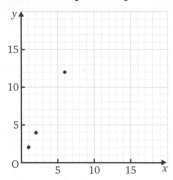

Exercise 7c

1 Represent each relation as a table of values of x and y and illustrate them on a graph.

   a {(1, 2), (2, 4), (3, 6), (4, 8)}   **c** {(10, 0), (7, 3), (5, 5), (0, 10)}

   b {(2, 1), (4, 2), (6, 3), (9, 4.5)}   **d** {(0, 0), (1, 4), (2, 6), (3, 8), (4, 6)}

2 A relation is represented by this table.

x	2	6	10
y	1	3	5

Illustrate the relation on a graph.

3 This graph illustrates a relation.

   a Represent the relation as a table.

   b Give the relation as a set of ordered pairs.

   c What type of relation is this?

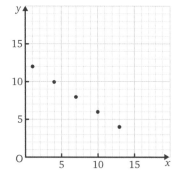

4 The points A, B, C, D and E illustrate a relation.

   a Represent these points as a table.

   b How is the y-coordinate of each point related to its x-coordinate?

   c The points A, B, C, D and E all lie on the same straight line.

   G is another point on this line. Its x-coordinate is 8; what is its y-coordinate?

   d F, H and I are also points on this line. Find the missing coordinates.

   (5,   ), (16,   ), (a,   )

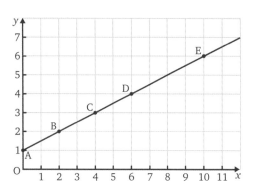

111

5 The points A, B, C and D illustrate a relation.

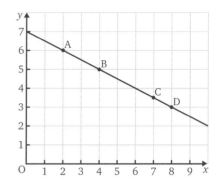

    a Represent these points as a table.

    b How is the *y*-coordinate of each point related to its *x*-coordinate?

    c The points A, B, C, and D all lie on the same straight line.

       E is another point on this line. Its *x*-coordinate is 5; what is its *y*-coordinate?

    d F, H and I are also points on this line. Find the missing coordinates.

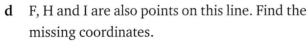

       (1,), (12,), (*a*,)

In the following questions we are going to investigate the properties of the diagonals of the special quadrilaterals. You will need your own set of axes for each question. Mark a scale on each axis from −5 to +5. Mark the points A, B, C and D and join them to form the quadrilateral ABCD.

6 A(5, −2) B(2, 4) C(−3, 4) D(0, −2)

    a What type of quadrilateral is ABCD?

    b Join A to C and B to D. These are the diagonals of the quadrilateral. Mark with an E the point where the diagonals cross.

    c Measure the diagonals. Are they the same length?

    d Is E the midpoint of either, or both, of the diagonals?

    e Measure the four angles at E. Do the diagonals cross at right angles?

For questions **7** to **10**, repeat question **6** for the following points.

7 A(2, −2) B(2, 4)   C(−4, 4) D(−4, −2)

8 A(2, −2) B(5, 4)   C(−3, 4) D(−1, −2)

9 A(2, 0)   B(0, 4)   C(−2, 0) D(0, −4)

10 A(1, −4) B(1, −1) C(−5, −1) D(−5, −4)

11 Name the quadrilaterals in which the two diagonals are of equal length.

12 Name the quadrilaterals in which the diagonals cut at right angles.

13 Name the quadrilaterals in which the diagonals cut each other in half.

Investigation

Draw your own set of x- and y-axes and scale each of them from −6 to +8.

Plot the points A(−1, 3), B(3, −1) and C(−1, −5).

1 Can you write

    a the coordinates of a point D such that ABCD is a square

    b the coordinates of a point E such that ACBE is a parallelogram

    c the coordinates of a point F such that CDEF is a rectangle?

2 Can you give the name of the special quadrilateral EDBF?

The equation of a straight line

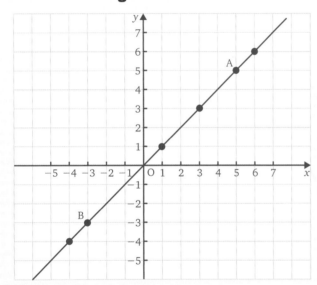

If we plot the points with coordinates (−4, −4), (1, 1), (3, 3) and (6, 6), we can see that a straight line can be drawn through these points that also passes through the origin.

For each point the y-coordinate is the same as the x-coordinate.

This is also true for any other point on this line,

e.g. the coordinates of A are (5, 5) and the coordinates of B are (−3, −3).

Hence y-coordinate $= x$-coordinate

or simply $y = x$

This is called the equation of the line.

We can also think of a line as a set of points, i.e. this line is the set of points, or *ordered number pairs*, such that $\{(x, y)\}$ satisfies the relation $y = x$.

It follows that if another point on the line has an x-coordinate of -5, then its y-coordinate is -5 and if a further point has a y-coordinate of 4, its x-coordinate is 4.

In a similar way we can plot the points with coordinates $(-2, -4)$, $(1, 2)$, $(2, 4)$ and $(3, 6)$.

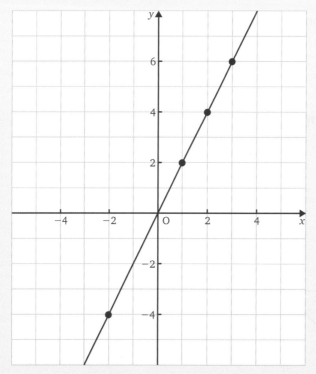

These points also lie on a straight line passing through the origin.

In each case the y-coordinate is twice the x-coordinate.

The equation of this line is therefore $y = 2x$ and we often refer to it simply as 'the line $y = 2x$'.

If another point on this line has an x-coordinate of 4,

$$\text{its } y\text{-coordinate is } 2 \times 4, \text{ i.e. } 8,$$

and if a further point has a y-coordinate of -5,

$$\text{its } x\text{-coordinate must be } -2\tfrac{1}{2}.$$

Exercise 7d

1   Find the y-coordinates of points on the line $y = x$ that have
    x-coordinates of
    a 2   **b** 3   **c** 7   **d** 12.

2   Find the y-coordinates of points on the line $y = x$ that have
    x-coordinates of
    a −1   **b** −6   **c** −8   **d** −20.

3   Find the y-coordinates of points on the line $y = -x$ that have
    x-coordinates of
    a $3\frac{1}{2}$ **b** $-4\frac{1}{2}$ **c** 6.1   **d** −8.3

4   Find the x-coordinates of points on the line $y = -x$ that have
    y-coordinates of
    a 7   **b** −2   **c** $5\frac{1}{2}$ **d** −4.2.

5   Find the y-coordinates of points on the line $y = 2x$ that have
    x-coordinates of
    a 5   **b** −4   **c** $3\frac{1}{2}$ **d** −2.6.

6   Find the x-coordinates of points on the line $y = -3x$ that have
    y-coordinates of
    a 3   **b** −9   **c** 6   **d** −4.

7   Find the x-coordinates of points on the line $y = \frac{1}{2}x$ that have
    y-coordinates of
    a 6   **b** −12   **c** $\frac{1}{2}$ **d** −8.2.

8   Find the x-coordinates of points on the line $y = -4x$ that have
    y-coordinates of
    a 8   **b** −16   **c** 6   **d** −3.

9   If the points $(-1, a)$, $(b, 15)$ and $(c, -20)$
    lie on the straight line with equation
    $y = 5x$, find the values of a, b and c.

A$(-1, a)$ lies on $y = 5x$. Replace y by a and x by -1. Then solve the equation to find a.

10 If the points $(3, a)$, $(-12, b)$ and $(c, -12)$ lie on the straight line with
    equation $y = -\frac{2}{3}x$, find the values of a, b and c.

11 Using 1 cm to 1 unit on each axis, plot the points $(-2, -6)$, $(1, 3)$,
    $(3, 9)$ and $(4, 12)$. What is the equation of the straight line that passes
    through these points?

12 Using 1 cm to 1 unit on each axis, plot the points (−3, 6) (−2, 4), (1, −2) and (3, −6). What is the equation of the straight line that passes through these points?

13 Using the same scale on each axis, plot the points (−6, 2), (0, 0), (3, −1) and (9, −3). What is the equation of the straight line that passes through these points?

14 Using the same scale on each axis, plot the points (−6, −4), (−3, −2), (6, 4) and (12, 8). What is the equation of the straight line that passes through these points?

15 Which of the points (−2, −4), (2.5, 4), (6, 12) and (7.5, 10) lie on the line $y = 2x$?

16 Which of the points (−5, −15), (−2, 6), (1, −3) and (8, −24) lie on the line $y = -3x$?

17 Consider these points:
(2, 2), (−2, 1), (3, 0), (−4.2, −2) and (−6.4, −3.2).
Which of the points lie

   a above the line $y = \frac{1}{2}x$

   b below the line $y = \frac{1}{2}x$?

Plotting the graph of a given equation

If we want to draw the graph of $y = 3x$ for values of x from −3 to +3, then we need to find the coordinates of some points on the line.

As we know that it is a straight line, two points are enough. However, it is sensible to find three points, the third point acting as a check on our working. It does not matter which three points we find, so we will choose easy values for x, one at each extreme and one near the middle.

If $x = -3,\quad y = 3 \times (-3) = -9$

If $x = 0,\quad y = 3 \times 0 = 0$

If $x = 3,\quad y = 3 \times 3 = 9$

These look neater if we write them in table form:

x	−3	0	3
y	−9	0	9

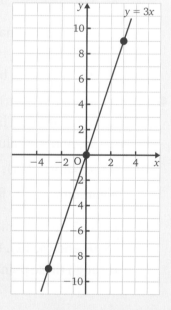

Exercise 7e

In questions **1** to **6**, draw the graphs of the given equations on the same set of axes. Use the same scale on both axes, taking values of x between -4 and 4, and values of y between -6 and 6. You should take at least three x values and record the corresponding y values in a table. Write the equation of each line somewhere on it.

1 $y = x$

3 $y = \frac{1}{2}x$

5 $y = \frac{1}{3}x$

2 $y = 2x$

4 $y = \frac{1}{4}x$

6 $y = \frac{3}{2}x$

In questions **7** to **12**, draw the graphs of the given equations on the same set of axes.

7 $y = -x$

9 $y = -\frac{1}{2}x$

11 $y = -\frac{1}{3}x$

8 $y = -2x$

10 $y = -\frac{1}{4}x$

12 $y = -\frac{3}{2}x$

We can conclude from these exercises that the graph of an equation of the form $y = mx$ is a straight line that:

- passes through the origin
- gets steeper as m increases
- makes an acute angle with the positive x-axis if m is positive
- makes an obtuse angle with the positive x-axis if m is negative.

Gradient of a straight line

The *gradient* or slope of a line is defined as the amount the line rises vertically divided by the distance moved horizontally,

i.e. gradient or slope of $AB = \dfrac{CB}{AC}$

The gradient of any line is defined in a similar way.

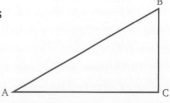

Considering any two points on a line, the gradient of the line is given by

$$\frac{\text{the increase in } y \text{ value}}{\text{the increase in } x \text{ value}}$$

If we plot the points $O(0, 0)$, $B(4, 4)$ and $C(5, 5)$, all of which lie on the line with equation $y = x$, then:

$$\text{gradient of } OC = \frac{LC}{OL} = \frac{5}{5} = 1$$

$$\text{gradient of } OB = \frac{NB}{ON} = \frac{4}{4} = 1$$

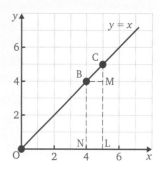

$$\text{gradient of BC} = \frac{MC}{BM} = \frac{5-4}{5-4} = \frac{1}{1} = 1$$

These show that, whichever two points are taken, the gradient of the line is 1.

Similarly, if we plot the points P(−3, 6), Q(−1, 2) and R(4, −8), all of which lie on the line with equation $y = -2x$, then:

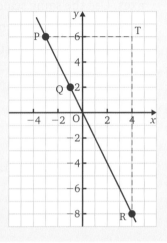

$$\text{gradient of PR} = \frac{\text{increase in } y \text{ value from P to R}}{\text{increase in } x \text{ value from P to R}}$$

$$= \frac{y\text{-coordinate of R} - y\text{-coordinate of P}}{x\text{-coordinate of R} - x\text{-coordinate of P}}$$

$$= \frac{(-8)-(6)}{(4)-(-3)}$$

$$= \frac{-8-6}{4+3} = \frac{-14}{7} = -2$$

Exercise 7f

Draw axes for x and y, for values between −6 and +6, taking 1 cm as 1 unit on each axis.

Plot the points A(−4, 4), B(2, −2) and C(5, −5), all of which lie on the line $y = -x$. Find the gradient of

a AB   **b** BC   **c** AC

a Gradient of AB
$$= \frac{(-2)-(4)}{(2)-(-4)} = \frac{-6}{6} = -1$$

b Gradient of BC
$$= \frac{(-5)-(-2)}{(5)-(2)} = \frac{-3}{3} = -1$$

c Gradient of AC
$$= \frac{(-5)-(4)}{(5)-(-4)} = \frac{-9}{9} = -1$$

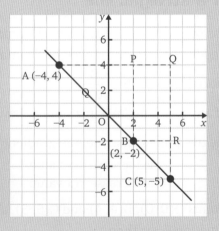

1 Using 2 cm to 1 unit on each axis, draw axes that range from 0 to 6 for x and from 0 to 10 for y. Plot the points A(2, 4), B(3, 6) and C(5, 10), all of which lie on the line $y = 2x$. Find the gradient of

     a AB   **b** BC   **c** AC

2 Draw the x-axis from −4 to 4 taking 2 cm as 1 unit, and the y-axis from −16 to 12 taking 0.5 cm as 1 unit. Plot the points X(−3, 12), Y(−1, 4) and Z(4, −16), all of which lie on the line $y = -4x$. Find the gradient of

    a XY   **b** YZ   **c** XZ

3 Choosing your own scale and range of values for both x and y, plot the points D(−2, −6), E(0, 0) and F(4, 12), all of which lie on the line $y = 3x$. Find the gradient of

    a DE   **b** EF   **c** DF

4 Taking 2 cm as 1 unit for x and 1 cm as 1 unit for y, draw the x-axis from −1.5 to 2.5 and the y-axis from −10 to 6. Plot the points A(−1.5, 6), B(0.5, −2) and C(2.5, −10), all of which lie on the line $y = -4x$. Find the gradient of

    a AB   **b** BC   **c** AC

Copy and complete the following table and use it to draw the graph of $y = 1.5x$.

x	−6	−4	0	2	4	6
y						

Choosing your own points, find the gradient of this line using two different sets of points.

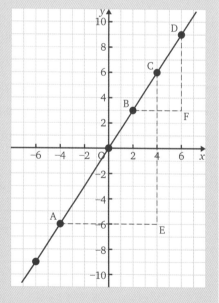

x	−6	−4	0	2	4	6
y	−9	−6	0	3	6	9

Four points, A, B, C and D, have been chosen.

$$\text{Gradient of line} = \frac{EC}{AE} = \frac{6-(-6)}{4-(-4)} = \frac{12}{8} = 1.5$$

$$\text{Gradient of line} = \frac{FD}{BF} = \frac{9-3}{6-2} = \frac{6}{4} = 1.5$$

(Finding the gradient using any other two points also gives a value of 1.5.)

5   Copy and complete the following table and use it to draw the graph of
    $y = 2.5x$.

x	−3	−1	0	2	4
y					

Choose your own pairs of points to find the gradient of this line at least
twice.

6   Copy and complete the following table and use it to draw the graph of
    $y = -0.5x$.

x	−6	−2	3	4
y				

Choose your own pairs of points to find the gradient of this line at least
twice.

7   Determine whether the straight lines with the following equations have
    positive or negative gradients:

a $y = 5x$ c $y = 12x$ e $3y = -x$

b $y = -7x$ d $y = -\dfrac{1}{4}x$ f $5y = -12x$

These exercises, together with the worked examples, confirm our conclusions on
page 117, namely that

- the larger the value of m the steeper is the slope
- lines with positive values for m make an acute angle with the positive x-axis
- lines with negative values for m make an obtuse angle with the positive x-axis.

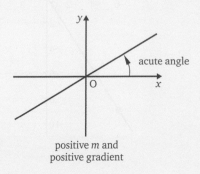

positive m and
positive gradient

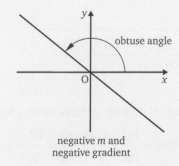

negative m and
negative gradient

Exercise 7g

For each of the following pairs of lines, state which line is the steeper. Show both lines on the same sketch.

1 $y = 5x$, $y = \frac{1}{5}x$

4 $y = -2x$, $y = -3x$

7 $y = -6x$, $y = -3x$

2 $y = 2x$, $y = 5x$

5 $y = 10x$, $y = 7x$

8 $y = 0.5x$, $y = 0.75x$

3 $y = \frac{1}{2}x$, $y = \frac{1}{3}x$

6 $y = -\frac{1}{2}x$, $y = \frac{1}{4}x$

Determine whether each of the following straight lines makes an acute angle or an obtuse angle with the positive x-axis.

9 $y = 4x$

12 $y = 3.6x$

15 $y = 10x$

18 $y = -\frac{2}{3}x$

10 $y = -3x$

13 $y = \frac{1}{3}x$

16 $y = 0.5x$

19 $y = -\frac{3}{4}x$

11 $y = -\frac{1}{2}x$

14 $y = 0.7x$

17 $y = -6x$

20 $y = -0.4x$

21 Estimate the gradient of each of the lines shown in the sketch.

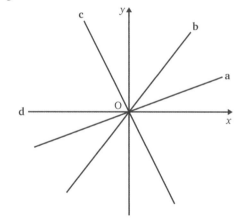

? Puzzle

Here is a very ingenious method of guessing the values of three dice thrown by a friend, without seeing them.

- Tell your friend to think of the first die.
- Multiply by 2. Add 5. Multiply by 5.
- Add the value of the second die.
- Multiply by 10. Add the value of the third die.
- Now ask for the total. From this total subtract 250.
- The three digits of your answer will be the values of the three dice.

As an example, if the total was 706, then $706 - 250 = 456$. The three dice were therefore 4, 5 and 6. Try it and see. Why does it work?

Lines that do not pass through the origin

If we plot the points $(-3, -1)$, $(1, 3)$, $(3, 5)$, $(4, 6)$ and $(6, 8)$, and draw the straight line that passes through these points, we can use it to find

a the equation of the line

b its gradient

c the distance from the origin to the point where the line crosses the y-axis.

a In each case, the y-coordinate is 2 more than the x-coordinate, i.e. all the points lie on the line with equation $y = x + 2$.

b Using the points A and B, the gradient of the line is given by

$$\frac{CB}{AC}, \quad \text{i.e.} \frac{3}{3} = 1$$

c The line crosses the y-axis at the point $(0, 2)$ which is 2 units above the origin. This quantity is called the *y-intercept*.

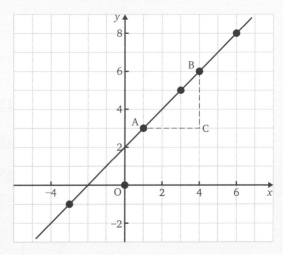

Exercise 7h

Draw the graph of $y = -4x + 3$ for values of x between -4 and $+4$.
Hence find

a the gradient of the line

b its y-intercept.

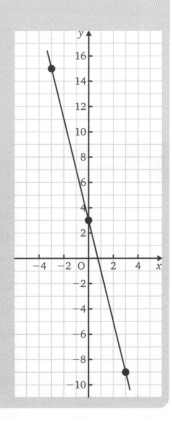

x	-3	0	3
y	15	3	-9

a Moving from the point $(0, 3)$ to $(-3, 15)$ the gradient is

$$\frac{3-15}{0-(-3)} = \frac{-12}{3} = \frac{-4}{1} = -4$$

b The y-intercept is 3.

In the following questions, draw the graph of the given equation using the given x values. Hence find the gradient of the line and its intercept on the y-axis. Use 1 cm as 1 unit on each axis with x values ranging from -8 to $+8$ and y values ranging from -10 to $+10$.

Compare the values you get for the gradient and the y-intercept with the numbers in the right-hand side of each equation.

1 $y = 3x + 1$; x values -3, 1, 3
Use your graph to find the value of y when x is   **a** -2 **b** 2

2 $y = -3x + 4$; x values -2, 2, 4
Use your graph to find the value of y when x is   **a** -1 **b** 3

3 $y = \frac{1}{2}x + 4$; x values -8, 0, 6
Use your graph to find
   a the value of y when x is -2 **b** the value of x when y is 6

4 $y = x - 3$, x values -4, 2, 8
Use your graph to find the value of x when y is   **a** 4 **b** -5

5 $y = \frac{3}{4}x + 3$; x values -4, 0, 8
Use your graph to find the value of x when y is   **a** 6 **b** 4.5

Draw the graph of $y = -2x + 3$ for values of x between -4 and $+4$.
Hence find

a the gradient of the line   **b** its y-intercept.

Compare the values for the gradient and the y-intercept with the number of x's and the number term on the right-hand side of the equation.

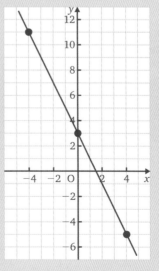

x	-4	0	4
y	11	3	-5

a Gradient of line $= \dfrac{3-11}{0-(-4)} = -\dfrac{8}{4}$
$$= -2$$

b The y-intercept is 3.

The number of x's on the right-hand side is -2, which is the same as the gradient of the line.

The number term on the right-hand side is 3, which is the same as the y-intercept.

In the following questions, draw a graph for each of the given equations. In each case find the gradient and the y-intercept for the resulting straight line. Take 1 cm as 1 unit on each axis, together with suitable values of x within the range −4 to +4. Choose your own range for y when you have completed the table.

Compare the values you get for the gradient and the y-intercept with

a the number of x's

b the number term on the right-hand side of the equation.

6 $y = 2x - 2$ **8** $y = 3x - 4$ **10** $y = -\dfrac{3}{2}x + 3$ **12** $y = -2x - 7$

7 $y = -2x + 4$ **9** $y = \dfrac{1}{2}x + 3$ **11** $y = 2x + 5$ **13** $y = -3x + 2$

Lines parallel to the axes

Now we will see what happens when the gradient of a line is zero.

Think, for example, of the equation $y = 3$.

For every value of x the y-coordinate is 3. This means that the graph of $y = 3$ is a straight line parallel to the x-axis at a distance 3 units above it.

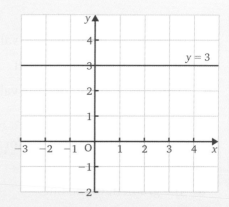

$y = c$ is therefore the equation of a straight line parallel to the x-axis at a distance c units away from it. If c is positive, the line is above the x-axis, and if c is negative, the line is below the x-axis.

Similarly $x = b$ is the equation of a straight line parallel to the y-axis at a distance b units from it.

Exercise 7i

Draw, on the same diagram, the straight-line graphs of $x = -3$, $x = 5$, $y = -2$ and $y = 4$.

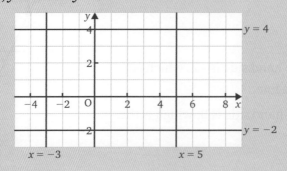

In the following questions, take both x and y in the range -8 to $+10$, Let 1 cm be 1 unit on each axis.

1 Draw the straight-line graphs of the following equations in a single diagram:

$x = 2, x = -5, y = \frac{1}{2}, y = -3\frac{1}{2}$

2 Draw the straight-line graphs of the following equations in a single diagram:

$y = -5, x = -3, x = 6, y = 5.5$

3 On one diagram, draw graphs to show the following equations:

$x = 5, y = -5, y = 2x$

Write down the coordinates of the three points where these lines intersect. What kind of triangle do they form?

4 On one diagram, draw the graphs of the straight lines with equations

$x = 4, y = -\frac{1}{2}x, y = 3$

Write down the coordinates of the three points where these lines intersect. What kind of triangle is it?

5 On one diagram, draw the graphs of the straight lines with equations

$y = 2x + 4, y = -5, y = 4 - 2x$

Write down the coordinates of the three points where these lines intersect. What kind of triangle is it?

Illustrating inequalities in the Cartesian plane

In Chapter 6 we represented inequalities on a number line. Now we look at them in a more visual way.

If we have the inequality $x \geqslant 2$, x can take any value greater than or equal to 2. This can be represented by the following diagram.

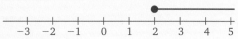

On this number line, x can take any value on the heavy part of the line including 2 itself, as indicated by the solid circle at 2.

If $x > 2$ then the diagram is as shown below.

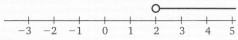

In this case, x cannot take the value 2 and this is shown by the open circle at 2.

It is sometimes more useful to use two-dimensional space with x and y axes, rather than a one-dimensional line. We represent $x \geqslant 2$ by the set of points whose x-coordinates are greater than or equal to 2. (y is not mentioned in the inequality so y can take any value.)

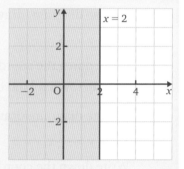

The boundary line represents all the points for which $x = 2$ and the region to the right contains all points with x-coordinates greater than 2.

To indicate this, and to make future work easier, we use a continuous line for the boundary when it is included and we shade the region we do *not* want.

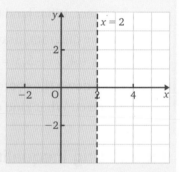

The inequality $x > 2$ tells us that x may not take the value 2. In this case we use a broken line for the boundary.

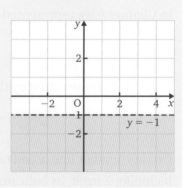

We can draw a similar diagram for $y > -1$

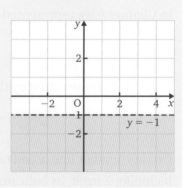

Exercise 7j

Draw diagrams to represent these inequalities:

a $x \leqslant 1$ 　　　　　　**b** $2 < y$

a $x \leqslant 1$

　　The boundary line is $x = 1$ (included).

　　The unshaded region represents $x \leqslant 1$

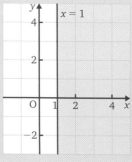

b $2 < y$

　　The boundary line is $y = 2$
　　(not included).

　　The unshaded region represents $2 < y$

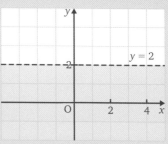

Draw diagrams to represent the following inequalities:

1 $x \geqslant 2$ 　　**3** $x > -1$ 　　**5** $x \geqslant 0$ 　　**7** $x \leqslant -4$

2 $y \leqslant 3$ 　　**4** $y < 4$ 　　**6** $0 > y$ 　　**8** $2 < x$

Draw a diagram to represent $-3 < x < 2$ and state whether or not the points $(1, 1)$ and $(-4, 2)$ lie in the given region.

$-3 < x < 2$ gives two inequalities, $-3 < x$ and $x < 2$, so the boundary lines are $x = -3$ and $x = 2$ (neither included). Shade the regions not wanted.

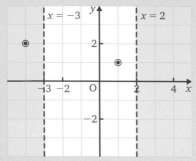

The unshaded region represents $-3 < x < 2$

Plot the points. Then you see that $(-4, 2)$ does not lie in the given region.

$(1, 1)$ lies in the given region.

Draw diagrams to represent the following pairs of inequalities:

9 $2 \leqslant x \leqslant 4$　　　**12** $4 < y < 5$　　　**15** $-\frac{1}{2} \leqslant x \leqslant 1\frac{1}{2}$

10 $-3 < x < 1$　　　**13** $0 \leqslant x < 4$　　　**16** $-2 \leqslant y < -1$

11 $-1 \leqslant y \leqslant 2$　　　**14** $-2 < y \leqslant 3$　　　**17** $3 \leqslant x < 5$

18　In each of the questions **9** to **11**, state whether or not the point (1, 4) lies in the unshaded region.

Give the inequality that defines the unshaded region.

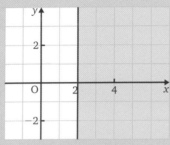

Boundary line $x = 2$ (included)

Inequality is $x \leqslant 2$

Give the inequalities that define the unshaded region.

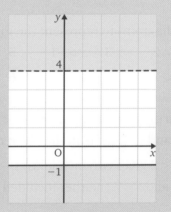

Boundary lines $y = 4$ (not included)

and　　　　　$y = -1$ (included)

The inequalities are $y < 4$ and $y \geqslant -1$　or　$-1 \leqslant y < 4$.

Give the inequalities that define the unshaded regions:

19 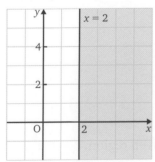　　　　**20**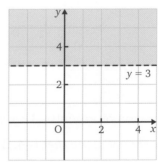

21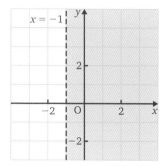

23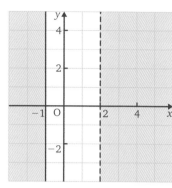

22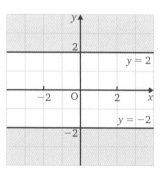

24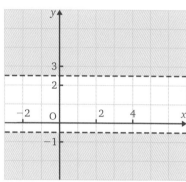

25 In each of the questions **19** to **24** state whether or not the point $(2, -1)$ is in the unshaded region.

In questions **26** to **29** give the inequalities that define the *shaded* regions:

26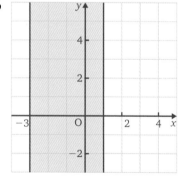

28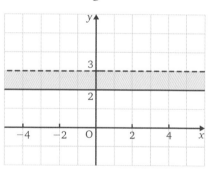

27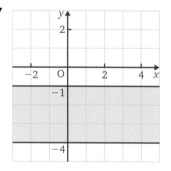

29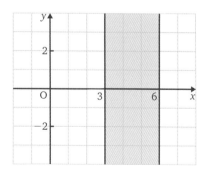

30 In each of the questions **26** to **29** state whether or not the point $(0, 2)$ is in the shaded region.

Exercise 7k

Draw a diagram to represent the region defined by the set of inequalities
$-1 \le x \le 2$ and $-5 \le y \le 0$

There are four inequalities here: $-1 \le x$, $x \le 2$, $-5 \le y$ and $y \le 0$.

The boundary lines are

$x = -1$: for $-1 \le x$, shade the region on the left of the line

$x = 2$: for $x \le 2$, shade the region on the right of the line

$y = -5$: for $-5 \le y$, shade the region below this line

$y = 0$: for $y \le 0$, shade the region above the line

The unshaded region represents the inequalities.

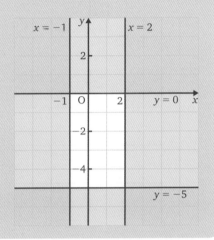

Draw diagrams to represent the regions described by the following sets of inequalities. In each case, draw axes for values of x and y from -5 to 5.

1   $2 \le x \le 4, -1 \le y \le 3$

2   $-2 < x < 2, -2 < y < 2$

3   $-3 < x \le 2, -1 \le y$

4   $0 \le x \le 4, 0 \le y \le 3$

5   $-4 < x < 0, -2 < y < 2$

6   $-1 < x < 1, -3 < y < 1$

7   $x \ge 0; y \ge 0$

8   $x \ge 1, -1 \le y \le 2$

Give the sets of inequalities that describe the unshaded regions:

9

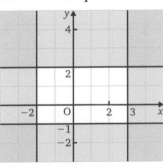

10

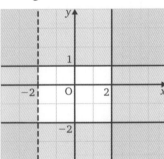

11   Is the point $(2\frac{1}{2}, 0)$ in either of the unshaded regions in questions **9** and **10**?

Give the sets of inequalities that describe the unshaded regions:

12

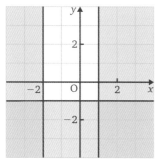

14

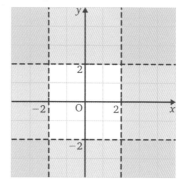

13

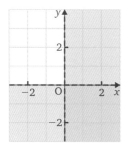

15

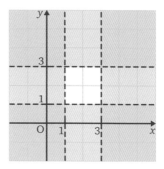

Solve each of the following inequalities and find the range of values that satisfies them both. Illustrate your solution as a region of the xy plane.

16 $x + 3 > 1$ and $x + 2 < 3$

17 $y + 4 \geqslant 5$ and $y + 3 \leqslant 5$

18 $2x > -4$ and $3 - x > 0$

19 $x > 0$ and $y \leqslant 3$

20 $x + 1 \geqslant 1$, $2x \leqslant 6$, $y \geqslant 0$ and $2y \leqslant 8$

Exercise 7I

Select the letter that gives the correct answer.
Use this diagram for questions **1** to **7**.

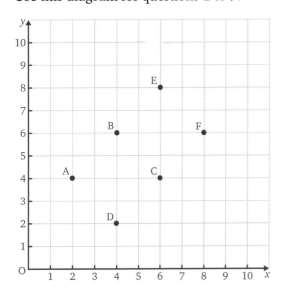

1   The coordinates of B are

    A   (3, 6)   **B**   (4, 5)   **C**   (4, 6)   **D**   (5, 6)

2   The coordinates of F are

    A   (5, 6)   **B**   (5, 8)   **C**   (6, 8)   **D**   (8, 6)

3   When the points A, B, C, D, A are joined in order the resulting shape is a

    A   rectangle   **B**   rhombus   **C**   square   **D**   trapezium

4   When the points A, E, F, D, A are joined in order to give a quadrilateral
    the resulting shape is a

    A   rectangle   **B**   rhombus   **C**   square   **D**   trapezium

5   The coordinates of the midpoint of the line segment AF are

    A   (4, 5)   **B**   (5, 4)   **C**   (5, 5)   **D**   (6, 6)

6   The angle between the line segments BF and BE is

    A   30°   **B**   45°   **C**   60°   **D**   90°

7   The angle ACF between the line segments AC and CF is

    A   acute   **B**   a right angle   **C**   obtuse   **D**   reflex

Use this diagram for questions **8** to **12**.

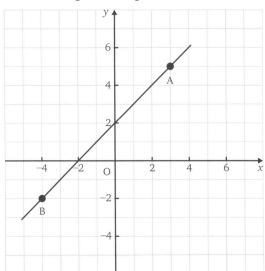

8 The coordinates of the point A are

    A $(2, 5)$ **B** $(2, 6)$ **C** $(3, 4)$ **D** $(3, 5)$

9 The coordinates of the point B are

    A $(-4, -2)$ **B** $(-4, 2)$ **C** $(-2, 2)$ **D** $(-2, 4)$

10 The gradient of the line AB is

    A -2 **B** -1 **C** 1 **D** 2

11 The y-intercept is

    A -2 **B** -1 **C** 1 **D** 2

12 The coordinates of the midpoint of the line segment AB are

    A $(-1, 1)$ **B** $\left(-\dfrac{1}{2}, 1\dfrac{1}{2}\right)$ **C** $(0, 2)$ **D** $\left(\dfrac{1}{2}, 2\dfrac{1}{2}\right)$

13

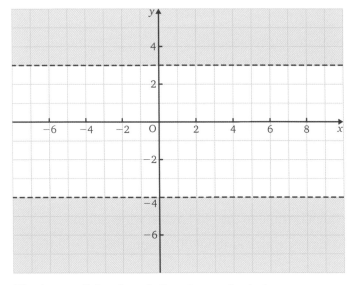

The inequalities that define the unshaded area are

    A $-4 < y < 3$ **B** $-4 < y \leqslant 3$ **C** $-4 \leqslant y < 3$ **D** $-4 \leqslant y \leqslant 3$

14

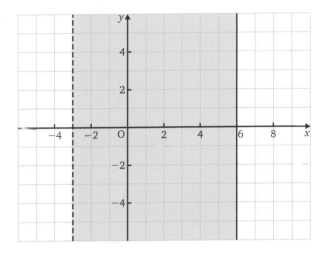

The inequalities that define the shaded area are

A $-4 < x < 6$ **B** $-4 < x \leqslant 6$ **C** $-4 \leqslant x < 6$ **D** $-4 \leqslant x \leqslant 6$

15

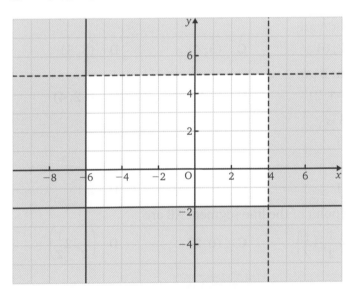

The inequalities that define the unshaded area are

A $-6 < x < 4$ and $-2 \leqslant y < 5$

B $-6 < x \leqslant 4$ and $-2 < y < 5$

C $-6 \leqslant x < 4$ and $-2 \leqslant y < 5$

D $-6 \leqslant x < 4$ and $-2 < y < 5$

Did you know?

A US gallon is 231 cubic inches, which is equal to the old English wine gallon.

An imperial gallon is 277.42 cubic inches, which is about 20% more than a US gallon.

In this chapter you have seen that...

✔ you can write down the coordinates of a point as an ordered pair of numbers

✔ the first number (x-coordinate) gives distance across and the second number (y-coordinate) gives distance up or down

✔ you can find the missing coordinate of a point on a line, given the equation of the line and one coordinate, by substituting the given coordinate into the equation and solving it

✔ you can draw a straight-line graph, given its equation, by finding the coordinates of three points on the line

✔ you can find the gradient of a straight line by calculating $\dfrac{\text{increase in } y}{\text{increase in } x}$ from one point to another point on the line

✔ the equation of a straight line parallel to the x-axis is $y = a$ and the equation of a straight line parallel to the y-axis is $x = b$.

8 Reflections and translations

At the end of this chapter you should be able to...

1 identify shapes that have lines of symmetry

2 complete drawings of shapes, given their lines of symmetry

3 draw in lines of symmetry for given shapes

4 find the mirror line given a reflection

5 represent a vector by a straight line

6 write a vector as an ordered pair in a column

7 describe a translation using a vector.

Did you know?

Many well-known trademarks have line symmetry, for example logos on cars.
Which trademarks can you find that have line symmetry?

You need to know...

✔ how to plot points on a set of x and y axes

✔ the equations of lines parallel to the x and y axes

✔ the meaning of image and object

✔ the meaning of a translation and of a reflection

✔ how to use a protractor to draw an angle.

Key words

bilateral symmetry, displacement, image, invariant point, line symmetry, line of symmetry, mapped, midpoint, mirror line, object, parallel, perpendicular, reflection, right angle, scalar, translation, vector

Transformations

A transformation of a shape moves it or reflects it or rotates it or enlarges it. This diagram shows different transformations of a triangle marked A.

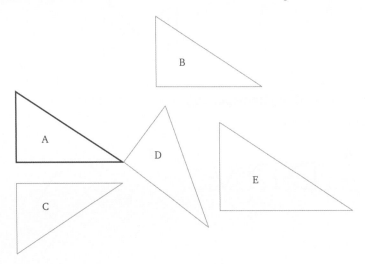

The *object* is triangle A. The *images* are transformations of A. Triangle B is a translation of A, triangle C is a reflection of A, triangle D is a rotation and triangle E is an enlargement.

In this chapter we concentrate on *reflections* and *translations*.

Line symmetry

 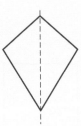 

As we saw in Book 1, shapes like these are *symmetrical*. They have *line symmetry* (or *bilateral symmetry*); the dashed line is the *line of symmetry* because if the shape were folded along the dashed line, one half of the drawing would fit exactly over the other half.

Exercise 8a

1 Which of the following shapes have a line of symmetry?

A    B   C

Copy the following drawings on square grid paper and complete them so that the dashed line is the line of symmetry.

2 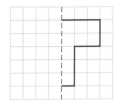   4    6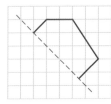

3    5 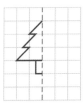   7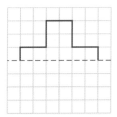

Two or more lines of symmetry

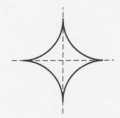   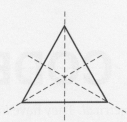   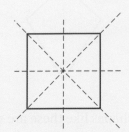

Shapes can have more than one line of symmetry. In the drawings above, the lines are shown by dashed lines and it is clear that the first shape has two lines of symmetry, the second has three and the third has four.

Exercise 8b

Sketch or trace the shapes in questions **1** to **12**. Mark in the lines of symmetry and say how many there are. (Some shapes may have no line of symmetry.)

1

5

9

2

6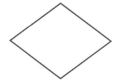

10

3

7

11

4

8

12

Copy and complete the following drawings on square grid paper. The dashed lines are the lines of symmetry.

13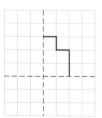

15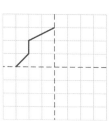

<u>17</u>

14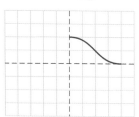

16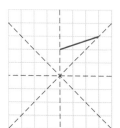

<u>18</u>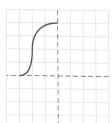

19   Draw, on square grid paper or on plain paper, shapes of your own with more than one line of symmetry.

Puzzle

Show how sixteen counters can be arranged in ten rows with exactly four counters in each row.

Reflections

We saw in Book 1 that when we reflect an object in a line (called the *mirror line*), the object and its image together form a symmetrical shape.

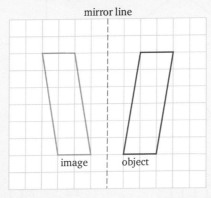

Exercise 8c

In each question copy the object and the mirror line on to square grid paper and draw the image of each object.

1
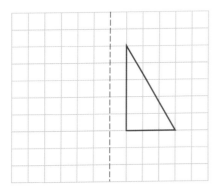

2
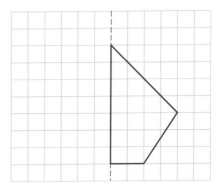

3

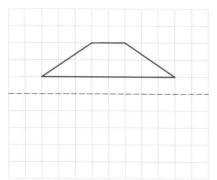

4

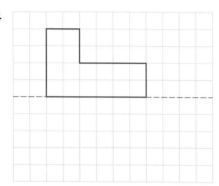

5

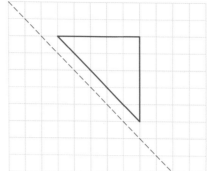

6

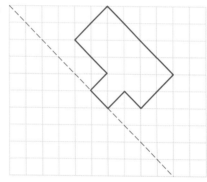

In questions **7** to **11** use graph paper and a scale of 1 cm to 1 unit.

7 Draw axes, for x from −5 to 5 and for y from 0 to 5. Draw triangle ABC by plotting A(1, 2), B(3, 2) and C(3, 5). Draw the image A′B′C′ when ABC is reflected in the y-axis.

8 Draw axes, for x from 0 to 5 and for y from −2 to 2. Draw triangle PQR where P is (1, −1), Q is (5, −1) and R is (4, 0). Draw the image P′Q′R′ when △PQR is reflected in the x-axis.

9 Draw axes for x and y from −5 to 1. Draw rectangle WXYZ: W is (−3, −1), X is (−3, −2), Y is (−5, −2) and Z is (−5, −1). Draw the mirror line $y = x$. Draw the image W′X′Y′Z′ when WXYZ is reflected in the mirror line.

10 Draw axes for x and y from −1 to 9. Plot the points A(2, 1), B(5, 1), C(7, 3) and D(4, 3). Draw the parallelogram ABCD and its image by reflection in the line $y = x$.

11 Draw axes for x and y from −6 to 8. Draw triangle ABC when A is (−6, −2), B is (−3, −4) and C is (−2, −1). Draw the following images of triangle ABC:

  a triangle $A_1B_1C_1$ by reflection in the y-axis

  b triangle $A_2B_2C_2$ by reflection in the line $y = -x$ (this is the straight line through the points (2, −2), (−4, 4))

  c triangle $A_3B_3C_3$ by reflection in the x-axis

  d triangle $A_4B_4C_4$ by reflection in the line $x = -1$.

Finding the mirror line

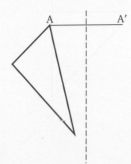
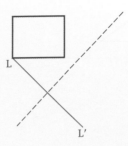

We can see from these diagrams, and from the work in the previous exercise, that the object and image points are at equal distances from the mirror line, and the lines joining them (e.g. AA′ and LL′) are perpendicular (at right angles) to the mirror line.

Exercise 8d

Find the mirror line if △A′B′C′ is the image of △ABC.

The mirror line is halfway between an object point and its image and perpendicular to the line through them.

So the mirror line is halfway between B and B′ and perpendicular to the line BB′. Check that it also goes through the midpoint of CC′.

The mirror line is the line $x = 1$.

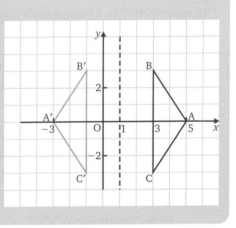

Copy the diagrams in questions **1** to **4** and draw in the mirror lines.

1

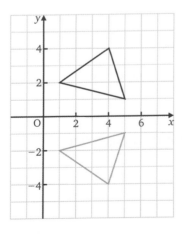

2

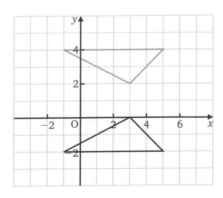

3 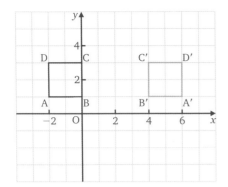 4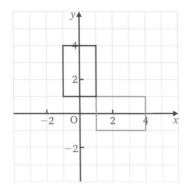

Draw axes for *x* and *y* from –5 to 5 for each of questions **5** to **8**.

5   Draw square PQRS: P(1, 1), Q(4, 1), R(4, 4), S(1, 4). Draw square
    P′Q′R′S′: P′(–2, 1), Q′(–5, 1), R′(–5, 4), S′(–2, 4). Draw the mirror line so
    that P′Q′R′S′ is the reflection of PQRS and write its equation.

6   Draw △XYZ: X(2, 1), Y(4, 4), Z(–2, 4),
    and △X′Y′Z′: X′(2, 1), Y′(4, –2), Z′(–2, –2).
    Draw the mirror line so that △X′Y′Z′ is the
    reflection of △XYZ and write its equation.
    Are there any invariant points? If there are,
    name them.

 An *invariant point* is where
a point on the object and the
corresponding point on the
image are in the same place.

7   Draw △ABC: A(–2, 0), B(0, 2), C(–3, 3), and △PQR: P(3, –1), Q(4, –4),
    R(1, –3). Draw the mirror line so that △PQR is the reflection of △ABC.
    Which point is the image of A? Are there any invariant points? If there
    are, name them.

<u>8</u>   Draw lines AB and PQ: A(2, –1), B(4, 4), P(–2, –1), Q(–5, 4). Is PQ a
    reflection of AB? If it is, draw the mirror line. If not, give a reason.

If A′B′C′ is the reflection of ABC,
draw the mirror line.

(Join AA′ and BB′ and find their midpoints,
marking them P and Q. Then PQ is the
mirror line.)

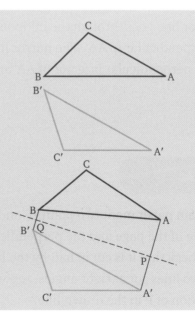

Whenever you attempt to draw a mirror line in this way, always check that the mirror line is at right angles to AA' and BB'. If it is not, then A'B'C' cannot be a reflection of ABC.

9 Trace the diagrams and draw the mirror lines.

a

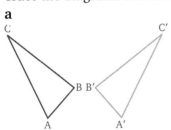

b

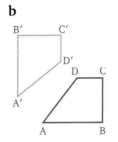

c

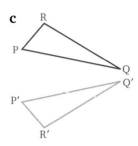

10 Draw axes for x and y from –4 to 5. Draw △ABC: A(3, 1), B(4, 5), C(1, 4), and △A'B'C': A'(0, –2), B'(–4, –3), C'(–3, 0). Draw the mirror line so that △A'B'C' is the image of △ABC.

11 Draw axes for x and y from –4 to 4. Draw lines AB and PQ: A(–4, 3), B(0, 4), P(1, –2), Q(2, 2). Draw the mirror line so that AB is the image of PQ.

12 Draw axes for x and y from –3 to 5. Draw △XYZ: X(3, 2), Y(5, 2), Z(3, 5), and △LMN: L(0, –3), M(0, –1), N(–3, –1). Draw the mirror line so that △LMN is the image of △XYZ.

Construction of the mirror line

If we have only one point and its image, and we cannot use squares to guide us, we can use the fact that the mirror line goes through the midpoint of AA' and is perpendicular to AA'. The mirror line is therefore the perpendicular bisector of AA' and can be drawn.

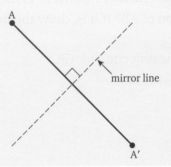

Exercise 8e

1 On plain paper mark two points P and P' about 10 cm apart in the middle of the page and the perpendicular bisector of PP'. Join PP' and check that it is cut in half by the line you have drawn and that the two lines cut at right angles. Are we correct in saying that P' is the reflection of P in the drawn line?

2   On square grid paper draw axes for x and y from –5 to 5, using 1 cm to 1 unit. A is the point (5, 2) and A′ is the point (–3, –3). Draw the mirror line so that A′ is the reflection of A.

3   Draw axes for x and y from –1 to 8, using 1 cm to 1 unit. B is the point (–1, 0) and B′ is the point (6, 3). Draw the mirror line so that B′ is the reflection of B.

Vectors

Before we look at transformations again we introduce a shorter way of describing movement using vectors.

If you arranged to meet your friend 3 km from your home, this information would not be enough to ensure that you both went to the same place. You would also need to know which way to go.

Two pieces of information are required to describe where one place is in relation to another: the distance and the direction. Quantities that have both *size* (magnitude) and *direction* are called *vectors*.

A quantity that has magnitude but not direction is called a *scalar*. For example, the amount of money in your pocket or the number of pupils in your school are scalar quantities. On the other hand, the velocity of a hurricane, which states the speed and the direction in which it is moving, is a vector quantity.

Exercise 8f

State whether the following sentences refer to vector or scalar quantities:

1   There are 24 pupils in my class.

2   To get to school I walk $\frac{1}{2}$ km due north.

3   There are 11 players in a cricket team.

4   John walked at 6 km per hour.

5   The vertical cliff face is 50 m high.

6   Give other examples of

   a   vector quantities

   b   scalar quantities.

Representing vectors

Because a vector has both size and direction we can represent a vector by a straight line and indicate its direction with an arrow. For example

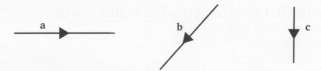

We use **a**, **b**, **c**,... to name the vectors.

When writing by hand it is difficult to write **a**, which is in heavy type, so we use $\underline{a}$.

In the diagram on the right, the movement along **a** corresponds to 4 across and 2 up and we can write

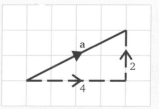

$$\mathbf{a} = \begin{pmatrix} 4 \\ 2 \end{pmatrix}$$

The vector **b** can be described as 8 across and 4 down. As with coordinates, which we looked at in Book 1, we use negative numbers to indicate movement down or movement to the left.

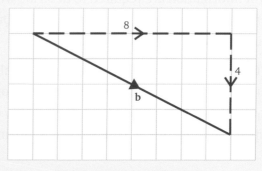

Therefore
$$\mathbf{b} = \begin{pmatrix} 8 \\ -4 \end{pmatrix}$$

Notice that the top number represents movement across and that the bottom number represents movement up or down.

Exercise 8g

Write the following vectors in the form $\begin{pmatrix} p \\ q \end{pmatrix}$:

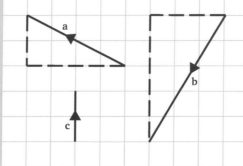

To move from the start to the end of **a**, you go 4 squares back (to the left) and 2 squares up: $\mathbf{a} = \begin{pmatrix} -4 \\ 2 \end{pmatrix}$.

For **b** you need to go 3 squares back and 5 squares down: $\mathbf{b} = \begin{pmatrix} -3 \\ -5 \end{pmatrix}$.

For **c** you do not need to go across, but you go 2 squares up: $\mathbf{c} = \begin{pmatrix} 0 \\ 2 \end{pmatrix}$.

Write the following vectors in the form $\begin{pmatrix} p \\ q \end{pmatrix}$:

1

> Move in the direction of the arrow and remember that the top number gives the distance across and the bottom number gives the distance up or down.

2

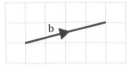

5

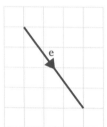

3

4

6

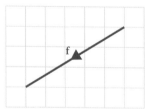

7

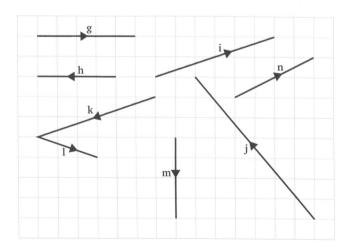

On square grid paper draw the following vectors. Label each vector with its letter and an arrow:

8 $a = \begin{pmatrix} 3 \\ 5 \end{pmatrix}$

9 $b = \begin{pmatrix} -4 \\ -3 \end{pmatrix}$

10 $c = \begin{pmatrix} 2 \\ -4 \end{pmatrix}$

11 $d = \begin{pmatrix} 6 \\ -12 \end{pmatrix}$

12 $e = \begin{pmatrix} -4 \\ 3 \end{pmatrix}$

13 $f = \begin{pmatrix} -2 \\ 5 \end{pmatrix}$

14 $g = \begin{pmatrix} 6 \\ 10 \end{pmatrix}$

15 $h = \begin{pmatrix} -1 \\ -5 \end{pmatrix}$

16 $i = \begin{pmatrix} -6 \\ 2 \end{pmatrix}$

17 What do you notice about the vectors in questions **8** and **14**, and in questions **10** and **11**?

Exercise 8h

$\begin{pmatrix} 5 \\ 2 \end{pmatrix}$ is a vector and (2, 1) is its starting point. Find the coordinates of its other end.

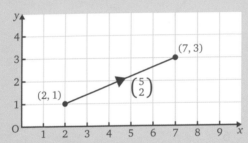

Starting at (2, 1) we need to go 5 squares to the right and 2 squares up.

The coordinates of its other end are (7, 3).

In each question you are given a vector followed by the coordinates of its starting point. Find the coordinates of its other end, or end point.

1 $\begin{pmatrix} 3 \\ 3 \end{pmatrix}$, (4, 1)

2 $\begin{pmatrix} 3 \\ 1 \end{pmatrix}$, (−2, −3)

3 $\begin{pmatrix} -6 \\ 2 \end{pmatrix}$, (3, 5)

4 $\begin{pmatrix} -4 \\ -3 \end{pmatrix}$, (5, −2)

5 $\begin{pmatrix} 5 \\ 2 \end{pmatrix}$, (3, −1)

6 $\begin{pmatrix} 4 \\ -2 \end{pmatrix}$, (4, 2)

7 $\begin{pmatrix} -3 \\ 4 \end{pmatrix}$, (2, −4)

8 $\begin{pmatrix} -6 \\ -6 \end{pmatrix}$, (−3, −2)

9 $\begin{pmatrix} 4 \\ 3 \end{pmatrix}$, (−2, −3)

10 $\begin{pmatrix} 5 \\ -3 \end{pmatrix}$, (2, −1)

11 $\begin{pmatrix} -5 \\ 2 \end{pmatrix}$, (−4, −3)

12 $\begin{pmatrix} -4 \\ -2 \end{pmatrix}$, (−3, −1)

$\begin{pmatrix} 6 \\ 4 \end{pmatrix}$ is a vector and (8, 6) are the coordinates of its end point.

Find the coordinates of its starting point.

From the end of the vector, you need to go backwards, i.e. 6 units left and 4 units down to get to the start of the vector.

The coordinates of the vector's starting point are (2, 2).

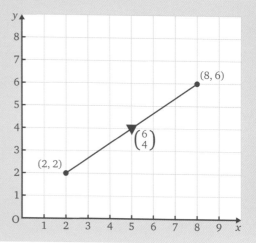

In each question a vector is given followed by the coordinates of its end point.
Find the coordinates of its starting point.

13 $\begin{pmatrix} 10 \\ 2 \end{pmatrix}$, (4, 1)   **17** $\begin{pmatrix} -3 \\ 4 \end{pmatrix}$, (−2, 1)

14 $\begin{pmatrix} 5 \\ -1 \end{pmatrix}$, (3, −4)   **18** $\begin{pmatrix} -6 \\ -3 \end{pmatrix}$, (−5, 2)

15 $\begin{pmatrix} -5 \\ -2 \end{pmatrix}$, (−2, −4)   **19** $\begin{pmatrix} 4 \\ -2 \end{pmatrix}$, (−3, 2)   **21** $\begin{pmatrix} 1 \\ 4 \end{pmatrix}$, (−5, −2)

16 $\begin{pmatrix} 8 \\ 6 \end{pmatrix}$, (6, 3)   **20** $\begin{pmatrix} -2 \\ 6 \end{pmatrix}$, (−3, −4)   **22** $\begin{pmatrix} 2 \\ -3 \end{pmatrix}$, (1, 7)

Remember that the point given is the end of the vector so you have to go in the opposite direction to get to its start point.

Capital letter notation

In the diagram A and B are two points.

We can denote the vector from A to B

as $\overrightarrow{AB}$ where $\overrightarrow{AB} = \begin{pmatrix} 7 \\ 1 \end{pmatrix}$.

Similarly $\overrightarrow{BC} = \begin{pmatrix} -4 \\ 6 \end{pmatrix}$.

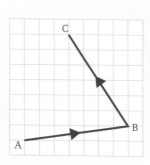

Exercise 8i

Write the vector $\overrightarrow{AB}$ where A is (2, 4), B is (3, 9).

Plot the start and end points of the vector.

Then you can see that you need to go 1 forward and 5 up.

Vector $\overrightarrow{AB}$ is $\begin{pmatrix} 1 \\ 5 \end{pmatrix}$.

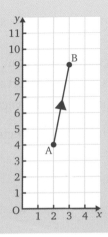

Write the vector $\overrightarrow{AB}$ where:

1   A is (1, 4),   B is (7, 6)

2   A is (−3, 4),   B is (2, 3)

3   A is (7, 3),   B is (1, 2)

4   A is (−1, 4),   B is (5, 9)

5   A is (2, 1),   B is (−3, −5)

6   A is (3, 0),   B is (5, −2)

7   A is (6, 3),   B is (4, 1)

8   A is (−1, −3),   B is (−5, −8)

9   A is (2, 6),   B is (2, −6)

10   A is (2, −3),   B is (4, 5)

Translations

In Book 1 we saw that a translation moves an object without reflecting it or rotating it or changing its size.

This diagram shows a triangle ABC translated by 6 units horizontally to the right and 2 units vertically downwards.

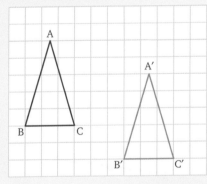

Using vectors to describe translations

The translation of triangle ABC in the previous diagram can be described more briefly by the vector $\begin{pmatrix} 6 \\ -2 \end{pmatrix}$.

Remember that the top number gives the *displacement* parallel to the x-axis and the bottom number gives the displacement parallel to the y-axis.

   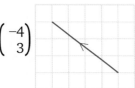

If the top number is negative, the displacement is to the left, and if the bottom number is negative, the displacement is downwards.

Consider the diagram:

$$\overrightarrow{AA'} = \begin{pmatrix} 5 \\ 3 \end{pmatrix}$$

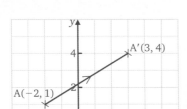

A' is the image of A under the translation described by the vector $\begin{pmatrix} 5 \\ 3 \end{pmatrix}$.

A is *mapped* to A' by the translation described by the vector $\begin{pmatrix} 5 \\ 3 \end{pmatrix}$.

Exercise 8j

Find the images of the points given in questions **1** to **10** under the translations described by the given vectors.

Draw the point (3, 1) then move 4 units to the right and 2 units up.

1 (3, 1), $\begin{pmatrix} 4 \\ 2 \end{pmatrix}$ **4** (3, 2), $\begin{pmatrix} -2 \\ 3 \end{pmatrix}$

$\begin{pmatrix} -2 \\ 3 \end{pmatrix}$ means 2 units to the left and 3 units up.

2 (4, 5), $\begin{pmatrix} 2 \\ 4 \end{pmatrix}$ **5** (4, 5), $\begin{pmatrix} -3 \\ -2 \end{pmatrix}$

3 (−2, 4), $\begin{pmatrix} 4 \\ 3 \end{pmatrix}$ **6** (4, −4), $\begin{pmatrix} 2 \\ -3 \end{pmatrix}$

7 $(-6, -3), \begin{pmatrix} 4 \\ 1 \end{pmatrix}$ **9** $(3, -2), \begin{pmatrix} 6 \\ -4 \end{pmatrix}$

8 $(1, 1), \begin{pmatrix} -5 \\ -3 \end{pmatrix}$ **10** $(7, 4), \begin{pmatrix} -5 \\ -4 \end{pmatrix}$

In questions **11** to **16**, find the vectors describing the translations that map A to A'.

11 A(1, 2), A'(5, 3)   **13** A(−4, −3), A'(0, 0)   **15** A(−3, −4), A'(−5, −6)

12 A(3, 8), A'(2, 9)   **14** A(−2, 6), A'(2, 6)   **16** A(4, −2), A'(5, −1)

In questions **17** to **19**, the given point A' is the image of an object point A under the translation described by the given vector. Find A.

17 $A'(7, 9), \begin{pmatrix} 2 \\ 3 \end{pmatrix}$ **18** $A'(0, 6), \begin{pmatrix} 2 \\ 3 \end{pmatrix}$ **19** $A'(-3, -2), \begin{pmatrix} 1 \\ 3 \end{pmatrix}$

 Investigation

This diagram shows the vectors $\mathbf{a} = \begin{pmatrix} 2 \\ 3 \end{pmatrix}$ and $\mathbf{b} = \begin{pmatrix} 2 \\ 1 \end{pmatrix}$.

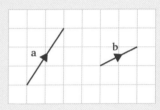

The point (6, 7) can be reached from the origin by adding **a** and **b**, and then adding **a** to the result. This is shown in the diagram.

1 In how many different ways can these vectors be combined to get from the origin to the point (6, 7)? Show them on a diagram.

2 The vector in the direction opposite to **a** is called −**a** so as

$\mathbf{a} = \begin{pmatrix} 2 \\ 3 \end{pmatrix}, -\mathbf{a} = \begin{pmatrix} -2 \\ -3 \end{pmatrix}$. Similarly $-\mathbf{b} = \begin{pmatrix} -2 \\ -1 \end{pmatrix}$.

Investigate how many of the points on this grid it is possible to get to from the origin if combinations of **a**, **b**, −**a** and −**b** are allowed.

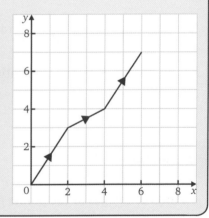

A translation moves each point of an object the same distance in the same direction.

$\overrightarrow{PP'} = \begin{pmatrix} 5 \\ 1 \end{pmatrix}$ $\overrightarrow{RR'} = \begin{pmatrix} 5 \\ 1 \end{pmatrix}$ $\overrightarrow{QQ'} = \begin{pmatrix} 5 \\ 1 \end{pmatrix}$

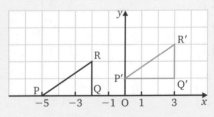

i.e. $\overrightarrow{PP'} = \overrightarrow{QQ'} = \overrightarrow{RR'}$

Exercise 8k

1 Given the following diagrams, find the vectors $\overrightarrow{AA'}$, $\overrightarrow{BB'}$ and $\overrightarrow{CC'}$. Are they all equal? Is the transformation a translation?

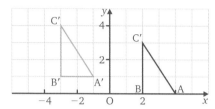

2 Given the following diagrams, find the vectors $\overrightarrow{LL'}$, $\overrightarrow{MM'}$ and $\overrightarrow{NN'}$. Are they all equal? Is the transformation a translation?

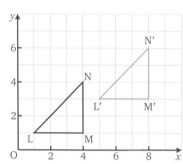

3 Find the vector that describes the translation mapping A to A′, B to B′ and C to C′.

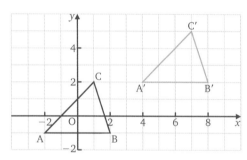

4 Give the vectors describing the translations that map
   a △ABC to △PQR
   b △PQR to △ABC.

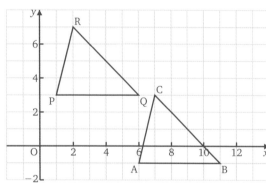

5 Give the vectors describing the translations that map
   a △ABC to △PQR
   b △ABC to △LMN
   c △XYZ to △ABC
   d △ABC to △ABC.

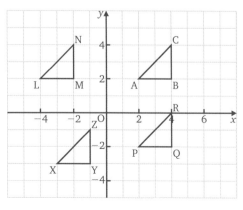

6 Draw axes for x and y from −4 to 5. Draw the following triangles:

△ABC with A(2, 2), B(4, 2), C(2, 5)

△PQR with P(1, −2), Q(3, −2), R(1, 1)

△XYZ with X(−3, 1), Y(−1, 1), Z(−3, 4).

Give the vectors describing the translations that map

a △ABC to △PQR

b △PQR to △ABC

c △PQR to △XYZ

d △ABC to △ABC.

7 Draw axes for x and y from 0 to 9. Draw △ABC with A(3, 0), B(3, 3), C(0, 3) and △A′B′C′ with A′(8, 2), B′(8, 5), C′(5, 5).

Is △A′B′C′ the image of △ABC under a translation? If so, what is the vector describing the translation?

Join AA′, BB′ and CC′. What type of quadrilateral is AA′B′B? Give reasons. Name other quadrilaterals of the same type in the figure.

8 a Square ABCD is translated parallel to AB a distance equal to AB. Sketch the diagram and draw the image of ABCD.

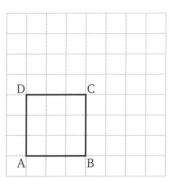

b Square ABCD is translated parallel to AC a distance equal to AC. Sketch the diagram and draw the image of ABCD.

9 Draw axes for x and y from −2 to 7.

Draw △ABC with A(−2, 5), B(1, 3), C(1, 5).

Translate △ABC using the vector $\begin{pmatrix} 5 \\ 1 \end{pmatrix}$. Label this image $A_1B_1C_1$.

Then translate △$A_1B_1C_1$ using the vector $\begin{pmatrix} -1 \\ -3 \end{pmatrix}$. Label this new image $A_2B_2C_2$.

Give the vectors describing the translations that map

a △ABC to △$A_2B_2C_2$

b △$A_2B_2C_2$ to △ABC

c △$A_2B_2C_2$ to △$A_1B_1C_1$.

Exercise 8I

Select the letter that gives the correct answer.

1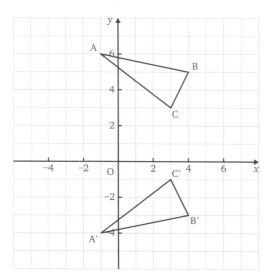

Triangle A′B′C′ is the image of triangle ABC under reflection.
The equation of the mirror line is

A $x = 1$ B $y = 1$ C $x = 2$ D $y = 2$

2 Which of these sentences refer to a vector quantity?
   i   Clive walked to school at 6 km/h.
   ii The number of pupils in my class is 27.
   iii The nearest post office from my home is 1 km away in the direction
       northwest.
   iv To get to the leisure centre my journey takes me due east.
   A i and ii   B i and iii   C iii   D iii and iv

3 Which of the sentences in question **2** refer to a scalar quantity?
   A i and ii   B i and iii   C iii   D iii and iv

4 The starting point of the vector $\begin{pmatrix} 2 \\ 4 \end{pmatrix}$ is the point (3, 1).
   The coordinates of this vector's other end are
   A (1, 3)   B (5, 1)   C (5, 3)   D (5, 5)

5 The coordinates of the end point of the vector $\begin{pmatrix} -2 \\ 3 \end{pmatrix}$ are (−1, 5). The
   coordinates of this vector's starting point are
   A (1, 2)   B (2, 3)   C (3, 2)   D (3, 3)

6 If A is the point (2, 6) and B is the point (−1, 4) the vector $\overrightarrow{AB}$ is
   A $\begin{pmatrix} -3 \\ -2 \end{pmatrix}$ B $\begin{pmatrix} -3 \\ 2 \end{pmatrix}$ C $\begin{pmatrix} 3 \\ -2 \end{pmatrix}$ D $\begin{pmatrix} 3 \\ 2 \end{pmatrix}$

7 The coordinates of the image of the point (2, 5) under a translation described by the vector $\begin{pmatrix} 4 \\ 3 \end{pmatrix}$ is

A (2, −3) B (2, 2) C (6, 2) D (6, 3)

Use this diagram for questions **8** and **9**.

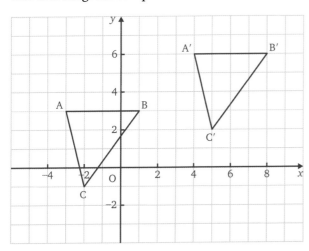

8 The vector that describes the translation mapping △ABC to △A′B′C′ is

A $\begin{pmatrix} 5 \\ 3 \end{pmatrix}$ B $\begin{pmatrix} 6 \\ 3 \end{pmatrix}$ C $\begin{pmatrix} 7 \\ 3 \end{pmatrix}$ D $\begin{pmatrix} 8 \\ 3 \end{pmatrix}$

9 The vector that describes the translation mapping △A′B′C′ to △ABC is

A $\begin{pmatrix} -8 \\ -3 \end{pmatrix}$ B $\begin{pmatrix} -7 \\ -3 \end{pmatrix}$ C $\begin{pmatrix} -7 \\ -2 \end{pmatrix}$ D $\begin{pmatrix} -6 \\ 3 \end{pmatrix}$

10

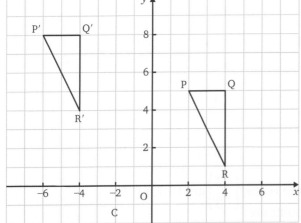

The vector that describes the translation mapping △PQR to △P′Q′R′

A $\begin{pmatrix} -9 \\ -3 \end{pmatrix}$ B $\begin{pmatrix} -8 \\ -3 \end{pmatrix}$ C $\begin{pmatrix} -8 \\ 3 \end{pmatrix}$ D $\begin{pmatrix} 9 \\ 3 \end{pmatrix}$

Investigation

Palindromes

A palindrome is a word or sentence or number that reads the same from right to left as it does from left to right.

Examples of single word palindromes are DID and CIVIC.

An example of a sentence is

ABLE WAS I ERE I SAW ELBA.

Examples with numbers are much easier to find.

For example: 242, 1551 and 3672763.

These numbers are called palindromic numbers.

Consider the times that appear on a digital watch or clock. For a clock set for a 12-hour cycle midday is shown as 1200. The time shown on the face continues 1201, 1202, 1203, … until it gets around to midnight and starts again at 1200.

1   For a clock set for a 12-hour cycle investigate:

   a all the possible palindromic times

   b the shortest number of minutes between two consecutive palindromic times

   c the longest time between two consecutive palindromic times.

2   Repeat these questions for a digital clock set for a 24-hour cycle. For a watch or clock set in 24-hour mode the cycle ends at midnight with the face showing 0000.

   There are therefore many more possible palindromic times when the timepiece is set in this way.

3   The dates when important buildings were opened are often shown on them, for example 1754 or 1991. The second of these dates is a palindrome. What do you notice if you turn this date upside down?

   Is it possible to find a date in the last 200 years that is not only a palindrome but reads the same when turned upside down? Investigate.

If you find this investigation interesting try it with words; it is more difficult. The more letters in the word the more difficult it becomes. Should you want a really difficult challenge, try to create a palindromic sentence.

In this chapter you have seen that...

✔ when an object is reflected in a mirror line, the object and the image are symmetrical about the mirror line

✔ the mirror line is the perpendicular bisector of the line joining a point on the object to the corresponding point on the image

✔ a vector has size (magnitude or length) and direction

✔ a scalar has size only

✔ a vector can be represented by an ordered pair of numbers written vertically. The top number gives movement across and the bottom number gives movement up or down

✔ a translation moves an object without turning it or reflecting it

✔ a translation can be described by a vector.

9 Measurement

At the end of this chapter you should be able to...

1 convert between metric units of length

2 convert between metric units of mass

3 know the different imperial units of length and mass

4 use approximations to convert between metric and imperial measures

5 use and draw conversion graphs.

Did you know?

According to legend, Euclid, who was the father of geometry, posed this puzzle.

A mule and a donkey were carrying a load of sacks. When the donkey groaned the mule looked at him and said, 'Why are you complaining? If you gave me one sack, I would have twice as many as you; and if I gave you one of my sacks, we would have equal loads.'

How many sacks was each carrying?

You need to know...

✔ how to multiply and divide decimals

✔ how to read values from scales and graphs

✔ how to draw a conversion graph.

Key words

approximate, Celsius, centimetre, dollar, equivalent, Fahrenheit, foot, gallon, gram, hundredweight, imperial, inch, kilogram, kilometre, litre, mass, metre, mile, milligram, millilitre, millimetre, ounce, pound (lb), pound (£), scale, ton, tonne, yard

In Book 1 we looked at units of length and mass and we revise this work here.

Units of length

There are two commonly used systems of units of length.

The metric system is used in most countries. The metric units of length in everyday use are

the millimetre (mm), the centimetre (cm), the metre (m) and the kilometre

where

$$10\,\text{mm} = 1\,\text{cm}, \quad 100\,\text{cm} = 1\,\text{m}, \quad 1000\,\text{m} = 1\,\text{km}$$

Imperial units are used in the USA and, for some lengths, in the UK. The imperial units in everyday use are

the inch (in), the foot (ft), the yard (yd) and the mile

where

$$12\,\text{in} = 1\,\text{ft}, \quad 3\,\text{ft} = 1\,\text{yd}, \quad 1760\,\text{yd} = 1\,\text{mile}$$

A rough conversion between metric and imperial units of length gives

- 1 in = 2.5 cm (good enough for most purposes; for a better approximation 1 in = 2.54 cm)

- 5 miles = 8 km.

Many rulers show both inches and centimetres.

Most of us use rulers and tapes for everyday measurement. More specialised measuring instruments are Vernier callipers. These are used for measurements such as internal and external diameters of pipes, and for measurements that are required to 0.1 mm. The picture shows a digital Vernier calliper.

Also used are electronic instruments for measuring distances, for example lengths of rooms. These typically use lasers or ultrasound and give the lengths digitally.

Exercise 9a

Express 2.4 cm in millimetres.

1 cm = 10 mm, so 2.4 cm = 2.4 × 10 mm
= 24 mm

Express 2400 m in kilometres.

1 km = 1000 m or 1 m = $\frac{1}{1000}$ km, so 2400 m = 2400 ÷ 1000 km
= 2.4 km

Express the given quantity in terms of the unit in brackets.

Remember that to change to a smaller unit, multiply, and to change to a larger unit, divide.

1 5 cm (mm)	**7** 54 cm (mm)
2 30 mm (cm)	**8** 5000 m (km)
3 0.5 km (m)	**9** 56 cm (m)
4 300 cm (m)	**10** 1350 mm (m)
5 1.5 m (cm)	**11** 2 ft (in)
6 345 mm (cm)	**12** 2 yd (ft)

13 48 in (ft)

14 12 ft (yd)

15 1.5 miles (yd)

Use 1 in ≈ 2.54 cm to express 1 ft as an approximate number of centimetres.

1 ft = 12 in and as 1 in ≈ 2.54 cm,   12 in ≈ 12 × 2.54 cm
= 30.5 cm (correct to 1 d.p.)

Express the given quantity approximately in terms of the unit in brackets.
Use 1 in ≈ 2.5 cm and 5 miles ≈ 8 km.

16 6 in (cm)

17 20 cm (in)

18 60 km (miles)

19 50 miles (km)

20 1 ft (cm)

21 5 m (in)

22 2 yd (cm)

23 450 mm (in)

24 1.5 m (ft)

25 600 yd (m)

First change feet to inches.

First change metres to centimetres.

Units of mass

The metric units of mass in everyday use are the milligram (mg), gram (g), kilogram (kg) and tonne (t)

where

$$1\,t = 1000\,kg, \quad 1\,kg = 1000\,g, \quad 1\,g = 1000\,mg$$

The imperial units of mass in everyday use are ounces (oz), pounds (lb), hundredweights (cwt) and tons

where

$$1\,ton = 20\,cwt, \quad 1\,cwt = 112\,lb, \quad 1\,lb = 16\,oz$$

Imperial units of mass are not all quite equivalent in the UK and the USA. The approximations given here are for UK units.

You can use the following approximations to convert between metric and imperial units of mass:

- a rough conversion between kilograms and pounds is $1\,kg \approx 2\,lb$
- a more accurate conversion is $1\,kg \approx 2.2\,lb$
- a metric tonne is very nearly the same as an imperial ton, so $1\,tonne \approx 1\,ton$

Instruments for measuring mass are called *scales* or balances and they come in a variety of forms.

A spring balance is used for weighing heavy objects such as luggage and gas cylinders. The scale is marked in kilograms and pounds.	These kitchen scales are also calibrated in kilograms and pounds.	These are digital kitchen scales. Most digital scales give the option of weighing in grams or pounds and ounces.

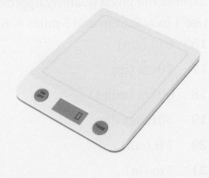

Exercise 9b

Express the given quantity in terms of the unit in brackets.

Remember that to change to a smaller unit, multiply, and to change to a larger unit, divide.

1　6 kg (g)

2　2000 g (kg)

3　0.5 t (kg)

4　0.5 kg (g)

5　1.5 t (kg)

6　3400 kg (t)

7　300 g (kg)

8　32 oz (lb)

9　2 cwt (lb)

10　2 t (cwt)

11　392 lb (cwt)

12　1.5 lb (oz)

Express the given quantity approximately in terms of the unit in brackets.
Use 1 kg ≈ 2.2 lb and give your answers correct to 1 decimal place.

13　3 kg (lb)

14　8 lb (kg)

15　500 g (lb)

16　2 t (tons)

17　3 t (cwt)

18　60 lb (kg)

Write the masses shown on the following scales in kilograms and grams **and** in pounds and ounces.

19

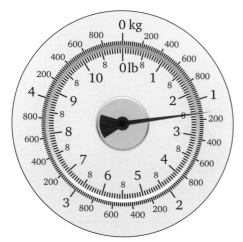

21

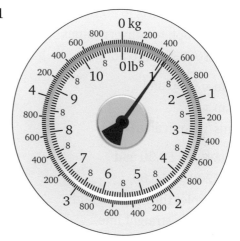

20

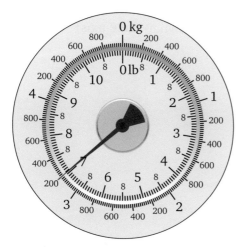

22　Use the scales shown to find approximately the number of grams in 1 ounce.

23　Using the scales, can you give a better approximation for the number of pounds in 1 kilogram?

Conversion graphs

There are many quantities that we may need to convert apart from length and mass. For example, many countries measure temperature using degrees Celsius, but the USA uses degrees Fahrenheit. If you go to another country you will need to convert your home currency to the that of the country you visit. Straight-line graphs are a useful way of doing this.

If you were to go to England for a holiday, you would probably have a little difficulty in knowing the cost of things in dollars and cents. If we know the rate of exchange, we can use a simple straight-line graph to convert a given number of pounds into dollars or a given number of dollars into pounds.

Given that $1 converts to £0.083, we can draw a graph to convert values from, say, $0–$300 into pounds.

Take 5 cm ≡ $100 and
    2 cm ≡ £5.
(≡ means 'is equivalent to'.)

Because $100 ≡ £8.30 and
    $200 ≡ £16.60,
we can now plot these points and join them with a straight line.

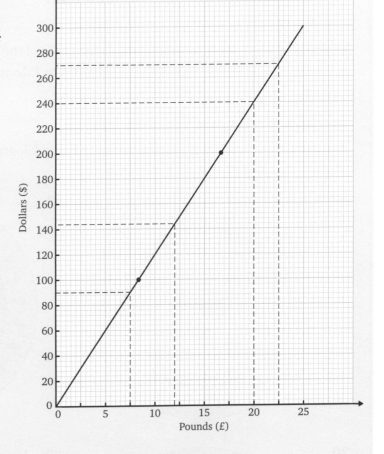

From the graph:

   $144 ≡ £12 (going from $144 across the graph then down to the £-axis)

   $240 ≡ £20

   £7.50 ≡ $90

   £22.50 ≡ $270

1 The table gives temperatures in degrees Fahrenheit (°F) and the equivalent values in degrees Celsius (°C).

Temperature in °F	57	126	158	194
Temperature in °C	14	52	70	90

Plot these points on a graph for Celsius values from 0 to 100 and Fahrenheit values from 0 to 220. Let 2 cm represent 20 units on each axis.

Use your graph to convert:

a 97 °F into °C   **c** 25 °C into °F

b 172 °F into °C   **d** 80 °C into °F

2 The table shows the conversion of various sums of money from US dollars to EC dollars.

US dollars (US $)	100	270	350
EC dollars (EC $)	270	729	945

Plot these points on a graph and draw a straight line to pass through them. Take 2 cm to represent 50 units on the US $-axis and 100 units on the EC $-axis.

Use your graph to convert:

a 160 US $ into EC $ **c** 440 EC $ into US $

b 330 US $ into EC $ **d** 980 EC $ into US $

 When you choose scales for axes, make them easy to read. On graph paper, you have 5 subdivisions between each centimetre, so choose a multiple of 5.

3 The table shows the distance a girl walks in a given time.

Time walking in hours	0	1	$2\frac{1}{2}$	4	5
Distance walked in km	0	6	15	24	30

Draw a graph of these results. What do you conclude about the speed at which she walks?

How far has she walked in   **a** 2 hours   **b** $3\frac{1}{2}$ hours?

How long does she take to walk   **c** 10 km   **d** 21 km?

4 Marks in an examination range from 0 to 65. Draw a graph that enables you to express the marks in percentages from 0 to 100. Note that a mark of 0 is 0% while a mark of 65 is 100%.

Use your graph

a to express marks of 35 and 50 as percentages

b to find the original mark for percentages of 50% and 80%.

5 Deductions from the wages of a group of employees amount to $35 for every $100 earned. Draw a graph to show the deductions made from gross pay in the range $0–$400 per week.

How much is deducted from an employee whose gross weekly pay is

a $125   b $240   c $335?

How much is earned each week by an employee whose weekly deductions amount to

d $40   e $88?

6 The table shows the fuel consumption figures for a car in both miles per gallon (X) and in kilometres per litre (Y).

mpg (X)	30	45	60
km/litre (Y)	10.5	15.75	21

Plot these points on a graph taking $2\,cm \equiv 10$ units on the X-axis and $4\,cm \equiv 5$ units on the Y-axis. Your scale should cover 0–70 for X and 0–25 for Y.

Use your graph to find:

a 12 km/litre in mpg

b 64 mpg in km/litre.

7 The table gives various speeds in kilometres per hour with the equivalent values in metres per second.

Speed in km/h (S)	0	80	120	200
Speed in m/s (V)	0	22.2	33.3	55.5

Plot these values on a graph taking $4\,cm \equiv 50$ units on the S-axis and $4\,cm \equiv 10$ units on the V-axis.

Use your graph to convert:

a 140 km/h into m/s

b 46 m/s into km/h

c 18 m/s into km/h

d 175 km/h into m/s.

<u>8</u> A number of rectangles, measuring l cm by b cm, all have a perimeter of 24 cm.

Copy and complete the following table:

l	1	2	3	4	6	8
b			9			4

Draw a graph of these results using your own scale. Use your graph to find l if b is

a 2.5 cm   **b** 6.2 cm

and to find b if l is

c 5.5 cm   **d** 2.8 cm.

Exercise 9d

Select the letter that gives the correct answer.

1 654 mm in cm is

    A 0.0654   **B** 0.654   **C** 6.54   **D** 65.4

2 8500 mm in km is

    A 0.000 85   **B** 0.0085   **C** 0.085   **D** 0.85

3 24 ft in yards is

    A 6   **B** 8   **C** 10   **D** 12

4 750 cm in metres is

    A 0.075   **B** 0.75   **C** 7.5   **D** 75

5 If 1 inch is approximately 2.5 cm, 12 inches is approximately

    A 18 cm   **B** 20 cm   **C** 24 cm   **D** 30 cm

6 5000 g in kilograms is

    A 0.05 kg   **B** 0.5 kg   **C** 5 kg   **D** 50 kg

7 2.75 kg in grams is

    A 27.5 g   **B** 275 g   **C** 2750 g   **D** 27500 g

Use this graph for questions **8** and **9**.

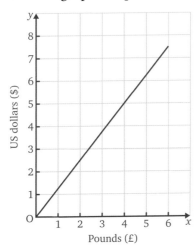

Pounds (£)

8   The graph enables you to convert pounds sterling (£) into US dollars ($).
From the graph, the equivalent value of £4 is

    A $4   **B** $5   **C** $6   **D** $8

9   The equivalent value of £6 in US dollars is

    A $6.50   **B** $7   **C** $7.50   **D** $8

10   Using your answer to question **9** the equivalent of £600 is

    A $750   **B** $800   **C** $850   **D** $900

? **Puzzle**

Trains leave London for Edinburgh every hour on the hour. Trains leave
Edinburgh for London every hour on the half-hour. The journey takes five
hours each way.

Carrie takes a train from London to Edinburgh. How many trains from
Edinburgh bound for London pass her train? Do not count any trains that
may be in the stations at either end of the journey.

In this chapter you have seen that...

✔ the metric units of length in common use are the kilometre, the metre, the centimetre and the millimetre, where

$$1\,cm = 10\,mm$$
$$1\,m = 100\,cm$$
$$1\,km = 1000\,m$$

✔ the metric units of mass in common use are the tonne, the kilogram, the gram and the milligram, where

$$1\,g = 1000\,mg$$
$$1\,kg = 1000\,g$$
$$1\,t = 1000\,kg$$

✔ you can convert approximately between metric and imperial units using

$$1\,kg \approx 2.2\,lb$$
$$10\,cm \approx 4\,in$$
$$8\,km \approx 5\,miles$$

✔ you can draw a graph and use it to convert a quantity from one unit to another.

10 Circles: circumference and area

Did you know?

Circumference means 'the perimeter of a circle'. The word comes from the Latin *circumference* – 'to carry around'. The symbol π is the first letter of the Greek word for circumference – *perimetron*. In Germany, π is identified as the ludolphine number, because of the work of Ludolph van Ceulen, who tried to find a better estimate of the number.

You need to know...

✔ the meaning of significant figures

✔ the units of area

✔ how to find one quantity as a fraction of another

✔ how to find the area of a rectangle

✔ how to find the area of a triangle.

Key words

annulus, approximate, area, centre, circumference, cone, cylinder, decimal place, diameter, formula, fraction, grid line, minimum, perimeter, pi (π), quadrant, radius, rectangle, revolution, sector, semicircle, significant figure, square unit

Diameter, radius and circumference

When you use a pair of compasses to draw a circle, the place where you put the point is the *centre* of the circle. The length of the curve that the pencil draws is the *circumference* of the circle.

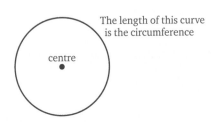

The length of this curve is the circumference

centre

Any straight line joining the centre to a point on the circumference is a *radius*.

A straight line across the full width of a circle (i.e. going through the centre) is a *diameter*.

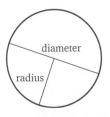

diameter

radius

The diameter is twice as long as the radius. If d stands for the length of a diameter and r stands for the length of a radius, we can write this as a formula:

$$d = 2r$$

Exercise 10a

In questions **1** to **6**, write down the length of the diameter of the circle whose radius is given

1

6 cm

2

5 m

3 15 mm

4 3.5 cm

5 1 km

6 4.6 cm

 Activity

For this activity you will need some thread and a cylinder (e.g. a tin of soup, a soft drink can, the cardboard tube from a roll of kitchen paper).

Measure across the top of the cylinder to get a value for the diameter. Wind the thread 10 times round the can. Measure the length of thread needed to do this and then divide your answer by 10 to get a value for the circumference. If C stands for the circumference and d for the length of the diameter, find, approximately, the value of $C \div d$.

(Note that you can also use the label from the cylindrical tin. If you are careful you can reshape it and measure the diameter and then unroll it to measure the circumference.)

Compare the results from the whole class for the value of $C \div d$.

Introducing π

From the activity on page 171 you will see that, for any circle,

$$\text{circumference} \approx 3 \times \text{diameter}$$

The number that you have to multiply the diameter by to get the circumference is slightly larger than 3.

This number is unlike any number that you have met so far. It cannot be written down exactly, either as a fraction or as a decimal: as a fraction it is approximately, but *not* exactly, $\frac{22}{7}$; as a decimal it is approximately 3.142, correct to 3 decimal places.

Now with a computer to do the arithmetic we can find its value to as many decimal places as we choose: it is a never-ending, never-repeating decimal fraction. To sixty decimal places, the value of this number is

3.141592653589793238462643383279502884197169399375105820974944 ...

Because we cannot write it down exactly we use the Greek letter π (pi) to stand for this number. Then we can write a formula connecting the circumference and diameter of a circle in the form $C = \pi d$. But $d = 2r$ so we can rewrite this formula as

$$C = 2\pi r$$

where C = circumference and r = radius

The symbol π was first used by an English writer, William Jones, in 1706. It was later adopted in 1737 by Euler.

Calculating the circumference

Exercise 10b

Using 3.142 as an approximate value for π, find the circumference of a circle of radius 3.8 m.

To get your answer correct to 3 s.f. you must work to 4 s.f.

3.8 m

Using $C = 2\pi r$

with $\pi = 3.142$ and $r = 3.8$

gives $C = 2 \times 3.142 \times 3.8$

            $= 23.9$ to 3 s.f.

Circumference $= 23.9$ m to 3 s.f.

Using 3.142 as an approximate value for π and giving your answers correct to 3 s.f., find the circumference of a circle of radius:

1	2.3 m	**4**	53 mm	**7**	36 cm	**10**	0.014 km	**13**	1.4 m
2	4.6 cm	**5**	8.7 m	**8**	4.8 m	**11**	7 cm	**14**	35 mm
3	2.9 cm	**6**	250 mm	**9**	1.8 m	**12**	28 mm	**15**	5.6 cm

For questions **16** to **23** you can use $C = 2\pi r$ or $C = \pi d$.
Read the question carefully before you decide which one to use.

Using $\pi \approx 3.14$ and giving your answer correct to 2 s.f., find the circumference of a circle of:

16	radius 154 mm	**20**	radius 34.6 cm
17	diameter 28 cm	**21**	diameter 511 mm
18	diameter 7.7 m	**22**	diameter 630 cm
19	radius 210 mm	**23**	diameter 9.1 m

In early times, $\sqrt{10}$ was used as an approximation for π.

 Investigation

Count Buffon's experiment

Count Buffon was an 18th-century scientist who carried out many probability experiments. The most famous of these is his 'Needle Problem'. He dropped needles on to a surface ruled with parallel lines and considered the drop successful when a needle fell between two lines. His amazing discovery was that the number of successful drops divided by the number of unsuccessful drops was an expression involving π.

You can repeat his experiment and get a good approximation for the value of π from it:

* Take a matchstick or a similar small stick and measure its length.
* Take a sheet of paper measuring about $\frac{1}{2}$ m each way and fill the sheet with a set of parallel lines whose distance apart is equal to the length of the stick.
* With the sheet on the floor, drop the stick on to it from a height of about 1 m.
* Repeat this about a hundred times and keep a tally of the number of times the stick touches or crosses a line and of the number of times it is dropped.
* Find the value of

$$\frac{2 \times \text{number of times it is dropped}}{\text{number of times it crosses or touches a line}}$$

Problems

Exercise 10c

Use the value of π on your calculator and give your answers correct to 3 s.f.

Find the perimeter of the given semicircle.

(The prefix 'semi' means half.)

Remember that perimeter means distance all round, so you need to find half the circumference then add the length of the straight edge.

The complete circumference of the circle is $2\pi r$

The curved part of the semicircle is $\frac{1}{2} \times 2\pi r$

$$= \frac{1}{\cancel{2}} \times \cancel{2} \times \pi \times 4\,\text{m}$$

$$= 12.57\,\text{m (correct to 4 s.f.)}$$

The perimeter = curved part + straight edge

$$= (12.57 + 8)\,\text{m}$$

$$= 20.57\,\text{m}$$

$$= 20.6\,\text{m to 3 s.f.}$$

Find the perimeter of each of the following shapes:

1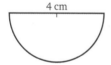
4 cm

2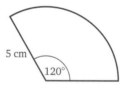
3 cm

This is called a *quadrant*: it is one quarter of a circle.

3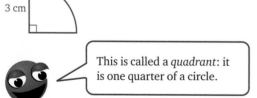
2 cm
4 cm
4 cm

4
5 cm
120°

This is one-third of a circle because 120° is $\frac{1}{3}$ of 360°.

5
10 cm
45°

A 'slice' of a circle is called a *sector*. $\frac{45}{360} = \frac{1}{8}$, so this sector is $\frac{1}{8}$ of a circle.

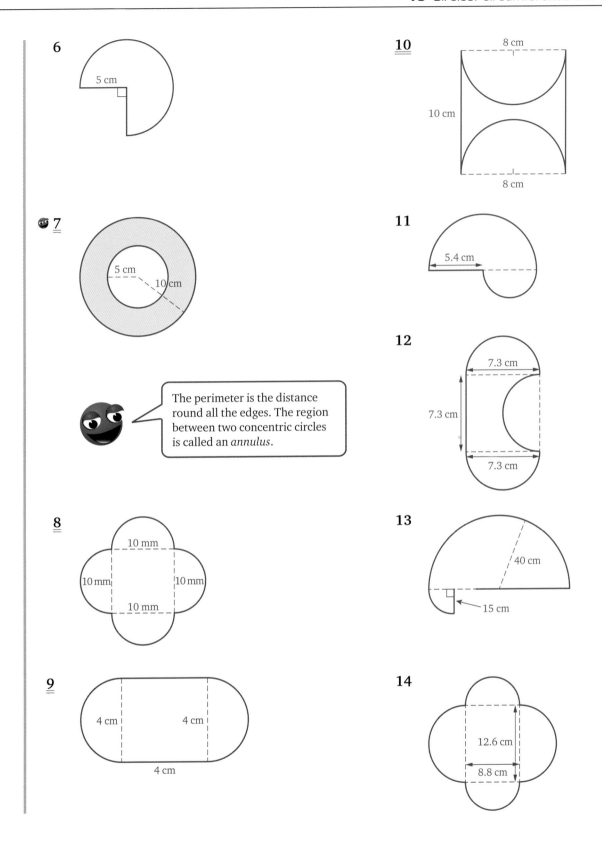

6

5 cm

10

8 cm

10 cm

8 cm

7

5 cm

10 cm

The perimeter is the distance round all the edges. The region between two concentric circles is called an *annulus*.

11

5.4 cm

12

7.3 cm

7.3 cm

7.3 cm

8

10 mm

10 mm

10 mm

10 mm

13

40 cm

15 cm

9

4 cm

4 cm

4 cm

14

12.6 cm

8.8 cm

Exercise 10d

Use the value of π on your calculator and give your answers correct to 3 s.f.

A circular flower bed has a diameter of 1.5 m. A metal edging is to be placed round it. Find the length of edging needed and the cost of the edging if it is sold by the metre (i.e. you can only buy a whole number of metres) and costs 60 c a metre.

First find the circumference of the circle, then how many metres you need.

Using $C = \pi d$,

$$C = \pi \times 1.5$$

$$= 4.712 \ldots$$

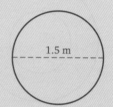

Length of edging needed = 4.71 m to 3 s.f.

(Note that if you use $C = 2\pi r$, you must remember to halve the diameter.)

As the length is 4.71 m we have to buy 5 m of edging.

$$\text{Cost} = 5 \times 60\,\text{c}$$

$$= 300\,\text{c or } \$3.00$$

1   Measure the diameter, in millimetres, of a 25 c coin. Use your measurement to find the circumference of a 25 c coin.

2   Repeat question **1** with a 10 c coin and a 5 c coin.

3   A circular tablecloth has a diameter of 1.4 m. How long is the hem of the cloth?

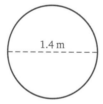

4   A rectangular sheet of metal measuring 50 cm by 30 cm has a semicircle of radius 15 cm cut from each short side as shown. Find the perimeter of the shape that is left.

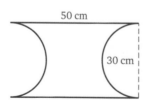

5 A bicycle wheel has a radius of 28 cm. What is the circumference of the wheel?

6 How far does a bicycle wheel of radius 28 cm travel in one complete revolution? How many times will the wheel turn when the bicycle travels a distance of 352 m?

7 A cylindrical tin has a radius of 2 cm. What length of paper is needed to put a label on the tin if the edges of the paper just meet?

8 A square sheet of metal has sides of length 30 cm. A quadrant (one quarter of a circle) of radius 15 cm is cut from each of the four corners. Sketch the shape that is left and find its perimeter.

9 A boy flies a model aeroplane on the end of a wire 10 m long. If he keeps the wire horizontal, how far does his aeroplane fly in one revolution?

10 If the aeroplane described in question **9** takes 1 second to fly 10 m, how long does it take to make one complete revolution? If the aeroplane has enough power to fly for 1 minute, how many turns can it make?

11 A cotton reel has a diameter of 2 cm. There are 500 turns of thread on the reel. How long is the thread?

12 A bucket is lowered into a well by unwinding rope from a cylindrical drum. The drum has a radius of 20 cm and with the bucket out of the well there are 10 complete turns of the rope on the drum. When the rope is fully unwound the bucket is at the bottom of the well.
How deep is the well?

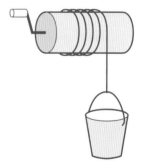

13 A garden hose is 100 m long. For storage it is wound on a circular hose reel of diameter 45 cm. How many turns of the reel are needed to wind up the hose?

14 The cage that takes miners up and down the shaft of a coal mine is raised and lowered by a rope wound round a circular drum of diameter 3 m. The rope does not wind on top of itself. It takes 10 revolutions of the drum to lower the cage from ground level to the bottom of the shaft. How deep is the shaft?

Investigation

Kevin entered a 50 km sponsored cycle ride. He wondered how many pedal strokes he made. The diameter of each wheel is 70 cm.

1 Investigate this problem if one pedal stroke gives one complete turn of the wheels.

2 What happens if Kevin uses a gear that gives two turns of the wheel for each pedal stroke?

3 Find out how the gears on a racing bike affect the ratio of the number of pedal strokes to the number of turns of the wheels.

Discuss the assumptions made in order to answer parts **1** and **2**.

Write a short report on how these assumptions affect the reasonableness of your answers.

Finding the radius of a circle given the circumference

If a circle has a circumference of 24 cm, we can find its radius from the formula
$C = 2\pi r$

i.e. $24 = 2 \times 3.142 \times r$

and solving this equation for r.

Exercise 10e

Use the value of π on your calculator and give your answers correct to 3 s.f.

The circumference of a circle is 36 m. Find the radius of this circle.

Using $C = 2\pi r$ gives

$$36 = 2 \times \pi \times r$$

$$36 = 6.283 \times r$$

(writing down the first 4 digits in the calculator display)

$$\frac{36}{6.283} = r \quad \text{(dividing both sides by 6.283)}$$

$$= 5.729\ldots$$

$$r = 5.73 \text{ m} \quad \text{to 3 s.f.}$$

Find the radius of the circle whose circumference is:

1	44 cm	**3**	550 m	**5**	462 mm	**7**	36.2 mm	**9**	582 cm
2	121 mm	**4**	275 cm	**6**	831 cm	**8**	391 m	**10**	87.4 m

11 Find the diameter of a circle whose circumference is 52 m.

12 A roundabout at a major road junction is to be built. It has to have a minimum circumference of 188 m. What is the corresponding minimum diameter?

13 A bicycle wheel has a circumference of 200 cm. What is the radius of the wheel?

14 A car has a turning circle whose circumference is 63 m. What is the narrowest road that the car can turn round in without going on the sidewalk?

15 When the label is taken off a tin of soup it is found to be 32 cm long.

If there was an overlap of 1 cm when the label was on the tin, what is the radius of the tin?

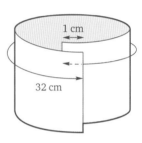

16 The diagram shows a quadrant of a circle. If the curved edge is 15 cm long, what is the length of a straight edge?

15 cm

17 A tea cup has a circumference of 24 cm. What is the radius of the cup? Six of these cups are stored edge to edge in a straight line on a shelf. What length of shelf do they occupy?

18 Make a cone from a sector of a circle as follows:

On a sheet of paper draw a circle of radius 8 cm. Draw two radii at an angle of 90°. Make a tab on one radius as shown. Cut out the larger sector and stick the straight edges together. What is the circumference of the circle at the bottom of the cone?

> A sector of a circle is the shape enclosed between an arc and the two radii at the ends of that arc (it looks like a slice of cake).

19 A cone is made by sticking together the straight edges of the sector of a circle, as shown in the diagram.

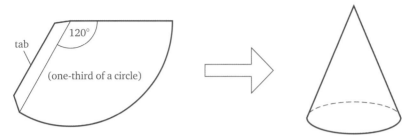

The circumference of the circle at the bottom of the finished cone is 10 cm. What is the radius of the circle from which the sector was cut?

20 The shape in the diagram on the right is made up of a semicircle and a square.
Find the length of a side of this square.

15 cm

21 The curved edge of a sector which is $\frac{1}{6}$ of a circle is 10 cm.
Find the radius and the perimeter of the sector.

(?) Puzzle

What is the exact time after 1 o'clock when the minute hand of a clock is immediately over the hour hand?

The area of a circle

The formula for finding the area of a circle is

$$A = \pi r^2$$

You can see this if you cut a circle up into sectors and place the pieces together as shown to get a shape which is roughly rectangular. Consider a circle of radius r whose circumference is $2\pi r$.

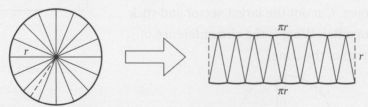

Area of circle = area of 'rectangle'
= length × width
= $\pi r \times r = \pi r^2$

Exercise 10f

Use the value of π on your calculator and give your answers correct to 3 s.f.

Find the area of a circle of radius 2.5 cm.

Using $A = \pi r^2$

with $r = 2.5$

gives $A = \pi \times (2.5)^2$

   $= 19.63...$

   $= 19.6$ to 3 s.f.

Area is 19.6 cm² to 3 s.f.

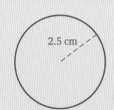

Find the areas of the following circles:

1 4 cm

4 10 mm

7 3.8 m

Be careful!

2 8 cm

5 3.5 m

8 3.5 km

3 5 m

6 60 cm

9 80 m

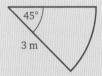

This sector is $\frac{1}{8}$ of a circle.

$\therefore$ area of sector $= \frac{1}{8}$ of area of circle of radius 3 m

$$\text{Area of sector} = \frac{1}{8} \text{ of } \pi r^2$$

$$= \frac{1}{8} \times \pi \times 9 \text{ m}^2$$

$$= 3.534 \text{ m}^2$$

$$= 3.53 \text{ m}^2 \text{ to 3 s.f.}$$

Find the areas of the following shapes:

10

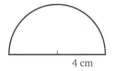

4 cm

11

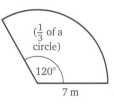

($\frac{1}{3}$ of a circle)

120°

7 m

12

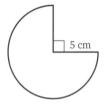

5 cm

13

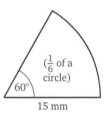

($\frac{1}{6}$ of a circle)

60°

15 mm

14

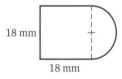

18 mm

18 mm

15

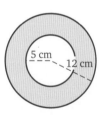

5 cm

12 cm

16

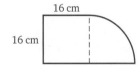

16 cm

16 cm

17

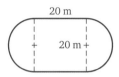

20 m

20 m

18

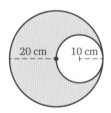

20 cm   10 cm

19

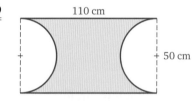

110 cm

50 cm

20

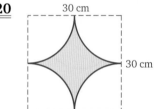

30 cm

30 cm

21

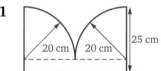

20 cm   20 cm

25 cm

22

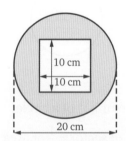

10 cm

10 cm

20 cm

23

8 cm

5 cm

12 cm

24

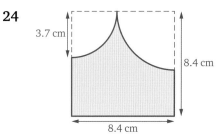

26

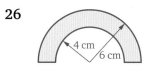

25

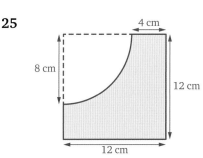

27

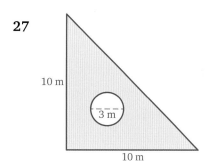

Problems

Exercise 10g

Use the value of π on your calculator and make a rough sketch to illustrate each problem. Give your answers to 3 s.f.

A circular table has a radius of 75 cm. Find the area of the table top.
The top of the table is to be varnished. One tin of varnish covers 4 m².
Will one tin be enough to give the table top three coats of varnish?

The area to varnish is three times the area of the top of the table.

Area of table top is πr^2

$= \pi \times 75 \times 75 \text{ cm}^2$

$= 17\,671.4 \ldots$

$= 17\,670 \text{ cm}^2$ to 4 s.f.

$= (17\,670 \div 100^2) \text{ m}^2$

$= 1.767 \text{ m}^2$ to 4 s.f.

(To give an answer correct to 3 s.f. work to 4 s.f.)

For three coats, enough varnish is needed to cover

$$3 \times 1.767 \text{ m}^2 = 5.30 \text{ m}^2 \text{ to 3 s.f.}$$

So one tin of varnish is not enough.

1   The minute hand on a clock is 15 cm long. What area does it pass over in 1 hour?

2   What area does the minute hand described in question **1** cover in 20 minutes?

3   The diameter of a 25 c coin is 25 mm. Find the area of one of its flat faces.

4   The hour hand of a clock is 10 cm long. What area does it pass over in 1 hour?

5   A circular lawn has a radius of 5 m. A bottle of lawn weedkiller says that the contents are sufficient to cover 50 m². Is one bottle enough to treat the whole lawn?

6   The largest possible circle is cut from a square of paper 10 cm by 10 cm. What area of paper is left?

7   Circular place mats of diameter 8 cm are made by stamping as many circles as possible from a rectangular strip of card measuring 8 cm by 64 cm. How many mats can be made from the strip of card and what area of card is wasted?

8   A wooden counter top is a rectangle measuring 280 cm by 45 cm. There are three circular holes in the counter, each of radius 10 cm. Find the area of the wooden top.

9   The surface of the counter top described in question **8** is to be given four coats of varnish. If one tin covers 3.5 m², how many tins will be needed?

10   Take a cylindrical tin of food with a paper label:

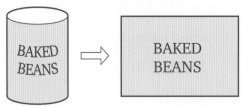

Measure the diameter of the tin and use it to find the length of the label. Find the area of the label. Now find the total surface area of the tin (two circular ends and the curved surface).

11   You need 5 mm squared paper for this question.

In Book 1 we counted squares to find estimates for the areas of several different shapes. Let us now apply the method to finding the area of a circle.

   a   Draw a circle, of radius 3 cm, taking its centre at the intersection of two grid lines

b Count the number of squares within the circle. Include a square if at least half is inside the circle, otherwise do not.

c What is the area of one grid square? Give your answer
  i in square millimetres   **ii** in square centimetres.

d What area do the total number of squares you have counted cover?

e Use the formula for the area of a circle to calculate the area of a circle of radius 3 cm.
  Give your answer correct to 1 decimal place.

f Now compare your answers for parts **d** and **e**. Does counting squares give a good estimate for the area of a circle?

 Investigation

In addition to using the formula $A = \pi r^2$ to calculate the area of a circle, there are other methods that provide reasonably good results. One such method is by weighing.

This method requires floor tiles, linoleum, or other material of measurable weight that can be easily cut. Trace the circle whose area is required on the tile and cut out the resulting circular region.

Use the remaining tiles to cut out three 10 cm squares, five 10 cm by 1 cm rectangles, and ten 1 cm squares. You will need more cutouts if the circle is large. These rectangular cutouts will be used as weights.

Place the circular cutout in the scale pan and use the rectangular pieces as weights. When the scale balances, remove the rectangular pieces and find their total area. This area will be the area of the circular cutout.

Why does this method of weighing to find area make sense?

Mixed exercises

Use the value of π on your calculator. Give your answers to 3 s.f.

Exercise 10h

1 Find the circumference of a circle of radius 2.8 mm.

2 Find the radius of a circle of circumference 60 m.

3 Find the circumference of a circle of diameter 12 cm.

4 Find the area of a circle of radius 2.9 m.

5 Find the area of a circle of diameter 25 cm.

6 Find the perimeter of the quadrant in the diagram.

8 mm

7 Find the area of the sector in the diagram, which is $\frac{1}{8}$ of a circle.

45°
4.5 cm

Exercise 10i

1 Find the circumference of a circle of diameter 20 m.

2 Find the area of a circle of radius 12 cm.

3 Find the radius of a circle of circumference 360 cm.

4 Find the area of a circle of diameter 8 m.

5 Find the diameter of a circle of circumference 280 mm.

6 Find the perimeter of the sector, which is $\frac{1}{3}$ of a circle.

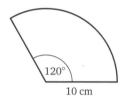

120°
10 cm

7 Find the area of the shaded part of the diagram.

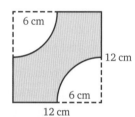

6 cm
12 cm
6 cm
12 cm

Exercise 10j

1 Find the area of a circle of radius 2 km.

2 Find the circumference of a circle of radius 49 mm.

3 Find the radius of a circle of circumference 88 m.

4 Find the area of a circle of diameter 14 cm.

5 Find the area of a circle of radius 3.2 cm.

6

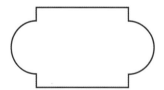

An ornamental pond in a garden is a rectangle with a semicircle on each short end. The rectangle measures 5 m by 3 m and the radius of each semicircle is 1 m. Find the area of the pond.

Exercise 10k

Select the letter that gives the correct answer.

1 The circumference of a circle of radius 8 cm is

    A 25.1 cm   **B** 50.2 cm   **C** 50.3 cm   **D** 50.4 cm

2 The radius of a circle of circumference 25 cm is

    A 3.97 cm   **B** 3.98 cm   **C** 3.99 cm   **D** 7.96 cm

3 The circumference of a circle of diameter 12 cm is

    A 37.6 cm   **B** 37.7 cm   **C** 37.8 cm   **D** 37.9 cm

4 The area of a circle of radius 15 cm is

    A 707 cm²   **B** 717 cm²   **C** 827 cm²   **D** 2830 cm²

5 The area of a circle of diameter 12 m is

    A 113 m²   **B** 114 m²   **C** 453 m²   **D** 454 m²

6 When the label is taken off a cylindrical tin it is 35 cm long. There was an overlap of 1 cm when the label was on the tin. The radius of the circular cross-section of the tin, correct to 3 s.f., is

    A 5.39 cm   **B** 5.40 cm   **C** 5.41 cm   **D** 5.44 cm

7 The perimeter of this quadrant of a circle, correct to 3 s.f., is

    A 20.6 cm   **B** 25 cm   **C** 28.5 cm   **D** 28.6 cm

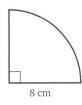

8 cm

8 The shaded area of the shape shown below correct to 3 s.f., is

    A 100 cm²   **B** 129 cm²   **C** 135 cm²   **D** 164 cm²

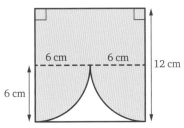

9 The circumference of a circle is 46 cm. Its area, correct to 3 s.f., is

    A 168 cm²   **B** 172 cm²   **C** 176 cm²   **D** 184 cm²

10 The area of a circle is 200 cm². The length of its circumference, correct to 2 s.f., is

    A 50 cm   **B** 51 cm   **C** 58 cm   **D** 60 cm

Did you know?

Over the centuries mathematicians have spent a lot of time trying to find the true value of π. The ancient Chinese used 3. Three is also the value given in the Old Testament (1 Kings 7 : 23). The Egyptians (*c.* 1600 BCE) used $4 \times \left(\dfrac{8}{9}\right)^2$. Archimedes (*c.* 225 BCE) was the first person to use a sound method for finding its value and a mathematician called Van Ceulen (1540–1610) spent most of his life finding it to 35 decimal places!

In this chapter you have seen that...

✔ for any circle the circumference divided by the diameter gives a fixed value; this value is denoted by π and its approximate value is 3.142

✔ you can find the circumference of a circle using either the formula $C = 2\pi r$ or the formula $C = \pi d$ when you know the radius or diameter of the circle

✔ you can use the formula $A = \pi r^2$ to find the area of a circle

✔ a sector of a circle is shaped like a slice of cake.

11 Volume and capacity

At the end of this chapter you should be able to...

1 recognise volume as a measure of space

2 measure volume using standard units

3 calculate the volume of solids given the necessary dimensions

4 convert from one standard metric unit of volume to another

4 construct a net to make a solid.

Did you know?

Archimedes, one of the greatest mathematicians, lived on the island of Sicily during the 3rd century BC. While taking a bath in a tub he discovered a law about things floating in water. He saw how this law could help the king, who thought that the man who made his crown had cheated him, know whether his crown was pure gold or not.

He was so excited that he ran out of the house naked shouting 'Eureka', which means 'I have found it'.

You need to know...

✔ how to change from one metric unit of length to another

✔ how to find the area of a square

✔ how to find the area of a parallelogram.

Key words

capacity, cube, cubic unit, cuboid, dimension, litre, millilitre, net, prism, volume

Volume

In the science laboratory you may well have seen a container with a spout similar to the one shown in the diagram (some people call this a Eureka can; do you know why?).

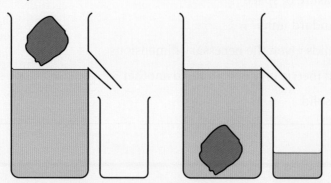

The container is filled with water to the level of the spout. Any solid which is put into the water will force a quantity of water into the measuring jug. The volume of this water will be equal to the volume of the solid. The volume of a solid is the amount of space it occupies.

Cubic units

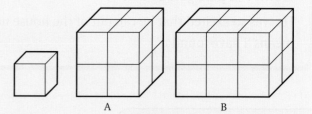

As with area, we need a convenient unit for measuring volume. The most suitable unit is a cube. A cube has six faces. Each face is a square.

How many of the smallest cubes are needed to fill the same space as each of the solids A and B? Careful counting will show that 8 small cubes fill the same space as solid A and 12 small cubes fill the same space as solid B.

A cube with a side of 1 cm has a volume of one cubic centimetre which is written 1 cm³.

Similarly a cube with a side of 1 mm has a volume of 1 mm³ and a cube with a side of 1 m has a volume of 1 m³.

Volume of a cuboid

A *cuboid* is the mathematical name for a rectangular block. Each face of a cuboid is a rectangle.

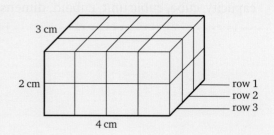

The diagram shows a rectangular block or cuboid measuring 4 cm by 3 cm by 2 cm. To cover the area on which the block stands we need three rows of cubes measuring 1 cm by 1 cm by 1 cm, with four cubes in each row, i.e. 12 cubes. A second layer of 12 cubes is needed to give the volume shown, so the volume of the block is 24 cubes.

But the volume of one cube is 1 cm³.

Therefore the volume of the solid is 24 cm³.

This is also given when we calculate length × breadth × height,

i.e.   the volume of the block = $4 \times 3 \times 2$ cm³

or   the volume of the block = length × breadth × height

Exercise 11a

Find the volume of a cuboid measuring 12 cm by 10 cm by 5 cm.

Volume of cuboid = length × breadth × height

$$= 12 \times 10 \times 5 \text{ cm}^3$$

i.e.   Volume = 600 cm³

Find the volume of each of the following cuboids:

	Length	Breadth	Height			Length	Breadth	Height
1	4 cm	4 cm	3 cm	**7**	4 m	3 m	2 m
2	20 mm	10 mm	8 mm	**8**	8 m	5 m	4 m
3	45 mm	20 mm	6 mm	**9**	8 cm	3 cm	$\frac{1}{2}$ cm
4	5 mm	4 mm	0.8 mm	**10**	12 cm	1.2 cm	0.5 cm
5	6.1 m	4 m	1.3 m	**11**	4.5 m	1.2 m	0.8 m
6	3.5 cm	2.5 cm	1.2 cm	**12**	1.2 m	0.9 m	0.7 m

Find the volume of a cube with the given side:

13 4 cm

14 5 cm

15 2 m

16 $\frac{1}{2}$ cm

17 2.5 cm

18 3 km

19 8 km

20 $1\frac{1}{2}$ km

21 3.4 m

The edges of a cube are all the same length so the volume is $(4 \times 4 \times 4)$ cm³.

 **Puzzle**

Which two of these shapes will fit together to form a cube?

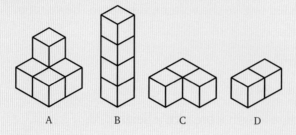

A   B   C   D

Exercise 11b

Draw a cube of side 8 cm. How many cubes of side 2 cm would be needed to fill the same space?

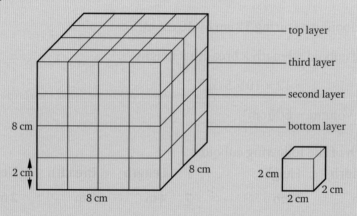

The bottom layer requires 4×4, i.e. 16 cubes of side 2 cm, and there are four layers altogether.

Therefore 64 cubes are required.

1   Draw a cube of side 4 cm. How many cubes of side 2 cm would be needed to fill the same space?

2   Draw a cuboid measuring 6 cm by 4 cm by 2 cm. How many cubes of side 2 cm would be needed to fill the same space?

3   Draw a cube of side 6 cm. How many cubes of side 3 cm would be needed to fill the same space?

4   Draw a cuboid measuring 8 cm by 6 cm by 2 cm. How many cubes of side 2 cm would be needed to fill the same space?

Puzzle

The outer surface of the large cube in the worked example on page 192 is painted red. How many of the 64 small cubes are unpainted?

Changing units of volume

Consider a cube of side 1 cm. If each edge is divided into 10 mm the cube can be divided into 10 layers each layer with 10×10 cubes of side 1 mm.

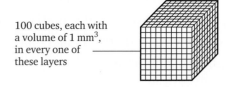

100 cubes, each with a volume of 1 mm³, in every one of these layers

So

$$1\,cm^3 = 10 \times 10 \times 10\,mm^3$$

i.e.

$$1\,cm^3 = 1000\,mm^3$$

Similarly, since 1 m = 100 cm

$$1 \text{ cubic metre} = 100 \times 100 \times 100\,cm^3$$

i.e.

$$1\,m^3 = 1\,000\,000\,cm^3$$

Exercise 11c

Express 2.4 m³ in **a** cm³ **b** mm³.

a Since $1\,m^3 = 100 \times 100 \times 100\,cm^3$

$2.4\,m^3 = 2.4 \times 100 \times 100 \times 100\,cm^3$

$= 2\,400\,000\,cm^3$

b Since $1\,m^3 = 1000 \times 1000 \times 1000\,mm^3$

$2.4\,m^3 = 2.4 \times 1000 \times 1000 \times 1000\,mm^3$

$= 2\,400\,000\,000\,mm^3$

1 Which metric unit would you use to measure the volume of
a a room **b** a teaspoon **c** a can of cola?

Express in mm³:

2 8 cm³ **3** 14 cm³ **4** 6.2 cm³ **5** 0.43 cm³ **6** 0.092 m³ **7** 0.04 cm³

Express in cm³:

8 3 m³ **10** 0.42 m³ **12** 22 mm³

9 2.5 m³ **11** 0.0063 m³ **13** 731 mm³

Capacity

When we buy a bottle of milk or a can of engine oil we are not usually interested in the external measurements or volume of the container. What really concerns us is the *capacity* of the container, i.e. how much milk the bottle can hold, or how much engine oil is inside the can.

The most common unit of capacity in the metric system is the *litre*. (A litre is usually the size of a large bottle of water.) A litre is much larger than a cubic centimetre but much smaller than a cubic metre. The relationship between these quantities is:

$$1000 \, cm^3 = 1 \, litre$$

i.e. a litre is the volume of a cube of side 10 cm

and $$1000 \, litres = 1 \, m^3$$

When the amount of liquid is small, such as dosages for medicines, the *millilitre* (ml) is used. A millilitre is a thousandth part of a litre, i.e.

$$1000 \, ml = 1 \, litre \quad or \quad 1 \, ml = 1 \, cm^3$$

Exercise 11d

Express 5.6 litres in cm^3.

$$1 \, litre = 1000 \, cm^3$$

so $$5.6 \, litres = 5.6 \times 1000 \, cm^3$$

$$= 5600 \, cm^3$$

Express in cm^3:

1	2.5 litres	**3**	0.54 litres	**5**	35 litres
2	1.76 litres	**4**	0.0075 litres	**6**	0.028 litres

Express in litres:

7	7000 cm^3	**8**	4000 cm^3	**9**	24 000 cm^3	**10**	600 cm^3

Express in litres:

11	5 m^3	**12**	12 m^3	**13**	4.6 m^3	**14**	0.067 m^3

Nets

Any solid with flat faces can be made from a flat sheet.

(We are using the word 'solid' for any object that takes up space, i.e. for any three-dimensional object, and such an object can be hollow.)

A cube can be made from six separate squares.

We can avoid a lot of unnecessary sticking if we join some squares together before cutting out.

This is called a *net*.

There are other arrangements of six squares that can be folded up to make a cube. Not all arrangements of six squares will work however, as we will see in the next exercise.

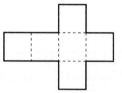

1   Below is the net of a cube of edge 5 cm.

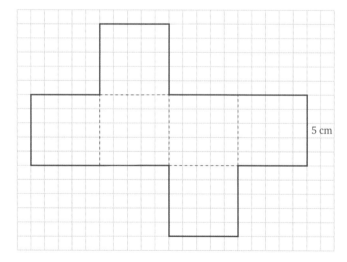

5 cm

Draw the net on 1 cm squared paper and cut it out. Fold it along the broken lines. Fix it together with sticky tape.

If you mark the faces with the numbers 1 to 6 you can make a dice.

2 Draw this net full-size on 1 cm squared paper.

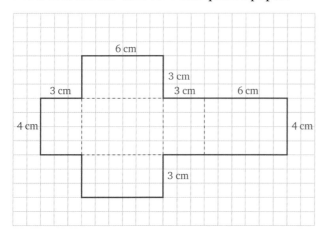

Cut the net out and fold it along the dotted lines. Stick the edges together.

a **i** How many faces are rectangles measuring 6 cm by 3 cm?

ii How many faces are rectangles measuring 6 cm by 4 cm?

iii What are the measurements of the remaining faces?

b Draw another arrangement of the rectangles that will fold up to make the same cuboid.

3 This cuboid is 6 cm long, 4 cm wide and 3 cm high.

a How many faces does this cuboid have?

b Sketch the faces, showing their measurement.

c On 1 cm grid paper, draw a net that will make this cuboid.

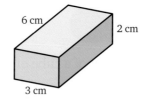

4 Draw this net full-size on 1 cm squared paper. The longest edge is 8 cm long.

a Cut the net out and fold it along the dotted lines. Stick the edges together.

b What name do we give to this solid?

c What shape is the cross-section?

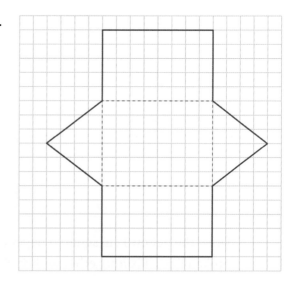

5 Draw this net full-size on 1 cm squared paper. The square, which is shown with dotted lines has an edge of 4 cm.

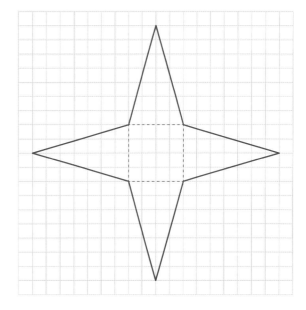

a Cut the net out and fold it along the dotted lines. Stick the edges together.

b Does the solid have a uniform cross-section? Justify your answer.

c What name do we give to this solid?

6 Draw this net full-size on 1 cm squared paper.

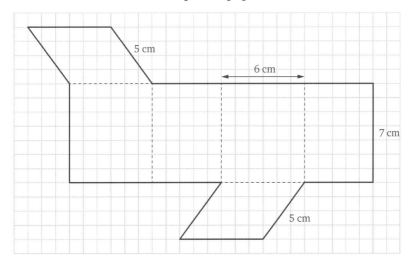

5 cm

6 cm

7 cm

5 cm

a Cut the net out and fold it along the dotted lines. Stick the edges together.

b What name do we give to this solid?

c What shape is the cross-section?

d Find the length of the perimeter of the shape at one end.

7 The diagram shows a pyramid with a square base.

a Sketch a net for this solid. Label it and insert the measurements.

b How many triangles are exactly the same shape and size as triangle AED? Name them.

c How many triangles are exactly the same shape and size as triangle ECD? Name them.

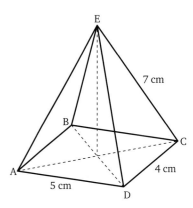

7 cm

5 cm

4 cm

8 This net will make a cuboid.

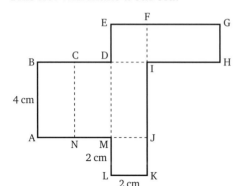

a Sketch the cuboid, and show its measurements.

b Which edge joins HI?

c Which corners meet at A?

9 This cube is cut along the edges drawn with a coloured line and flattened out.
Draw the flattened shape.

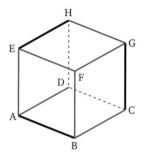

10 Here are two arrangements of six squares.

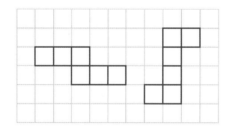

a Draw as many other arrangements of six squares as you can find.

b Which of your arrangements, including the two given here, will fold up to make a cube? If you cannot tell by looking, cut them out and try to make a cube

---

🔍 Investigation

A rectangular piece of card measuring 12 cm by 9 cm is to be used to make a small rectangular box.

The diagram shows one way of doing this.

1 How many different open boxes can be made from this piece of card if the length and breadth of the base is to be a whole number of centimetres?
Draw each possibility on squared paper.

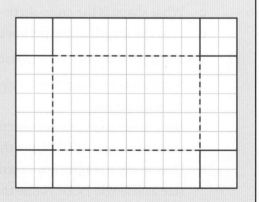

2   For each different box find

    a   its dimensions   **b**   its total external surface area   **c**   its capacity.

3   Use the information you have found in part **2** to state whether each of these statements is true (T) or false (F).

    A   The box with the largest base has the greatest capacity.

    B   The box with the smallest total external surface area has the smallest capacity.

    C   The box with the greatest capacity is as deep as it is wide.

4   Find the dimensions of the largest cubical open box that can be made from a rectangular card measuring 12 cm by 9 cm. How much card is wasted?

5   Investigate other sizes of card to find the dimensions of the box with the largest volume that can be made from each size.

Mixed units

Before we can find the volume of a cuboid, *all* measurements must be expressed in the same unit.

Exercise 11f

Find the volume of a cuboid measuring 2 m by 70 cm by 30 cm.

Give your answer in   **a** cm³   **b** m³.

a   (All the measurements must be in centimetres so we first convert the 2 m into centimetres.)

$$\text{Length of cuboid} = 2\,\text{m} = 2 \times 100\,\text{cm} = 200\,\text{cm}$$

$$\text{Volume of cuboid} = \text{length} \times \text{breadth} \times \text{height}$$

$$= 200 \times 70 \times 30\,\text{cm}^3$$

$$= 420\,000\,\text{cm}^3$$

b   (We convert all the measurements to metres before finding the volume.)

$$\text{Breadth of cuboid} = 70\,\text{cm} = \frac{70}{100}\,\text{m} = 0.7\,\text{m}$$

$$\text{Height of cuboid} = 30\,\text{cm} = \frac{30}{100}\,\text{m} = 0.3\,\text{m}$$

$$\therefore \quad \text{Volume of cuboid} = 2 \times 0.7 \times 0.3\,\text{m}^3$$

$$= 0.42\,\text{m}^3$$

Find the volumes of the following cuboids, giving your answers in the units stated in brackets:

	Length	Breadth	Height	
1	50 mm	30 mm	20 mm	(cm³)
2	400 cm	100 cm	50 cm	(m³)
3	1 m	4 cm	2 cm	(cm³)
4	15 cm	80 mm	50 mm	(cm³)
5	6 cm	12 mm	8 mm	(mm³
6	2 m	50 cm	40 mm	(cm³)
7	4 cm	35 mm	2 cm	(cm³)
8	20 m	80 cm	50 cm	(m³)
9	3.5 cm	25 mm	20 mm	(cm³)
10	$\frac{1}{2}$ m	45 mm	8 mm	(cm³)

Problems involving cuboids

Exercise 11g

Find the volume of a rectangular block of wood measuring 8 cm by 6 cm which is 2 m long. Give your answer in cubic centimetres.

Working in centimetres:

$$\text{Length of block} = 2\,\text{m} = 2 \times 100\,\text{cm} = 200\,\text{cm}$$
$$\text{Volume of block} = \text{length} \times \text{breadth} \times \text{height}$$
$$= 200 \times 8 \times 6\,\text{cm}^3$$
$$= 9600\,\text{cm}^3$$

A rectangular metal water tank is 3 m long, 2.5 m wide and 80 cm deep.

Find its capacity in   **a** m³   **b** litres.

To find the capacity of the tank you need to find the volume inside the tank.

a   Working in metres:

$$\text{Depth of tank} = 80\,\text{cm} = \frac{80}{100}\,\text{m} = 0.8\,\text{m}$$
$$\text{Capacity of tank} = \text{length} \times \text{breadth} \times \text{height}$$
$$= 3 \times 2.5 \times 0.8\,\text{m}^3$$
$$= 6\,\text{m}^3$$

b
$$1\,m^3 = 1000 \text{ litres}$$
$$\text{Capacity of tank} = 6 \times 1000 \text{ litres}$$
$$= 6000 \text{ litres}$$

1   Which unit would you use to give the volume of

    a this book   **d** a spoonful of water   **g** a petrol can

    b the room you are in   **e** a lorry load of rubble   **h** a 25 c coin

    c one vitamin pill   **f** a packet of cornflakes   **i** a concrete building block?

2   Find the volume of air in a room measuring 4 m by 5 m which is 3 m high.

3   Find the volume, in cm³, of a concrete block measuring 36 cm by 18 cm by 12 cm.

4   Find the volume of a school hall which is 30 m long and 24 m wide if the ceiling is 9 m high.

5   An electric light bulb is sold in a box measuring 10 cm by 6 cm by 6 cm. If the shopkeeper receives them in a carton measuring 50 cm by 30 cm by 30 cm, how many bulbs would be packed in a carton?

6   A classroom is 10 m long, 8 m wide and 3 m high. How many pupils should it be used for if each pupil requires 5 m³ of air space?

7   How many cubic metres of water are required to fill a rectangular swimming bath 15 m long and 10 m wide which is 2 m deep throughout? How many litres is this?

8   How many rectangular packets, measuring 8 cm by 6 cm by 4 cm, may be packed in a rectangular cardboard box measuring 30 cm by 24 cm by 16 cm?

9   A water storage tank is 3 m long, 2 m wide and $1\frac{1}{2}$ m deep. How many litres of water will it hold?

10   How many lead cubes of side 2 cm could be made from a lead cube of side 8 cm?

11   How many lead cubes of side 5 mm could be made from a rectangular block of lead measuring 10 cm by 5 cm by 4 cm?

? **Puzzle**

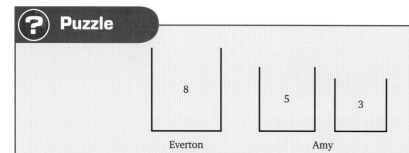

Everton is returning from the local farm with an 8-pint can which is full of milk. He meets Amy who is going to the same farm for milk. She has an empty 5-pint can and an empty 3-pint can. Everton knows that there is no milk left at the farm, so being the kind boy he is, decides to share his milk equally with Amy. How do they do it using only the three containers they have?

Volume of a prism

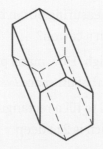

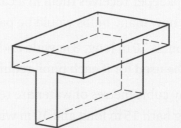

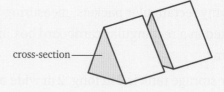

When we cut through any one of the solids above, parallel to the ends, we always get the same shape as the end.

This shape is called the *cross-section*.

It is said to be uniform or constant.

First consider a cuboid (which can also be thought of as a rectangular prism).

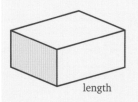

Volume = length × width × height

= (width × height) × length

= area of shaded end × length

= area of cross-section × length

Now consider a triangular prism. If we enclose it in a cuboid we can see that its volume is half the volume of the cuboid.

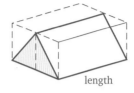

$$\text{Volume} = \left(\frac{1}{2} \times \text{width} \times \text{heigth}\right) \times \text{length}$$

$$= \text{area of shaded triangle} \times \text{length}$$

$$= \text{area of cross-section} \times \text{length}$$

This is true of any prism so that

> Volume of a prism = area of cross-section × length

Exercise 11h

Find the volume of the solid below.

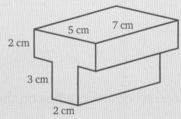

To find the volume you need first to find the area of the cross-section.

Draw the cross-section, then divide it into two rectangles.

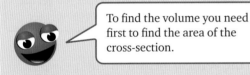

Area of A = $2 \times 5\,\text{cm}^2 = 10\,\text{cm}^2$

Area of B = $2 \times 3\,\text{cm}^2 = 6\,\text{cm}^2$

Area of cross-section = $16\,\text{cm}^2$

Volume = area × length

$= (16 \times 7)\,\text{cm}^3$

$= 112\,\text{cm}^3$

Find the volumes of the following prisms. Draw a diagram of the cross-section but do *not* draw a picture of the solid.

1

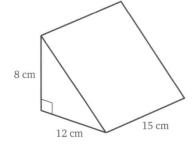

2

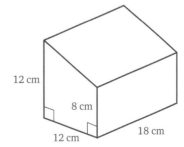

3

5

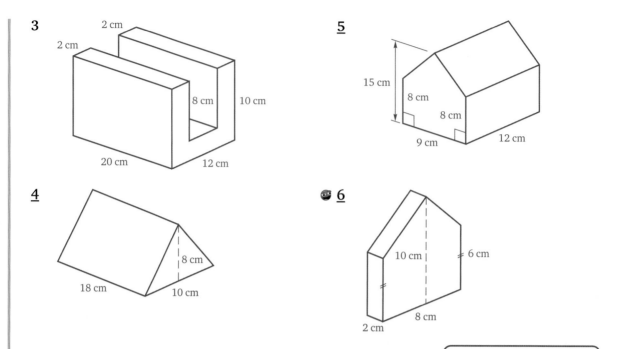

4

6

Be careful that you get the right cross-section.

The following two solids are standing on their ends so the vertical measurement is the length.

7

8

In questions **9** to **10**, the cross-sections of the prisms and their lengths are given. Find their volumes.

9

10

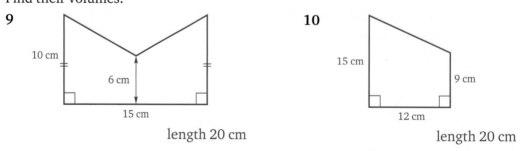

length 20 cm

length 20 cm

11

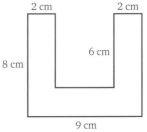

2 cm   2 cm

8 cm

6 cm

9 cm

length $7\frac{1}{2}$ cm

14

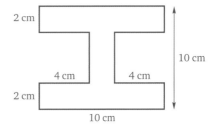

2 cm

2 cm

4 cm   4 cm

10 cm

10 cm

length 12 cm

12

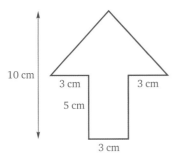

10 cm

3 cm   3 cm

5 cm

3 cm

length 12 cm

15

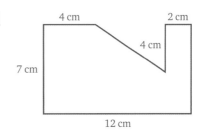

4 cm   2 cm

4 cm

7 cm

12 cm

length 12 cm

13

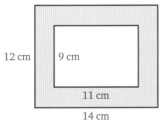

12 cm   9 cm

11 cm

14 cm

length 10 cm

16

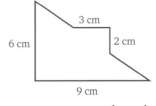

3 cm

6 cm   2 cm

9 cm

length 24 cm

You need the area between the two rectangles.

17 A tent is in the shape of a triangular prism. Its length is 2.4 m, its height 1.8 m and the width of the triangular end is 2.4 m. Find the volume enclosed by the tent.

18 The area of the cross-section of the given solid is 42 cm² and the length is 32 cm. Find its volume.

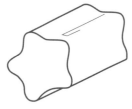

19 A solid of uniform cross-section is 12 m long. Its cross-section is shown in the diagram. Find its volume.

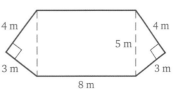

4 m   4 m

5 m

3 m   3 m

8 m

20

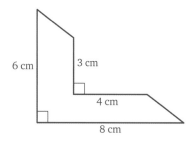

The diagram shows the uniform cross-section of a prism. The prism is 30 cm long. Find its volume.

21

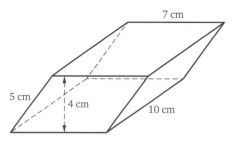

This solid has a constant cross-section and is 10 cm long.

  a What name do we give to the shape of the cross-section?

  b Find the area of the cross-section.

  c Find the volume of the solid.

22 This solid has a constant cross-section.

  a How high is it?

  b What name do we give to the shape of the cross-section?

  c Find the area of the cross-section.

  d Find the volume of the solid.

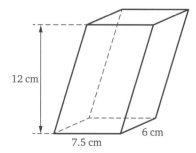

(?) Puzzle

Leela has a bag of identical triangular wooden blocks.

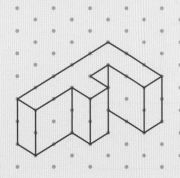

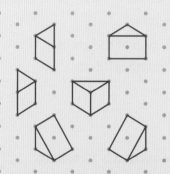

She uses some of them to make the letter F.

How many blocks does she need?

Volume of a cylinder

Reminder: The circumference of a circle is given by $C = 2\pi r$ and the area of a circle by $A = \pi r^2$.

A cylinder can be thought of as a circular prism so its volume can be found using

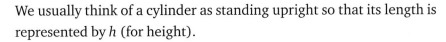

volume = area of cross-section × length

= area of circular end × length

(cross-section is the circular end of a cylinder)

From this we can find a formula for the volume.

We usually think of a cylinder as standing upright so that its length is represented by h (for height).

If the radius of the end circle is r, then the area of the cross-section is πr^2

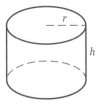

∴   volume = $\pi r^2 \times h$

= $\pi r^2 h$

Exercise 11i

Find the volume inside a cylindrical mug of internal diameter 8 cm and height 6 cm. Use the π button on your calculator

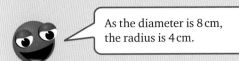
As the diameter is 8 cm, the radius is 4 cm.

The volume is given by the formula

$V = \pi r^2 h$

= $\pi \times 4 \times 4 \times 6 = 301.59...$

Therefore the volume of the mug is 302 cm² (correct to 3 s.f.).

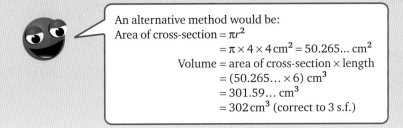
An alternative method would be:
Area of cross-section = πr^2
= $\pi \times 4 \times 4$ cm² = $50.265...$ cm²
Volume = area of cross-section × length
= $(50.265... \times 6)$ cm³
= $301.59...$ cm³
= 302 cm³ (correct to 3 s.f.)

Use the value of π on your calculator and give all your answers correct to 3 s.f.

Find the volumes of the following cylinders:

1	Radius 2 cm, height 10 cm		**11**	Radius 3.2 cm, height 10 cm
2	Radius 3 cm, height 4 cm		**12**	Radius 6 cm, height 3.6 cm
3	Radius 5 cm, height 4 cm		**13**	Diameter 10 cm, height 4.2 cm
4	Radius 3 cm, height 2.1 cm		**14**	Radius 7.2 cm, height 4 cm
5	Diameter 2 cm, height 1 cm		**15**	Diameter 64 cm, height 22 cm
6	Radius 1 cm, height 4.8 cm		**16**	Diameter 2.4 cm, height 6.2 cm
7	Diameter 4 cm, height 3 cm		**17**	Radius 4.8 mm, height 13 mm
8	Diameter 6 cm, height 1.8 cm		**18**	Diameter 16.2 cm, height 4 cm
9	Radius 12 cm, height 10 cm		**19**	Radius 76 cm, height 88 cm
10	Radius 7 cm, height 9 cm		**20**	Diameter 0.02 m, height 0.14 m

Compound shapes

Exercise 11j

Find the volumes of the following solids. Use the value of π on your calculator and give your answers correct to 3 s.f.

Draw diagrams of the cross-sections but do *not* draw pictures of the solids.

Find the area of the cross-section first.

1

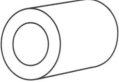

A tube of length 20 cm. The inner radius is 3 cm and the outer radius is 5 cm.

3

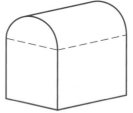

A solid of length 6.2 cm, whose cross-section consists of a square of side 2 cm surmounted by a semicircle.

2

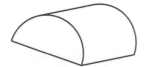

A half-cylinder of length 16 cm and radius 4 cm.

4

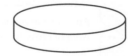

A disc of radius 9 cm and thickness 0.8 cm.

5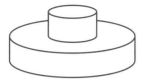

A solid made of two cylinders each of height 5 cm. The radius of the smaller one is 2 cm and of the larger one is 6 cm.

6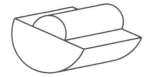

A solid made of two half-cylinders each of length 11 cm. The radius of the larger one is 10 cm and the radius of the smaller one is 5 cm.

> **(?) Puzzle**
>
> A set of three encyclopaedias is placed in the normal way on a shelf. A bookworm takes $\frac{1}{4}$ day to eat through a cover and $\frac{1}{2}$ day to eat through the pages of one book.
>
> How long will it take this bookworm to eat its way from the first page of Volume 1 to the last page of Volume 3?
>
>

Mixed exercises

Exercise 11k

1 Express 3.2 m³ in
   a cm³   **b** mm³.

2 Express 1.6 litres in cm³.

3 Find the volume of a cube of side 4 cm.

4 Find the volume, in cm³, of a cuboid measuring 2 m by 25 cm by 10 cm.

5 Find the volume, in mm³, of a cuboid measuring 5 cm by 3 cm by 9 mm.

6 Find the volume of this prism.

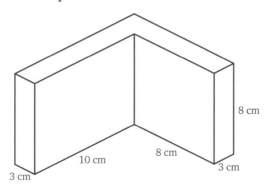

Exercise 11l

1   Express 8 cm³ in
    a   mm³   b   m³.

2   Express 3500 cm³ in litres.

3   Find the volume of a cuboid measuring 10 cm by 5 cm by 6 cm.

4   Find, in cm³, the volume of a cube of side 8 mm.

5   Find the volume, in cm³, of a cuboid measuring 50 cm by 1.2 m by 20 cm.

6   The diagram shows the uniform cross-section of a prism. The prism is
    12 cm long. Find its volume.

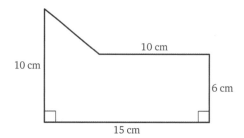

Exercise 11m

1   Express 0.009 m³ in
    a   cm³   b   mm³.

2   Express 0.44 litres in cm³.

3   Find the volume of a cube of side 6 cm.

4   Find the volume of a cuboid measuring 12 cm by 6 cm by 4 cm.

5   Find the capacity, in litres, of a rectangular tank measuring 2 m by 1.5 m
    by 80 cm.

6   Find the volume if this disc with radius 10 cm and thickness 2.5 mm

Exercise 11n

1 Express 900 cm³ in m³.

2 Express 10 800 cm³ in litres.

3 Express 0.075 m³ in litres.

4 Find, in cm³, the volume of a cube of side 20 mm.

5 Find, in m³, the volume of a cuboid measuring 150 cm by 100 cm by 80 cm.

6 Find the volume in cubic metres of a cylinder of radius 30 cm and height 1.5 m.

Exercise 11p

Select the letter that gives the correct answer.

1 The volume of a cube with a side of 6 cm is

   A   108 cm³   B   188 cm³   C   216 cm³   D   324 cm³

2 The volume, correct to 3 s.f., of a cuboid measuring 5.5 cm by 4.2 cm by 3 cm is

   A   57.9 cm³   B   68.5 cm³   C   69.3 cm³   D   70.2 cm³

3 How many cubes of side 3 cm will fit into a rectangular box measuring 9 cm by 6 cm by 6 cm?

   A   6   B   8   C   10   D   12

4 Expressed in mm³, 0.53 cm³ is

   A   5.3 mm³   B   53 mm³   C   530 mm³   D   5300 mm³

5 Expressed in cm³, 0.000 75 m³ is

   A   7.5 cm³   B   75 cm³   C   750 cm³   D   7500 cm³

6 Expressed in cm³, 0.65 litres is

   A   6.5 cm³   B   65 cm³   C   650 cm³   D   6500 cm³

7 300 cm³ expressed in litres is

   A   0.03 l B   0.3 l C   3 l D   30 l

8 The diagram shows a pyramid with a square base.
The number of edges this pyramid has is

A 6 **B** 7 **C** 8 **D** 9

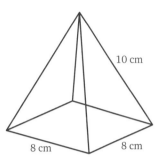

9 The number of identical triangular faces the pyramid shown in
question **8** has is

A 2 **B** 3 **C** 4 **D** 6

10

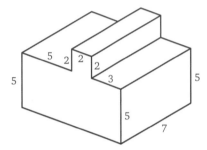

The diagram shows the cross-section of a prism which is 7 cm wide.
All the measurements are in centimetres.
The volume of this prism is

A 350 cm³ **B** 375 cm³ **C** 378 cm³ **D** 385 cm³

11

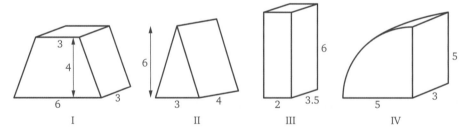

All measurements for these four solids are in centimetres.
Which solid has the largest volume?

A I **B** II **C** III **D** IV

12 Which of the solids shown in question **11** has the smallest volume?

A I **B** II **C** III **D** IV

Did you know?

A Moebius strip is named after the German mathematician August Ferdinand Moebius. You can make one: take a strip of paper, twist it once and join the ends together. It has only one surface and only one edge (try it – draw a line along its surface – what happens?).

In this chapter you have seen that...

✔ volume and capacity are measures of space

✔ the volume of a cube or a cuboid is found by multiplying the length by the breadth by the height

✔ if the dimensions are given in different units you must change some of them so that they are all in the same unit before multiplying

✔ you should be familiar with the common metric units used to measure large and small volumes

These are cubic millimetres (mm^3), cubic centimetres (cm^3), cubic metres (m^3), litres and millilitres (ml). The relationships between them are

$$1\,cm^3 = 10 \times 10 \times 10\,mm^3 = 1000\,mm^3$$

$$1\,m^3 = 100 \times 100 \times 100\,cm^3 = 1\,000\,000\,cm^3$$

$$1\,litre = 1000\,cm^3 = 1000\,ml$$

✔ any solid with a uniform cross-section is called a prism and its volume is equal to the area of the cross-section multiplied by its length

✔ in particular the volume of a cylinder is given by $V = \pi r^2 h$.

✔ REVIEW TEST 2: CHAPTERS 7–11

In questions **1** to **9**, choose the letter for the correct answer.

1 Which of the four lines, whose equations are given below, makes the greatest angle with the *x*-axis?

A $y = \frac{1}{2}x$ B $y = 2x$ C $y = -3x$ D $y = -\frac{1}{3}x$

2 For the vector $\begin{pmatrix} 8 \\ 3 \end{pmatrix}$ the coordinates of its end point are (4, 2).

The coordinates of its starting point are

A (4, 1)   B (4, –1)   C (–4, 1)   D (–4, –1)

3 The vector describing the translation of a point A(–2, 4) to a point A′(3, –3) is

A $\begin{pmatrix} -5 \\ -7 \end{pmatrix}$ B $\begin{pmatrix} -5 \\ 7 \end{pmatrix}$ C $\begin{pmatrix} 5 \\ -7 \end{pmatrix}$ D $\begin{pmatrix} 5 \\ 7 \end{pmatrix}$

4 For the vector $\begin{pmatrix} 2 \\ -4 \end{pmatrix}$ the coordinates of its starting point are (3, 2).

The coordinates of its end point are

A (–5, –2)   B (–5, 2)   C (5, –2)   D (5, 2)

5 P′ is the image of P under reflection in a mirror line *l*. At what angle does PP′ cut *l*?

A 30°   B 45°   C 60°   D 90°

6 The circumference of a circle is 88 cm. What is its radius? (Take $\pi = \frac{22}{7}$.)

A 11 cm   B 14 cm   C 22 cm   D 44 cm

7 Expressed in cm³, 0.047 m³ is

A 47 cm³   B 470 cm³   C 4700 cm³   D 47000 cm³

8 A cuboid measures 8 cm by 6 cm by 4 cm. The number of cubes of side 2 cm that would be required to fill the same space is

A 18   B 24   C 32   D 48

9 Expressed in litres, 36 000 cm³ is

A 3.6 litres   B 36 litres   C 360 litres   D 3600 litres

10 **a** Find, in millimetres,   **i** $3\,\text{m} + 55\,\text{cm} + 8\,\text{mm}$ **ii** $6\,\text{m} - 62\,\text{cm}$.

     b Find, in kg, $3 \times 4\,\text{kg}\ 345\,\text{g}$.

     c Find the difference, in grams, between $6\,\text{g}$ and $475\,\text{mg}$.

     d Express   **i** $734\,\text{m}$ in km   **ii** 216 hours in days.

11 The points $(4, a)$, $(-6, b)$ and $(c, -3)$ lie on the straight line with equation $y = -\dfrac{3}{2}x$.

    Find the values of a, b and c.

12 **a** Give the inequalities that define the shaded region.

     b Is the point $(2, -5)$ within the shaded region?

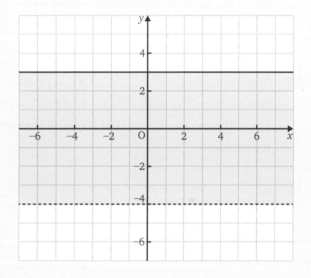

13 The points A, B, C and D illustrate a relation.

     a Represent these points as a table.

     b How is the y-coordinate of each point related to the x-coordinate?

     c The points A, B, C and D all lie on the same line. E is another point on this line. Its x-coordinate is 3; what is its y-coordinate?

     d F is a point on the line whose y-coordinate is 4. What is its x-coordinate?

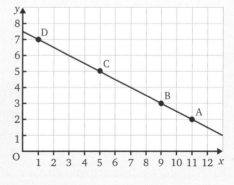

14   ABCD is a square. The coordinates of A, B and C are respectively A(3, 0),
      B(2, 4) and C(6, 5).
      Write
      a   the coordinates of D
      b   the coordinates of E, the midpoint of AC
      c   the coordinates of F, the midpoint of BD.
      What do you notice?

15   Draw triangle PQR with vertices P(1, 5), Q(6, 4) and R(5, 1).
      Draw the image of PQR after reflection in
      a   the x-axis   b   the y-axis   c   the line $y = x$.
      Name the coordinates of the image in each case.

16   Draw square PQRS: P(1, −1), Q(5, −1), R(5, 3) and S(1, 3).
      Draw square P′Q′R′S′: P′(−3, −1), Q′(−7, −1), R′(−7, 3) and S′(−3, 3).
      Draw the mirror line so that P′Q′R′S′ is a reflection of PQRS and write
      its equation.

17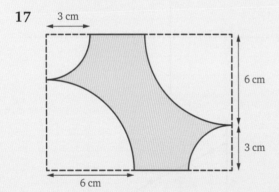
      3 cm
      6 cm
      3 cm
      6 cm

      A rectangular sheet measuring 16 cm by 9 cm has its corners cut off as
      shown in the diagram. Each corner is the quadrant of a circle. Find,
      correct to 3 s.f., the area of the sheet remaining.

18   The circumference of a circle is 30 cm.
      Calculate, correct to 2 d.p.,
      a   its diameter   b   its radius   c   its area.

19 Express

    a $80\,000\,\text{cm}^3$ in m^3

    b $0.007\,\text{m}^3$ in litres

    c $0.0006\,\text{m}^3$ in mm^3.

20 The diagram shows a square ABCD of side 12 cm.

    ABCE is a quadrant of a circle.

    Find, correct to 3 s.f., the area of

    a the quadrant ABCE   **b** ABCF   **c** AECF.

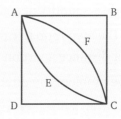

21 This net will make a cuboid.

    a Sketch the cuboid and show its measurements.

    b Which edge joins with

        i GH   **ii** AB?

    c Which corners meet at G?

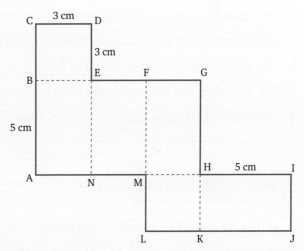

At the end of this chapter you should be able to...

1 express the ratio of one number to another

2 express the ratio of one unit of measurement to another

3 write a ratio equivalent to a given ratio

4 divide a quantity in a given ratio

5 use the map ratio to calculate the actual distance between two places given their distance apart on a map

6 solve problems on direct proportion using the unitary method

7 read from a distance–time graph the distance or time of motion of a moving object

8 draw distance–time graphs using suitable scales

9 calculate the distance travelled in a given time by an object moving at a constant speed

10 calculate the time taken to travel a given distance at a constant speed

11 calculate the average speed of a body, given the distance travelled and time taken

12 calculate the average speed for a body covering different distances at different speeds

13 read information from a distance–time graph.

You need to know...

✔ the meaning of equivalent fractions

✔ how to simplify fractions

✔ how to multiply a fraction by a whole number

✔ the meaning of lowest common multiple

✔ the angle sum of a triangle.

Key words

average speed, constant speed, denominator, direct proportion, equivalent fraction, lowest common multiple, map ratio, numerator, proportion, ratio, rectangle, representative fraction, speed, square, triangle

Simplifying ratios

Suppose that Peter makes a model of his father's boat. If the model is 1 m long while the actual boat is 20 m long, we say that the ratio of the length of the model to the length of the actual boat is 1 m : 20 m or, more simply, 1 : 20. We can also write the ratio as the fraction $\frac{1}{20}$.

If Peter built a larger model which was 2 m long then the ratio would be

$$\frac{\text{length of model}}{\text{length of actual boat}} = \frac{2\text{ m}}{20\text{ m}} = \frac{1}{10}$$

or   length of model : length of boat = 1 : 10

Ratios are therefore comparisons between related quantities.

Exercise 12a

Express the ratios   **a** 24 to 72   **b** 2 cm to 1 m   in their simplest form.

a $\frac{24}{72} = \frac{3}{9} = \frac{1}{3}$ (dividing both numbers by 8 and then by 3)

or   24 : 72 = 3 : 9 = 1 : 3

so   24 : 72 = 1 : 3

b   (Before we can compare 2 cm and 1 m they must be expressed in the same unit.)

$\frac{2\text{ cm}}{1\text{ m}} = \frac{2\text{ cm}}{100\text{ cm}}$ or   2 cm : 1 m = 2 cm : 100 cm

= 2 : 100

$= \frac{1}{50}$ = 1 : 50

so   2 cm : 1 m = 1 : 50

Express the following ratios in their simplest form:

1   8 : 10
2   20 : 16
3   12 : 18
4   2 cm : 8 cm
5   32 c : 96 c

6   45 g : 1 kg
7   $4 : 75 c
8   48 c : $2.88
9   288 : 306
10   10 cm² : 1 m²

Simplify the ratio $24:18:12$

(As there are three numbers involved, this ratio cannot be expressed as a single fraction.)

$$24:18:12 = 4:3:2 \quad \text{(dividing each number by 6)}$$

11	$4:6:10$	**16**	$7:56:49$
12	$18:24:36$	**17**	$15:20:35$
13	$2:10:20$	**18**	$16:128:64$
14	$9:12:15$	**19**	$144:12:24$
15	$20:24:32$	**20**	$98:63:14$

We know that we can produce equivalent fractions by multiplying or dividing both numerator and denominator by the same number,

so that $\quad \dfrac{2}{3} = \dfrac{4}{6} \quad$ or $\quad \dfrac{12}{18} \quad$ or $\quad \dfrac{20}{30}$.

We can do the same with a ratio in the form $3:6$.

$$3:6 = 6:12 \quad \text{(multiplying both numbers by 2)}$$

and $\quad 2:\dfrac{1}{3} = 6:1 \quad$ (multiplying both numbers by 3)

We can use this to simplify ratios containing fractions.

Exercise 12b

Express in their simplest form the ratios

a $\quad 3:\dfrac{1}{4}$ **b** $\quad \dfrac{2}{3}:\dfrac{4}{5}$

a $\quad 3:\dfrac{1}{4} = 12:1 \quad$ (multiplying both numbers by 4)

b $\quad \dfrac{2}{3}:\dfrac{4}{5} = {}^{5}\cancel{15} \times \dfrac{2}{\cancel{3}_1} : \cancel{15}^{3} \times \dfrac{4}{\cancel{5}_1} \quad$ (multiplying both numbers by 15 which is the lowest common multiple of 3 and 5)

$$= 10:12$$
$$= 5:6$$

Express the following ratios in their simplest forms:

1 $5:\frac{1}{3}$ **5** $\frac{1}{3}:\frac{3}{4}$ **9** $2\frac{2}{3}:1\frac{1}{6}$ **13** $4:\frac{9}{10}$ **17** $1\frac{1}{2}:3:4\frac{1}{2}$

2 $2:\frac{1}{4}$ **6** $\frac{7}{12}:\frac{5}{6}$ **10** $\frac{2}{3}:\frac{7}{15}$ **14** $\frac{4}{5}:6$ **18** $6:4\frac{1}{2}$

3 $\frac{1}{2}:\frac{1}{3}$ **7** $\frac{5}{4}:\frac{6}{7}$ **11** $24:15:9$ **15** $7\frac{1}{2}:9\frac{1}{2}$ **19** $\frac{1}{6}:\frac{1}{8}:\frac{1}{12}$

4 $\frac{3}{4}:\frac{1}{4}$ **8** $3:\frac{4}{3}$ **12** $\frac{4}{9}:\frac{2}{3}$ **16** $\frac{1}{4}:\frac{1}{5}$ **20** $6:8:12$

Relative sizes

Exercise 12c

Which ratio is the larger, $6:5$ or $7:6$?

(Express each ratio as a fraction. We need to compare the sizes of $\frac{6}{5}$ and $\frac{7}{6}$ so we express both with the same denominator.)

$$\frac{6}{5} = \frac{36}{30} \quad \text{and} \quad \frac{7}{6} = \frac{35}{30}$$

so $6:5$ is larger than $7:6$

1   Which ratio is the larger, $5:7$ or $2:3$?

2   Which ratio is the smaller, $7:4$ or $13:8$?

3   Which ratio is the larger, $\frac{5}{8}$ or $\frac{7}{12}$?

4   Which ratio is the smaller, $\frac{3}{4}$ or $\frac{7}{10}$?

In the following sets of ratios some are equal to one another. In each question identify the equal ratios.

5 $6:8$, $24:32$, $\frac{3}{4}:1$

6 $10:24$, $\frac{5}{9}:\frac{4}{5}$, $\frac{5}{9}:\frac{4}{3}$

Simplify each ratio, then you can see which are equal.

7 $8:64$, $2:14$, $\frac{1}{16}:\frac{1}{2}$

8 $\frac{2}{3}:3$, $4:18$, $2:6$

Problems

Exercise 12d

A family has 12 pets of which 6 are cats or kittens, 2 are dogs and the rest are birds. Find the ratio of the numbers of
a birds to dogs   **b** birds to pets.

a There are 4 birds and 2 dogs

So number of birds : number of dogs $= 4 : 2$
$$= 2 : 1$$

b There are 4 birds and 12 pets

So number of birds : number of pets $= 4 : 12$
$$= 1 : 3$$

In each question give your answer in its simplest form.

1 A couple have 6 grandsons and 4 granddaughters. Find
    a the ratio of the number of grandsons to that of granddaughters
    b the ratio of the number of granddaughters to that of grandchildren.

2 Square A has side 6 cm and square B has side 8 cm. Find the ratio of
    a the length of the side of square A to the length of the side of square B
    b the area of square A to the area of square B.

3 Tom walks 2 km to school in 40 minutes and John cycles 5 km to school in 15 minutes. Find the ratio of

    a Tom's distance to John's distance
    b Tom's time to John's time.

4 Mary has 18 sweets and Jane has 12. As Mary has 6 sweets more than Jane she tries to even things out by giving Jane 6 sweets. What is the ratio of the number of sweets Mary has to the number Jane has
    a to start with   **b** to end with?

5 If $p : q = 2 : 3$, find the ratio $6p : 2q$.

6 Rectangle A has length 12 cm and width 6 cm while rectangle B has length 8 cm and width 5 cm. Find the ratio of
    a the length of A to the length of B
    b the area of A to the area of B
    c the perimeter of A to the perimeter of B
    d the size of an angle of A to the size of an angle of B.

7 A triangle has sides of lengths 3.2 cm, 4.8 cm and 3.6 cm. Find the ratio of the lengths of the sides to one another.

8 Two angles of a triangle are 54° and 72°. Find the ratio of the size of the third angle to the sum of the first two.

9 For a school bazaar, Mrs Jones and Mrs Brown make marmalade in 1 lb jars. Mrs Jones makes 5 jars of lemon marmalade and 3 jars of orange. Mrs Brown makes 7 jars of lemon marmalade and 5 of grapefruit. Find the ratio of the numbers of jars of
   a   lemon to orange to grapefruit
   b   Mrs Jones' to Mrs Brown's marmalade
   c   Mrs Jones' lemon to orange.

Finding missing quantities

Some missing numbers are fairly obvious.

Exercise 12e

Find the missing numbers in the following ratios:

a $6:5 = \quad : 10$ b $\dfrac{4}{3} = \dfrac{}{9} = \dfrac{24}{}$

a   10 is 5×2, so the missing number is 6×2. Therefore $6:5 = 12:10$

b   Think of these as equivalent fractions. $\dfrac{4}{3} = \dfrac{12}{9} = \dfrac{24}{18}$

Find the missing numbers in the following ratios:

1   $2:5 = 4:$

2   $\quad : 6 = 12:18$

3   $24:14 = 12:$

4   $\dfrac{6}{} = \dfrac{9}{3}$

5   $3: \quad = 12:32$

6   $\quad : 15 = 8:10$

7   $9:6 = \quad :4$

8   $\dfrac{}{4} = \dfrac{15}{10}$

9   $\dfrac{6}{8} = \dfrac{}{12}$

10   $6:9 = 8:$

Problems

Exercise 12f

Two speeds are in the ratio $12:5$. If the first speed is 8 km/h, what is the second speed?

$8 = 12 \div 3 \times 2$

So the second speed is $5 \div 3 \times 2$ km/h

$$= \frac{10}{3} \text{ km/h} = 3\frac{1}{3} \text{ km/h}$$

1   The ratio of the amount of money in David's pocket to that in Indira's pocket is 9 : 10. Indira has 25 c. How much has David got?

2   Two lengths are in the ratio 3 : 7. The second length is 42 cm. Find the first length.

3   If the ratio in question **2** were 7 : 3, what would the first length be?

4   In a rectangle, the ratio of length to width is 9 : 4. The length is 24 cm. Find the width.

5   The ratio of the perimeter of a triangle to its shortest side is 10 : 3. The perimeter is 35 cm. What is the length of the shortest side?

6   A length, originally 6 cm, is increased so that the ratio of the new length to the old length is 9 : 2. What is the new length?

7   A class is making a model of the school building and the ratio of the lengths of the model to the lengths of the actual building is 1 : 20. The gym is 6 m high. How high, in centimetres, should the model of the gym be?

8   The ratio of lengths of a model boat to those of the actual boat is 3 : 50. Find the length of the actual boat if the model is 72 cm long.

Division in a given ratio

Exercise 12g

Share $60 between Anne and John so that Anne's share and John's share are in the ratio 3 : 2.

Anne's share   John's share

Anne has 3 portions and John has 2 portions so they have 5 portions between them. Therefore Anne has 3 out of 5 portions, i.e. $\frac{3}{5}$ of $60.

$$\therefore \qquad \text{Anne's share} = \frac{3}{5} \text{ of } \$60$$

$$= \$\frac{3}{5} \times 60^{12}$$

$$= \$36$$

$$\text{John's share} = \$\frac{2}{5} \times 60^{12}$$

$$= \$24$$

Check: $36 + $24 = $60

1 Divide 80 c into two parts in the ratio 3 : 2.

2 Divide 32 cm into two parts in the ratio 3 : 5.

3 Divide $45 into two shares in the ratio 4 : 5.

4 Dick and Tom share the contents of a bag of peanuts between them in the ratio 3 : 5. If there are 40 peanuts, how many do they each get?

5 Maria is 10 years old and Eleanor is 15 years old. Divide 75 c between them in the ratio of their ages.

6 In a class of 30 pupils the ratio of the number of boys to the number of girls is 7 : 8. How many girls are there?

<u>7</u> Divide $20 into two parts in the ratio 1 : 7.

<u>8</u> In a garden the ratio of the area of lawn to the area of flowerbed is 12 : 5. If the total area is 357 m², find the area of
   a the lawn   b the flowerbed.

<u>9</u> In a bowl containing oranges and apples, the ratio of the numbers of oranges to apples is 4 : 3. If there are 28 fruit altogether, how many apples are there?

Gabriella and Ronnel get a share of an inheritance in the ratio of 4 : 3. Gabriella receives $50 more than Ronnel. Find the total inheritance.

You can visualise this problem by drawing a block for each part of the money that each receives.

$50   Gabriella's share

Ronnel's share

Now you can see that the $50 is one of seven equal shares.

Therefore the total inheritance is 7 × $50 = $350

10 A wooden plank was sawn into two pieces in the ratio 5 : 7. What remained was 44 cm longer than the length cut off.
   a How long was the original plank?
   b What length was cut off?

11 After Jo had peeled an orange she found the ratio of what she could eat to what was wasted was 3 : 2. If she could eat 42 g more than she wasted what was the mass of
   a the original orange
   b the part she could eat?

12 The Education and Social Services departments of a region divide the total grant they receive from the government between the two departments in the ratio 5 : 4. As a result the Education department receives $546 000 more than Social Services.

How much does each receive?

13 Uncle Rohan gives Misha and John a sum of money to share between them so that Misha gets $100 more than John. He says, 'Divide it in the ratio 5 : 7.'

How much does each receive?

14 A plank of wood is cut into two pieces. The shorter piece is $\frac{3}{8}$ of the original plank.

What is the ratio of the lengths of the two pieces?

Divide 6 m into three parts in the ratio 3 : 7 : 2.

There are 3 + 7 + 2, i.e. 12 portions altogether,

$$\therefore \qquad \text{first part} = \frac{3}{12} \times 600\,\text{cm}$$

$$= 150\,\text{cm}$$

$$\text{Similarly second part} = \frac{7}{12} \times 600\,\text{cm}$$

$$= 350\,\text{cm}$$

$$\text{and third part} = \frac{2}{12} \times 600\,\text{cm}$$

$$= 100\,\text{cm}$$

Check: 150 + 350 + 100 = 600 cm = 6 m

---

15 Divide $26 amongst three people so that their shares are in the ratio 4 : 5 : 4.

16 The perimeter of a triangle is 24 cm and the lengths of the sides are in the ratio 3 : 4 : 5. Find the lengths of the three sides.

17 In a garden, the ratio of the areas of lawn to beds to paths is $3 : 1 : \frac{1}{2}$. Find the three areas if the total area is 63 m².

(?) Puzzle

A man left $799 500 to be divided between his widow, four sons and five daughters. He directed that every daughter should have three times as much as a son and that every son should have twice as much as their mother. What was the widow's share?

Map ratio (or representative fraction)

The *map ratio* of a map is the ratio of a length on the map to the length it represents on the ground. This ratio or fraction is given on most maps in addition to the scale. It is sometimes called the *representative fraction* of the map, or RF for short.

If two villages are 6 km apart and on the map this distance is represented by 6 cm, then the ratio is

$$6 \, \text{cm} : 6 \, \text{km} = 6 \, \text{cm} : 600\,000 \, \text{cm}$$
$$= 1 : 100\,000$$

so the map ratio is $1 : 100\,000$ or $\dfrac{1}{100\,000}$

Any length on the ground is 100 000 times the corresponding length on the map.

Exercise 12h

Find the map ratio of a map if 12 km is represented by 1.2 cm on the map.

$$\text{RF} = 1.2 \, \text{cm} : 12 \, \text{km}$$

$$= 1.2 \, \text{cm} : 1\,200\,000 \, \text{cm} \quad \text{(changing both to the same unit)}$$

$$= 12 : 12\,000\,000 \quad \text{(multiplying both numbers by 10)}$$

$$= 1 : 1\,000\,000 \quad \text{(dividing both numbers by 12)}$$

Find the map ratio of the maps in the following questions:

1   2 cm on the map represents 1 km.

2   The scale of the map is 1 cm to 5 km.

3   10 km is represented by 10 cm on the map.

4   3.2 cm on the map represents 16 km.

5    $\frac{1}{2}$ cm on the map represents 500 m.

6   100 km is represented by 5 cm on the map.

If the map ratio is 1 : 5000 and the distance between two points on the map is 12 cm, find the actual distance between the two points.

1 cm on the map represents 5000 cm on the ground.

12 cm on the map represents 12 × 5000 cm on the ground,

i.e. 60 000 cm = 600 m

7 The map ratio of a map is 1 : 50 000. The distance between A and B on the map is 6 cm. What is the true distance between A and B?

8 The map ratio of a map is 1 : 1000. A length on the map is 7 cm. What real length does this represent?

9 The map ratio of a map is 1 : 10 000. Find the actual length represented by 2 cm.

<u>10</u> The map ratio of a map is 1 : 200 000. The distance between two towns is 20 km. What is this in centimetres? Find the distance on the map between the points representing the towns.

<u>11</u> The map ratio of a map is 1 : 2 000 000. Find the distance on the map which represents an actual distance of 36 km.

 Puzzle

If four hens lay four eggs in four days, how long will it take twelve hens to lay 36 eggs?

Proportion

When comparing quantities, words other than ratio are sometimes used. If two varying quantities are *directly proportional* they are always in the same ratio.

Sometimes it is obvious that two quantities are directly proportional, e.g. the cost of buying oranges is proportional to the number of oranges bought. In cases like this you would be expected to know that the quantities are in direct proportion.

A book of 250 pages is 1.5 cm thick (not counting the covers).

a   How thick is a book of 400 pages?

b   How many pages are there in a book 2.7 cm thick?

a   If 250 pages are 15 mm thick then 1 page is $\dfrac{15}{250}$ mm thick

so 400 pages are $\dfrac{15^{\,3}}{250_{\,50}} \times 400^{\,8}$ mm thick that is, 24 mm or 2.4 cm thick

b   If 15 mm contains 250 pages then 1 mm contains $\dfrac{250}{15}$ pages

so 27 mm contains $\dfrac{250^{\,50}}{15_{\,3}} \times 27^{\,9}$ pages that is, 450 pages

1   Sam covers 9 m when he walks 12 paces. How far does he travel when he walks 16 paces?

2   I can buy 24 bottles of a cold drink for $25 when buying in bulk. How many bottles can I buy at the same rate for $75?

3   If 64 seedlings are allowed 24 cm² of space, how much space should be allowed for 48 seedlings? How many seedlings can be planted in 27 cm²?

4   A ream (500 sheets) of paper is 6 cm thick. How thick a pile would 300 sheets make?

5   At a school picnic 15 sandwiches are provided for every 8 children. How many sandwiches are needed for 56 children?

A family with two pets spends $7.50 a week on pet food. If the family gets a third pet, how much a week will be spent on pet food?

We are not told what sort of animals the pets are. Different animals eat different types and quantities of food so the amount spent is not in proportion to the number of pets.

Beware! Some of the quantities in the following questions are not in direct proportion. Some questions need a different method and some cannot be answered at all from the given information.

6 Two tea towels dry on a clothes line in 2 hours. How long would 5 tea towels take to dry?

7 Three bricklayers build a wall in 6 hours. How long would two bricklayers take to build the wall working at the same rate?

8 House contents insurance is charged at the rate of $4.50 per thousand dollars worth of the contents. How much is the insurance if the contents are worth $13 600?

9 If the insurance paid on the contents of a house is $90.00, at the rate of $5 per thousand dollars worth, what are the house contents worth?

10 It takes Margaret 45 minutes to walk 4 km. How long would it take her to walk 5 km at the same speed? How far would she go in 1 hour?

11 It takes a gardener 45 minutes to dig a flower bed of area 7.5 m². If he digs at the same rate, how long does he take to dig 9 m²?

12 Fencing costs $12.00 per 1.8 m length. How much would 7.5 m cost?

13 Mrs Brown and Mrs Jones make 4 dozen sandwiches in half an hour in Mrs Jones' small kitchen. If they had 30 friends in to help, how many sandwiches could be made in the same time?

14 A recipe for 12 scones requires 2 teaspoons of baking powder and 240 g of flour. If a larger number of scones are made, using 540 g of flour, how much baking powder is needed?

Investigation

People come in all shapes and sizes but we expect the relative sizes of different parts of our bodies to be more or less the same.

For example, we do not expect a person's arms to be twice as long as their legs! We might expect the ratio of arm length to leg length to be about 2 : 3.

1 Gather some evidence and use it to find out if the last statement is roughly true.

2 Does the age of the person make any difference?

3 Investigate the ratio of shoe size to height.

Speed, time and distance

When Wesley drives on the freeway he aims to travel at a steady (or *constant*) speed of 80 kilometres per hour (km/h).

This means that   in 1 hour he travels 80 km, i.e. at 80 km/h

in 2 hours he travels $80 \times 2 = 160$ km

and in 3 hours he travels $80 \times 3 = 240$ km.

More generally   Distance travelled = Speed × Time

The icon ◺ $\frac{D}{S\,|\,T}$ may help you to remember how these quantities are related.

Put your finger over the quantity you want to find. What is left is the formula you need.

It follows that $\qquad D = S \times T, \quad S = \dfrac{D}{T} \quad \text{and} \quad T = \dfrac{D}{S}$

If the speed is measured in kilometres per hour and the time is measured in hours, the distance travelled will be measured in kilometres.

Exercise 12j

A coach travels at 60 km/h. How far will it travel in

a   3 hours   **b** $5\frac{1}{2}$ hours?

a   Distance = speed × time

Therefore distance travelled in 3 hours $= 60 \times 3$ km

$= 180$ km

b   Distance travelled in $5\frac{1}{2}$ hours $= 60 \times 5\frac{1}{2}$ km

$= 60 \times \dfrac{11}{2}$ km

$= 330$ km

1   An express train travels at 200 km/h. How far will it travel in

     a   4 hours   **b** $5\frac{1}{2}$ hours?

2   Ken cycles at 24 km/h. How far will he travel in

     a   2 hours   **b** $3\frac{1}{2}$ hours   **c** $2\frac{1}{4}$ hours?

3   An aeroplane flies at 300 mph. How far will it travel in

     a   4 hours   **b** $5\frac{1}{2}$ hours?

 mph means miles per hour.

4 A bus travels at 60 km/h. How far will it travel in

    a $1\frac{1}{2}$ hours   **b** $2\frac{1}{4}$ hours?

5 Susan can cycle at 12 mph. How far will she ride in

    a $\frac{3}{4}$ hour   **b** $1\frac{1}{4}$ hours?

6 An athlete can run at 10.5 m/s. How far will he travel in

    a 5 seconds   **b** 8.5 seconds?

m/s means metres per second.

7 A boy cycles at 12 mph. How far will he travel in

    a 2 hours 40 minutes   **b** 3 hours 10 minutes?

8 Majid can walk at 8 km/h. How far will he walk in

    a 30 minutes   **b** 20 minutes   **c** 1 h 15 minutes?

9 A racing car travels at 111 mph. How far will it travel in

    a 20 minutes   **b** 1 hour 40 minutes?

10 A bullet travels at 100 m/s. How far will it travel in

    a 5 seconds   **b** $8\frac{1}{2}$ seconds?

11 A Boeing 747 travels at 540 mph. How far does it travel in

    a 3 hours 15 minutes   **b** 7 hours 45 minutes?

12 A racing car travels around a 2 km circuit at 120 km/h. How many laps will it complete in

    a 30 minutes   **b** 1 hour 12 minutes?

Calculating the time taken

If you know the speed something is travelling at, then you can find out how long it takes to travel a given distance. For example, suppose Georgina walks at 6 km/h. How long will it take her to walk 24 km?

If she takes 1 hour to walk 6 km, she will take $\frac{24}{6}$ hours, i.e. 4 hours, to walk 24 km.

Similarly, if the distance is 15 km, then she will take $\frac{15}{6}$ hours, i.e. $2\frac{1}{2}$ hours, to walk 15 km.

So $$\text{Time}=\frac{\text{Distance}}{\text{Speed}}$$

Exercise 12k

1   How long will Zena, walking at 5 km/h, take to walk

    a   10 km   **b**   15 km?

2   How long will a car travelling at 80 km/h take to travel

    a   400 km   **b**   260 km?

3   How long will it take David, running at 10 mph, to run

    a   5 miles   **b** $12\frac{1}{2}$ miles?

4   How long will it take an aeroplane flying at 450 mph to fly

    a   1125 miles   **b**   2400 miles?

5   A cowboy rides at 14 km/h. How long will it take him to ride

    a   21 km   **b**   70 km?

6   A rally driver drives at 50 mph. How long does it take him to cover

    a   75 miles   **b**   225 miles?

7   An athlete runs at 8 m/s. How long does it take her to cover

    a   200 m   **b**   1600 m?

8   A dog runs at 20 km/h. How long will it take him to travel

    a   8 km   **b**   18 km?

9   A liner cruises at 28 nautical miles per hour. How long will it take to travel

    a   6048 nautical miles   **b**   3528 nautical miles?

10   A car travels at 56 mph. How long does it take to travel

    a   70 miles   **b**   154 miles?

11   A cyclist cycles at 12 mph. How long will it take her to cycle

    a   30 miles   **b**   64 miles?

12   How long will it take a car travelling at 64 km/h to travel

    a   48 km   **b**   208 km?

Average speed

Russell Compton left home at 8 a.m. to travel the 50 km to his place of work. He arrived at 9 a.m. Although he had travelled at many different speeds during his journey he covered the 50 km in exactly 1 hour. We say that his *average speed* for the journey was 50 kilometres per hour, or 50 km/h. If he had travelled at the same speed all the time, he would have travelled at 50 km/h.

Judy Smith travelled the 135 miles from her home to Georgetown in 3 hours. If she had travelled at the same speed all the time, she would have travelled at $\frac{135}{3}$ mph., i.e. 45 mph. We say that her average speed for the journey was 45 mph.

In each case:
$$\text{average speed} = \frac{\text{total distance travelled}}{\text{total time taken}}$$

This formula can also be written:
$$\text{distance travelled} = \text{average speed} \times \text{time taken}$$
and
$$\text{time taken} = \frac{\text{distance travelled}}{\text{average speed}}$$

Suppose that a car travels 35 km in 30 min, and we wish to find its speed in kilometres per hour. To do this we must express the time taken in hours instead of minutes,

i.e.
$$\text{time taken} = 30 \text{ min} = \frac{1}{2} \text{ hour}$$

Then
$$\text{average speed} = \frac{35}{\frac{1}{2}} \text{ km/h} = 35 \times \frac{2}{1} \text{ km/h}$$
$$= 70 \text{ km/h}$$

Great care must be taken with units. If we want a speed in kilometres per hour, we need the distance in kilometres and the time in hours. If we want a speed in metres per second, we need the distance in metres and the time in seconds.

Exercise 12I

Find the average speed for each of the following journeys:

1 80 km in 1 hour
2 120 km in 2 hours
3 60 miles in 1 hour
4 480 miles in 4 hours
5 80 m in 4 seconds
6 135 m in 3 seconds
7 150 km in 3 hours
8 520 km in 8 hours
9 245 miles in 7 hours
10 104 miles in 13 hours
11 252 m in 7 seconds
12 255 m in 15 seconds

Find the average speed in km/h for a journey of 39 km which takes 45 minutes.

To find a speed in km/h you need the distance in kilometres and the time in hours.

First, convert the time taken to hours:

$$45 \text{ min} = \frac{45}{60} \text{ hour} = \frac{3}{4} \text{ hour}$$

Then

$$\text{average speed} = \frac{\text{distance travelled}}{\text{time taken}}$$

$$= \frac{39 \text{ km}}{\frac{3}{4} \text{ hour}}$$

$$= 39 \times \frac{4}{3} \text{ km/h}$$

$$= 52 \text{ km/h}$$

Find the average speed in km/h for a journey of:

13 40 km in 30 min   **15** 48 km in 45 min

14 60 km in 40 min   **16** 66 km in 33 min

Find the average speed in km/h for a journey of:

17 4000 m in 20 min   **19** 40 m in 8 s

18 6000 m in 45 min   **20** 175 m in 35 s

Make sure that the time is in hours and the distance is in kilometres.

Find the average speed in mph for a journey of:

21 27 miles in 30 min   **23** 25 miles in 25 min

22 18 miles in 20 min   **24** 28 miles in 16 min

The following table shows the distances in kilometres between various towns in the West Indies.

	St John's	Roseau	Castries	Basseterre	Kingstown	St Georges	Port of Spain	Georgetown
Roseau	174							
Castries	382	211						
Basseterre	100	478	621					
Kingstown	446	272	74	557				
St Georges	549	570	554	1040	118			
Port of Spain	723	659	534	1218	528	176		
Georgetown	1234	1224	1099	1694	1093	741	565	

Use this table to find the average speeds for journeys between:

25 St John's, leaving at 1025 h, and Kingstown, arriving at 1625 h

26 St Georges, leaving at 0330 h, and Castries, arriving at 0730 h

27   Basseterre, leaving at 1914 h, and St Georges, arriving at 2044 h

28   Port of Spain, leaving at 0620 h, and St Johns, arriving at 0750 h

29   Roseau, leaving at 1537 h, and St Georges, arriving at 1907 h

30   Castries, leaving at 1204 h, and Georgetown, arriving at 1624 h

31   Roseau, leaving at 1014 h, and Port of Spain, arriving at 1638 h

Problems frequently occur where different parts of a journey are travelled at different speeds in different times but we wish to find the average speed for the whole journey.

Consider for example a motorist who travels the first 50 miles of a journey at an average speed of 25 mph and the next 90 miles at an average speed of 30 mph.

One way to find his average speed for the whole journey is to complete the following table by using the relationship:

$$\text{time in hours} = \frac{\text{distance in miles}}{\text{speed in mph}}$$

	Speed in mph	Distance in miles	Time in hours
First part of journey	25	50	2
Second part of journey	30	90	3
Whole journey		**140**	**5**

We can add the distances to give the total length of the journey, and add the times to give the total time taken for the journey.

$$\text{average speed for whole journey} = \frac{\text{total distance}}{\text{total time}}$$

$$= \frac{140 \text{ miles}}{5 \text{ hours}} = 28 \text{ mph}$$

Note: Never add or subtract average speeds.

We could also solve this problem, without using a table, as follows:

$$\text{time to travel 50 miles at 25 mph} = \frac{\text{distance}}{\text{speed}}$$

$$= \frac{50 \text{ miles}}{25 \text{ mph}} = 2 \text{ hours}$$

$$\text{time to travel 90 miles at 30 mph} = \frac{\text{distance}}{\text{speed}}$$

$$= \frac{90 \text{ miles}}{30 \text{ mph}} = 3 \text{ hours}$$

∴ total distance of 140 miles is travelled in 5 hours

i.e. $$\text{average speed for whole journey} = \frac{\text{total distance}}{\text{total time}}$$

$$= \frac{140 \text{ miles}}{5 \text{ hours}} = 28 \text{ mph}$$

Exercise 12m

1 I walk for 24 km at 8 km/h, and then jog for 12 km at 12 km/h. Find my average speed for the whole journey.

To find the average speed you need the *total distance* travelled and the *total time* taken.

2 A cyclist rides for 23 miles at an average speed of $11\frac{1}{2}$ mph before his cycle breaks down, forcing him to push his cycle the remaining distance of 2 miles at an average speed of 4 mph. Find his average speed for the whole journey.

3 An athlete runs 6 miles at 8 mph, then walks 1 mile at 4 mph. Find her average speed for the total distance.

4 A woman walks 3 miles at an average speed of $4\frac{1}{2}$ mph and then runs 4 miles at 12 mph. Find her average speed for the whole journey.

5 A motorist travels the first 30 km of a journey at an average speed of 120 km/h, the next 60 km at 60 km/h, and the final 60 km at 80 km/h. Find the average speed for the whole journey.

6 Phil Sharp walks the 1 km from his home to the bus stop in 15 min, and catches a bus immediately which takes him the 9 km to the airport at an average speed of 36 km/h. He arrives at the airport in time to catch the plane which takes him the 240 km to Antigua at an average speed of 320 km/h. Calculate his average speed for the whole journey from home to Antigua.

7 A liner steaming at 24 knots takes 18 days to travel between two ports. By how much must it increase its speed to reduce the length of the voyage by 2 days? (A knot is a speed of 1 nautical mile per hour.)

Finding distance from a graph

When we went on holiday we travelled by car to our holiday resort at a constant speed of 30 kilometres per hour (km/h), i.e. in each hour we covered a distance of 30 km.

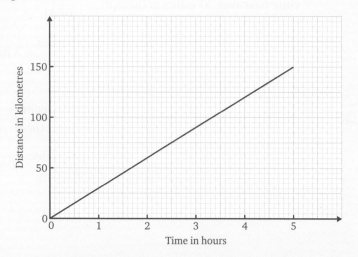

This graph shows our journey. It plots distance against time and shows that

in 1 hour we travelled 30 km   in 4 hours we travelled 120 km
in 2 hours we travelled 60 km   in 5 hours we travelled 150 km
in 3 hours we travelled 90 km

Using this graph, which represents our journey, we can read off how far we travelled for any given time and, how long it took to travel any distance.

Exercise 12n

The graphs that follow show four different journeys.
For each journey find:

a   the distance travelled

b   the time taken

c   the distance travelled in 1 hour

Make sure you understand what the subdivisions on the scales represent.

1

Distance in kilometres

Time in hours

2

Distance in kilometres

Time in hours

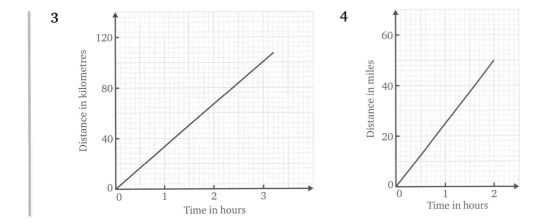

3

4

Time in hours

Time in hours

Drawing travel graphs

If Peter walks at 6 km/h, we can draw a graph to show this, using 2 cm to represent 6 km on the distance axis and 2 cm to represent 1 hour on the time axis.

Plot the point which shows that in 1 hour he has travelled 6 km. Join the origin to this point and produce the straight line to give the graph shown. From this graph we can see that in 2 hours Peter travels 12 km and in 5 hours he travels 30 km.

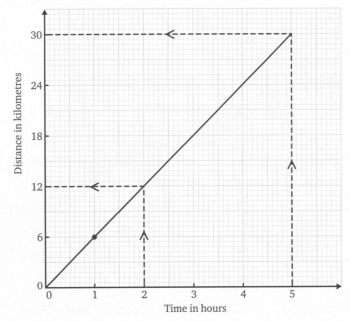

Exercise 12p

Draw a travel graph to show a journey of 150 km in 3 hours. Plot distance along the vertical axis and time along the horizontal axis.

Let 4 cm represent 1 hour and 2 cm represent 50 km.

Draw a line from 0 to the point above 3 on the time axis and along from 150 on the distance axes.

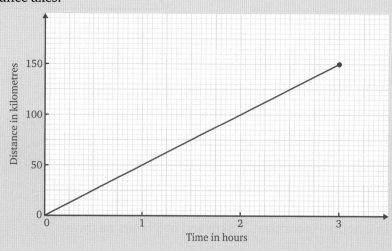

Draw travel graphs to show the following journeys. Plot distance along the vertical axis and time along the horizontal axis. Use the scales given in brackets.

1 60 km in 2 hours
($4 \text{ cm} \equiv 1$ hour, $1 \text{ cm} \equiv 10$ km)

2 180 km in 3 hours
($4 \text{ cm} \equiv 1$ hour, $2 \text{ cm} \equiv 50$ km)

3 300 km in 6 hours
($1 \text{ cm} \equiv 1$ hour, $1 \text{ cm} \equiv 50$ km)

4 80 miles in 2 hours
($6 \text{ cm} \equiv 1$ hour, $1 \text{ cm} \equiv 10$ miles)

5 140 miles in 4 hours
($2 \text{ cm} \equiv 1$ hour, $1 \text{ cm} \equiv 25$ miles)

6 100 km in $2\frac{1}{2}$ hours
($2 \text{ cm} \equiv 1$ hour, $2 \text{ cm} \equiv 25$ km)

7 105 km in $3\frac{1}{2}$ hours
($2 \text{ cm} \equiv 1$ hour, $4 \text{ cm} \equiv 50$ km)

8 75 miles in $1\frac{1}{4}$ hours
($8 \text{ cm} \equiv 1$ hour, $2 \text{ cm} \equiv 25$ miles)

9 90 m in 5 seconds
($2 \text{ cm} \equiv 1$ seconds, $2 \text{ cm} \equiv 10$ m)

10 240 m in 12 seconds
($1 \text{ cm} \equiv 1$ second, $2 \text{ cm} \equiv 50$ m)

11 Alan walks at 5 km/h. Draw a graph to show him walking for 3 hours. Take 4 cm to represent 5 km and 4 cm to represent 1 hour. Use your graph to find how far he walks in   **a** $1\frac{1}{2}$ hours   **b** $2\frac{1}{4}$ hours.

12 Julie can jog at 10 km/h. Draw a graph to show her jogging for
2 hours. Take 1 cm to represent 2 km and 8 cm to represent 1 hour.
Use your graph to find how far she jogs in   **a** $\frac{3}{4}$ hour   **b** $1\frac{1}{4}$ hours.

13 Jo drives at 35 mph. Draw a graph to show her driving for 4 hours.
Take 1 cm to represent 10 miles and 4 cm to represent 1 hour. Use your
graph to find how far she drives in   **a** 3 hours   **b** $1\frac{1}{4}$ hours.

14 John walks at 4 mph. Draw a graph to show him walking for 3 hours.
Take 1 cm to represent 1 mph and 4 cm to represent 1 hour. Use your
graph to find how far he walks in   **a** $\frac{1}{2}$ hour   **b** $3\frac{1}{2}$ hours.

Information from a travel graph

Exercise 12q

The graph shows the journey of a coach that calls at three service stations A, B
and C on a motorway. B is 60 km north of A and C is 20 km north of B. Use the
graph to answer the following questions:

a   At what time does the coach leave A?

b   At what time does the coach arrive at C?

c   At what time does the coach pass B?

d   How long does the coach take to travel from A to C?

e   What is the average speed of the coach for the whole journey?

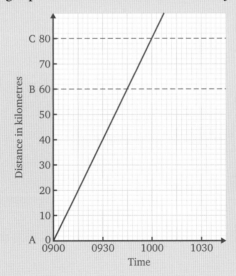

a   The coach leaves A at 0900.

b   It arrives at C at 1000. (Go from C on the distance axis across to the
graph then down to the time axis.)

c It passes through B at 0945.

d Time taken to travel from A to C is 1000 − 0900, i.e. 1 hour.

e Distance from A to C = 80 km (reading from the vertical axis)

Time taken to travel from A to C = 1 hour.

$$\text{average speed} = \frac{\text{distant travelled}}{\text{time taken}} = \frac{80 \text{ km}}{1 \text{ hour}} = 80 \text{ km/h}$$

1 The graph shows the journey of a car through three towns, Axeter, Bexley and Canton, which lie on a straight road. Axeter is 100 km south of Bexley and Canton is 60 km north of it. Use the graph to answer the following questions:

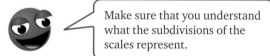

Make sure that you understand what the subdivisions of the scales represent.

a At what time does the car

   i leave Axeter   **ii** pass through Bexley   **iii** arrive at Canton?

b How long does the car take to travel from Axeter to Canton?

c How long does the car take to travel

   i the first 80 km of the journey   **ii** the last 80 km of the journey?

d What is the average speed of the car for the whole journey?

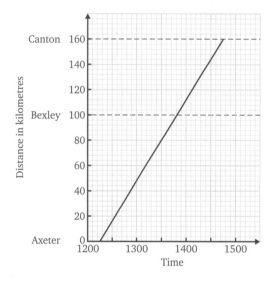

2 A car leaves Kingston at noon on its journey to Port Antonio via Morant Bay. The graph shows its journey.

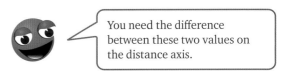

You need the difference between these two values on the distance axis.

a How far is it from
  i Kingston to Morant Bay
  ii Morant Bay to Port Antonio?

b How long does the car take to travel from Kingston to Port Antonio?

c What is the car's average speed for the whole journey?

d How far does the car travel between 1.30 p.m. and 2.30 p.m.?

e After travelling for $1\frac{1}{2}$ hours, how far is the car from
  i Kingston
  ii Morant Bay?

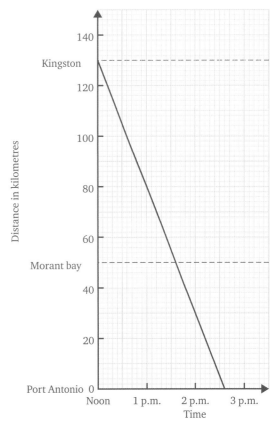

Go up from 1.30 p.m. on the time axis to the graph then across to the distance axis. Do the same for 2.30 p.m. Then find the difference between these readings or the distance axis.

3 The graph shows the journey of a car through three towns A, B and C.

a Where was the car at
  i 0900 h
  ii 0930 h?

b What was the average speed of the car between
  i A and B
  ii B and C?

c For how long does the car stop at B?

d How long did the journey take?

e What was the average speed of the car for the whole journey? Give your answer correct to 1 s.f.

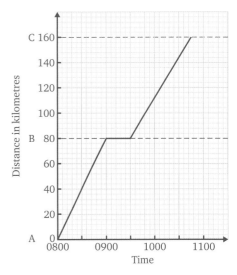

The car arrives at B at the point where the graph stops going uphill and leaves B at the point where the graph starts going uphill again.

Mixed exercises

Exercise 12r

1 Express the ratio $10\,\text{mm}^2 : 1\,\text{cm}^2$ in its simplest form.

2 Simplify the ratio $\dfrac{7}{8} : \dfrac{3}{4}$.

3 Adrian has $24\,c$ and Brian has $36\,c$. Give the ratio of the amount of Adrian's money to the total amount of money.

4 Which ratio is the larger, $16 : 13$ or $9 : 7$?

5 What is the map ratio of a map with a scale of $1\,\text{cm}$ to $5\,\text{km}$?

6 Find the missing number in the ratio $7 : 12 = \quad : 9$.

7 Share $26 amongst three people in the ratio $6 : 3 : 4$.

8 The ratio of boys to girls in a school is $10 : 9$. There are 459 girls. How many boys are there?

9 **a** Nina takes 3 hours to pedal 42 kilometres. Find her average speed.

   b An animal runs at $20\,\text{km/h}$. How long will it take to run **i** $6\,\text{km}$ **ii** $9\,\text{km}$?

10 An aircraft travels for 4 hours at an average speed of $400\,\text{mph}$, but then, because of a headwind, reduces its average speed to $350\,\text{mph}$ for the remaining hour of the journey. Find

   a the total distance travelled

   b the total time taken

   c the average speed for the whole journey.

Exercise 12s

1 Express the ratio $96 : 216$ in its simplest form.

2 Simplify the ratio $\dfrac{1}{4} : \dfrac{2}{5}$.

3 Divide $100 into three parts in the ratio $10 : 13 : 2$.

4 Two cubes have edges of lengths $8\,\text{cm}$ and $12\,\text{cm}$. Find the ratio of
   a the lengths of their edges
   b their volumes.

5 Find the missing number in the ratio $\square : 18 = 11 : 24$.

6 What does $1\,\text{cm}$ represent on a map with map ratio $1 : 10\,000$?

7 If $x : y = 3 : 4$, find the ratio $4x : 3y$.

8 It costs $22.50 to feed a dog for 12 days. At the same rate, how much will have to be spent to feed it for 35 days?

9 a   An athlete takes 4 minutes to run 1500 metres. Find his average
        speed in metres per second.

   b   Bob walks at 5 km/h. How long will it take him to walk

        i   1.5 km   ii   8 km?

10   Benny wants to make the 110 km trip to Singleton in 2 hours. He
     travelled the first 60 kilometres at an average speed of 45 km/h, and
     the next 30 kilometres at an average speed of 90 km/h. What must his
     average speed for the final 20 kilometres be if he is to arrive on time?

Exercise 12t

1   Express the ratio 1028 : 576 in its simplest form.

2   Which ratio is the smaller, 32 : 24 or 30 : 22?

3   An alloy is made of copper and zinc in the ratio 11 : 2. How much zinc
     does 65 kg of alloy contain?

4   Increase a length of 24 m so that the ratio of the new length to the old length is 11 : 8.

5   Anne has twice as many crayons as Martin, who has three times as many as Susan.
     Give the ratio of the number of crayons owned by the three children.

6   The map ratio of a map is 1 : 50 000. Find the length on the ground represented by
     6.4 cm on the map.

7   Simplify the ratio $\frac{13}{12} : \frac{5}{21}$.

8   Carpet to cover a floor of area 15 m² costs $550. How much would you expect to
     pay for a similar carpet measuring 5 m by 4.2 m?

9 a   A lorry travels 275 km at 50 km/h. How long does the journey take?

   b   Freda cycles at 12 km/h. How far will she cycle in

        i   5 minutes

        ii 12 minutes?

10   Neal walks the $\frac{1}{2}$ mile from his home to the bus stop at an average speed of 4 mph
     and immediately catches the bus that takes him the 10 miles to the city centre at
     an average speed of 20 mph. Find his average speed for the whole journey.

11   The ratio of Mr Khan's cell phone bill to Mr Newton's is 5 : 6. Mr Khan's bill is $44
     less than Mr Newton's. How much does each pay?

Exercise 12u

Select the letter that gives the correct answer.

1   In its simplest form, the ratio 102 : 136 is equal to

     A   3 : 4   B   3 : 5   C   4 : 5   D   4 : 7

2 The ratio $\frac{3}{7}:\frac{4}{5}$

    A $3:4$ **B** $4:3$ **C** $15:28$ **D** $28:15$

3 $210 is shared between A, B and C in the ratio $5:2:7$. B's share will be

    A $28   **B** $30   **C** $60   **D** $90

4 The missing number in the ratio $17:6 =$ $:12$ is

    A 8   **B** 12   **C** 21   **D** 34

5 The ratio of men to women working in a factory is $2:3$.
There are 155 workers altogether.
How many more men than women are there?

    A 27   **B** 31   **C** 33   **D** 45

6 The map ratio of a map with a scale of $1\,cm:4\,km$ is

    A $1:400$ **B** $1:4000$ **C** $1:40\,000$ **D** $1:400\,000$

7 Scott takes 2 hours to pedal 17 kilometres. His average speed is

    A $7\,km/h$ **B** $7\frac{1}{2}\,km/h$ **C** $8\frac{1}{2}\,km/h$ **D** $9\,km/h$

8 Zoe runs at $8\,km/h$. How long will it take her to run $18\,km$?

    A $1\frac{3}{4}$ hours   **B** 2 hours   **C** $2\frac{1}{4}$ hours   **D** $2\frac{1}{2}$ hours

9 If $x:y = 7:6$ and $y = 24$, then $x =$

    A 28   **B** 30   **C** 144   **D** 168

10 The map ratio of a map is $1:20\,000$. The distance represented by $2\,cm$ on the map is

    A $0.2\,km$ **B** $0.4\,km$ **C** $2\,km$ **D** $4\,km$

11 One cube has an edge of $4\,cm$ and another cube has an edge of $6\,cm$.
The ratio of the number of edges of the first cube to the number of edges of the second cube is

    A $1:1$ **B** $2:3$ **C** $3:2$ **D** $3:4$

12 The ratio of the volume of the first cube to the volume of the second cube given in question **11** is

    A $2:3$ **B** $4:9$ **C** $8:27$ **D** $64:81$

? Puzzle

A train, $400\,m$ long and travelling at $120\,km/h$, enters a tunnel that is $5.6\,km$ long. For what time is any part of the train in the tunnel?

Did you know?

Bhaskara, who lived in India around CE 1150, did some very interesting work in arithmetic.

Bhaskara's work was full of puzzles and stories. He had a problem about Hari, a god who had four hands. He wanted to pick up a hammer, a shell, a flower and a discus. Hari wanted to know in how many ways he can pick up these four things. Can you figure it out? A chart like the one below will help you.

	Hand 1	Hand 2	Hand 3	Hand 4
1st way	Hammer	Shell	Flower	Discus
2nd way	Hammer	Shell	Discus	Flower
3rd way				

Complete the table. How many ways are possible?

In this chapter you have seen that...

✔ a ratio can be simplified by dividing (or multiplying when fractions are involved) all parts in the ratio by the same number

✔ you can compare ratios by expressing them with the same denominator

✔ you can divide a quantity in the ratio $a : b$ by first dividing it into $(a + b)$ equal parts

✔ a journey at constant speed can be represented by a straight line on a graph

✔ when you read values from a graph you need to make sure that you understand the meaning of the subdivisions on the scales on the axes

✔ the formula 'distance = speed × time' can be used to find one quantity when the other two are known

✔ the scale of a map is sometimes given as a ratio, e.g. $1 : 25\,000$, and it is called the map ratio; it is sometimes given as a fraction, e.g. $1/25\,000$, when it is called the representative fraction

✔ two quantities that are directly proportional are always in the same ratio

✔ when you are working out speeds, you must make sure that the units are consistent, e.g. to find a speed in kilometres per hour, the distance must be in kilometres and the time must be in hours

✔ the average speed for a journey is equal to the total distance travelled divided by the total time taken.

At the end of this chapter you should be able to...

1   calculate percentage increase and decrease
2   calculate the cost of buying an item using hire-purchase
3   calculate workers' wages, salaries and commission
4   calculate sales tax and exchange rates
5   calculate the amount due on telephone and electricity bills.

? Puzzle

The clock strikes 12 and both hands point upwards. How many times will
the minute hand and hour hand coincide before the hands point upwards
at 12 again?

You need to know...

✔ how to work with decimals and fractions
✔ how to use a calculator
✔ how to find a percentage of a quantity
✔ how to find one quantity as a percentage of another.

Key words

commission, exchange rate, gross and net wages, income tax, kilowatt-hour, salary,
standing charge

Percentage increase

My telephone bill is to be increased by 8% from the first quarter of the year
to the second quarter. It amounted to $64.50 for the first quarter. From this
information I can find the value of the bill for the second quarter.

If $64.50 is increased by 8%, the increase is 8% of $64.50,

i.e. $\dfrac{8}{100} \times \$64.50 = \$5.16$

The bill for the second quarter is therefore

$$\$64.50 + \$5.16 = \$69.66$$

The same result is obtained if we take the original sum to be 100%. The increased amount is $(100+8)\%$, or $\dfrac{108}{100}$, of the original sum,

i.e. the bill for the second quarter is $\dfrac{108}{100} \times \$64.50 = \$69.66$

The quantity $\dfrac{108}{100}$ is called the multiplying factor.

To increase a quantity by 12%, the multiplying factor would be $\dfrac{112}{100}$.

Percentage decrease

Similarly if we wish to decrease a quantity by 8%, the decreased amount is $(100-8)\%$, or $\dfrac{92}{100}$, of the original sum.

If we wish to decrease a quantity by 15%, the new quantity is 85% of the original quantity, and the multiplying factor is $\dfrac{85}{100}$.

Exercise 13a

If a number is increased by 40%, what percentage is the new number of the original number?

The new number is $100\% + 40\% = 140\%$ of the original.

If a number is increased by the given percentage, what percentage is the new number of the original number?

1	50%	3	20%	5	75%	7	48%	9	175%	11	57%
2	25%	4	60%	6	35%	8	300%	10	$12\frac{1}{2}\%$	12	15%

What multiplying factor increases a number by 44%?

The multiplying factor is $\dfrac{100+44}{100} = \dfrac{144}{100}$

Give the multiplying factor which increases a number by:

13 30% 14 80% 15 65% 16 130%

If a number is decreased by 65%, what percentage is the new number of the original number?

The new number is 100% − 65% = 35% of the original.

If a number is decreased by the given percentage what percentage is the new number of the original number?

17 50%	**19** 70%	**21** 35%	**23** 4%	**25** $62\frac{1}{2}$%	**27** 53%
18 25%	**20** 85%	**22** 42%	**24** 66%	**26** $33\frac{1}{3}$%	**28** 10%

What multiplying factor decreases a number by 30%?

The multiplying factor is $\frac{100-30}{100} = \frac{70}{100}$

What multiplying factor decreases a number by:

29 40%   **30** 75%   **31** 34%   **32** 12%

Increase 180 by 30%.

The new value is 130% of the old

i.e. the new value is $\frac{130}{100} \times 180 = 234$

Increase:

33 100 by 40%	**37** 1600 by 73%	**40** 111 by $66\frac{2}{3}$%
34 200 by 85%	**38** 745 by 14%	**41** 145 by 120%
35 340 by 45%	**39** 64 by $62\frac{1}{2}$%	**42** 644 by 275%
36 550 by 36%		

Decrease 250 by 70%.

The new value is 100% − 70% = 30% of the original value

i.e. the new value is $\frac{30}{100} \times 250 = 75$

Decrease:

43 100 by 30%	**47** 3400 by 28%	**50** 273 by $66\frac{2}{3}$%
44 200 by 15%	**48** 3450 by 4%	**51** 208 by $87\frac{1}{2}$%
45 350 by 46%	**49** 93 by $33\frac{1}{3}$%	**52** 248 by $37\frac{1}{2}$%
46 750 by 13%		

Problems

Exercise 13b

The number of cases of mumps reported this year is 4% lower than the number of cases reported last year. There were 250 cases last year. How many cases were reported this year?

There were 4% fewer cases this year so to find the number of cases this year, we need to decrease 250 by 4%.

The multiplying factor is $\dfrac{100-4}{100} = \dfrac{96}{100}$.

The number of cases this year is $\dfrac{96}{100} \times 250 = 240$.

1   A boy's weight increased by 15% between his fifteenth and sixteenth birthdays. If he weighed 55 kg on his fifteenth birthday, what did he weigh on his sixteenth birthday?

Read the question carefully to make sure that you understand whether you are being asked to increase or to decrease a quantity.

2   The water rates due on my house this year are 8% more than they were last year.
    Last year I paid $640. What must I pay this year?

3   There are 80 teachers in a school. It is anticipated that the number of staff next year will increase by 5%. How many staff should there be next year?

4   Pierre is 20% taller now than he was 2 years ago. If he was 150 cm tall then, how tall is he now?

5   A factory employs 220 workers. Next year this number will increase by 15%. How many extra workers will be taken on?

6   A living room suite is priced at $26 000 plus value added tax (VAT) at 15%. How much does the suite actually cost the customer?

7   A CD costs $35 plus value added tax at 20%. How much does the CD actually cost?

8   The cost of a meal is $64 plus service charge at 15%. How much must I pay for the meal?

9   Miss Kendall earns $1080 per week from which income tax is deducted at 30%. Find how much she actually gets. (This is called her *net* pay.)

10   In a certain week a factory worker earns $900 from which income tax is deducted at 30%. Find his net income after tax, i.e. how much he actually gets.

11 Mr Hall earns $2000 per month. If income tax is deducted at 25%, find his net pay after tax.

12 As a result of using Alphamix fertiliser, my potato crop increased by 32% compared with last year. If I grew 150 kg of potatoes last year, how many kilograms of potatoes did I grow this year?

13 The number of children attending White Sands village school is 8% fewer this year than last year. If 450 attended last year, how many are attending this year?

14 The marked price of a man's suit is $750. In a sale the price is reduced by 12%. Find the sale price.

15 In a sale all prices are reduced by 10%. What is the sale price of an article marked
   a $40   b $85?

16 Last year in a school there were 75 reported cases of measles. This year the number of reported cases has dropped by 16%. How many cases have been reported this year?

17 Mr Connah was 115 kg when he decided to go on a diet. He lost 10% of his weight in the first month and a further 8% of his original weight in the second month. How much did he weigh after 2 months of dieting?

18 A car is valued at $48 000. It depreciates by 20% in the first year and thereafter each year by 15% of its value at the beginning of that year. Find its value
   a after 2 years   b after 3 years.

19 In any year the value of a motorcycle depreciates by 10% of its value at the beginning of that year. What is its value after two years if the purchase price was $7200?

20 When John Short increases the speed at which he motors from an average of 40 mph to 50 mph, the number of miles travelled per gallon decreases by 25%. If he travels 36 miles on each gallon when his average speed is 40 mph, how many miles per gallon can he expect at an average speed of 50 mph?

21 When petrol was $2.00 per litre I used 700 litres in a year. The price rose by 12% so I reduced my yearly consumption by 12%. Find
   a the new price of a litre of petrol
   b my reduced annual petrol consumption
   c how much more (or less) my petrol bill is for the year.

Puzzle

Ed bought a watch for $50. He marked it up by 30% and put it in the window of his shop. He could not sell it, so in a sale marked it '30% off'. Molly bought the watch and claimed she had paid less than Ed bought it at. Was this true?

Mixed exercise

Exercise 13c

1 Express 85%
   a as a decimal   b as a common fraction in its lowest terms.
2 Express 6 mm as a percentage of 3 cm.
3 Find 35% of 120 m².
4 If a number is increased by 25%, what percentage is the new number of the original number?
5 What multiplying factor would increase a quantity by 45%?
6 a Increase 56 cm by 75%.   b Decrease 1200 sheep by 20%.
7 The annual cost of insuring the contents of a house is 0.3% of the value of the contents. How much will it cost to insure contents valued at $29 000?

Hire-purchase

Hire-purchase (HP) is a popular and convenient way of buying things when you cannot afford the full price out of your income and don't wish to spend your savings. It is frequently used to buy such things as a washing machine, camera, motorcycle or car. As the term implies, you don't really own the article until you have made the last payment. An article bought on HP always costs more, sometimes much more, than if you can pay cash.

Exercise 13d

A motorcycle is priced at $22 500. If bought on hire-purchase the terms are:
$\frac{1}{3}$ deposit plus 36 monthly payments of $640. Find the HP price.

Deposit of $\frac{1}{3}$ of $22 500 = $7500

Total of 36 monthly payments of $640 = $640 × 36
$$= \$23\,040$$

Total HP price = $7500 + $23 040
$$= \$30\,540$$

Find the total hire-purchase cost in each of the following cases:
1   No deposit, 12 monthly payments of $124

2   No deposit, 12 monthly payments of $252

3   No deposit, 12 monthly payments of $744

4   Deposit $5120 plus 12 monthly payments of $461

5   Deposit $3120 plus 24 monthly payments of $258

6   Deposit $17 370 plus 24 monthly payments of $940

7   Deposit $624 plus 52 weekly payments of $103

8   Deposit $8670 plus weekly payments of $521 for 3 years

9   Deposit $24 130 plus monthly payments of $2123 for 2 years

10   Deposit $19 370 plus monthly payments of $1650 for 3 years.

The complete furnishings for a lounge display in a department store amount to $128 160. If cash is paid a 5% discount is given, but if sold on hire-purchase the terms are: a deposit of 25% plus a monthly payment of $3472 for three years.

Find   **a**   the cash price

   b   the deposit

   c   the total HP price

   d   the amount saved by paying cash.

a   Cash price = $128 160 – discount of 5%

Discount = $128 160 $\times \frac{5}{100}$ = $6408

Cash price = $128 160 – $6408

= $ 121 752

b Deposit = $128 160 $\times \frac{25}{100}$ = $32 040

c Total HP price = deposit + 36 monthly payments of $3472

= $32 040 + 36 $\times$ $3472

= $32 040 + $124 992

= $157 032

d Saving by paying cash = HP cost – cash price

= $157 032 – $121 752

= $35 280

11   The cash price of a dining suite is $7840. Hire-purchase terms require 25% deposit together with 24 monthly repayments of $282. Calculate the amount saved by paying cash.

12   An electric lawn mower is offered for sale at $1855. If bought on hire-purchase a deposit of $\frac{1}{5}$ is required, followed by 24 equal monthly payments of $119. How much is saved by paying cash?

13   A camera is advertised at $2240. If bought on HP, the terms are: 25% deposit plus 12 monthly payments of $179. How much is saved by paying cash?

14   A grand piano is advertised at $220 000. If bought on hire-purchase, the terms are: 20% deposit plus 18 monthly payments of $12 600. How much is saved by paying cash?

15   The cash price of a cut-glass water set is $1710. The hire-purchase terms are $\frac{1}{5}$ deposit plus 52 weekly payments of $34.50. How much is saved by paying cash?

16   A man's suit can be bought for $2520 cash or for a deposit of $840 plus 12 monthly instalments of $194.
   a   How much more does the suit cost if bought on the instalment plan compared with the cash price?
   b   Express the additional cost as a percentage of the cash price.

17   A motorcycle is offered for sale at $11 200. If bought on hire-purchase a deposit of $\frac{1}{4}$ is required, together with 24 monthly payments of $435. Calculate the difference between the cash price and the hire-purchase price.

18   The marked price of a three-piece suite is $25 800. A 5% discount is offered for a cash sale, but if bought on HP, the deposit is $\frac{1}{3}$, followed by 18 monthly payments of $1166. Find the cash difference in the two ways of paying for the suite and express this difference as a percentage of the cash price, giving your answer correct to three significant figures.

19   The marked price of an electric cooker is $3660. If bought for cash, a discount of $2\frac{1}{2}$% is given, but if bought on hire-purchase, the terms are: $\frac{1}{3}$ deposit plus 24 monthly payments of $132. How much more does the cooker cost if bought on hire-purchase?

20   A bus company is offered a second-hand coach for $200 700. Since it cannot afford to pay cash it has two options:

   Option 1: 6 half-yearly payments of $38 880

   Option 2: a deposit of $\frac{1}{3}$ plus 12 three-monthly payments of $14 580.

   Which option is the cheaper, and by how much?

21 Retiling a house will cost $114000. If paid for on hire-purchase, a deposit of $\frac{1}{5}$ is required together with 60 monthly payments of $2128. Find the additional cost when bought on HP and express this as a percentage of the cash price .

22 A motorist decides to buy a new car, the list price of which is $223 200. If he sells his old car privately for $69 000 and then pays cash for the new car, he is given a discount of $12\frac{1}{2}$%. However, if he offers his car in part-exchange, it is valued at $75 000 and in addition he must make 36 monthly payments of $5760. How much will he save if he sells his car privately and pays cash?

23 A carpet, which is suitable for use in a lounge measuring 5 m by 4 m, is offered for sale at $428 per square metre. Hire-purchase terms are as follows: $33\frac{1}{3}$% deposit, the balance to be increased by 12% and divided by 12 to give the monthly repayments for 1 year.

Find:
a the monthly repayments
b the increased cost if bought on hire-purchase
c the increased cost expressed as a percentage of the cash price.

24 A food mixer may be bought by paying a deposit of $292 together with 26 equal payments of $43.40. If this is $170.80 more than the cash price, find the cash price.

25 A professional standard football may be bought by paying a deposit of $114.80 together with 52 equal instalments of $9.20. If this is $78.80 more than the cash price, find the cash price.

26 The cash price of an outfit is $5292. Alternatively it may be paid for with a cash deposit of $1323 followed by 23 monthly payments of $241. How much cheaper is it to pay cash?

27 The cash price of a colour television set is $11 550. On the instalment plan a deposit of 20% is followed by monthly payments of $839 for one year. For the second and subsequent years the set may be insured against failure for $960 p.a. If the same set had been rented, the rental fee would have been $284 per month for the first year and $278 for every additional month. Compare the hire-purchase costs with the rental costs over a 6-year period. Which is the cheaper and by how much?

28 An electrical discount store calculates its HP prices as follows:

   i   a deposit of 25% of the cash price

   ii the balance is charged interest at $12\frac{1}{2}\%$

   iii the balance plus interest is divided by the number of monthly instalments paid.

Using this information calculate

   a the monthly repayments over one year on a video recorder marked $7872

   b the total cost of a music centre, the list price of which is $4464, if it is paid for over an 8-month period.

Wages

Everybody who goes to work expects to get paid. Some are paid an annual amount or *salary*, but many people are paid a wage at a fixed sum per hour. There is usually an agreed length to the working week and any hours worked over and above this may be paid for at a higher rate.

If John Duffy works for 37 hours for an agreed hourly rate of $9.00, he receives payment of $9.00 × 37, i.e. $333.00. This figure is called his *gross wage* for the week. From this, deductions are made for such things as National Insurance contributions and *income tax*. After the deductions have been made he receives his *net wage* or 'take-home' pay.

All this information is gathered together by the employer on a pay slip, an example of which is given below.

STAFF NO.	DATE	Basic Salary	Additional Payts. A	Deduction for Absence	Gross Pay
01035932	JAN 2015	130.34	24.44		154.78
Loan Repayts/ Adv. Recovered	Vol. Dedns. B	Nat. Ins.		Income Tax	Total Deducted
		13.54		46.50	60.04
A—Acting Allow.	Commission	Bonuses	Other	Non-Taxable. Alices	NET PAY
24.44					94.74
Detail	Detail	Detail	Detail	B–Voluntary Deductions	
				Union Dues	

Exercise 13e

Calculate the gross weekly wage for each of the following factory workers.

	Name	Number of hours worked	Hourly rate of pay
1	E. D. Nisbett	40	$10
2	A. Dexter	35	$11.00
3	T. Wilson	$38\frac{1}{2}$	$11.20
4	A. Smith	44	$10.80
5	D. Thomas	$39\frac{1}{2}$	$14.80

In the questions that follow, it is assumed that the meal breaks are unpaid.

Sally Green works a five-day week Monday to Friday. She starts work every day at 8 a.m. and finishes at 4.30 p.m. She has 1 hour off for lunch. How many hours does she work in a week? Find her gross pay if her rate is $9.84 for each hour worked.

Number of hours from 8 a.m. to 4.30 p.m. is $8\frac{1}{2}$.

She has 1 hour off for lunch, so number of hours worked each day is $7\frac{1}{2}$.

$$\text{Number of hours worked each week} = 7\frac{1}{2} \times 5 = 37\frac{1}{2}$$

$$\text{Gross pay for the week} = \$9.84 \times 37\frac{1}{2} = \$369.00$$

6   Edna Owen works a five-day week. She starts work each day at 7.30 a.m. and finishes at 4.15 p.m. She has 45 minutes for lunch and a 10-minute break each morning and afternoon. How long does she actually work
   a   in a day   b   in a week?
   c   If her hourly rate is $9.32, calculate her gross wage for the week.

7   Martin Jones starts work each day at 7 a.m. and finishes at 4.30 p.m. He has a 45-minute lunch break. How many hours does he work in a normal five-day week? Find his gross weekly wage if his rate of pay is $10.48 per hour.

8   Elaine Mock works 'afternoons'. She starts every day at 2 p.m. and finishes at 10.30 p.m., and is entitled to a meal break from 6 p.m. to 6.45 p.m. How many hours does she work
   a   in a day   b   in a five-day week?
   c   Calculate her gross weekly wage if she is paid $9.04 per hour.

Mary Killick gets paid $8.24 per hour for her normal working week of $37\frac{1}{2}$ hours. Any overtime is paid at time-and-a-half. Find her gross pay in a week when she works $45\frac{1}{2}$ hours.

$$\text{Basic weekly pay} = \$8.24 \times 37.5 = \$309.00$$

$$\text{Number of hours overtime} = (45\tfrac{1}{2} - 37\tfrac{1}{2}) \text{ hours} = 8 \text{ hours}$$

Because overtime is paid at time-and-a-half, which is one-and-a-half times the hourly rate, the rate of overtime pay is $\$8.24 \times 1.5 = \$12.86$ per hour

$$\text{Payment for overtime} = \$12.86 \times 8 = \$98.88$$

$$\text{Total gross pay} = \text{basic pay} + \text{overtime pay}$$

$$= \$309.00 + \$98.88$$

$$= \$407.88$$

9 Tom Shepherd works for a builder who pays $6.20 per hour for a basic week of 38 hours. If overtime worked is paid at time-and-a-half, how much will he earn in a week when he works for

   a 38 hours

   b 48 hours

   c 50 hours?

10 Maxine Brown works in a factory where the basic hourly rate is $3.92 for a 35-hour week. Any overtime is paid at time-and-a-half. How much will she earn in a week when she works for 46 hours?

11 Walter Markland works a basic week of $37\frac{1}{2}$ hours. Overtime is paid at time-and-a-quarter. How much does he earn in a week when he works $44\frac{1}{2}$ hours if the hourly rate is $6.80?

12 Peter Ambler's time sheet showed that he worked 7 hours overtime in addition to his basic 38-hour week. If his basic hourly rate is $6.32 and overtime is paid at time-and-a-half, find his gross pay for the week.

13 During a certain week Adelle Dookham worked $8\frac{1}{2}$ hours Monday to Friday together with 4 hours on Saturday. The normal working day was 7 hours and any time worked in excess of this was paid at time-and-a-half, with Saturday working being paid at double time. Calculate her gross wage for the week if her basic pay is $8.64 per hour.

14 Diana Read works a basic week of 39 hours. Overtime is paid at time-and-a-half. How much does she earn in a week when she works $47\frac{1}{2}$ hours if the basic hourly rate is $7.28?

15 Joan Danby's pay slip showed that she worked $5\frac{1}{2}$ hours overtime in addition to her basic 37-hour week. If her basic rate of pay is $5.92 and overtime is paid at time-and-a-half, find her gross pay for the week.

16 The timesheet for Anne Stent showed that during the last week in November she worked as follows:

Day	Morning		Afternoon	
	In	**Out**	**In**	**Out**
Monday	7.45 a.m.	12 noon	1.00 p.m.	5.45 p.m.
Tuesday	7.45 a.m.	12 noon	1.00 p.m.	4.15 p.m.
Wednesday	7.45 a.m.	12 noon	1.00 p.m.	4.15 p.m.
Thursday	7.45 a.m.	12 noon	1.00 p.m.	4.15 p.m.
Friday	7.45 a.m.	12 noon	1.00 p.m.	4.15 p.m.

  a What is the length of her normal working day?

  b How many hours make up her basic working week?

  c Calculate her basic weekly wage if the hourly rate is $5.68.

  d How much overtime was worked?

  e Calculate her gross wage if overtime is paid at time-and-a-half.

Commission

Some workers, such as salesmen and representatives, are paid in a different way. They are given a fairly low basic wage but they also get *commission* on every order they secure. The commission is usually a percentage of the value of the order.

Other workers get paid a fixed wage plus an amount that depends on the amount of work they do.

For example, Pete gets paid $240 a week plus 80 c for every article he produces after the first 30.

Exercise 13f

1 In addition to a basic weekly wage of $80, Miss Black receives a commission of 1% for selling second-hand cars. Calculate her gross wage for a week when she sells cars to the value of $100 000.

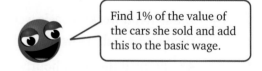

Find 1% of the value of the cars she sold and add this to the basic wage.

2 A salesman receives a basic wage of $100 per week plus commission at 6% on the value of the goods he sells. Find his income in a week when sales amount to $10 600.

3 Tom Hannah receives a basic wage of $110 per week and receives a commission of 2% on all sales over $2000. Find his income for a week when he sells goods to the value of $17 600.

4 Sue Renner receives a basic wage of $200 per week plus a commission of 2% on her sales. Find her income for a week when she sells goods to the value of $42 400.

5 Penny George is paid a basic wage of $190 per week plus a commission of $1\frac{1}{2}$% on her sales over $3000. Find her income for a week when she sells goods to the value of $42 600.

6 Alan McKay is paid a basic wage of $100 per week plus a commission of 3% on all sales over $4800. Find his income for a week when he sells goods to the value of $34 800.

7 In addition to a weekly wage of $340, Olive MacCarthy receives commission of $1\frac{1}{2}$% on the sales of antique furniture. Calculate her gross wage in a week when she sells furniture to the value of $31 000.

8 Don Smith receives a guaranteed weekly wage of $520 plus a bonus of 40 c for every circuit board he completes each day after the first 20. During a particular week the number of boards he produced are as follows:

First find the total number on which the bonus is paid: 33 the first day, 28 the second, and so on. Next calculate the total bonus and add it to the gross wage.

Monday 53, Tuesday 48, Wednesday 55, Thursday 51, Friday 47. Calculate his gross wage for the week.

9 Audley Davis gets paid 80 c for each article he completes up to 100 per day. For every article above this figure he receives 90 c. In a particular week his production figures are

Mon	Tues	Wed	Thurs	Fri
216	192	234	264	219

a How many articles does he produce in the week?
b For how many of these is he paid 80 c each?
c For how many of these is he paid 90 c each?
d Find his earnings for the week.

10 The table shows the number of electric light fittings produced by five factory workers each day for a week.

	Mon	Tues	Wed	Thurs	Fri
Ms Arnold	34	38	34	39	41
Mr Beynon	37	40	37	44	–
Miss Capstick	35	40	43	37	39
Mr Davis	42	45	40	52	46
Mrs Edmunds	39	38	37	35	42

The rate of payment is: $1.90 for each fitting up to 20 per day and $2.70 for each fitting above 20 per day.

a How many fittings does each person produce in the week?

b For each person find

  i how many fittings are paid at $1.90 each

  ii how many fittings are paid at $2.70 each.

c Find each person's income for the week.

d On which day of the week does this group of workers produce the greatest number of fittings?

Exchange rates

When we shop abroad, prices quoted in the local currency often give us little idea of value so we tend to convert prices into the currency we are familiar with. To do this we need to know the *exchange rate*.

This tells us how many units of currency are equivalent to 1 unit of our own currency.

For example, using an exchange rate of 1 US dollar (US$1) = 0.8 euros

means that $100 = 100 \times 0.8$ euros = 80 euros

and that 100 euros = $\frac{100}{0.8}$ US$ = US$125.

Exercise 13g

This table gives the equivalent of US$ in various currencies.

US$	UK£	Barbadian $	Canadian $	Trinidad $	Jamaican $
1	0.76	2	1.29	6.7	130

Use this table to convert

1 US$45 into Jamaican dollars

2 US$550 into Canadian dollars

3 US$400 into UK pounds

4 US$68.90 into Barbadian dollars

For the amounts of money shown in questions **5** to **14**, use the table
- **a**   to estimate the equivalent value in US$
- **b**   to calculate, to the nearest whole number, the equivalent value in US$.

5   £100

6   345 Barbadian dollars

7   5567 Jamaican dollars

8   500 Barbadian dollars

9   £642

10   462 Canadian dollars

11   1000 Jamaican dollars

The table shows that £0.76 is equivalent to US$1 so £1 is equivalent to $\frac{1}{0.76}$ US$

∴ £100 is equivalent to US$100 × $\frac{1}{0.76}$

12   £246.40

13   1188 Barbadian dollars

14   860 Trinidad and Tobago dollars

Use the table to convert

15   £200 into Barbadian dollars

16   500 Canadian dollars into Jamaican dollars

17   3000 Barbadian dollars into UK pounds

18   275 Jamaican dollars into Barbadian dollars

19   £754 into Jamaican dollars

20   560 Trinidad and Tobago dollars into UK pounds

Start with £0.76 = 2 Barbadian dollars, so £1 = $\frac{2}{0.76}$ Barbadian dollars. The equivalent of £200 will be 200 times this value.

Telephone bills

The cost of a telephone call on a landline depends on four factors:
1 the line rental
2 the distance between the caller and the person being called
3 the time of day and/or the day of the week on which the call is being made
4 the length of the call.
These factors are put together in various ways to give metered units of time, each unit being charged at a fixed rate.

Today, very many people use a cell phone. Users may buy such a telephone outright and pay a monthly charge to their service provider or, they can hire a phone, two years being a typical contract period. At the end of the two years the phone is theirs. Their choice is then to pay a much smaller charge to the service provider, or upgrade to a more up-to-date device.

For example, suppose that Chris Reynolds' landline telephone account for the last quarter showed that his telephone had been used for 546 metered units. If the line rental was $31.00 and each unit cost 5 c, his telephone bill for the quarter can be worked out as follows:

$$\text{cost of 546 units at 5 c per unit} = 546 \times 5\,c$$

$$= \$27.30$$

$$\text{line rental} = \$31$$

$$\therefore \text{ the telephone bill for the quarter was } \$58.30$$

In some islands, for example Barbados, telephone bills are calculated at a fixed rate. Additional charges are made only for overseas calls, which will depend on the three factors above. Details similar to the following will be shown on such a bill.

Date	Country	Area Code	Number	Minutes	Amount
06/11	Tdad & Tobago	000	645-3272	7	$18.92
06/19	Tdad & Tobago	000	622-0000	12	$30.74
06/29	Jamaica	000	927-9751	8	$17.60
06/29	Jamaica	000	927-8798	4	$8.80
07/03	Jamaica	000	927-9751	12	$34.32
07/20	Miami	305	279-1319	1	$3.96
07/20	Miami	305	949-4616	9	$35.64

Balance Forward	$177.30
Payments	$177.80
Overseas Calls	$149.98
Other Charges	$ 0.00
Service Charge	$ 25.40
TOTAL DUE	$175.38

Exercise 13h

Find the quarterly telephone bill for each of the following households.

	Name	Number of units used	Line rental	Cost per unit
1	Mrs Keeling	750	$28	5 c
2	Mr Hodge	872	$32	6 c
3	Miss Hutton	1040	$33	7 c
4	Miss Jacob	1134	$37.60	8.5 c
5	Mrs Buckley	1590	$36.80	8.3 c
6	Mr Leeson	765	$42	7.68 c
7	Mrs Solly	965	$51	10.5 c

Calculate the monthly telephone bill for each of the following people.

	Name	1st 3 min	Each additional min	Number of min	Service charge
8	Singh	$3.90	$1.30	70	$25.40
9	Bird	$6.45	$2.15	28	$30.00
10	Lee	$9.15	$3.05	105	$25.40

11 Colin has agreed to pay $112 each month for two years for his cell phone with unlimited calls. There are no other charges. Find the total cost to Colin during the period of the contract.

12 Paul buys a SIM-free cell phone for $2550 and has to spend $80 each month for the SIM card to operate it. How much does he spend for his cell phone during the first two years?

If he had taken out a two-year contract the cost would have been $199 per month with no other charges. Would this have been a cheaper way of having a cell phone? Justify your answer.

13 Amy and Bernadette decide the buy cell phones. Amy agrees a contract for $212 per month for 2 years with free calls, texts, and all the data she could possibly need. Bernadette pays $2999 for her phone but, in addition, pays $95 a month for the SIM card. Which of the two girls has the cheaper way of having a cell phone? Justify your answer.

14 Penny's cell phone costs $96 a month but there are extra costs when she exceeds the agreed usage. They are 15 c a minute for each extra call, 10 c for sending each extra text and 55 c for each extra 10 MB of data downloaded.

Find Penny's total bill for a month when she makes 22 extra calls totalling 182 extra minutes, sends 45 additional texts and uses 40 MB for downloading extra data.

Electricity: kilowatt-hours

A *kilowatt-hour* is electric power of one kilowatt used for one hour. Electricity companies charge one rate for the first number of kilowatt-hours and a lower rate for additional usage.

In an attempt to encourage consumers to use less electricity some suppliers increase their unit cost after a certain number of kilowatt-hours have been used.

We all use electricity in some form and we know that some appliances cost more to run than others. For example, an electric fire costs much more to run than a light bulb. Electricity is sold in units called kilowatt-hours (kWh) and each appliance has a rating that tells us how many kilowatt-hours it uses each hour.

A typical rating for an electric fire is 2 kW. This tells us that it will use 2 kWh each hour, i.e. 2 units per hour. On the other hand, a light bulb can have a rating of 100 W. Because 1 kilowatt = 1000 watts (kilo means 'thousand' as we have already seen in kilometre and kilogram), the light bulb uses $\frac{1}{10}$ kWh each hour, or $\frac{1}{10}$ of a unit.

How many units (i.e. kilowatt-hours) will each of the given appliances use in 1 hour?

1 a 3 kW electric fire

2 a 100 W bulb

3 a $1\frac{1}{2}$ kW fire

4 a 1200 W hair dryer

5 a 60 W DVD player

6 a 20 W radio

7 an 8 kW cooker

8 a 2 kW dishwasher

With the help of an adult, find the rating of any of the following appliances that you might have at home. The easiest place to find this information is probably from the instructions.

9   an electric kettle

10   the refrigerator

11   the washing machine

12   the television set

13   a bedside lamp

14   the electric cooker

How many units of electricity would

15   a 2 kW fire use in 8 hours

16   a 100 W bulb use in 10 hours

17   an 8 kW cooker use in $1\frac{1}{2}$ hours

18   a 60 W bulb use in 50 hours

19   a 150 W refrigerator use in 12 hours

20   a 12 W radio use in 12 hours

21   an 8 W night bulb use in a week at 10 hours per night

22   a 5 W clock use in 1 week?

For how long could each of the following appliances be run on one unit of electricity?

23   a 250 W bulb

24   a 2 kW electric fire

25   a 100 W television set

26   a 360 W electric drill

In the following questions assume that 1 unit of electricity costs 6 c.
How much does it cost to run

27   a 100 W bulb for 5 hours

28   a 250 W television set for 8 hours

29   a 3 W clock for 1 week

30   a 3 kW kettle for 5 minutes?

Electricity bills

It is clear from the questions in the previous exercise that lighting from electricity is cheap but heating is expensive. While electricity is a difficult form of energy to store, it is convenient to produce it continuously at power stations, 24 hours a day. There are, therefore, some times of the day when more electricity is produced than is normally required. The electricity providers are able to solve this problem by selling off-peak electricity to users at a cheaper rate. Most of the electricity consumed in this way is for domestic heating.

Domestic electricity bills are calculated by charging every household a fixed amount, together with a charge for each unit used. Off-peak electricity is sold at approximately half price. The amount used is recorded on a meter, the difference between the readings at the beginning and end of a month or quarter showing how much has been used.

The following shows an electricity bill that might be received by a customer in a Caribbean Island.

LIGHT & POWER COMPANY   August 2017

Meter No.	Meter reading & date		kWh Used	Fuel Cts/kWh
	Previous	Present		
F12906	09118 04-07-17	09218 04-08-17	100	5.5408

Charges	
Fixed	$20.60
Energy	5.54
Subtotal	26.14
Arrears	
TOTAL	$26.14

The above bill shows the number of kWh registered on the meter on 04-07-17 as 09118 and on 04-08-17 as 09218. The number used for the one-month period is calculated as the difference between 09118 and 09218, i.e. 100 kWh.

The cost of the energy is therefore 100 kWh at 5.5408 c per kWh = $5.54.

There is also a fixed charge of $20.60 to add, so the total is $20.60 + $5.54 = $26.14.

Sometimes a customer is unable to pay the full amount in a particular period and only pays a portion. The remainder is then added to his next bill as 'Arrears'. In the above bill, there were no arrears.

In some territories bills are sent quarterly instead of monthly.

Exercise 13j

Mrs Comerford uses 1527 units of electricity in a quarter. If the fixed charge is $9.45 and each unit costs 8 c, how much does electricity cost her for the quarter?

Cost of 1527 units at 8 c per unit = 1527×8 c

= $122.16

Fixed charge = $9.45

Total bill = $131.61

Find the quarterly electricity bills for each of the following households:

	Name	Number of units used	Fixed charge	Cost per unit
1	Mr George	500	$20	5 c
2	Mrs Newton	600	$24	5 c
3	Mr Churchman	950	$30	10 c
5	Mr Khan	750	$28	12 c
5	Mr Vincent	1427	$31.80	6.65 c
6	Mrs Jackson	684	$36	11 c
7	Mr Wilton	938	$32.80	7.36 c

Find the quarterly electricity bills for each of the following households. Assume in each case that there is a fixed charge of $20, and that off-peak units are bought at half price.

	Name	Number of units used		Basic cost per unit
		At the basic price	Off-peak	
8	Mr Bennett	1000	500	10 c
9	Miss Cann	800	600	8 c
10	Mr Hadley	640	1200	7.5 c

Investigation

1   Find an electricity bill for a domestic property in your area. Use the bill to work out how the company charges for the electricity used.

The questions you can try to answer are:

- is there a standing charge
- what is the cost of 1 kWh
- is there a cheaper rate for off-peak usage
- what period of time does the bill cover
- are there any taxes applied to the bill?

2   Investigate how the charges for a landline telephone are worked out in your area. You will need to find a telephone bill.

Mixed exercises

Exercise 13k

1 a Increase 260 by by 30%.   b Decrease 206 by 49%.

2 If a number is decreased by 42%, what percentage is the new number of the original number?

3 What mutliplying factor would decrease a quantity by 18%?

4 a Increase 70 m by 35%.   b Decrease 55 miles by 84%.

5 In a sale a shopkeeper reduces the prices of his goods by 10%. Find the sale price of goods marked
   a $97   b $492.

Exercise 13l

1 The cash price of a television set is $4800. If bought on hire-purchase there is a deposit of $1600 followed by 36 monthly payments of $154. Find
   a the total cost of the television set if bought on HP
   b the extra cost if bought on HP compared with the cash price.

2 Mounir Ekdawi works a basic week of 38 hours at an hourly rate of $12.84. Overtime is paid at time-and-a-half.
   How much does he earn in a week when he works $42\frac{1}{2}$ hours?

3 Convert
   a 750 Barbadian dollars into UK pounds if each Barbadian dollar is equivalent to £0.35
   b £550 into Barbadian dollars if £1 = 3.30 Barbadian dollars.

4 During the last quarter Mr Barrett's telephone bill showed that he had used 842 units at 12.5 c per unit. In addition there was a line rental charge of $54.50. Find the total amount due.

5 Electricity costs 26 c per unit. How much is Mildred's quarterly bill if she uses 750 units and there is a quarterly fixed charge of $55?

Exercise 13m

1   The cost of some furniture, if bought on hire-purchase, is:
a deposit of $344 plus 12 monthly payments of $146.
Find the total HP cost.

2   Mrs Esther works a basic 36-hour week. She is paid at an hourly rate of $45.
Any overtime is paid at time-and-a-half.
Find
   a   her gross earnings in a normal week
   b   the hourly rate when she works overtime
   c   the extra she would be paid if she worked 5 hours overtime
   d   her total wage for a week when she works 46 hours.

3   a   Convert US$200 into Trinidad and Tobago dollars when the exchange rate is
      US$1 = TT$6.8.
   b   At the same rate of exchange, how many US dollars would I get for TT$550?

4   Mrs Spencer's telephone bill records that she has used 2740 units during the
last three months. The cost of each unit is 89 c. There is no service charge. How
much is Mrs Spencer's telephone bill?

5   Mr Peter's quarterly electricity bill, including a fixed charge, is $516.80.
Electricity is charged at 56 c per unit.
He finds that he has used 840 units. Calculate his fixed charge.

Exercise 13n

Select the letter that gives the correct answer.

1   When 460 m is increased by 10% its value is
   A   470 m   B   506 m   C   560 m   D   660 m

2   When 240 km is decreased by 5% its value is
   A   210 km   B   216 km   C   228 km   D   235 km

3   The multiplying factor that increases a quantity by 35% is
   A $\frac{7}{20}$ B $\frac{3}{2}$ C $\frac{13}{10}$ D $\frac{27}{20}$

4   The multiplying factor that decreases a quantity by 15% is
   A $\frac{4}{5}$ B $\frac{17}{20}$ C $\frac{9}{10}$ D $\frac{19}{20}$

5   Expressed as a percentage of 7.4 m, 629 cm is
   A   75%   B   80%   C   85%   D   90%

6   If 1 Barbadian dollar is equivalent to 0.28 US dollars, the equivalent value of
US$500 in Barbadian dollars, correct to 3 s.f., is
   A $1760   B $1770   C $1780   D $1790

7 I get £518 when I exchange 700 US dollars into pounds sterling.

The rate of exchange I receive is US$1 is equivalent to

    A £0.70   **B** £0.74   **C** £0.84   **D** £1.35

8 How long can a 50 W light bulb burn on 1 unit of electricity?

    A 2 hours   **B** 5 hours   **C** 10 hours   **D** 20 hours

9 The cash price of an item of furniture is $5500 + sales tax of 15%. The total cost to the buyer is

    A $6050   **B** $6100   **C** $6325   **D** $6600

10 Clive Prior works a 40-hour week for which he is paid at $13.50 an hour. His weekly pay is

    A $500   **B** $540   **C** $560   **D** $580

 Investigation

These references to percentages were in a newspaper. Investigate what each means.

1 *'The annual rate of inflation has fallen from 3.5% last month to 3.46% this month.'*

Does this mean that prices are rising, falling or standing still?

2 *'Everyone in the company is to get a raise of 4.5%. This means that the annual increase ranges from $2350 to $500.'*

How can this be true if everybody gets the same raise? Can you explain?

Did you know?

If 320 players enter a singles knockout competition, then 319 matches must be played to find the winner.

In this chapter you have seen that...

✔ to increase a quantity by a%, multiply it by $\dfrac{100+a}{100}$; $\dfrac{100+a}{100}$ is called the multiplying factor

✔ to decrease a quantity by a%, multiply it by $\dfrac{100-a}{100}$; $\dfrac{100-a}{100}$ is called the multiplying factor

✔ a kWh is 1 kilowatt used for 1 hour

✔ bills for domestic utilities usually include a fixed charge and a charge for the number of units used

✔ exchange rates are used to convert from one currency to another.

14 Geometry

Parallel lines

Two straight lines that are always the same distance apart, however far they are drawn, are called *parallel lines*.

The lines in your exercise books are parallel. You can probably find many other examples of parallel lines.

1   Using the lines in your exercise book, draw three lines that are parallel. Do not make them all the same distance apart. For example

(We use arrows to mark lines that are parallel.)

2   Using the lines in your exercise book, draw two parallel lines. Make them fairly far apart. Now draw a slanting line across them. For example

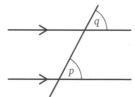

Mark the angles in your drawing that are in the same position as those in the diagram. Are they acute or obtuse angles? Measure your angles marked *p* and *q*.

3   Draw a grid of parallel lines like the diagram below. Use the lines in your book for one set of parallels and use the two sides of your ruler to draw the slanting parallels.

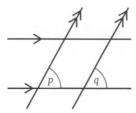

Mark your drawing like the diagram. Are your angles *p* and *q* acute or obtuse? Measure your angles *p* and *q*.

4   Repeat question **3** but change the direction of your slanting lines.

5   Draw three slanting parallel lines like the diagram below, with a horizontal line cutting them. Use the two sides of your ruler and move it along to draw the third parallel line.

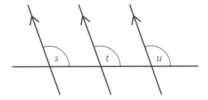

Mark your drawing like the diagram. Decide whether angles *s*, *t* and *u* are acute or obtuse and then measure them.

6   Repeat question **5** but change the slope of your slanting lines.

Corresponding angles

In the exercise above, lines were drawn that crossed a set of parallel lines.

> A line that crosses a set of parallel lines is called a *transversal*.

When you have drawn several parallel lines you should notice that:

> Two parallel lines on the same flat surface will never meet however far they are drawn.

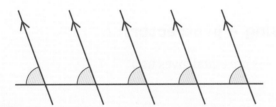

If you draw the diagram above by moving your ruler along you can see that all the shaded angles are equal. These angles are all in corresponding positions: in this diagram they are all above the transversal and to the left of the parallel lines. Angles like these are called *corresponding angles*.

> When two or more parallel lines are cut by a transversal, the corresponding angles are equal.

Exercise 14b

In the diagrams below write down the letter that corresponds to the shaded angle:

1

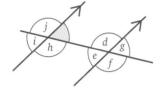

5

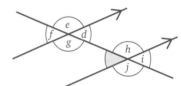

2

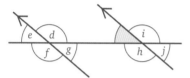

6

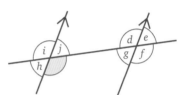

3

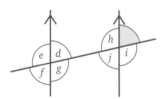

7

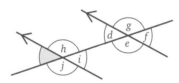

4

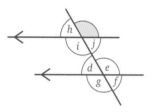

8

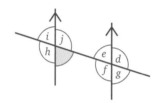

Drawing parallel lines (using a protractor)

The fact that the corresponding angles are equal gives us a method for drawing parallel lines.

If you need to draw a line through the point C that is parallel to the line AB, first draw a line through C to cut AB.

Use your protractor to measure the shaded angle. Place your protractor at C as shown in the diagram. Make an angle at C the same size as the shaded angle and in the corresponding position.

You can now extend the arm of your angle both ways, to give the parallel line.

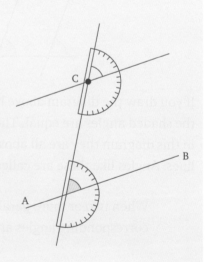

Exercise 14c

1   Using your protractor draw a grid of parallel lines like the one in the
    diagram. (It does not have to be an exact copy.)

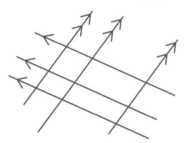

2   Trace the diagram below.

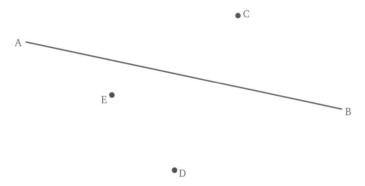

Now draw lines through the points C, D and E so that each line is
parallel to AB.

3   Draw a sloping line on your exercise book. Mark a point C above the
    line. Use your protractor to draw a line through C parallel to your
    first line.

4   Trace the diagram below.

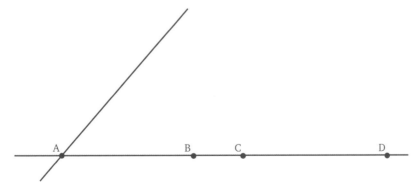

Measure the acute angle at A. Draw the corresponding angles at B, C
and D. Extend the arms of your angles so that you have a set of four
parallel lines.

In questions **5** to **8** remember to draw a rough sketch before doing the accurate drawing.

5 Draw an equilateral triangle with the equal sides each 8 cm long. Label the corners A, B and C. Draw a line through C that is parallel to the side AB.

6 Draw an isosceles triangle ABC with base AB which is 10 cm long and base angles at A and B which are each 30°. Draw a line through C which is parallel to AB.

7 Draw the triangle as given in question **5** again and this time draw a line through A which is parallel to the side BC.

8 Make an accurate drawing of the figure below where the side AB is 7 cm, the side AD is 4 cm and Â = 60°.

(A figure like this is called a *parallelogram.*)

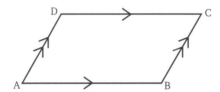

 Puzzle

Copy this grid.

How many different-shaped parallelograms can you draw on this grid?

Each vertex must be on a dot. One has been drawn for you.

Do not include squares and rectangles.

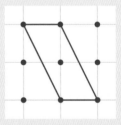

Problems involving corresponding angles

The simplest diagram for a pair of corresponding angles is an F shape.

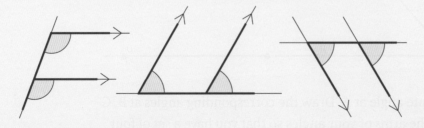

Looking for an F shape may help you to recognise the corresponding angles.

Exercise 14d

Write down the size of the angle marked *d* in each of the following diagrams:

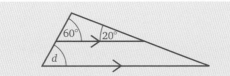

$d = 60°$ (*d* and the angle of 60° are corresponding angles.)

1

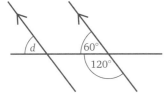

Look for an F shape round the angle you need to find.

2

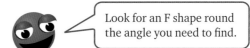

6

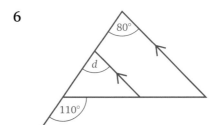

3

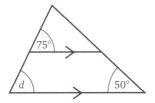

7

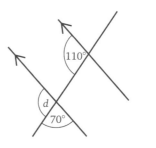

4

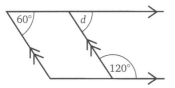

8

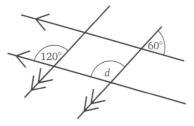

5

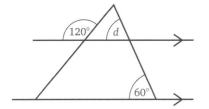

9

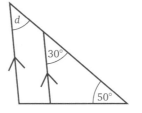

10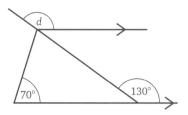

11

Using angle facts

Reminder:

Vertically opposite angles are equal.

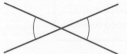

Angles on a straight line add up to 180°.

Angles at a point add up to 360°.

The angles of a triangle add up to 180°.

You will need these facts in the next exercise. If you cannot see immediately the angle you want, copy the diagram. On your diagram, write down the size of any angles you can, including those that are not marked. This should help you to find the size of other angles in the diagram, including those that you need. Remember you can use any facts you know about angles.

Exercise 14e

Find the size of each angle marked with a letter:

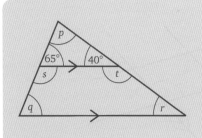

$p = 75°$ (angles of $\triangle$ add up to 180°)

$q = 65°$ (corresponding angles)

$s = 115°$ (s and 65° add up to 180°)

$r = 40°$ (corresponding angles)

$t = 140°$ (t and 40° add up to 180°)

1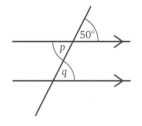

2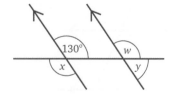

3

4

5

6

7

8

9

10

11

12

13

14

15

16

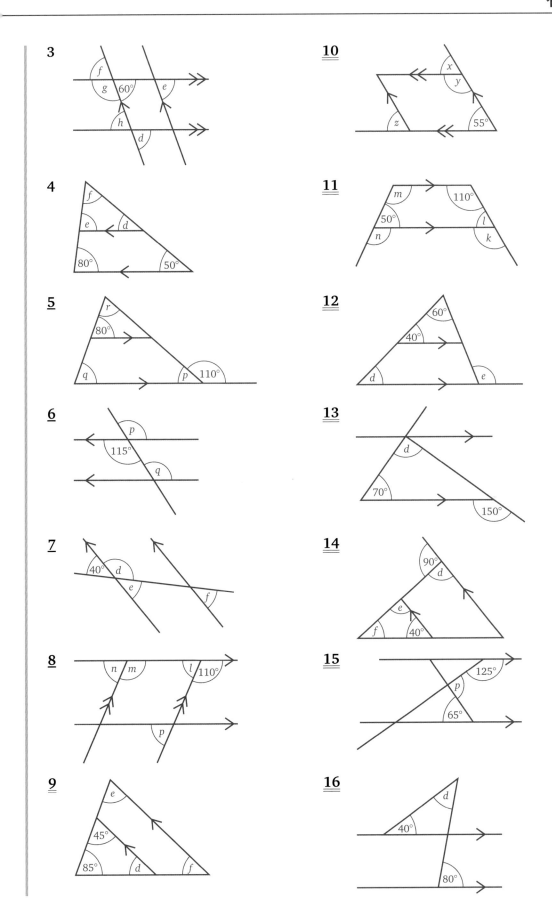

Find the size of angle *d* in questions **17** to **24**:

17

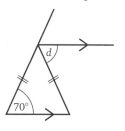

21

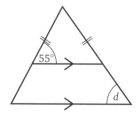

18

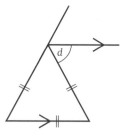

22

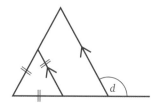

19

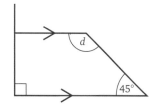

23

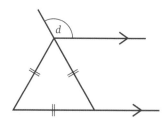

20

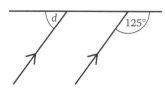

24

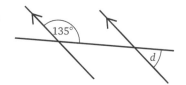

Alternate angles

Draw a large letter Z. Use the lines of your exercise book to make sure that the outer arms of the Z are parallel.

When this letter is turned through 180° about the point marked with a cross, the diagram looks exactly the same. This means that the two shaded angles are equal. Measure them to make sure.

Draw a large N, making sure that the outer arms are parallel.

Also when this letter is turned through 180° about the point marked with a cross, the diagram looks exactly the same, so once again the shaded angles are equal. Measure them to make sure.

The pairs of shaded angles like those in the Z and N are between the parallel lines and on alternate sides of the transversal.

Angles like these are called *alternate angles*.

> When two parallel lines are cut by a transversal, the alternate angles are equal.

The simplest diagram for a pair of alternate angles is a Z shape.

Looking for a Z shape may help you to recognise the alternate angles.

Exercise 14f

Write down the angle that is alternate to the shaded angle in the following diagrams:

Look for a Z shape around the angle you want to find.

1

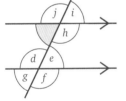

4

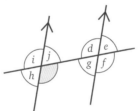

7

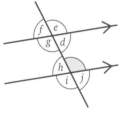

2

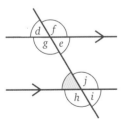

5

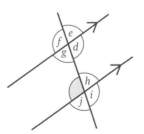

8

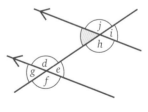

3

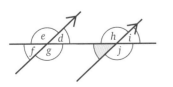

6

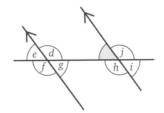

9

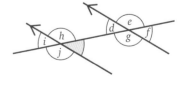

Problems involving alternate angles

Without doing any measuring we can show that alternate angles are equal by using the facts that we already know:

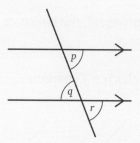

$p = r$ because they are corresponding angles

$q = r$ because they are vertically opposite angles

$\therefore \quad p = q$ and these are alternate angles

Exercise 14g

Find the size of each marked angle:

1

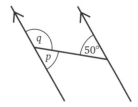

Remember that you can use any angle you know.

2

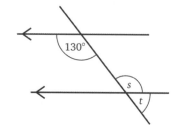

4

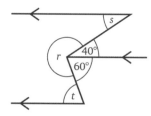

3

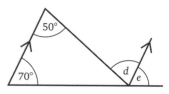

5

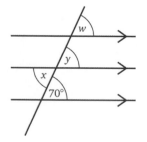

6

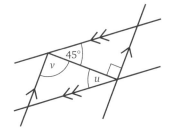

9

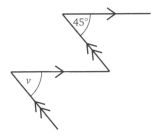

7

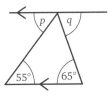

10

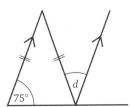

8

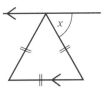

11

Investigation

This diagram represents a child's billiards table.

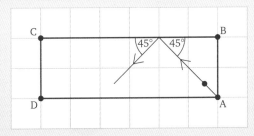

There is a pocket at each corner.

The ball is projected from the corner A at 45° to the sides of the table. It carries on bouncing off the sides at 45° until it goes down a pocket. (This is a very superior toy – the ball does not lose speed however many times it bounces!)

1   How many bounces are there before the ball goes down a pocket?

2   Which pocket does it go down?

3   What happens if the table is 2 squares by 8 squares?

4   Can you predict what happens for a 2 by 20 table?

5   Now try a 2 by 3 table.

6 Investigate for other sizes of tables. Start by keeping the width at 2 squares, then try other widths. Copy this table and fill in the results.

Size of table	Number of bounces	Pocket
2×6		
2×8		
2×3		
2×5		

7 Can you predict what happens with a 3×12 table?

Interior angles

In the diagram on the right, f and g are on the same side of the transversal and 'inside' the parallel lines.

Pairs of angles like f and g are called *interior angles*.

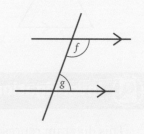

Exercise 14h

In the following diagrams, two of the marked angles are a pair of interior angles.
Name them:

You may find it helpful to look for a U shape.

1
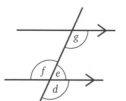

2
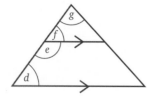

3
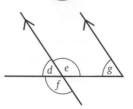

4
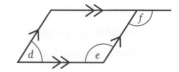

5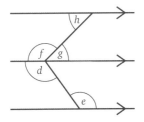

6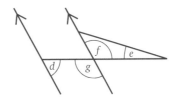

In the following diagrams, use the information given to find the size of *p* and of *q*. Then find the sum of *p* and *q*.

7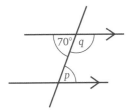

10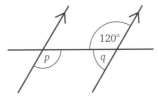

8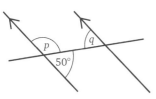

11 Make a large copy of the diagram below. Use the lines of your book to make sure that the outer arms of the 'U' are parallel.

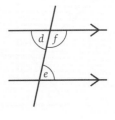

Measure each of the interior angles *p* and *q*. Add them together.

9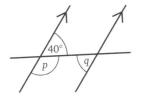

> The sum of a pair of interior angles is 180°.

You will probably have realised this fact by now.
We can show that it is true from the following diagram.

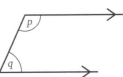

$d + f = 180°$ because they are angles on a straight line

$d = e$ because they are alternate angles

So $e + f = 180°$

The simplest diagram for a pair of interior angles is a U shape.

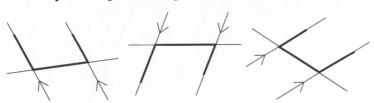

Looking for a U shape may help you to recognise a pair of interior angles.

Exercise 14i

Find the size of each marked angle:

1

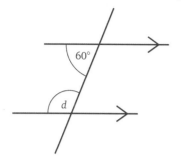

6

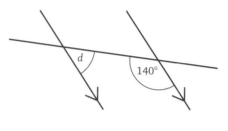

2

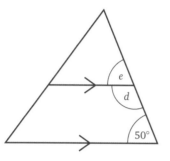

7

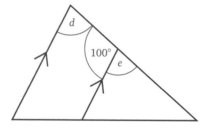

3

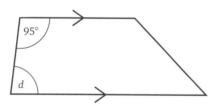

8

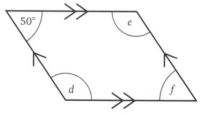

4

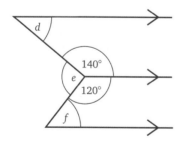

9

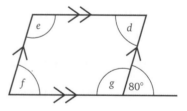

5

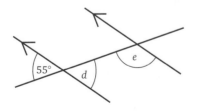

10

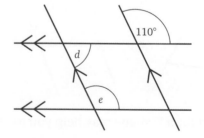

The exterior angle of a triangle

If any side of a triangle is produced, an exterior angle is formed. In the diagram AC is produced to a point D. Angle BCD is an example of an exterior angle of a triangle.

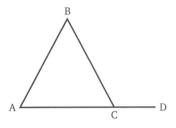

In this diagram the side AC is produced to D and the line CE is drawn parallel to the side AB.

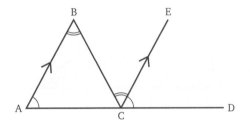

It follows that

        ∠BAC = ∠ECD   because they are corresponding angles

        ∠ABC = ∠BCE   because they are alternate angles

so that ∠BCD = ∠BAC + ∠ABC

i.e. the exterior angle shown equals the sum of the two opposite interior angles.

More generally in any triangle:

> The exterior angle equals the sum of the two interior and opposite angles.

Exercise 14j

Find angles *a* and *b*.

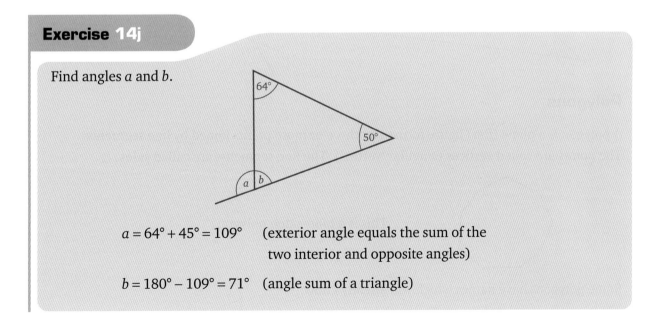

$a = 64° + 45° = 109°$ (exterior angle equals the sum of the two interior and opposite angles)

$b = 180° - 109° = 71°$ (angle sum of a triangle)

In each question find, in alphabetical order, the angles marked with letters:

1

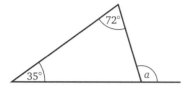

5

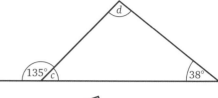

2

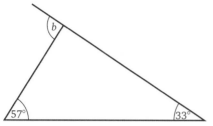

6

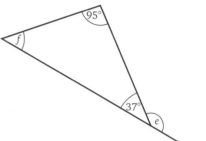

3

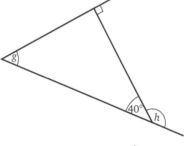

7

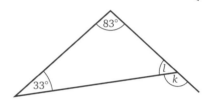

4

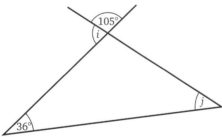

8

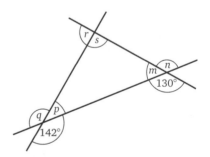

Polygons

A polygon is a plane (flat) figure formed by three or more points joined by line segments.
The points are called vertices (singular 'vertex'). The line segments are called sides.

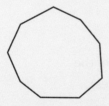

This is a nine-sided polygon.

Some polygons have names which you already know:

a three-sided polygon is a triangle

Regular polygons

A polygon is called regular when all its sides are the same length *and* all its angles are the same size. The polygons below are all regular:

Exercise 14k

State which of the following figures are regular polygons. Give a brief reason for your answer:

1 Square	**5** Right-angled triangle
2 Rectangle	**6** Equilateral triangle
3 Parallelogram	**7** Circle
4 Isosceles triangle	

Make a rough sketch of each of the following polygons. (Unless you are told that a polygon is regular, you must assume that it is *not* regular.)

8 A regular quadrilateral	**12** A regular hexagon
9 A hexagon	**13** A pentagon
10 A triangle	**14** A quadrilateral
11 A regular triangle	**15** A ten-sided polygon

Convex and concave polygons

When the vertices of a polygon all point outwards, the polygon is convex.

Sometimes one or more of the vertices point inwards, in which case the polygon is concave.

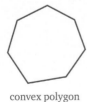

convex polygon   concave polygon

In this chapter we consider only convex polygons.

Interior angles

The angles enclosed by the sides of a polygon are the *interior angles*.
For example:

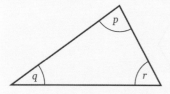

p, q and r are the interior angles of the triangle

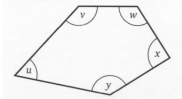

u, v, w, x and y are the interior angles of the pentagon.

Exterior angles

If we produce (extend) one side of a polygon, an angle is formed outside the
polygon. It is called an *exterior angle*.

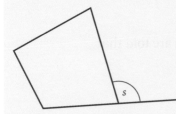

For example, s is an exterior angle of the quadrilateral.

If we produce all the sides in order we have
all the exterior angles.

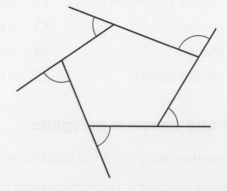

Exercise 14I

1 What is the sum of the interior angles of any triangle?

2 What is the sum of the interior angles of any quadrilateral?

3 In triangle ABC, find
   a the size of each marked angle
   b the sum of the exterior angles.

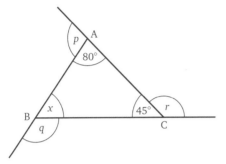

4 ABCD is a parallelogram. Find
   a the size of each marked angle
   b the sum of the exterior angles.

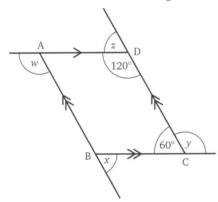

5 In triangle ABC, write down the value of
   a $x + q$
   b the sum of all six marked angles
   c the sum of the interior angles
   d the sum of the exterior angles.

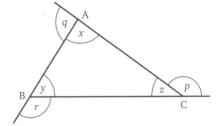

6 Draw a pentagon. Produce the sides in order to form the five exterior angles. Measure each exterior angle and then find their sum.

7 Construct a regular hexagon of side 5 cm. (Start with a circle of radius 5 cm and then with your compasses still open to a radius of 5 cm, mark off points on the circumference in turn.) Produce each side of the hexagon in turn to form the six exterior angles.

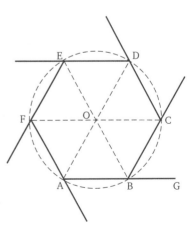

If O is the centre of the circle, joining O to each vertex forms six triangles.
   a What kind of triangle is each of these triangles?
   b What is the size of each interior angle in these triangles?
   c Write down the value of $A\hat{B}C$.
   d Write down the value of $C\hat{B}G$.
   e Write down the value of the sum of the six exterior angles of the hexagon.

The sum of the exterior angles of a polygon

In the last exercise, we found that the sum of the exterior angles is 360° in each case. This is true of any polygon, whatever its shape or size.

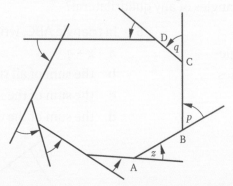

Consider walking round this polygon. Start at A and walk along AB. When you get to B you have to turn through angle p to walk along BC. When you get to C you have to turn through angle q to walk along CD, ... and so on until you return to A. If you then turn through angle z you are facing in the direction AB again. You have now turned through each exterior angle and have made just one complete turn, i.e.

> The sum of the exterior angles of a polygon is 360°.

Exercise 14m

Find the size of the angle marked p.

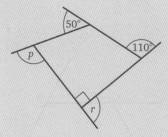

$p + r + 110° + 50° = 360°$ (sum of exterior angles of a polygon)

but $r = 90°$ (angles on a straight line)

∴ $p = 360° - 90° - 110° - 50°$

             $p = 110°$

In each case find the size of the angle marked *p:*

1

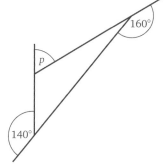

6

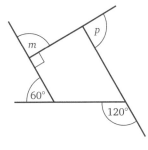

2

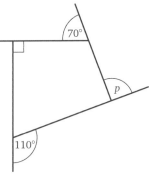

7

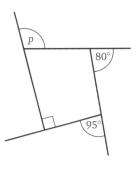

3

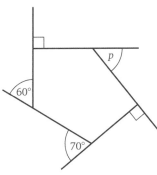

8

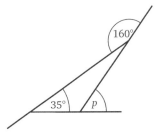

4

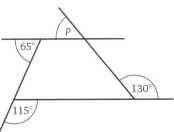

9

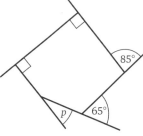

5

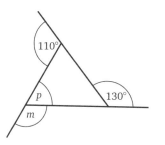

10

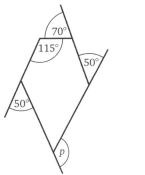

In questions **11** and **12** find the value of x.

11

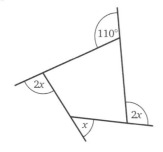

12

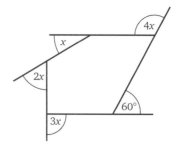

13 The exterior angles of a hexagon are x, $2x$, $3x$, $4x$, $3x$ and $2x$.
Find the value of x.

14 Find the number of sides of a polygon if each exterior angle is

    a 72°   **b** 45°.

 Puzzle

This flag is to be coloured red, white and blue.

Adjoining regions must have different colours.

How many different flags are possible?

Mixed exercises

You now know that when a transversal cuts a pair of parallel lines:

- the corresponding (F) angles are equal
- the alternate (Z) angles are equal
- the interior (U) angles add up to 180°.

You can use any of these facts, together with the other angle facts you know, to answer the questions in the following exercises.

Find the size of each marked angle:

1

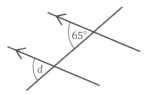

2

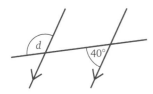

3

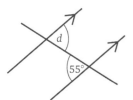

4

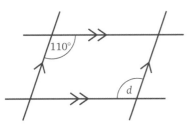

5

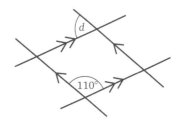

6

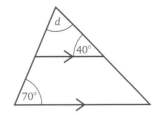

7

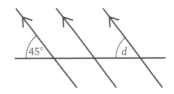

8 Construct a triangle ABC in which
AB = 12 cm, BC = 8 cm and AC = 10 cm.
Find the midpoint of AB and mark it D.
Find the midpoint of AC and mark it E.
Join ED. Measure AD̂E and AB̂C. What
can you say about the lines DE and BC?

Find the size of each marked angle:

1

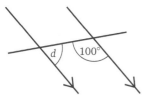

2

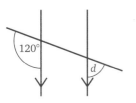

3

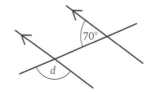

4

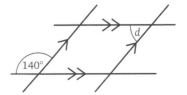

297

5

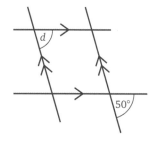

6

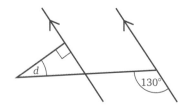

7

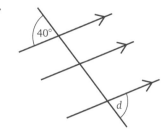

8 Construct the parallelogram below, making it full size.

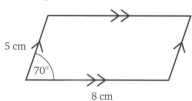

Exercise 14q

Select the letter that gives the correct answer.

Use this diagram for questions **1** to **6**.

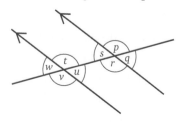

1 Which angle corresponds to w?

    A p **B** q **C** r **D** s

2 Which angle corresponds to r?

    A t **B** u **C** v **D** w

3 Which angle is alternate to s?

    A t **B** u **C** v **D** w

4 Which angle is alternate to t?

    A p **B** q **C** r **D** s

5 Which angle is vertically opposite q?

    A p **B** r **C** s **D** u

6 The angle interior to angle u is

    A p **B** q **C** r **D** s

7 The value of the angle marked *a* is

A   52°   B 80°   C 82°   D 90°

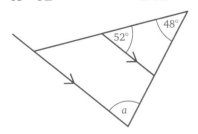

8 The angle marked *a* is

   A   63°
   B   107°
   C   117°
   D   127°

9 The angle marked *b* is

   A   65°
   B   81°
   C   99°
   D   115°

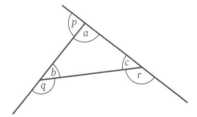

10 The angle marked *c* is

   A   45°
   B   47°
   C   52°
   D   58°

11 The sum of the six marked angles is

   A   360°
   B   450°
   C   510°
   D   540°

12 The angles of a pentagon, in anticlockwise order, are
5*x*, 3*x*, 4*x*, 90° and 114°.
The value of *x* is

   A   24°
   B   28°
   C   30°
   D   32°

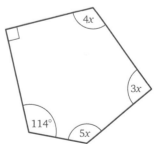

In this chapter you have seen that...

✔ you can draw parallel lines

✔ parallel lines cut by a transversal give different types of angles – some are called corresponding angles, some alternate angles and others interior angles

✔ corresponding angles are equal; they can be recognised by an F shape

✔ alternate angles are equal; they can be recognised by a Z shape

✔ interior angles add up to 180°; they can be recognised by a U shape

✔ geometry problems can often be solved by starting with a copy of the diagram and filling in the sizes of the angles you know

✔ the exterior angle of a triangle is equal to the sum of the two interior opposite angles

✔ the sum of the exterior angles of any polygon is 360°.

15 Constructions

Did you know?

Isaac Newton (1642–1727) wrote:

The description of right lines and circles, upon which geometry is founded, belongs to mechanics. Geometry does not teach us to draw these lines, but requires them to be drawn.

You need to know...

✔ what a right angle is

✔ how angles are measured

✔ how to use a protractor, a pair of compasses and a ruler

✔ how to use, to solve problems, the properties of:

   • vertically opposite angles

   • the sum of angles at a point

   • angles on a straight line

   • the sum of the three angles in a triangle

   • the sum of the four angles in a quadrilateral

   • corresponding, alternate, interior angles with respect to two parallel lines

✔ what an arc of a circle is

✔ the properties of equilateral and isosceles triangles.

Angles and triangles

Reminder:

Vertically opposite angles are equal.

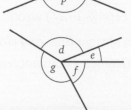

Angles at a point add up to 360°.

$$d + e + f + g = 360°$$

Angles on a straight line add up to 180°.

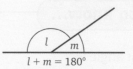

$$l + m = 180°$$

The sum of the three angles in any triangle is 180°.

$$x + y + z = 180°$$

The sum of the four angles in any quadrilateral is 360°.

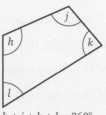

$$h + j + k + l = 360°$$

An equilateral triangle has all three sides the same length and each of the three angles is 60°.

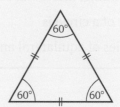

An isosceles triangle has two equal sides and the two angles at the base of the equal sides are equal.

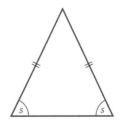

When a transversal cuts a pair of parallel lines:

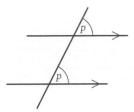

the corresponding angles, or F angles, are equal

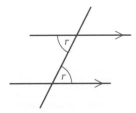

the alternate angles, or Z angles, are equal

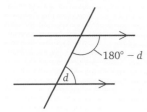

the interior angles are supplementary (add up to 180°).

Exercise 15a

Find the sizes of the marked angles. If two angles are marked with the same letter they are the same size.

1

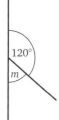

2

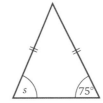

3

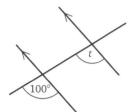

7

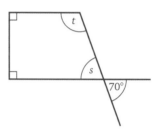

4

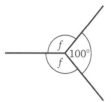

8

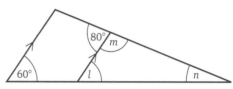

5

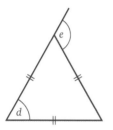

9

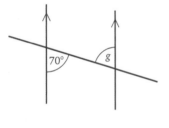

6

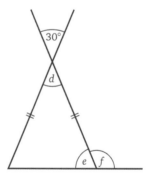

10

? **Puzzle**

In ten years' time the combined age of four brothers will be 100. What will it be in five years' time?

Constructing angles without using a protractor

Some angles can be made without using a protractor: one such angle is 60°.

Every equilateral triangle, whatever its size, has three angles of 60°. To make an angle of 60° we construct an equilateral triangle but do not draw the third side.

To construct an angle of 60°

Start by drawing a straight line and marking a point, A, near one end.

Next open your compasses to a radius of about 4 cm (this will be the length of the sides of your equilateral triangle).

With the point of your compasses on A, draw an arc to cut the line at B, continuing the arc above the line.

Move the point to B and draw an arc above the line to cut the first arc at C.

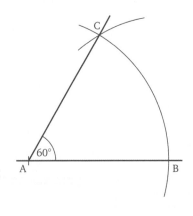

Draw a line through A and C. Then Â is 60°.

△ABC is the equilateral triangle so *be careful not to alter the radius on your compasses during this construction.* Why is △ABC always equilateral?

Bisecting angles

Bisect means 'cut exactly in half'.

The construction for bisecting an angle makes use of the fact that, in an isosceles triangle, the line of symmetry cuts Â in half.

To bisect Â, open your compasses to a radius of about 6 cm.

With the point on A, draw an arc to cut both arms of Â at B and C. (If we joined BC, △ABC would be isosceles.)

With the point on B, draw an arc between the arms of Â.

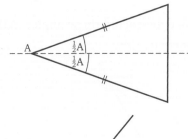

Move the point to C (being careful not to change the radius) and draw an arc to cut the other arc at D.

Join AD.

The line AD then bisects Â.

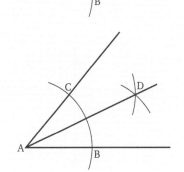

Exercise 15b

1   Construct an angle of 60°.

2   Draw an angle of about 50°. Bisect this angle.
    Measure both halves of your angle.

Make sure that your pencil is sharp.

3   Construct an angle of 60°. Now bisect this angle.
    What size should each new angle be? Measure both of them.

4   Use what you learnt from the last question to construct an angle of 30°.

5   Draw a straight line and mark a point A near the middle.

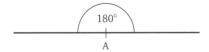

180°

A

You now have an angle of 180° at A.

Now bisect the angle of 180° you have drawn. What is the size of each
new angle? Measure each of them.

Construction of angles of 60°, 30°, 90°, 45°

You constructed these angles in the last exercise. Here is a summary of these
constructions.

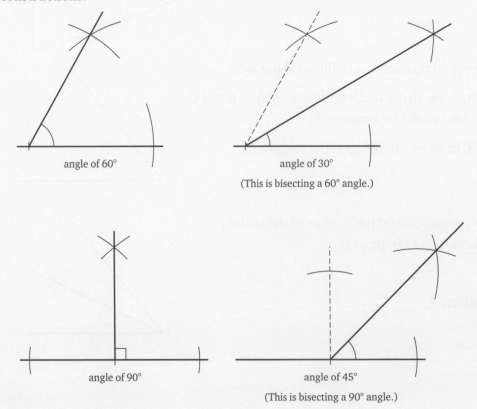

angle of 60°

angle of 30°
(This is bisecting a 60° angle.)

angle of 90°

angle of 45°
(This is bisecting a 90° angle.)

Exercise 15c

Construct the following figures using only a ruler and a pair of compasses:

Make sure that your pencil is sharp.

1

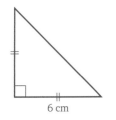

6 cm

6

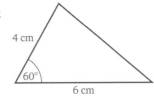

4 cm

60°

6 cm

2

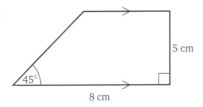

45°

8 cm

5 cm

7

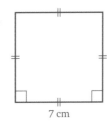

7 cm

3

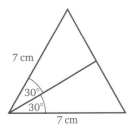

7 cm

30°
30°

7 cm

8

4 cm

8 cm

4

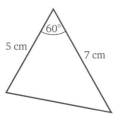

60°

5 cm

7 cm

9

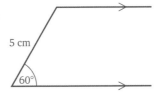

5 cm

60°

5

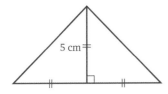

5 cm

10

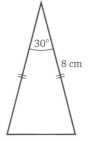

30°

8 cm

For questions **11** to **15**, draw a rough sketch before starting the construction.

11 Draw a line, AB, 12 cm long. Construct an angle of 60° at A. Construct an angle of 30° at B. Label with C the point where the arms of Â and B̂ cross. What size should Ĉ be? Measure Ĉ as a check on your construction.

12 Construct a triangle, ABC, in which AB is 10 cm long, Â is 90° and AC is 10 cm long. What size should Ĉ and B̂ be? Measure Ĉ and B̂ as a check.

13 Construct a square, ABCD, with a side of 6 cm.

14 Construct a quadrilateral, ABCD, in which AB is 12 cm, Â is 60°, AD is 6 cm, B̂ is 60° and BC is 6 cm. What can you say about the lines AB and DC?

15 Construct an angle of 120°. Label it BAC (so that A is the vertex and B and C are at the ends of the arms). At C, construct an angle of 60° so that Ĉ and Â are on the same side of AC. You have constructed a pair of parallel lines; mark them and devise your own check.

To construct an angle equal to a given angle

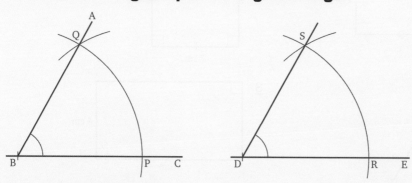

Draw any angle ABC. To construct an angle at D, on the line DE, equal to the angle ABC proceed as follows:

With the point of your compasses at B, draw an arc to cut the arms of angle ABC at P and Q. Next, with the point of your compasses at D, draw an arc of the same radius. With the point of your compasses at P open out your compasses until it reaches Q. Transfer the point to R and, keeping the same arc, draw an arc to cut the first arc at S. Then, angle RDS is equal to the angle ABC.

Construction to bisect a line

To bisect a line we have to find the midpoint of that line. To do this we construct a *rhombus* with the given line as one diagonal, but we do not join the sides of the rhombus.

To bisect XY, open your compasses to a radius that is about $\frac{3}{4}$ of the length of XY.

With the point of the compasses on X, draw arcs above and below XY.

Move the point to Y (being careful not to change the radius) and draw arcs to cut the first pair at P and Q.

Join PQ.

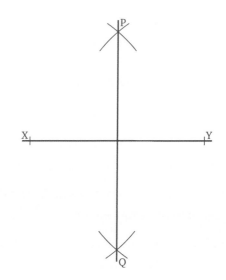

The point where PQ cuts XY is the midpoint of XY. PQ is called the *perpendicular bisector* of XY.

(XPYQ is a rhombus because the same radius is used to draw all the arcs, i.e. XP = YP = YQ = XQ. PQ and XY are the diagonals of the rhombus so PQ bisects XY.)

Note: When you are going to bisect a line, draw it so that there is plenty of space for the arcs above *and* below the line.

Dropping a perpendicular from a point to a line

If you are told to drop a perpendicular from a point, C, to a line, AB, this means that you have to draw a line through C which is at right angles to the line AB.

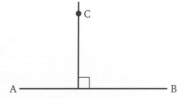

To drop a perpendicular from C to AB, open your compasses to a radius that is about $1\frac{1}{2}$ times the distance of C from AB.

With the point of the compasses on C, draw arcs to cut the line AB at P and Q.

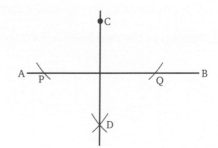

Move the point to P and draw an arc on the other side of AB. Move the point to Q and draw an arc to cut the last arc at D.

Join CD.

CD is then perpendicular to AB.

Remember to keep the radius unchanged throughout this construction: you then have a rhombus, PCQD, of which CD and PQ are the diagonals.

Constructing triangles

We now revise and extend some of the work we did in Book 1.

To construct a triangle given the lengths of the three sides, start by drawing one side, AB.

With the point of the compasses at A, and the radius equal to AC, draw an arc.

Then with the point of the compasses at B and the radius equal to BC, draw an arc to cut the first arc.

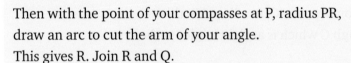

To construct a triangle given two sides and the angle between them, start by drawing one of the known sides, say PQ.

Next, use your protractor to measure and draw the angle at P.

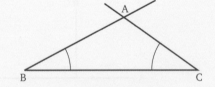

Then with the point of your compasses at P, radius PR, draw an arc to cut the arm of your angle.
This gives R. Join R and Q.

To construct a triangle given one side and two angles, start by drawing the side, say BC.

Now measure and draw the angle you want at B and the angle you want at C.

(If either ∠B or ∠C is not known you can find it using ∠A + ∠B + ∠C = 180°)

The point of intersection of the two lines drawn to make the angles gives A.

Exercise 15d

Before you start a construction, remember to make a rough sketch and to put all the information that you are given on to that sketch. Then decide which method to use.

Construct the following triangles:

1 △ABC in which AB = 5 cm, BC = 7 cm and AC = 6 cm

2 △PQR in which $\hat{P} = 60°$, $\hat{Q} = 40°$ and PQ = 8 cm

3 △LMN in which $\hat{M} = 45°$, LM = 7 cm and MN = 8 cm

4 △XYZ in which $\hat{X} = 100°$, $\hat{Y} = 20°$ and XY = 5 cm

5 △RST in which RS = 10 cm, ST = 6 cm and RT = 7 cm

6 Construct a triangle ABC, in which AB = 6 cm, BC = 8 cm and CA = 10 cm. Using a ruler and compasses only, drop a perpendicular from B to AC. Use a protractor to measure each of the interior angles of the triangle. Now find their sum. Is this the value you expected? Justify your answer.

7 Construct a triangle ABC, in which AB = 8 cm, AC = 10 cm and BC = 9 cm. Construct the perpendicular from C to AB and measure and record its length.

8 Construct a triangle XYZ, in which XY = 12 cm, XZ = 5 cm and YZ = 9 cm. Construct the perpendicular from Z to YX at P. Produce this line to a point Q.

Use your protracor to measure angles XZP, ZXP and XPQ. Hence verify that the exterior angle of triangle XZP is equal to the sum of the two opposite interior angles.

9 Construct the isosceles triangle LMN in which LM = 6 cm, LN = MN = 8 cm.

Construct the perpendicular bisector of the side LM. Explain why this line is a line of symmetry of △LMN.

10 Construct the isosceles triangle PQR, in which PQ = 5 cm, PR = RQ = 7 cm.

Construct the perpendicular bisector of the side PR. This line is not a line of symmetry of △PQR; why not?

11 The diagram shows a circle whose centre is C, with a line, AB, drawn across the circle.

(AB is called a *chord*.)

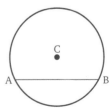

This figure has one line of symmetry that is not shown. Make a rough sketch of the figure and mark the line of symmetry. Explain what the line of symmetry is in relation to AB.

12 Draw a circle of radius 6 cm and mark the centre, C. Draw a chord, AB, about 9 cm long. (Your drawing will look like the one in question **11**.) Construct the line of symmetry.

13 Construct a triangle ABC, in which AB = 8 cm, BC = 10 cm and AC = 9 cm. Construct the perpendicular bisector of AB. Construct the perpendicular bisector of BC. Where these two perpendicular bisectors intersect (i.e. cross), mark G. With the point of your compasses on G and with a radius equal to the length of GA, draw a circle.

This circle should pass through B and C, and it is called the *circumcircle* of △ABC.

14 Repeat question **13** with a triangle of your own.

15 Construct a square ABCD, such that its sides are 5 cm long. Construct the perpendicular bisector of AB and the perpendicular bisector of BC. Label with E the point where the perpendicular bisectors cross. With the point of your compasses on E and the radius equal to the distance from E to A, draw a circle.

This circle should pass through all four corners of the square. It is called the circumcircle of ABCD.

16 Construct a triangle ABC, in which AB = 10 cm, AC = 8 cm and BC = 12 cm. Construct the bisector of $\hat{A}$ and the bisector of $\hat{B}$. Where these two angle bisectors cross, mark E. Drop the perpendicular from E to AB. Label G, the point where this perpendicular meets AB. With the point of your compasses on E and the radius equal to EG, draw a circle.

This circle should touch all three sides of △ABC and it is called the *incircle* of △ABC.

17 Repeat question **16** with the equilateral triangle ABC, with sides that are 10 cm long.

18 Repeat question **16** with a triangle of your own.

19 Construct a square ABCD, of side 8 cm. Construct the incircle (i.e. the circle that *touches* all four sides of the square) of ABCD. First decide how you are going to find the centre of the circle.

Puzzle

How many cubes can you see?

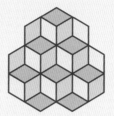

 Activity

You can use your construction skills to make three-dimensional polyhedron models.

The net above, which consists of four equilateral triangles, makes a regular *tetrahedron*. A regular solid is one in which all the faces are identical.

Construct the net accurately, making the sides of each triangle 4 cm long. Start by drawing one triangle of side 8 cm; mark the midpoints of the sides and join them up. Draw flaps on the edges as shown (they are not part of the net). To complete the model shown on page 314 you will require 8 identical tetrahedra like the one shown above.

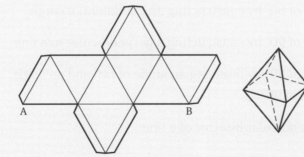

This net, which is also drawn with equilateral triangles of side 4 cm, gives the solid shown on the right. It is called an *octahedron*. This is another regular solid. All the faces are identical. Start by making AB 12 cm long.

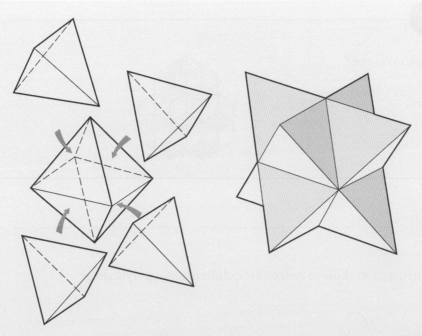

This shows how four of the tetradedra we made can be fixed to the four faces of the octahedron which are facing us. The other four are fixed to the faces on its opposite side.

It needs a great deal of patience to make this model, but is well worth the trouble.

You could make it even more interesting by colouring the tetrahedra or by using coloured paper.

The solid you have made is an eight-pointed star or stella octangula.

In this chapter you have seen that...

✔ you can construct an angle of 60° by constructing an equilateral triangle

✔ you can construct an angle of 90° by constructing a perpendicular to a line

✔ you can construct an angle of 30° by bisecting an angle of 60° and an angle of 45° by bisecting an angle of 90°

✔ you can construct the perpendicular bisector of a line

✔ you can bisect any angle

✔ you can construct the perpendicular from a point to a line

✔ you can construct an angle equal to a given angle.

16 Statistics

At the end of this chapter you should be able to...

1 draw pie charts and interpret information from them

2 find the mode, mean and median from data given in a frequency table

3 draw line graphs

4 understand the difference between discrete data and continuous data

5 draw histograms.

Did you know?

Statistics wasn't generally taught in schools until the introduction of the electronic calculator.

Imagine trying to do all the calculations you need to do using pencil and paper!

You need to know...

✔ how to add, subtract, multiply and divide whole numbers

✔ how to add, subtract, multiply and divide decimal numbers

✔ how to put a set of numbers in ascending or descending order

✔ how to use a protractor to draw and measure angles

✔ the meaning of a frequency table.

Key words

arithmetic average, bar chart, categorical data, continuous data, discrete data, frequency table, histogram, interval data, line graph, mean, median, mode, nominal data, numerical data, ordinal data, pie chart, ratio data

Pie charts

A *pie chart* is used to represent information when some quantity is shared out and divided into different categories.

Here is a pie chart to show the proportions, within a group, of people with eyes of certain colours.

The size of the 'pie slice' represents the size of the group. We can see without looking at the numbers that there are about the same number of people with brown eyes as with grey eyes and that there are about twice as many with grey eyes as with blue. The size of the pie slice is given by the size of the angle at the centre, so to draw a pie chart we need to calculate the sizes of the angles.

The number of people is 60.

As there are 12 blue-eyed people, they form $\frac{12}{60}$ of the whole group and are therefore represented by that fraction of the circle.

Blue: $\frac{12}{60} \times \frac{360°}{1} \times 1 = 72°$ Grey: $\frac{20}{60} \times \frac{360°}{1} = 120°$

Hazel: $\frac{6}{60} \times \frac{360°}{1} = 36°$ Brown: $\frac{22}{60} \times \frac{360°}{1} = 132°$

Total   360°

Now draw a circle of radius about 5 cm (or whatever is suitable). Draw one radius as shown and complete the diagram using a protractor, turning your page into the easiest position for drawing each new angle.

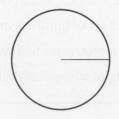

Label each 'slice'.

Exercise 16a

Draw pie charts to represent the following information, first working out the angles.

⟲ **1**   A box of 60 coloured balloons contains the following numbers of balloons of each colour:

Find the number of balloons in each category as a fraction of the total number of balloons. Then find this fraction of 360°.

Colour	Red	Yellow	Green	Blue	White
Number of balloons	16	22	10	7	5

2   Ninety people were asked how they travelled to work and the following information was recorded:

Transport	Car	Bus	Walk	Motorcycle	Bicycle
Number of people	32	38	12	6	2

3   On a cornflakes packet the composition of 120 g of cornflakes is given in grams as follows:

Protein	Fat	Carbohydrate	Other ingredients
101	1	10	8

4   Of 90 cars passing a survey point it was recorded that 21 had two doors, 51 had four doors, 12 had three (two side doors and a hatchback) and 6 had five doors.

5   A large flower arrangement contained 18 dark red roses, 6 pale pink roses, 10 white roses and 11 deep pink roses.

6   The children in a class were asked what pets they owned and the following information was recorded:

Animal	Dog	Cat	Bird	Rabbit	Fish
Frequency	8	10	3	6	3

The eye colours of 54 people were recorded:

Eye colour	Blue	Grey	Hazel	Brown
Frequency	10	19	5	20

The total number here is 54, which is not as convenient as in the previous problems. In problems like these we may have to find an angle correct to the nearest degree.

Blue: $\dfrac{10}{54} \times \dfrac{360°}{1} = \dfrac{200°}{3}$

$= 66\frac{2}{3}° = 67°$ (to the nearest degree)

Grey: $\dfrac{19}{54} \times \dfrac{360°}{1} = \dfrac{380°}{3}$

$= 126\frac{2}{3}° = 127°$ (to the nearest degree)

Hazel: $\dfrac{5}{\cancel{54}\,_3} \times \dfrac{\cancel{360°}^{\,20}}{1} = \dfrac{100°}{3}$

$= 33\dfrac{1}{3}° = 33°$ (to the nearest degree)

Brown: $\dfrac{20}{\cancel{54}\,_3} \times \dfrac{\cancel{360°}^{\,20}}{1} = \dfrac{400°}{3}$

$= 133\dfrac{1}{3}° = 133°$ (to the nearest degree)

Total $= 67 + 127 + 33 + 133 = 360°$

Draw pie charts to represent the following information, working out the angles first and, where necessary, giving the angles correct to the nearest degree.

7 300 people were asked whether they lived in a condo, a house, a studio, an apartment or in some other type of accommodation and the following information was recorded:

Type of accommodation	Condo	House	Studio	Apartment	Other
Frequency	90	150	33	15	12

8 In a street in which 80 people live the numbers in various age groups are as follows:

Age group (years)	0–15	16–21	22–34	35–49	50–64	65 and over
Number of people	16	3	19	21	12	9

Interpreting pie charts

Exercise 16b

1   This pie chart shows the uses of personal computers in 2018:

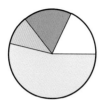 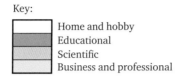

Key:
- Home and hobby
- Educational
- Scientific
- Business and professional

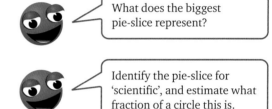

a For which purpose were computers used most?

What does the biggest pie-slice represent?

b Estimate the fraction of the total used for
  i scientific purposes
  ii home and hobbies.

Identify the pie-slice for 'scientific', and estimate what fraction of a circle this is.

2   The pie chart below shows how fuel is used for different purposes in the average house in the Caribbean:

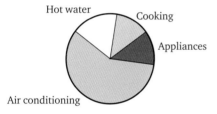

Hot water
Cooking
Appliances
Air conditioning

a For which purpose is most fuel used?

b How does the amount used for cooking compare with the amount used for hot water?

Is the angle of the slice for 'cooking' bigger or smaller than the angle of the slice for 'hot water' and by roughly how much?

3   The pie chart shows the age distribution of a population in years in 2018:

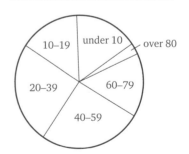

under 10
10–19
over 80
20–39
60–79
40–59

a Estimate the size of the fraction of the population in the age groups
  i under 10 years
  ii 20–39 years.

b State which groups are of roughly the same size.

Remember that a whole turn is 360°. What fraction of a whole turn represents each age group?

Mean, mode and median

In Book 1 we saw that, when we have a set of numbers, there are three different measures we can use that attempt to give a 'typical member' that is representative of the set.

Mean

The *mean* (arithmetic average) of a set of n numbers is the sum of the numbers divided by n. The mean of the set 2, 6, 8, 8, 10, 10, 12, is

$$\frac{2+6+8+8+10+10+12}{7} = \frac{56}{7} = 8$$

The mean value of a set of numbers is the most frequently used form of average, so much so that the word 'average' is often used for 'mean value'.

For example, if you were asked for your average mark in a set of examinations, you would total the marks and divide by the number of examinations, i.e. you would find the mean mark.

Mode

In a set of numbers, the *mode* is the number that occurs most often. For example, for the set 2, 2, 4, 4, 4, 5, 6, 6, the mode is 4 as the number 4 occurs more often than any of the other numbers.

The mode is easier to find if the numbers are arranged in order of size.
If the numbers in a set are all different, there is no mode.
For example, the set 1, 2, 3, 5, 8, 10, has no mode.

If there are two (or more) numbers which equally occur most often, there are two (or more) modes.

For example, in the set 1, 2, 2, 3, 5, 5, 8, both 2 and 5 are modes.

Median

If we arrange a set of numbers in order of size, the *median* is the number in the middle. For example, for the seven numbers in the set 2, 4, 5, 7, 7, 8, 9, the median is 7.

When there is an even number of numbers in the set, the median is the mean of the two middle numbers. For example, for the eight numbers in the set 2, 3, 4, 4, 5, 6, 7, 7, the median is the mean of 4 and 5, i.e. 4.5.

For a small set of numbers, say 15, it is easy to find the median and we can see that it is the $\left(\frac{15+1}{2}\right)$th value, i.e. the 8th value. From examples such as these we deduce that, for n numbers arranged in order of size, the median is the $\left(\frac{n+1}{2}\right)$th number.

For example, for 59 numbers, the median is the $\left(\frac{59+1}{2}\right)$th number,

i.e. the 30th number. For 60 numbers, the median is the $\left(\frac{60+1}{2}\right)$th number,

i.e. the $\left(30\frac{1}{2}\right)$th number. This means the average of the 30th and 31st numbers.

Exercise 16c

A page from a novel by George Lamming was chosen at random and the number of letters in each of the first twenty words on that page was recorded:

$$3,\ 4,\ 5,\ 3,\ 7,\ 8,\ 3,\ 3,\ 6,\ 2,\ 4,\ 6,\ 4,\ 6,\ 3,\ 13,\ 4,\ 3,\ 3,\ 2$$

Find the mean, mode and median of the number of letters per word.

Arranging the numbers in size order:

$$2,\ 2,\ 3,\ 3,\ 3,\ 3,\ 3,\ 3,\ 3,\ 4,\ 4,\ 4,\ 4,\ 5,\ 6,\ 6,\ 6,\ 7,\ 8,\ 13$$

10th 11th

The mean is $\frac{92}{20} = 4.6$

The mode is 3

The median is the value of the $\left(\frac{20+1}{2}\right)$th number,

i.e. the $\left(10\frac{1}{2}\right)$th number, which is the average of the 10th and 11th numbers

∴ the median is 4

Find the mean, mode and median of the sets of numbers in questions **1** to **4**. Remember to arrange the numbers in order of size first. Give answers correct to three significant figures where necessary:

1   3, 6, 2, 5, 9, 2, 4

2   13, 16, 12, 14, 19, 12, 14, 13

3   1.6, 2.4, 3.9, 1.7, 1.6, 0.2, 1.3, 2.0

4   1.3, 1.8, 1.7, 1.9, 1.4, 1.5, 1.3, 1.8, 1.2

5   Ten music students took a Grade 3 piano examination.
       They obtained the following marks:

$$106,\ 125,\ 132,\ 140,\ 108,\ 102,\ 75,\ 135,\ 146,\ 123$$

Find the mean and median marks. Which of these two representative measures would be most useful to the teacher who entered the students? (Give *brief* reasons – do not write an essay on the subject.)

6 A small firm employs ten people. The salaries of the employees are as follows:

$30 000, $8000, $5000, $5000, $5000, $5000, $5000, $4000, $3000, $1500

Find the mean, mode and median salary.

Which of these three figures is a trade union official unlikely to be interested in, and why?

7 Thirty 15-year-olds were asked how much pocket money they received each week and the following amounts (in cents) were recorded:

0, 0, 0, 50, 50, 50, 100, 100, 100, 100, 100, 100, 100, 150, 150, 200, 200, 200, 200, 200, 200, 200, 200, 200, 250, 250, 250, 500, 1000

Find the mean, mode and median amount.

If you were presenting your parents with an argument for an increase in pocket money, which of the three representative measures would you use and why?

8 The first eight customers at a supermarket one Saturday spent the following amounts:

$25.10, $3.80, $20.50, $15.70, $38.40, $9.60, $46.20, $10.46

Find the mean and median amount spent.

Finding the mode from a frequency table

The frequency table shows the number of houses in a village that are occupied by different numbers of people:

Number of people living in one house	0	1	2	3	4	5	6
Frequency	2	10	8	15	25	12	4

The highest frequency is 25 so there are more houses with four people living in them than any other number, i.e. the modal number of people living in one house is 4.

Finding the mean from a frequency table

The pupils in class 3G were asked to state the number of children in their own family and the following frequency table was made:

Number of children per family	1	2	3	4	5
Frequency	7	15	5	2	1

Adding the frequencies gives the total number of families as 30.

This information has not been grouped: all the numbers are here so we can total this set. We have seven families with one child giving seven children, 15 with two children giving 30 children and so on, giving the total number of children as

$$(7 \times 1) + (15 \times 2) + (5 \times 3) + (2 \times 4) + (1 \times 5) = 65$$

There are 30 numbers in the set, so the mean is

$$\frac{65}{30} = 2.2 \text{ (to 1 d.p.)}$$

i.e. there are, on average, 2.2 children per family.

To avoid unnecessary errors, this kind of calculation needs to be done systematically and it helps if the frequency table is written vertically.

We can then add a column for the number of children in each group and sum the numbers in this column for the total number of children.

Number of children per family x	Frequency f	fx
1	7	7
2	15	30
3	5	15
4	2	8
5	1	5
	No. of families = 30	No. of children = 65

$$\text{mean} = \frac{65}{30} = 2.2 \text{ (to 1 d.p.)}$$

Exercise 16d

1

Number of tickets bought per person for a football match	1	2	3	4	5	6	7
Frequency	250	200	100	50	10	3	1

Find the mean number of tickets bought per person.

Draw a vertical frequency table, like the one above, with a third column.

2

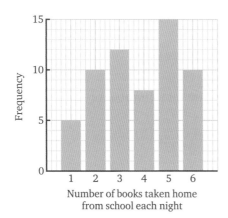

Number of books taken home from school each night

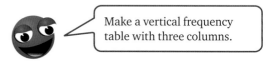

Make a vertical frequency table with three columns.

Find the mean for the number of books taken home each night.

3 This table shows the results of counting the number of prickles per leaf on 50 holly bushes.

Number of prickles	1	2	3	4	5	6
Frequency	4	2	8	7	20	9

Find

a the mean number of prickles per leaf   **b** the mode.

4 A six-sided die was thrown 50 times. The table gives the number of times each score was obtained.

Score	1	2	3	4	5	6
Frequency	7	8	10	8	5	12

Find

a the mean score per throw   **b** the mode.

5 Three coins were tossed together 30 times and the number of heads per throw was recorded.

Number of heads	0	1	2	3
Frequency	3	12	10	5

Find

a the mean number of heads per throw

b the mode.

Finding the median from a frequency table

Exercise 16e

1   A group of students gathered this information about themselves.

Number of children in each family	Frequency
1	8
2	12
3	4
4	2

You want to find the middle value.
First find the number of families (add up the frequencies).
You can find where in the order the middle value is by adding 1 to the total, then dividing this by 2.
This tells you which family or families you want.
Is it in the first 8 families? This would give a median of 1 child.
Is it in the next 12 families, i.e. 9 to 20?

Find the median number of children per family.

2   Once every five minutes, Debbie counted the number of people queuing at a checkout. Her results are shown in this table.

Number of people queuing at a supermarket checkout	Frequency
0	4
1	6
2	5
3	2
4	2

Write down the median number of people queuing.

3   This frequency table shows the distribution of scores when a die is rolled 20 times.

Score	1	2	3	4	5	6
Frequency	3	2	5	3	3	4

Find the median score.

4   In a shooting competition a competitor fired 50 shots at a target and got the following scores

Score	1	2	3	4	5
Frequency	3	4	18	16	9

Find

a   the median score   b   the mode   c   the mean.

5 The table shows the distribution of goals scored by the home teams one Saturday.

Score	0	1	2	3	4	5
Frequency	3	8	4	3	5	2

Find

a the median score   **b** the mode   **c** the mean.

Line graphs

A *line graph* is used to show how a quantity changes over time.
For example, temperature, share prices, cost of living and profits are all quantities that change over time.

This table shows the profits of AB Manufacturing Company as declared at the end of each year from 2010 to 2017.

2010	2011	2012	2013	2014	2015	2016	2017
$25 000 000	$15 000 000	$10 000 000	$12 000 000	$13 000 000	$18 000 000	$26 000 000	$29 000 000

We can draw a line graph to illustrate these figures by plotting the profits against the years and joining the points with straight lines.

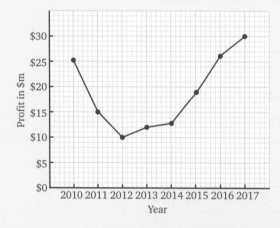

The lines help to show how the profits are changing but values between the lines mean nothing. For example, it is not possible to give the profits half way between the end of 2016 and the end of 2017 for two reasons: there is no point on the graph for this time and half-year profits may or may not be half the yearly profits.

Exercise 16f

1   When Sara went into hospital her temperature was taken every hour and recorded on this line graph.

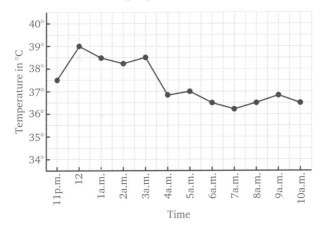

The graph shows that Sara's temperature at 1 a.m. was 38.4 °C.

Use the graph to answer these questions.

   a   What was Sara's highest recorded temperature and when did it occur?

   b   What was her lowest recorded temperature?

   c   By 6 a.m. her temperature had returned to normal.
       What is her normal temperature?

   d   How long was she in hospital before her temperature returned to normal?

   e   Can you say what her highest temperature was while she was in hospital?

2

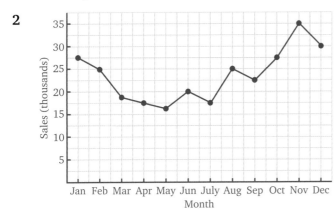

The graph shows the total monthly sales at Benshaw plc.

   a   In which month were the sales

       i   greatest   ii   least?

b Does the graph suggest gradually increasing sales?

c Does it look as though the sales improve around Christmas?

d Assuming that the sales graph has looked like this every year for the last five, can you think of a business that could have this sales pattern?

3 The line graph shows the price of a share in a privatised company at yearly intervals after privatisation.

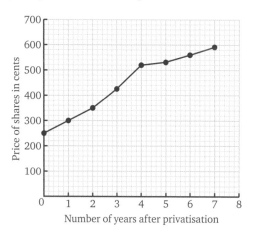

a What was the price of the share when issued?

b Copy and complete the following table.

Time after privatisation (years)	Value of share (cents)
1	
2	
3	
4	
5	
6	
7	

c In which year after privatisation did the price of the share rise most?

d What trend do you notice in the price of the share?

4   a   Use the graph given in question **3** to estimate the price of the share, 8 years after privatisation.

    b   Do you think that, 8 years after privatisation, the share price will be the same as your estimate?
Give a reason for your answer.

5   Use the graph for question **2** for these questions.

    a   Can the graph be used to find the half-monthly sales figures for the year? Explain your answer.

    b   Looking at this graph, the managing director asked why the sales had fallen in the first half of July. The sales director replied that they had not; they had in fact increased for the first two weeks of July. How could the sales director justify this statement and, assuming it is correct, describe what happened to the sales in the second half of July.

Categorical data

Categorical data is information about different categories such as eye colour or types of reptiles. There are two forms of categorical data.

1   This is a table from Book 1. It shows the different types of vehicle passing along a road.

Vehicle	Cars	Vans	Trucks	Motorcycles	Bicycles
Frequency	62	11	15	10	2

The vehicles listed are in categories and could be in any order. This is an example of *nominal* data.

Other examples of nominal data are different subjects taught in school, different vegetables on sale.

2   This table shows the highest educational qualifications of people living in a village.

Type of qualification	None	CSEC	Cape	Graduate	Postgraduate
Frequency	50	60	20	5	2

The qualifications are in categories but there is a clear order here from lowest to highest. This type of data is called *ordinal* data.

Examples of ordinal data are often found in questionnaires, such as when you are asked to tick boxes labelled

Agree, Neither agree nor disagree, Disagree.

Numerical data

Numerical data can be counted or measured, for example the numbers of children born each year and the heights of five-year-olds in a swimming class. There are two forms of numerical data.

1   This table shows the number of days the highest temperature in degrees Celsius was recorded in one week.

Temperature	20°	22°	24°	26°	28°
Frequency	1	0	3	2	1

The temperatures are numerical and there is a clear interval between them (2°). This type of data is called *interval data*.

Interval data has no absolute zero, for example zero degrees Celsius is not the same as zero degrees Fahrenheit.

Another example of interval data is years. Again there is no absolute zero because different cultures measure the number of years from different starting points.

2   This table shows the numbers of different lengths of wooden planks for sale at a DIY store,

Length	200 cm	300 cm	400 cm	500 cm	600 cm
Frequency	1	0	3	2	1

A plank of length 0 cm does not exist. This is not the same as a temperature of 0 °C because this does exist. Therefore the data in the table has an important difference from interval data because there is a zero where the quantity cannot exist.

This type of data is called *ratio data*.

Exercise 16g

State whether the quantities in the following questions could be nominal, ordinal, interval or ratio data.

1 Different types of fuel used in houses.

2 Numbers of rooms in houses.

3 The ages of dogs in a rescue centre.

4 The masses of mangos harvested from a tree.

5 The profit made by stores in your high street.

6 The different colours of rose bushes in a park.

7 The heights of students in your form.

Discrete and continuous data

Numerical data can have exact and distinct values such as numbers of objects or sizes of apparel.

For example: If you count the number of students in your class, you can give an exact value. For example, 28 students *is* exact. If we show this number on a number line, it can be marked at only one point. If we mark another number of students on the number line, it will be at a separate and distinct point (we cannot have 1.5 students, or any other part of a student!).

Also there is no such thing as two and a half cats or a size $10\frac{1}{4}$ dress. These are types of *discrete* numerical data.

Discrete data can be illustrated by a *bar chart* where the bars do not have to touch. For example this bar chart shows the number of different items that are on discount in several supermarkets.

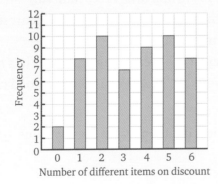

Some numerical data cannot have exact values.

For example, suppose that the length of a piece of wood is being measured.

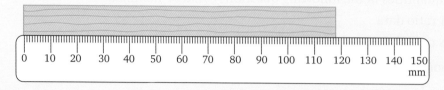

The length is close to 120 mm, so we can give the length as 120 mm to the nearest 10 mm.

If we magnify the scale where the end of the wood is, we can see that the length is 118 mm to the nearest millimetre.

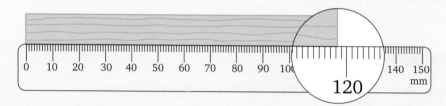

If we use stronger magnification, we can see that it becomes impossible to measure this length any more accurately because the edge is not smooth enough.

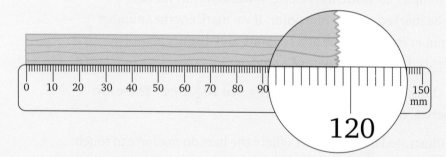

This means that we cannot give an exact value for the length of this wood; we can say that the length lies between 117.5 mm and 118.5 mm. Any other piece of wood will have a length that can be measured to the nearest centimetre, or millimetre, or tenth of a millimetre, depending on the smoothness of the ends and the accuracy of the measuring scale. But it is *not* possible to give a length exactly. In general the length of a piece of wood can be anywhere on a scale.

This is an example of *continuous* numerical data that can have any value within a range.

Mass, length and time are examples of continuous data as they can never be measured exactly, only correct to a given significant figure. For example, Usain Bolt ran the 100 m race in a world record time of 9.58 seconds in Berlin in 2009. The time of 9.58 seconds is not exact; it is correct to the nearest 0.01 seconds so lies in the range between 9.575 and 9.585.

Exercise 16h

1 Give some possible values for
   a the number of people standing at a bus stop
   b the shoe size of a 13-year-old boy
   c a person's weight
   d the world high jump record.

2 Discuss whether the values in question **1** are exact or can only be given correct to a number of significant figures.

3 Jane's height is 152 cm correct to the nearest centimetre. Amjad's height is 152 cm correct to the nearest centimetre.
   Discuss this statement: 'Jane and Amjad are exactly the same height.'

4 You probably have been, or soon will be, involved in a conversation like this:
   Bus driver: 'How old are you?'
   Sam: 'I'm 13.'
   Does Sam mean that he was 13 on his last birthday, or does he mean that he is 13 years old correct to the nearest year? (We will assume that Sam is telling the truth!)
   Discuss the difference between these possibilities.

This frequency table shows the heights of 55 children which have been rounded down to the nearest centimetre so 141.2 cm and 141.8 cm, for example, are both rounded down to 141 cm.

Height (to the nearest complete cm)	131	132	133	134	135	136	137	138	139	140	141	142	143	144	145	146	147	148	149	150	151	152	153
Frequency	1	2	2	3	2	4	3	2	3	3	2	5	2	5	3	1	3	2	3	2	0	1	1

There are 2 children whose heights are recorded as 132 cm.

This means that each child's height is in the range 132 cm up to (but not including) 133 cm.

However, the two children are unlikely to be exactly the same height. This can be shown in the frequency table by giving the heights, x cm, as

$131 \leqslant x < 132,\ 132 \leqslant x < 133$, and so on

Because of the space that this notation takes, it is sometimes simplified to 131–, 132–, and so on, where 131–, 132–, mean a number from 131 up to, but not including 132, etc.

Height (cm)	131–	132–	133–	134–	135–	136–	137–	138–	139–	140–	141–	142–	143–	144–	145–	146–	147–	148–	149–	150–	151–	152–	153–
Frequency	1	2	2	3	2	4	3	2	3	3	2	5	2	5	3	1	3	2	3	2	0	1	1

Now we can see that *continuous values are in groups.*

It is easier to understand this information if it is grouped into wider ranges, so we will start the first group at 130 cm, the second group at 135 cm, the third group at 140 cm, and so on. This will give us five groups which we can write as

$130 \leqslant x < 135,\quad 135 \leqslant x < 140,\quad 140 \leqslant x < 145,\quad 145 \leqslant x < 150,\quad 150 \leqslant x < 155$

Any height that is less than 135 cm belongs to the first group, but a height of 135 cm belongs to the second group.

Looking along the list of heights we can see that there are 8 children whose heights are in the first group, 14 children whose heights are in the second group, and so on.

We can write this information in a frequency table.

Height (cm)	Frequency
$130 \leqslant x < 135$	8
$135 \leqslant x < 140$	14
$140 \leqslant x < 145$	17
$145 \leqslant x < 150$	12
$150 \leqslant x < 155$	4
	Total: 55

Histograms

We can use the information in the frequency table to draw a chart.

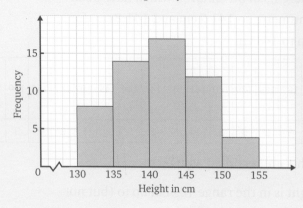

Notice that the horizontal axis gives the heights on a continuous scale, like part of a tape measure, so there are no gaps between the bars.

> A bar chart illustrating continuous data must have no gaps between the bars and is called a *histogram*.

Exercise 16i

1   This histogram summarises the times taken by all the students in Year 2 to complete a technology task.

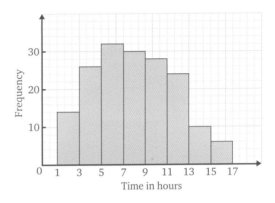

   a   How many students took more than 9 hours?

   b   How many students completed the task?

   c   There are 200 students in Year 2. How many of them did not complete the task?

   d   Jane was asked to estimate the number of students who spent less than 2 hours on this task. Which of these two answers do you think is the better estimate and why?

   i   14   **ii**   7

   e   Is it true to say that most students took between 5 and 7 hours?

2   Here is a frequency table showing the times, in minutes, taken by the students in a class on their journeys from home to school on a particular morning.

Time, t (minutes)	Frequency
$0 \leqslant t < 10$	2
$10 \leqslant t < 20$	9
$20 \leqslant t < 30$	5
$30 \leqslant t < 40$	4
$40 \leqslant t < 50$	2
$50 \leqslant t < 60$	1

Copy and complete this histogram, using the table.

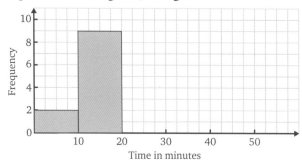

3 The heights of students belonging to a trampolining club were recorded; the histogram summarises the information gathered.

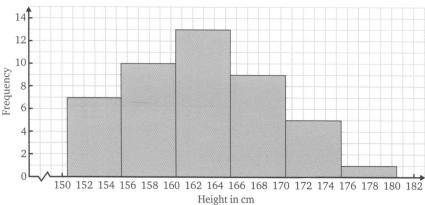

a How many heights were recorded?

b The heights were rounded when they were recorded. How do you think these heights were rounded and why do you think that?

c How many of these heights were more than 160 cm?

d In which group should a height recorded as 158 cm to the nearest centimetre, be placed?

e How would you reply if asked to give the height of the shortest student in the club?

f Estimate the number of students who are taller than 168 cm, and explain how you get your estimate.

g What can you say about the number of students whose heights are 155 cm to 160 cm?

h Can you tell how many students are 162 cm tall?

4 At the health-centre, some babies were weighed one afternoon. Their masses, in kilograms, were recorded by the nurse in this frequency table.

Mass, m (kg)	$4 \leqslant m < 8$	$8 \leqslant m < 12$	$12 \leqslant m < 16$
Frequency	7	12	6

The next two babies were weighed at just under 12 kg and just over 12 kg.

a Complete the frequency table including these two masses.

b Draw a histogram to illustrate this information.

5 This is a list of the masses in kilograms, rounded up to the nearest kilogram, of 30 14-year-old boys.

51	56	60	62	65	65	67	67	68	69
52	57	60	64	65	65	67	68	68	70
55	57	61	64	65	66	67	68	69	75

You are asked to draw a histogram to illustrate this data.

a Decide on the groups that you will use and make a frequency table.

b Draw the histogram.

c Which of your groups contains the largest number of masses?

6 These are two of the charts drawn to illustrate the data in question **5**.

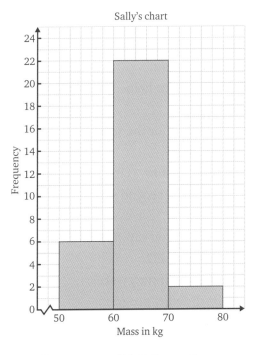

Sally's chart

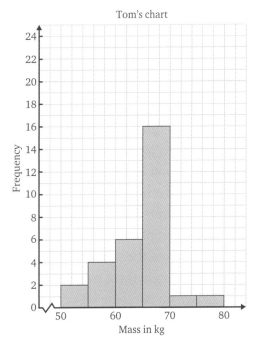

Tom's chart

a What groups did Sally use?

b What groups did Tom use?

c What are the advantages and disadvantages of Sally's choice of groups?

d What are the advantages and disadvantages of Tom's choice of groups?

e What are the advantages and disadvantages of your choice in question **5**?

7 The students in Class 8G were given two sets of five multiple choice questions to answer. They did the first set without any previous experience of this type of question. After the first set, they discussed the problems encountered and then they answered another set.

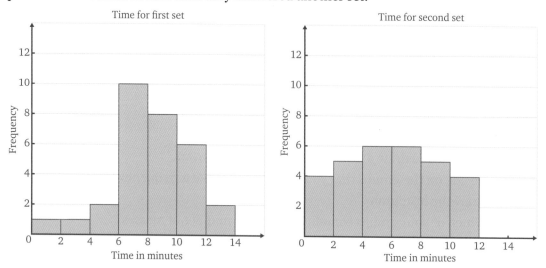

These histograms illustrate the times taken by the students in Class 8G to answer each set of multiple choice questions.

a Give two ways in which these distributions are different.

b Jenny looked at these two bar charts and said, 'Practice helped us to do the second set more quickly.' Is she right?
Can you think of another reason why the times taken for the second test were, on average, less than those for the first test?

c Khalil took 13 minutes to answer the first set of questions. Is it true to say that he took less than 13 minutes to answer the second set? Justify your answer.

d Sukei completed the first set in 8 minutes. What can you say, and why, about the time she took to complete the second set?

e Erol thought these times would be easier to compare if they were drawn on the same set of axes. He used a chart drawing program and came up with these two charts.

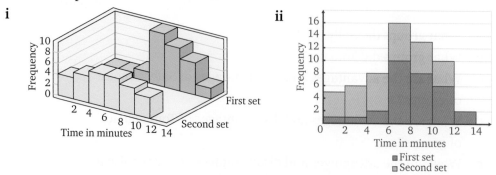

List some advantages and some disadvantages of each of these illustrations.

Exercise 16j

Select the letter that gives the correct answer.

1 The pie chart shows the pets owned by the families in a village.
The two pets that are almost equally popular are

  A a bird and a cat

  B a bird and a dog

  C a bird and a rabbit

  D a cat and a dog.

2 This pie chart shows the types of vehicles involved in road accidents in a city over a period of one month. The greatest number of accidents involved

  A buses

  B cars

  C trucks

  D motorcycles

Use the following data for questions **3** to **5**.

The number of letters in the first 20 words on a page from a novel were counted and gave the following numbers:

  2, 3, 8, 5, 4, 6, 7, 8, 8, 9

3 The mean number of letters per word is

  A 5   B 6   C 7   D 8

4 The median number of letters per word for this data is

  A 5   B $5\frac{1}{2}$ C $6\frac{1}{2}$ D 7

5 The modal number of letters per word is

  A 5   B 6   C 7   D 8

Use the following data for questions **6** to **9**.

This frequency table shows the number of goals scored by the teams in a football league one Saturday.

Number of goals	0	1	2	3	4	5
Frequency	12	15	4	6	2	1

6 How many teams were there in the league?

  A 18   B 20   C 22   D 40

7 The mean number of goals scored per team was

  A 1.35   B 1.65   C 2.2   D 2.8

8 The median value for the number of goals scored per team was

A 0   **B** 1   **C** 2   **D** 3

9 The modal number of goals scored per team was

A 1   **B** 2   **C** 3   **D** 4

Use this data for questions **10** to **12**.

In a competition 50 competitors received the scores shown in the frequency table.

Score	1	2	3	4	5	6
Frequency	3	8	16	13	9	1

10 The mean score is

A 3.4   **B** 3.6   **C** 3.8   **D** 3.9

11 The median score is

A 2   **B** 3   **C** 4   **D** 5

12 The modal score is

A 3   **B** 4   **C** 4.5   **D** 5

Use this histogram to answer questions **13** and **14**. It shows the time in minutes taken by the science students in a year group to complete a homework.

The time categories go from $0 \leq t < 10$ up to $60 \leq t < 70$.

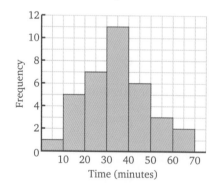

13 The number of students in the year group is

A 32   **B** 34   **C** 35   **D** 37

14 How many more students spent less than 30 minutes compared with the number who spent who spent 50 minutes or more?

A 5   **B** 6   **C** 7   **D** 8

Investigation

1   Count the number of letters in the surname of each of the teachers in your school.

Enter this information in a frequency table like this.

Number of letters in surname	3	4	5	6	7	8		
Frequency								

You do not have to start your table with 3. Start with the number of letters in the shortest surname. Go up as far as you need to.

2   Now find, from these data

   a the mode   **b** the median   **c** the mean.

3   Repeat this investigation for the students in your class. Compare the mode, median and mean for your class with that for the teachers. Are the values similar or quite different?

In this chapter you have seen that...

✔ the slices on a pie chart represent the fractions that the groups are of the total

✔ a line graph shows how a quantity changes over time

✔ you can draw a line graph by plotting the values of the quantity at given times and joining the points with straight lines

✔ you find the mean by adding all the values then dividing this sum by the number of values

✔ the mode is the value or values that occur most often, i.e. with the greatest frequency

✔ the median is the middle value after a set of values has been arranged in order of size; when there are two middle values the median is halfway between them.

REVIEW TEST 3: CHAPTERS 12–16

In questions **1** to **9**, choose the letter for the correct answer.

1   What percentage of 14 is 42?

   A $\frac{1}{3}\%$ B 3%   C $33\frac{1}{3}\%$ D 300%

2   $\frac{4}{25}$ as a percentage is

   A 0.16%   B 4%   C 16%   D 160%

3   In a sale, all marked prices are reduced by 10%. The sale price of goods marked $250 is

   A $25   B $125   C $225   D $240

4   The perimeter of a square is 24 cm. Its area is

   A 24 cm²   B 36 cm²   C 48 cm²   D 96 cm²

Use this diagram to answer questions **5** to **7**.

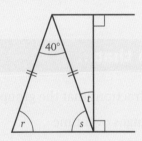

5   The measure of the angle *r* in degrees is

   A 40   B 50   C 60   D 70

6   The measure of the angle *s* in degrees is

   A 40   B 50   C 60   D 70

7   The measure of the angle *t* in degrees is

   A 20   B 30   C 40   D 90

8   The median of the numbers 2, 4, 6, 7 is

   A $4\frac{1}{2}$ B 4.75   C 5   D 6

9   A pie chart shows the age distribution of persons in Caricom countries. Twenty-five per cent of the people are in the age range 'over 60 years'. What is the size of the angle representing this group?

   A 25°   B 60°   C 75°   D 90°

10   a   Which ratio is the larger 7 : 5 or 12 : 7?

     b   Which ratio is the smaller $\frac{5}{8}$ or $\frac{7}{12}$?

     c   Divide $480 between two people in the ratio 3 : 7.

     d   What is the map ratio if 1 cm on the map represents 500 m?

11   It takes Ho Chan 45 minutes to walk 5 km.

     a   At the same rate, how long would it take him to walk 7 km?

     b   How far would he walk in 3 hours?

12   a   If a number is increased by 30% what percentage is the new number
         of the original number?

     b   If a number is decreased by 25% what percentage is the new number
         of the original number?

     c   Increase 135 by $66\frac{2}{3}$%.

     d   Decrease 366 by $33\frac{1}{3}$%.

13   A jug contains a mixture of fruit syrup and water in the ratio 1 : 5.
     How much syrup is there in a jug containing 3 litres of mixture?

14   a   The cost of my meal is $64 plus a service tax of 15%.
         How much does my meal cost me?

     b   The number of people employed at Tompson Bros is 12% fewer than
         this time last year. Last year there were 350 employees. How many
         are there this year?

15   The cost price of a car is $128 000. If bought on hire-purchase a deposit
     of $13 000 is required, followed by a monthly payment of $4695 for
     3 years.
     Find   a   the total HP price   b   the amount saved by paying cash.

16   Tommy Owen starts work each day at 7.30 a.m. and finishes at 4.15 p.m.
     He has an unpaid 45-minute lunch break.

     a   How many hours does he work in a normal 5-day week?

     b   Find his gross weekly wage if he is paid $12.40 per hour.

17 Sally Humble receives a basic weekly wage of $200. In addition she is paid 4% commission on the value of the goods she sells. Find her total income in a week when she sells goods to the value of $42 300.

18 a How many units (kilowatt-hours) will a 2 kW electric fire use in 5 hours?

b How long would a 50 W light bulb run on 1 unit of electricity?

c At 12 c per unit how much would it cost to run a 2 W electric clock for a week?

19 a In the figure below calculate the sizes of the angles marked x, y and z.

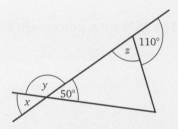

b A triangle ABC has three axes of symmetry. If AB = 6 cm, what are the lengths of BC and AC? What is the measure of the angle ABC? Explain your answers.

20 Find the angles marked with letters.

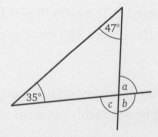

21 A worker digs a ditch with perpendicular sides. It is 1.05 m wide at the top and at the bottom. If it is 1.80 m deep and 21.6 m long, how many cubic metres of earth are removed? (Give your answer to 1 decimal place.)

22

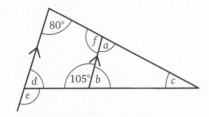

Find the size of each angle marked with a letter.

23 Construct a triangle ABC in which AB = 10 cm, angle BAC = 30° and angle ABC = 45°. Now construct CD, the perpendicular from C to AB. Measure and record the lengths of AC, BC and CD.

24 a Complete the following table showing the masses of students in a class.

Mass (kg)	Tally	Number
$40.5 \leqslant x < 45.5$	I	
$45.5 \leqslant x < 50.5$	III	
$50.5 \leqslant x < 55.5$	⊁⊁⊁ ⊁⊁⊁ I	11
$55.5 \leqslant x < 60.5$	⊁⊁⊁ IIII	
$60.5 \leqslant x < 65.5$	IIII	4
$65.5 \leqslant x < 70.5$	III	

b Draw a histogram showing this information.

25 The marks out of 20 in a maths test were
5, 7, 4, 15, 17, 12, 15, 13, 19, 20, 20, 15, 18, 4, 10, 11, 9, 17, 15, 8, 12, 14
Find
a the mean mark **b** the modal mark **c** the median mark.

✔ REVIEW TEST 4: CHAPTERS 1–16

Choose the letter for the correct answer.

1   The value of $-2 - (-4) + (-3)$ is

 A -9 B -7 C -1 D 5

2   The expression $3(4 - x) - (7 - x)$ simplifies to

 A $5 - 2x$ B $5 - 4x$ C $-2x$ D $5 + 2x$

3   The value of x that satisfies the equation $5 - 2x = 15 - 7x$ is

 A -2 B $\dfrac{1}{2}$ C 2 D $\dfrac{20}{9}$

4   The value of $7^4 \times 7^3 \div 7^6$ is

 A $\dfrac{1}{7}$ B 1 C 7 D 7^2

5   The angles marked p and q are

 A alternate

 B corresponding

 C supplementary

 D vertically opposite

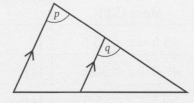

6

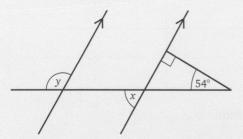

The values of x and y respectively are

 A $54°$ and $126°$ C $36°$ and $164°$

 B $36°$ and $144°$ D $54°$ and $146°$

7   The largest integer x such that $17 - x > 3x - 11$ is

 A 3 B 6 C 7 D 8

8   The map ratio of a map is $1 : 50\,000$. On the map the distance between
A and B is 2.5 cm. On the ground the distance between A and B, in
kilometres, is

 A 1.25 B 12.5 C 125 D 1250

9 Written in standard form, 450 000 000 is
   A 4.5×10^7 B 0.45×10^9 C 4.5×10^8 D 45×10^7

10 Correct to 3 significant figures, $0.034 93 \div 0.003 523 =$
   A 99.2   B 9.92   C 9.91   D 9.915

11 In a game, the score occurs with the frequency shown in the table.

Score	1	2	4	6	12
Frequency	12	6	3	2	1

   The mean score is
   A 1   B 2.5   C 11   D 12

12

x	1	3	3	5	5
y	1	0	2	0	6

   The table represents a relation. This type of relation is
   A one–one   B one–many   C many–one   D many–many

13 The equation of the straight line parallel to the y-axis passing through the point $(-3, 0)$ is
   A $x = 3$ B $x = -3$ C $y = 3$ D $y = -3$

14 The inverse of 4 under multiplication is
   A -4 B $-\frac{1}{4}$ C $\frac{1}{4}$ D $+4$

15 The lines $y = -3$ and $x = 2$ intersect at the point
   A $(-3, 2)$ B $(3, -2)$ C $(-2, 3)$ D $(2, -3)$

16 10% of 20 differs from 0.5 of 2 by
   A 1   B 2   C 4   D 5

17 $N = \{$positive integers from 2 to 15 inclusive$\}$.

Consider the following subsets of N:

$\qquad P = \{$prime numbers$)$

$\qquad Q = \{$numbers $\geqslant 10\}$

$\qquad R = \{$odd numbers $< 15\}$

$\qquad S = \{$multiples of 3$\}$

The set with the smallest number of members is

A P **B** Q **C** R **D** S

18 The equations of four straight lines are $y = 2x$, $y = -\dfrac{3x}{2}$, $y = -3x$ and $y = \dfrac{1}{2}x$.

The line that makes the smallest angle with the x-axis is

A $y = -3x$ **B** $y = -\dfrac{3x}{2}$ **C** $y = \dfrac{1}{2}x$ **D** $y = 2x$

19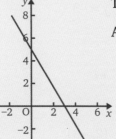

The area of this shape is

A $46\,\text{cm}^2$

B $94\,\text{cm}^2$

C $102\,\text{cm}^2$

D $80\,\text{cm}^2$

20 The gradient of this straight line is

A $-\dfrac{5}{3}$ **B** $-\dfrac{3}{5}$ **C** $\dfrac{3}{5}$ **D** $\dfrac{5}{3}$

21 The largest of the four fractions $\dfrac{21}{32}$, $\dfrac{32}{43}$, $\dfrac{43}{51}$ and $\dfrac{51}{72}$ is

A $\dfrac{21}{32}$ **B** $\dfrac{32}{43}$ **C** $\dfrac{43}{51}$ **D** $\dfrac{51}{72}$

22 The value of x that satisfies the equation $5x - 4 = 2(x + 7)$ is

A 6   **B** 4   **C** 3   **D** 2

Use this diagram for questions **23** and **24**.

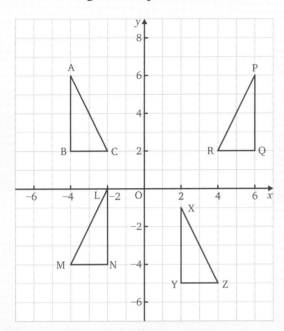

23 The vector that describes the translation of triangle ABC to triangle XYZ is

    A $\begin{pmatrix} 6 \\ 7 \end{pmatrix}$ **B** $\begin{pmatrix} 6 \\ -7 \end{pmatrix}$ **C** $\begin{pmatrix} -6 \\ 7 \end{pmatrix}$ **D** $\begin{pmatrix} -6 \\ -7 \end{pmatrix}$

24 The equation of the mirror line, given that triangle PQR is the reflection of triangle ABC, is

    A $x = 0$ **B** $x = 1$ **C** $x = 1\frac{1}{2}$ **D** $x = 2$

25 $R = \{$equilateral triangles$\}$ and $I = \{$isosceles triangles$\}$
    The diagram illustrating R and I is

A 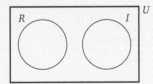   **C**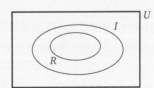

B 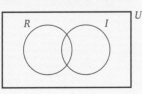   **D**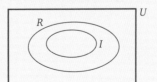

26 $P = \{1, 2. 3, \ldots 10\}$. In the set P, the largest odd number exceeds the largest prime number by

 A 0   B 1   C 2   D 3

27 Which one of the following statements defines an infinite set?
 A Vehicles that carry passengers.
 B Sixth form students who can sing well.
 C The fifth form students of a certain school.
 D Plane figures bounded by three or more straight lines.

28 Before a sale a store owner raises the price of an item by 10%. In the sale he offers a 10% discount. The cost of the item in the sale is
 A the same as before he raised the price
 B less than before he raised the price
 C more than before he raised the price.

29 The median of the set of numbers 6, 1, 2, 3, 7 and 5 is
 A 2   B 2.5   C 3   D 4

30 The square of 0.07 is
 A 0.49   B 0.049   C 0.0049   D 0.00049

31 Given that $2(x + 3) = 9$, x is
 A $1\frac{1}{2}$ B 3   C 6   D $7\frac{1}{2}$

32 The statement $9 \times (4 - 3) = 9 \times 4 - 9 \times 3$ is an example of
 A the associative law   C the distributive law
 B the commutative law   D none of these

33 A salesman is given commission of 5% of the amount by which his weekly sales exceed $1000. His sales in a certain week are $3500. His commission is
 A $20   B $125   C $175   D $50

34 Quadrants of radius 1 cm are cut from each corner of the square ABCD to leave the figure shaded in the diagram on the right.

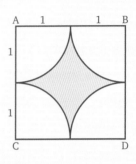

The area of the shaded region, in cm², is

A $4-\pi$ B $1-2\pi$ C $8-2\pi$ D $4-2\pi$

35 The range of values for which the inequalities $-3-x<2x+3\leqslant9$ are true is

A $2<x\leqslant3$ B $0\leqslant x<3$ C $-2<x\leqslant3$ D $-6<x\leqslant3$

36 The domain of the relation $\{(1,2),(1,3),(2,2)\}$ is

A $\{1,3\}$ B $\{1,2,3\}$ C $\{2,3\}$ D $\{1,2\}$

37 The set of inequalities that describe the unshaded region are

A $x\geqslant-2, x<3, y\leqslant2$

B $x>-2, x<3, y<2$

C $x>2, x\leqslant3, y<2$

D $x\geqslant-2, x<3, y\leqslant2$

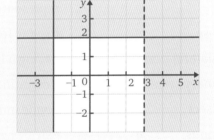

38 160 miles in kilometres is about

A $320\,\text{km}$ B $256\,\text{km}$ C $240\,\text{km}$ D $100\,\text{km}$

39 I think of a number, double it, and add 3. The result is 13. The number I first thought of was

A 5   B 6   C 7   D 8

40 The vector that translates ABC to DEF is

A $\begin{pmatrix} -6 \\ 3 \end{pmatrix}$ C $\begin{pmatrix} 6 \\ -3 \end{pmatrix}$

B $\begin{pmatrix} -6 \\ -3 \end{pmatrix}$ D $\begin{pmatrix} 6 \\ 3 \end{pmatrix}$

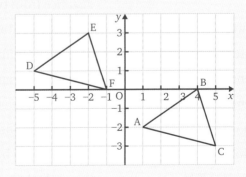

Glossary

acute angle	an angle less than 90°
alternate angles	equal angles on opposite sides of a transversal, e.g.
angles at a point	a group of angles round a point that make a complete revolution. e.g.
angles on a straight line	a group of angles that together make a straight line, e.g.
annulus	area between two concentric circles
approximation	an estimate of the value of a calculation or quantity
area	the amount of surface covered
arc	part of a curve
arithmetic average	the sum of a set of values divided by the number of values
associative law	this says that for the same operation brackets can be removed without changing the result, e.g. $2 + (3 + 4)) = (2 + 3) + 4 = 2 + 3 + 4$
average speed	the total distance travelled divided by the total time taken
bar chart	a diagram of bars; each represents a quantity. The height of the bar represents the number (frequency) of that quantity
base	the line from which the perpendicular height of a plane figure is measured
bilateral symmetry	having a line of symmetry that divides an object into two equal halves
binary system	a counting system based on 2
bisect	divide into two equal parts
bonus	extra wages that employees are paid
boundary line	a line showing the edge of an area or region
breadth	a measure of length
capacity	capacity
Cartesian cordinates	they give the position of a point in two-dimensions by stating its shortest distance from two fixed reference lines at right angles to each other.
Cartesian plane	the plane containing the x and y axes
categorical data	data about different categories such as eye colour or types of cars
centimetre	a metric measure of length
centre (of a circle)	the point that is the same distance from any point on the circumference
chord	the straight line joining two points on a curve
circle	a curve made by moving one point at a fixed distance from another
circumcircle	the circle that passes through the vertices of a plane figure
circumference	the edge of a circle

closure	a set is closed under an operation such as addition where the result is always a member of the set
commission	pay earned by successful selling
common factor	a number that divides exactly into two or more other numbers
commutative law	the law that says that order does not matter in an operation, e.g. $7 \times 6 = 6 \times 7$
complement of a set A	the set of members not in A
complementary angles	angles that add up to $90°$
composite number	a number that can be written as the product of two or more prime numbers
cone	a pyramid with a circular base
construction	drawing a figure exactly
continuous data	data that cannot be measured exactly but lies within a range of values
coordinates	an ordered pair of numbers giving the position of a point on a grid
corresponding angles	equal angles on the same side of a transversal, e.g.
cross-section	the shape formed by a plane cutting a solid
cube	a solid with six faces, each of which is a square, e.g.
cubic unit	a measure of volume
cuboid	a solid with six faces, each of which is a rectangle, e.g.
currency	the money used by a country
cylinder	a prism with a uniform circular cross-section
data	a collection of facts
decimal	a fraction expressed by numbers on the right of a point, e.g. 0.2
decimal place	the position of a figure after the decimal point
degree	unit of measure for an angle or for temperature
denary system	a counting system based on 10
denominator	the bottom of a fraction
deposit	an initial payment to secure a purchase
diagonal	a line from one corner to another in a figure
diameter	a line across a circle going through the centre
difference	the value of the larger number minus the smaller number
digit	one of the figures 0, 1, 2, 3, 4, 5, 6, 7, 8, 9
dimension	a measurable length in an object
directed numbers	positive and negative numbers collectively
disc	a thin circular solid

discount	reduction in the cost of an article
discrete data	separate or distinct
disjoint sets	sets that have no common elements
displacement	the distance and direction of an object from some fixed point
distance-time graph	a graph showing the relation between the distance travelled in a given time
distributive law	the law that says that one operation can be distributed over another, e.g. $3 \times (4 + 5) = 3 \times 4 + 3 \times 5$
domain	the set of the first objects in the set of the ordered pairs of a relation
element	a member of a set
empty set	a set with no members
equal set	two sets with identical members
equation	two expressions connected by an equals sign
equivalent fraction	measures the same part of a quantity
equilateral triangle	a triangle whose sides are all the same length
estimate	an approximate value
exchange rate	the number of units of one currency equal to one unit of another
expression	a collection of algebraic terms connected with plus and minus signs, without an equals sign
exterior angle	the angle between the extension of one side of a polygon and another side, e.g.
factor	a number or letter that divides exactly into another number or algebraic term
finite set	a set whose members are limited in number
foot	an imperial measure of length
formula	a general rule for expressing one quantity in terms of other quantities
fraction	part of a quantity
frequency	the number of times that a value occurs
frequency table	a table listing the number of each quantity
gallon	an imperial unit of capacity
gradient	a measure of the slope of a line
gram	a metric measure of mass
gross and net wages	gross is the amount before any deductions, net is the amount after deductions

hexagon	a plane figure bounded by six straight line segments
highest common factor	the largest number that divides exactly into two or more other numbers
hire-purchase	paying a deposit to hire an article and the balance in instalments after which it becomes yours
histogram	a bar chart used for continuous data where the bars touch on a number line
horizontal	parallel to the surface of the earth
hundredweight	an imperial measure of mass
hypotenuse	the longest side in a right-angled triangle
identity element	a number that preserves the identity of a given number under an operation
image	the resulting shape after a transformation of an object
improper fraction	a fraction whose numerator is larger than its denominator
inch	an imperial measure of length
incircle	the circle inside a shape that touches all its sides
income tax	a tax due on income levied by the government
index (pl. indices)	a superscript to a number that tells you how many of those numbers are multiplied together
inequality	the relationship between two quantities that are not equal
intercept	the distance from the origin to where a line crosses an axis
infinite set	a set with an unlimited number of members
integer	a whole number
interior angles	angles between a transversal and two parallel lines that add to $180°$, e.g.
intersection of sets	the set of elements common to two or more sets
interval data	data that has a clear interval between them
invariant	a line or point that does not change under a transformation
inverse	the reverse of an operation
isosceles triangle	a triangle with two equal sides
kilogram	a metric measure of mass
kilometre	a metric measure of length
kilowatt-hour	a unit of energy
like terms	terms that contain the same combination of letters, e.g. $3xy^2$ and $7xy^2$ but not xy^2 and xy
line of symmetry	a line that divides a figure into two identical shapes

line segment	a line with a beginning and an end
litre	a measure of capacity
lowest common multiple	the lowest number that two or more other numbers divide into
magnitude	the size of a quantity
map ratio	the ratio between the distance of two points on a map and the corresponding two points on the ground
mapping	describes the relation of the first and second elements in an ordered pair
mass	the quantity of matter in an object
mean	the sum of a set of values divided by the number of values
median	the middle item of a set of items arranged in order of size
member	an item that belongs to a set of items
metre	a metric measure of length
midpoint	halfway between the two given points on a straight line
mile	an imperial measure of length
milligram	a metric measure of mass
millilitre	a metric measure of capacity
millimetre	a metric measure of length
mirror line	the line in which an object is reflected to give its image
mixed number	the sum of a whole number and a fraction
mixed operations	a calculation involving two or more of addition, subtraction, multiplication and division
mode	the most frequent item in a set
multiple	a particular number multiplied by any other number is a multiple of that particular number
multiplying factor	a number that multiplies to increase or decrease a quantity
natural number	a counting number, i.e. 1, 2, 3, 4,...
negative number	all the real numbers which are less than zero
net	a flat shape that can be folded to make a polyhedron
net pay	pay received after deductions for tax and other purposes
nominal data	categorical data that could be put in any order
null set	a set with no members
number base	the number of distinct digits, including zero, used to represent numbers, e.g. numbers to base five use the digits 0, 1, 2, 3 and 4

number line	a line on which numbers can be marked to show their relative size
number pair	a pair of numbers in a particular order, e.g. the coordinates of a point
number pattern	a pattern of numbers with a rule for getting the next number in the pattern
numerator	the top number of a fraction
numerical data	data that can be counted or measured
object	the original shape before a transformation is performed
obtuse	an angle whose size is between 90° and 180°
octagon	a plane figure bounded by eight straight line segments
octahedron	a solid with eight faces
order of rotation	the number of different positions in which an object looks the same when rotated about a fixed point
ordered pair	a pair of objects in a defined order
ordinal	the natural numbers used to describe the position of an object in a set
origin	the point where the x-axis and y-axis cross
pair of compasses	an instrument used for drawing circles or parts of circles
parallel	two lines that are always the same distance apart
parallelogram	a four-sided figure whose opposite sides are parallel
pentagon	a plane figure bounded by five straight line segments
perpendicular bisector	a line that bisects a given line segment at right angles
percentage	out of a hundred
perimeter	the total distance round the edge of a figure
perpendicular	at right angles to a line or surface
pi (π)	the ratio of the circumference of a circle to its diameter
pie chart	a circle divided into slices where each slice shows the fraction that one category is of the whole information
place value	the position of a digit in a number that shows its value
plane figure	a closed shape made by lines drawn on a surface
polygon	a plane figure drawn with three or more straight lines
polyhedron	a solid with many plane faces
pound	a measure of mass or the currency of the UK
prime number	a number whose only factors are 1 and itself (1 is not a prime number)
prism	a solid whose cross-section is the same everywhere along its length
product	the result of multiplying two or more numbers together

proper subset	a subset that is not the whole set
proper fraction	a fraction whose numerator is less than its denominator
proportion	the ratio of one quantity to the other
protractor	an instrument for measuring angles
pyramid	a solid with a polygon as a base and triangular sides that meet at a common point
quadrant	a quarter of a circle
quadrilateral	a plane figure bounded by four straight lines
radius	the distance from the centre of a circle to the edge
range of a relation	the set of the second objects in the ordered pairs in a relation
ratio	the comparison between the sizes of two quantities
ratio data	data where there is no zero
rectangle	a four sided figure whose angles are each 90°
rectilinear solid	a solid whose edges are straight lines and faces are flat
reflection	a transformation in which any two corresponding points in the object and the image are both the same distance from a fixed straight line
reflex angle	an angle whose size is between 180° and 360°
regular polygon	a polygon which has all angles equal and all sides of equal length
relation	a set of ordered pairs
remainder	the amount left over when one number is divided by another
representative fraction	the scale of a map
right angle	one quarter or a revolution (90°)
rotational symmetry	a figure has rotational symmetry when it can be turned about a point to another position and still look the same
salary	an agreed amount of pay, usually for a year
scalar	a quantity that has size but not direction, e.g. speed
sector	part of a circle enclosed by two radii and an arc
semicircle	half a circle
set	a collection of items
significant figure	position of a figure in a number, e.g. in 2731 the third significant figure is 3
solution	the correct answer to a problem or equation
speed	the rate at which an object covers distance

square	a four-sided figure whose sides are all the same length and each of whose angles is a right angle
square unit	a measure of area
standard form	a number between 1 and 10 multiplied by a power of 10
standing charge	an initial charge made by a service company
subset	a set whose members are also members of another set
supplementary angles	two angles whose sum is 180°
symmetry	having congruent parts each side of a line or around a point
table of values	a table giving corresponding values to two or more variables
tetrahedron	a solid with four triangular plane faces
ton	an imperial measure of mass
tonne	a metric measure of mass
transformation	a change in position and/or size
translation	a movement in one direction
transversal	a line that crosses two or more parallel lines
trapezium	a four-sided figure with one pair of sides parallel
triangle	a plane figure bounded by three straight lines
uniform	everywhere the same
union	the set containing all the different elements of two or more sets
unit	a standard quantity used to measure, e.g. a metre, a litre, a square inch
universal set	a set that contains all the elements of the sets being considered
unlike terms	terms containing different combinations of letters
variable	a quantity that can vary in value
vector	a quantity that has size and direction e.g. velocity
Venn diagram	a diagram used to show the elements in two or more sets
vertex (pl. vertices)	corner
vertically opposite	the pair of angles opposite each other where two lines cross
volume	a measure of space
x and y axes	two fixed lines Cartesian coordinates at right angles to each other
yard	a imperial measure of length

Answers

CHAPTER 1

Exercise 1a   page 2

1 -6

2 6

3 5

4 $\frac{1}{2}$

5 -72

6 2

7 84

8 $3\frac{1}{3}$

9 3

10 $-\frac{1}{3}$

11 $-1\frac{2}{3}$

12 $105\frac{1}{4}$

Exercise 1b   page 3

1 associative for multiplication
2 associative for addition
3 commutative
4 distributive
5 commutative
6 associative for multiplication
7 distributive
8 distributive
9 commutative
10 distributive

Exercise 1c   page 4

1 identity for addition
2 identity for multiplication
3 inverse of 10 under addition
4 -9
5 divide by 9
6 $+5$
7 A
8 C
9 B
10 A
11 A
12 D
13 C
14 A

15 **a** true   **d** true   **g** true
    b false   **e** sometimes
    c true   **f** usually false

Exercise 1d   page 7

1 **a** 0.75   **c** 0.3   **e** 0.875
    b 0.6   **d** 0.15   **f** 0.24

2 0.47

3 **a** $\frac{3}{50}$ **b** $\frac{1}{250}$ **c** $15\frac{1}{2}$ **d** $2\frac{1}{100}$ **e** $3\frac{1}{4}$

4 $\frac{43}{50}$

5 $\frac{1}{20}$

6 **a** 30%   **c** 70%   **e** 92.5%
    b 20%   **d** 3.5%

7 **a** 132%   **c** 240%   **e** 255.5%
    b 150%   **d** 105%

8 **a** 0.45   **c** 0.95   **e** 0.125
    b 0.6   **d** 0.055

9 **a** $\frac{2}{5}$ **b** $\frac{13}{20}$ **c** $\frac{27}{50}$ **d** $\frac{1}{4}$

10 **a** 40% **b** 15% **c** 42% **d** 37.5%

11 $\frac{3}{5}$ 13 $\frac{19}{20}$ 15 85%   17 60%

12 $\frac{7}{20}$ 14 $\frac{8}{25}$ 16 34%   18 12.5%

19

Fraction	Percentage	Decimal
$\frac{3}{5}$	60%	0.6
$\frac{4}{5}$	80%	0.8
$\frac{3}{4}$	75%	0.75
$\frac{7}{10}$	70%	0.7
$\frac{11}{20}$	55%	0.55
$\frac{11}{25}$	44%	0.44

20 **a** $\frac{1}{20}$ **b** 5%

21 **a** 42%   **b** 0.42

22 **a** $\frac{7}{25}$ **b** 60%   **c** 12%

23 **a** $\frac{3}{5}$ **b i** 35% **ii** 95%   **c** 0.05

Exercise 1e   page 9

1 9   7 128   13 7200   19 46.3
2 4   8 10   14 893   20 503.2
3 100   9 64   15 65 000   21 709
4 125   10 10 000   16 3820   22 69.78
5 1000   11 1 000 000   17 27.5
6 81   12 27   18 537 000

Exercise 1f   page 10

1 3^7 4 2^{11} 7 12^9 10 r^8
2 7^8 5 b^5 8 p^{14}
3 9^{10} 6 5^8 9 4^{16}

Exercise 1g   page 10

1 4^2 6 15^4 11 6^{11} 16 2^9
2 7^6 7 6^5 12 3^3 17 4^1
3 5^1 8 b^2 13 2^1 18 a^1
4 10^5 9 9^1 14 a^{12} 19 3^8
5 q^4 10 p^1 15 c^3 20 b^9

Exercise 1h   page 11

1 4   5 4   9 783.4   13 3^6
2 64   6 2410   10 30 500   14 a^7
3 125   7 497.1   11 2^7 15 a^4
4 81   8 59 200   12 4^3

Exercise 1i   page 12

1 3780   6 3 670 000
2 1260   7 30 400
3 5 300 000   8 85 030
4 740 000 000 000 000   9 4 250 000 000 000
5 13 000   10 643 000 000

Exercise 1j   page 13

1	2.5×10^3	12	5.47×10^5	23	4.05×10^1
2	6.3×10^2	13	3.06×10^4	24	5.03×10^8
3	1.53×10^4	14	4.06×10^6	25	9.9×10^7
4	2.6×10^5	15	7.04×10^2	26	8.4×10^1
5	9.9×10^3	16	7.93×10^1	27	3.51×10^2
6	3.907×10^4	17	8.06×10^4	28	3.6×10^1
7	4.5×10^6	18	6.05×10^1	29	5.09×10^3
8	5.3×10^8	19	7.08×10^6	30	2.68×10^5
9	4×10^4	20	5.608×10^5	31	3.07×10^1
10	8×10^{10}	21	5.3×10^{12}		
11	2.603×10^4	22	7.08×10^5		

Exercise 1k   page 14

1	1550, 1500, 2000	10	6010, 6000, 6000
2	8740, 8700, 9000	11	4980, 5000, 5000
3	2750, 2800, 3000	12	8700, 8700, 9000
4	36 840, 36 800, 37 000	13	54, 45
5	68 410, 68 400, 68 000	14	45 499, 44 500
6	5730, 5700, 6000	15	1549, 1450
7	4070, 4100, 4000	16	$2 500 000
8	7510, 7500, 8000	17	1950
9	53 800, 53 800, 54 000		

Exercise 1l   page 16

1	2.76, 2.8, 3	9	6.90, 6.9, 7
2	7.37, 7.4, 7	10	55.58, 55.6, 56
3	16.99, 17.0, 17	11	5.1
4	23.76, 23.8, 24	12	0.009
5	9.86, 9.9, 10	13	7.90
6	3.90, 3.9, 4	14	34.8
7	8.94, 8.9, 9	15	0.0078
8	73.65, 73.6, 74	16	0.975
17	5.551	19	6.7
18	285.6	20	10.00

Exercise 1m   page 17

1	3	5	7	9	0
2	8	6	8	10	8
3	6	7	0		
4	8	8	0		

Exercise 1n   page 18

1	60 000	19	73 000	37	600 000
2	4000	20	440	38	500
3	4 000 000	21	50 000	39	7.82
4	600 000	22	54 000	40	5000
6	80 000	23	480	41	37.9
6	500	24	600	42	7000
7	50 000	25	0.00846	43	0.0709
8	4000	26	0.826	44	0.07
9	700 000	27	5.84	45	3.3
10	900	28	78.5	46	1.7
11	30	29	46.8	47	13
12	1000	30	0.00785	48	13
13	4700	31	7.51	49	14
14	57 000	32	370	50	29
15	60 000	33	0.990	51	24
16	890 000	34	54.0	52	0.23
17	7000	35	47	53	0.026
18	10 000	36	0.006845	54	0.00043

Exercise 1p   page 19

1	100	11	600	21	10
2	36	12	4.5	22	0.36
3	0.014	13	2	23	10
4	20	14	0.7	24	2
6	180 000	15	17	25	32
6	0.8	16	0.003	26	1.2
7	0.48	17	0.0056	27	15
8	3.6	18	80	28	0.25
9	1.3	19	90 000	29	0.12
10	3 500 000	20	1.5	30	140

Exercise 1q   page 21

1	7.08	26	36.8	51	49.0
2	7.55	27	1950	52	11 200
3	7.02	28	38.0	53	83.6
4	8.54	29	1350	54	2.28
6	9.19	30	14 400	55	0.672
6	7.71	31	2.70	56	9.83
7	7.49	32	0.0196	57	0.693
8	9.15	33	0.0549	58	0.742
9	1.61	34	526	59	0.128
10	1.56	35	4.65	60	10 300
11	3.80	36	0.0481	61	6340
12	1.50	37	1.79	62	0.00608
13	2.94	38	0.005 15	63	34.8
14	1.54	39	3.97	64	484 000
16	1.44	40	0.548	65	0.361
16	1330	41	0.121	66	0.0203
17	8370	42	0.0825	67	0.000 123
18	6580	43	0.393	68	631
19	15.5	44	0.103	69	0.000 000 0961
20	6.65	45	0.139	70	4950
21	172	46	124	71	0.174
22	14.7	47	55.8	72.	16.7
23	11.2	48	91.7	73	0.000 146
24	1170	49	186	74	13.4
25	12 600	50	957		

Exercise 1r   page 22

1	64	4	3.64×10^4	7	3.71
2	b^3	5	60 000	8	2.88
3	1	6	0.0614		

Exercise 1s   page 22

1	216	6	46 000
2	2^3	7	7500
3	5^3	8	1350
4	a^7	9	0.699
5	6.5×10^8	10	a $\frac{7}{20}$ b 0.35

Exercise 1t   page 23

1	$5^5 = 3125$	6	0.0508
2	a^3	7	9
3	1	8	9.89
4	7.826×10^4	9	4.70
5	10 000	10	a 62.5% b 0.625

Exercise 1u   page 23

1	B	5	C	9	B	13	A
2	A	6	A	10	C	14	B
3	B	7	C	11	B		
4	C	8	D	12	D		

CHAPTER 2

Exercise 2a   page 28

1 213_5 **2** 2014_5 **3** 41240_5 **4** 30201_5

	5^3	5^2	5	Units
5			3	1
6			4	2
7		4	1	0
8		2	3	1
9			3	4
10			1	0
11		2	0	4
12		4	0	0

13 16_{10} **19** 17_{10} **25** 13_5 **31** 12_5
14 14_{10} **20** 10_{10} **26** 23_5 **32** 41_5
15 20_{10} **21** 4_{10} **27** 20_5 **33** 110_5
16 36_{10} **22** 100_{10} **28** 124_5 **34** 1003_5
17 54_{10} **23** 70_{10} **29** 133_5 **35** 312_5
18 23_{10} **24** 75_{10} **30** 1100_5 **36** 400_5

Exercise 2b   page 30

1 a

4	1
2	3

b 11_{10}

2 a

7	1
1	5

b 12_{10}

3 a

4^2	4	1
1	3	1

b 29_{10}

4 a

2^2	2	1
1	0	1

b 5_{10}

5 a

8	1
5	7

b 47_{10}

6 a

5^2	5	1
2	0	4

b 54_{10}

7 a

3^2	3	1
2	1	0

b 21_{10}

8 a

9^2	9	1
5	7	4

b 472_{10}

9 a

	3	1
	2	1

b 7_{10}

10 a

9	1
1	8

b 17_{10}

11 a

6	1
2	4

b 16_{10}

12 a

8^2	8	1
1	7	5

b 125_{10}

13 a

4^2	4	1
3	0	3

b 51_{10}

14 a

2^3	2^2	2	1
1	0	0	1

b 9_{10}

15 a

3^3	3^2	3	1
1	2	1	1

b 49_{10}

16 a

6^3	6^2	6	1
1	0	0	0

b 216_{10}

17 21_4 **28** 1001_3 **39** 1100011_2
18 22_5 **29** 110_7 **40** 1102_7
19 33_7 **30** 108_9 **41** 131_4
20 111_2 **31** 101101_2 **42** 15_6
21 23_5 **32** 110100_3 **43** 1111_2
22 52_6 **33** 243_8 **44** 11100_3
23 65_8 **34** 22000_4 **45** 11302_4
24 100_7 **35** 10001110_2 **46** 234_5
25 22_3 **36** 422_6 **47** 33_8
26 23_6 **37** 111_6 **48** 102122_3
27 37_9 **38** 210_5 **49** 310_8

Exercise 2c   page 32

1 43_5 **19** 3_4 **37** 32_6
2 20_3 **20** 35_7 **38** 31_5
3 30_4 **21** 202_3 **39** 105_7
4 11_2 **22** 11_5 **40** 180_9
5 103_6 **23** 226_8 **41** 330_4
6 102_3 **24** 1_2 **42** 4105_6
7 115_8 **25** 133_4 **43** 1111_3
8 1000_2 **26** 56_7 **44** 1032_5
9 122_5 **27** 33_6 **45** 414_7
10 333_4 **28** 10_2 **46** 130_4
11 1151_6 **29** 51_6 **47** 242_5
12 10100_2 **30** 101_2 **48** 105_7
13 1000_3 **31** 646_8 **49** 1015_6
14 1000_4 **32** 101_3 **50** 123_4
15 1030_7 **33** 22_5 **51** 143_5
16 100001_2 **34** 12_4 **52** 560_8
17 125_6 **35** 101_3 **53** 2_3
18 101_3 **36** 120_4 **54** 214_8

Exercise 2d   page 34

1 10221_4
2 22022_5
3 1110101_2
4 2422_8
5 2011210_3
6 2116_8
7 222142_5
8 220041_7
9 a 2254_8 **c** 1196_{10}
   b 52, 23   **d** 2254_8
10 a 31026_9 **c** 20436
   b 393, 52   **d** 31026_9
11 3047_8

Exercise 2e   page 35

1 13, 11, 25, 4, 12, 29

2 a

+	0	1
0	0	1
1	1	10

b 10010000_2

3 a 6   **b** 101_2

4

×	0	1
0	0	0
1	0	1

Exercise 2f   page 36

1 a 12_3 **b** 22_3 **c** 110_3 **d** 1011_3

2 three

3

×	0	1	2
0	0	0	0
1	0	1	2
2	0	2	11

4 11_3

5 a 102_5 **b** 33_5 **c** 1103_5

6 $31_5 + \frac{2}{5}$ or 16.4_{10}

7 0

8 no

9 four, $5^3 = 1000_5$

10 eight, $3^7 = 10000000_3$

11 a 2, 3, 4, 5, 6, 7, 8

b i 11010_2 **ii** 1210_3 **iii** 1750_8

c The figures move one column to the left; i.e. the effect is the same as multiplying a denary number by ten.

12 6   **15** 7   **18** 5
13 4   **16** 5   **19** 6
14 3   **17** 9   **20** False

Exercise 2g   page 37

1 a 6   **b** 5   **c** 147
2 a 40_5 **b** 202_3 **c** 24_8
3 a 341_5 **b** 101_3 **c** 636_8
4 part **c**

Exercise 2h   page 38

1 B   **3** C   **5** C   **7** C   **9** B
2 D   **4** A   **6** B   **8** C   **10** B

CHAPTER 3

Exercise 3a   page 41

1 4   **5** 3   **9** 2
2 4   **6** 4   **10** 3
3 12   **7** 1
4 2   **8** 3

Exercise 3b   page 42

1 4   **7** 6   **14** 1
2 1   **8** 5   **15** 3
3 3   **9** 4   **16** 8
4 5   **10** 5   **17** −2
5 7   **13** 3   **18** 1
6 $-\frac{3}{4}$ **12** 4
    13 1

Exercise 3c   page 43

1 1   **15** 2   **29** 4
2 1   **16** 1   **30** 1
3 4   **17** 7   **31** $4\frac{1}{2}$
4 $1\frac{6}{7}$ **18** 2   **32** $1\frac{1}{2}$
5 6   **19** 5   **33** 2
6 2   **20** 1   **34** 1
7 $4\frac{1}{2}$ **21** $\frac{1}{2}$ **35** $\frac{2}{3}$
8 2   **22** 10   **36** 2
9 $\frac{1}{2}$ **23** 2   **37** 3
10 2   **24** 4   **38** 2
11 $1\frac{2}{3}$ **25** 2   **39** $5\frac{1}{2}$
12 2   **26** 1   **40** $\frac{4}{5}$
13 $1\frac{1}{5}$ **27** 1   **41** 1
14 3   **28** 1   **42** 2

Exercise 3d   page 45

1 $6x + 24$ **17** $28x + 27$ **33** 1
2 $6x + 3$ **18** $18x - 44$ **34** 2
3 $4x - 12$ **19** $4x + 25$ **35** $\frac{1}{2}$
4 $6x - 10$ **20** $-30x + 47$ **36** $1\frac{1}{2}$
5 $12 - 8x$ **21** $10x + 5$ **37** $1\frac{1}{4}$
6 $20x + 10$ **22** $-x + 12$ **38** 1
7 $6 - 9x$ **23** $17x - 33$ **39** −1
8 $35 - 28x$ **24** $-4x + 14$ **40** −4
9 $10x - 14$ **25** $-10x + 14$ **41** $1\frac{1}{2}$
10 $42 + 12x$ **26** $36x + 26$ **42** $-\frac{2}{3}$
11 $8x + 18$ **27** $-7x + 32$ **43** 3
12 $26x + 13$ **28** $x + 22$ **44** 1
13 $34x - 13$ **29** $21x - 19$ **45** 3
14 $8x + 4$ **30** $-6x + 2$ **46** $\frac{1}{2}$
15 $21x + 5$ **31** 2
16 $13x + 19$ **32** $1\frac{1}{2}$

Exercise 3e   page 46

1 −8   **9** 3   **18** $5x - 17$
2 15   **10** $-2x + 17$ **19** 1
3 −24   **11** $17x - 20$ **20** 3
4 −3   **12** $-15x - 30$ **21** 2
5 2   **13** $25 - 14x$ **22** 13
6 28   **14** $15x - 20$ **23** $\frac{13}{11}$
7 −4   **15** $-9x + 6$
8 $\frac{1}{3}$ **16** 2   **24** $\frac{13}{16}$
    17 $25x - 46$

Exercise 3f   page 48

1 $2l + 2w$ **12** $C = nx$
2 $2l + d$ **13** $L = l - d$
3 $3l$ **14** $p = 6l$
4 $5l$ **15** $A = 2l^2$
5 $2l + s + d$ **16** $N = S - T$
6 $W = x + y$
7 $P = 2l + 2b$ **17** $W = T + S$
8 $T = N + M$
9 $T = N - L$ **18** $S = N - L - R$
10 $A = l^2$ **19** $r = p - q$ or $r = q - p$
11 $N = 10n$ **20** $W = Kn$

21 $q = \frac{x}{5}$

22 $L = \frac{ny}{100}$

23 $A = 100lb$

24 $T = t + \frac{s}{60}$

Exercise 3g   page 50

1 10	**11** −1	**21** 15
2 100	**12** −12	**22** 200
3 30	**13** 5	**23** $3\frac{1}{3}$
4 2	**14** 33	
5 20	**15** 50	**24** 7
6 200	**16** 19	
7 24	**17** 16	**25** $1\frac{3}{4}$
8 15	**18** 2	**26** 0
9 25	**19** 105	
		27 $\frac{5}{24}$
10 $7\frac{1}{2}$	**20** $3\frac{1}{3}$	
		28 −3

Exercise 3h   page 52

1 a 48 **b** −18 **c** 6 **d** 5
2 a 4 **b** 20 **c** 8 **d** −12
3 a 52 **b** 20 **c** 96 **d** −4
4 a 15 **b** −1.1 **c** −15.9 **d** 0.38
5 $C = 50n$, 600 c or $6

6 $L = \frac{n}{2}$, $5

7 $P = 2a + 2b$, 70 cm
8 $P = 6x$, 6 cm
9 $P = L − Nr$, 5 m
10 $P = 3a$, 24 cm
11 $W = Na + p$, 45
12 $A = 2lw + 2lh + 2hw$, 6200 cm²

Exercise 3i   page 54

1 formula	**5** formula	**9** equation
2 equation	**6** expression	**10** formula
3 equation	**7** expression	**11** formula
4 expression	**8** equation	**12** expression

Exercise 3j   page 55

1 $2\frac{1}{2}$

2 $3\frac{1}{3}$

3 $6x − 24$

4 $5x − 8$
5 $P = 4l + f + g$
6 −3

Exercise 3k   page 55

1 $\frac{1}{3}$

2 $\frac{2}{3}$

3 $−8x + 10$

4 15
5 $N = a + b + c$
6 4

Exercise 3l   page 56

1 $\frac{1}{3}$

2 2
3 10

4 $P = 6a$
5 $12a − 21$
6 $p = 3$

Exercise 3m   page 56

1 C	**3** A	**5** B	**7** B	**9** D
2 C	**4** D	**6** B	**8** D	**10** D

CHAPTER 4

Exercise 4a   page 59

1 $a < 20$ where a is the number of library books a school can afford to buy.
2 $b < 100$ where b is the number of people who attended a rally.
3 $c > 20$ where c is the number of albums sold on the first day.
4 $d \geqslant 50$ where d is the number of cars that passed the school between 9 a.m. and 10 a.m.
5 $p \leqslant 50$ where p is the perimeter of a rectangle in cm.
6 $c < 5$ where c is the cost in dollars of making a widget.
7 $g \geqslant 3$ where g is the number of goats Ceejay owns.
8 $d > 50$ where d is the number of $1 coins in a bag.
9 $d \geqslant 250$ where d is the number of days it takes to build a bungalow.
10 $p > 5$ where p is the number of pens Victoria has in her school bag.
11 $r < 5$, where r is the number of rubbers Jesse has in his school bag.
12 $f \geqslant 50$, where f is the number of fireworks there are in a box.
13 $t \leqslant 10$, where t is the number of minutes a bus takes to get to school.
14 $n \leqslant 20$ where n is the number of $5 bills in a cash box.
15 $a \geqslant 6$ where a is Anna's age in years.

Exercise 4b   page 60

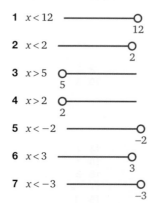

10 a 2, 3, 4, 6, 7   **d** 2, 3, 4, 6, 7
 b 2, 5, 7, 8, 9   **e** 2, 3, 4, 7, 9
 c 2, 3, 7, 9
12 a 5 > 3; yes   **c** −2 > −4; yes
 b 1 > −1; yes   **d** 7 > 5; yes
13 a 0 > −1; yes   **c** −7 > −8; yes
 b −4 > −5; yes   **d** 2 > 1; yes
14 a 1 < 6; yes   **c** −6 < −1; yes
 b −3 < 2; yes   **d** 3 < 8; yes

Exercise 4c   page 61

1 $x < 12$
2 $x < 2$
3 $x > 5$
4 $x > 2$
5 $x < −2$
6 $x < 3$
7 $x < −3$

8 $x < -7$ ———○ -7

9 $x < -5$ ———○ -5

10 $x < -2$ ———○ -2

11 $x > -1$ ○——— -1

12 $x < 3$ ———○ 3

13 $x > 0$ ○——— 0

14 $x > -3$ ○——— -3

15 $x < -3$ ———○ -3

16 $x < 1$ ———○ 1

17 $x > -2$ ○——— -2

18 $x < -5$ ———○ -5

19 $x < 5$ ———○ 5

20 $x < 1$ ———○ 1

21 $x < -1$ ———○ -1

22 $x > 0$ ○——— 0

23 $x > 7$ ○——— 7

24 $x > -5$ ○——— -5

25 $x > -3$ ○——— -3

26 $x < 13$ ———○ 13

27 $x > 12$ ○——— 12

28
a	$24 < 72$	c	$6 < 18$	e	$-24 < -72$
b	$3 < 9$	d	$2 < 6$	f	$-4 < -12$

a	yes	c	yes	e	no
b	yes	d	yes	f	no

29
a	$72 > -24$	c	$18 > -6$	e	$-72 > 24$
b	$9 > -3$	d	$6 > -2$	f	$-12 > 4$
c	$18 > -6$				

a	yes	c	yes	e	no
b	yes	d	yes	f	no

30
a	$-36 < -12$	c	$-9 < -3$	e	$36 < 12$
b	$-4\frac{1}{2} < -1\frac{1}{2}$	d	$-3 < -1$	f	$6 < 2$

a	yes	c	yes	e	no
b	yes	d	yes	f	no

32 Only when you are multiplying by a positive number.

Exercise 4d   page 63

1 ———○ $x < 3$ 3

2 ○——— $x > 1$ 1

3 ○——— $x > 2$ 2

4 ———○ $x < 1$ 1

5 ———○ $x < \frac{1}{2}$ $\frac{1}{2}$

6 ○——— $x > 1\frac{1}{3}$ $1\frac{1}{3}$

7 ———○ $x < 2\frac{1}{4}$ $2\frac{1}{4}$

8 ○——— $x > 1\frac{1}{2}$ $1\frac{1}{2}$

9 ———● $x \leqslant 1$ 1

10 ———● $x \leqslant 4$ 4

11 ●——— $x \geqslant -2$ -2

12 ●——— $x \geqslant 1$ 1

13 ———○ $x < -1$ -1

14 ———● $x \leqslant 2$ 2

15 ○——— $x > 1$ 1

16 ●——— $x \geqslant 1\frac{1}{3}$ $1\frac{1}{3}$

17 ●——— $x \geqslant 0$ 0

18 ———● $x \leqslant 1$ 1

19 ———○ $x < 1$ 1

20 ———○ $x < -3$ -3

21
a	$x > 3$	b	$2 \leqslant x \leqslant 3$	c	no values of x

22
a	$0 \leqslant x \leqslant 1$	b	$x \leqslant 0$	c	no values of x

23
a	$-2 < x \leqslant 4$	b	no values of x	c	$x < -2$

24
a	$-3 < x < -1$	b	$x < -3$	c	no values of x

25 $x < 12; x > -1; -1 < x < 12$

26 $x \leqslant -1; x \geqslant 3$; no values of x

27 $x \leqslant 7; x \geqslant -2; -2 \leqslant x \leqslant 7$

28 $x > 1; x < 2; 1 < x < 2$

29 $x > 2; x < 3; 2 < x < 3$

30 $x < 2; x > -1; -1 < x < 2$

31 $x \geqslant -1; x < 2; -1 \leqslant x < 2$

32 $x > \frac{1}{2}; x \leqslant 3; \frac{1}{2} < x \leqslant 3$

33 $2 < x < 5$

34 $-3 \leqslant x \leqslant 2$

35 $x < -2$

36 $0 < x < 2$

37 $x \geqslant 1$

38 $-4 < x < 2$

39 $x < -3$

40 $x < -1$

41 $1\frac{4}{5} < x < 3$

42 $\frac{1}{2} < x < 1$

Exercise 4e   page 66

1 $\{x \mid x > 12\}$
2 $\{x \mid x < 2\}$
3 $\{x \mid x \geqslant -2\}$
4 $\{x \mid x \leqslant 10\}$
5 $\{x \mid 2 < x < 6\}$
6 $\{x \mid -2 < x < 1\}$
7 $\{x \mid 3 \leqslant x < 5\}$
8 $\{x \mid 5 < x \leqslant 8\}$
9 $\{x \mid -3 \leqslant x \leqslant 0\}$
10 $\{x \mid 30 < x \leqslant 4\}$

11 ○──────── (5)
16 ○────────● (−2, 1)
12 ────────● (−1)
17 ●────────● (0, 3)
13 ────────● (4)
18 ●────────○ (−1, 0)
14 ●──────── (3)
19 ○────────● (−2, 2)
15 ●──────── (−1)
20 ○────────● (−2, −1)

Exercise 4f   page 66

1 D	3 D	5 A	7 D
2 A	4 C	6 A	8 C

CHAPTER 5

Exercise 5a   page 69

1 a {teachers in my school}
   b {books I have read}
3 a odd numbers up to 9
   b the days of the week from Monday to Friday
4 a {European countries}, France
   b {multiples of 10}, 60
5 John ∈ {boys' names}
6 English ∈ {school subjects}
7 June ∉ {days of the week}
8 Monday ∉ {domestic furniture}
9 false   10 true   11 true   12 true

Exercise 5b   page 70

1 infinite	7 6	13 no
2 infinite	8 21	14 yes
3 finite	9 11	15 yes
4 infinite	10 no	16 no
5 5	11 yes	
6 8	12 yes	

Exercise 5c   page 71

1 cutlery
2 whole numbers less than 50
3 whole numbers less than 25
4 $n(A) = 8, n(B) = 6$
   $B = \{3, 6, 9, 12, 15, 18\}$
5 $A = \{1, 2, 3, 4, 6, 12\}$ $B = \{2, 3, 5, 7, 11, 13\}$
   $C = \{6, 12\}$
6 $n(A) = 4, n(B) = 2, n(C) = 5$

Exercise 5d   page 72

1 {Joy, Anora}, {Joy, Tissha}, {Tissha, Anora}
2 $A = \{1, 3, 5, 7, 9, 11, 13, 15\}$,
   $B = \{2, 3, 5, 7, 11, 13\}, C = \{3, 6, 9, 12, 15\}$
   yes, 3, 5, 7, 11, 13

3 $B = \{6, 12, 18\}, C = \{2\}$,
   $D = \{13, 14, 15, 16, 17, 18, 19, 20\}$

Exercise 5e   page 74

1 your own answers
2 my friends who do not like coming to my school
3 my friends who like coming to my school
4 all pupils at my school except those who are not my friends and like coming to school
5 my friends who like coming to school and the pupils who are not my friends who do not like coming to school

Exercise 5f   page 75

1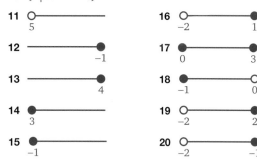

$A \cup B = \{\text{Janet, Jill, Jamila, Judith, Jacky}\}$

2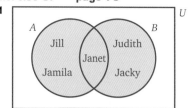

$X \cup Y = \{2, 4, 6, 8, 10, 12, 14, 16\}$

3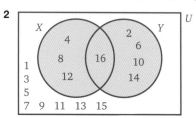

$P \cup Q = \{e, g, i, m, n, o, t, r, y\}$

4 a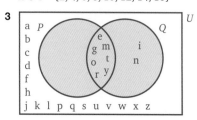

$A \cup B = \{\text{all parallelograms and trapeziums}\}$

   b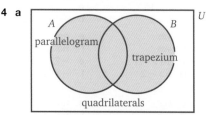

$P \cup Q = \{\text{angles that are either obtuse or reflex}\}$

5

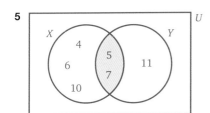

$X \cap Y = \{5, 7\}$

6

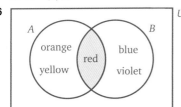

$A \cap B = \{\text{red}\}$

7

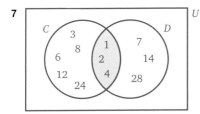

$C \cap D = \{1, 2, 4\}$

8

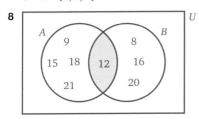

$A \cap B = \{12\}$

Exercise 5g   page 76

1 a Lenny, Sylvia
   b Adam, Richard
   c Jack, Scott, Lee
2 a David, Joe, Tariq, Paul
   b Tariq, Paul
   c Claude, Alan, Clive
3 a Emma, Majid, Clive, Sean, Ann
   b Emma, Majid, Clive
   c Sean, Ann

4

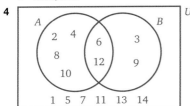

a 6, 12   **b** $n(A) = 6, n(B) = 4$

5

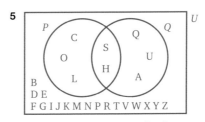

  a 5   **b** 8   **c** 2
6 a 26, 6, 6
   b

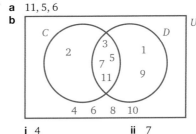

  c i 4   **ii** 8
7 a 11, 5, 6
   b

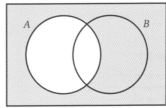

   i 4   **ii** 7
8 a 35, 8, 5
   b i 2   **ii** 11
9 10

Exercise 5h   page 80

1 {10, 20}
2 {5, 6, 11}
3 {b, c, d, f, g, h, j, k, l, m, n, p, q, r, s, t, v, w, x, y, z}
4 {a, e, i, o, u}
5 {Sunday, Tuesday, Thursday, Saturday}
6 {adults}
7 {non-British motor cars}
8 {female tennis players}
9 {Caribbean towns not in Jamaica}
10 {quadrilaterals that are not squares}
11 {adults aged 80 or younger}
12 {female doctors}
13 {all homes}
14 a $n(A) = 5, n(A') = 21$ **b** 26
15 a $n(X) = 5, n(X') = 5, U = \{a, b, c, d, e, f, g, h, i, j\}$ **b** 10
16 a

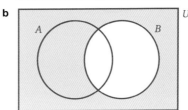

   b

17 a 6   **c** 8   **e** 12
   b 8   **d** 4   **f** 12; they are equal

18

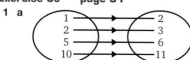

   a 3   **c** 13   **e** 15
   b 12   **d** 3   **f** 15; they are equal

Exercise 5i   page 83

1 a $3x + 9 = 33$ **b** $x = 8$; 8 in neither club
2 a $3x + 2 = 11$ **b** $x = 3$; $n(U) = 20$
3 a $n(A \cup B) = 6x + 12$, $n(A \cup B)' = x$
   b $7x + 12 = 40$
   c $x = 4$; $n(A \cap B) = 8$
4 a $n(P) = 10 - x$, $n(Q) = 8 - x$
   b $18 - x = 24$, $x = 6$ **c** 54
5 a $48 + x$ **c** $x = 12$; $n(B) = 12$
   b $48 + x = 60$
6 a $13 + 4x = 21$, $x = 2$ **b** $n(B) = 6$, $n(A \cap B)' = 6$

Exercise 5j   page 84

1 C   **3** D   **5** C   **7** B   **9** B
2 C   **4** D   **6** A   **8** A   **10** D

CHAPTER 6

Exercise 6a   page 89

1 The second number is one more than the first.
2 The second number is two more than the first.
3 The second number is the square of the first.
4 {(Maths, Spanish), (Science, Spanish), (Science, Maths)}
5 {(4, □), (5, ◠), (3, ▲)}
6 {(Tnd, Jma), (Bds, Jma), (St Lucia, Jma), (St Lucia, Tnd), (St Lucia, Bds)}
7 25, 8
8 7, 2, 17

Exercise 6b   page 90

1 {1, 2, 5, 10}, {2, 3, 6, 11}
2 a {a, b}, {b, c}   **b** {□, △, □}, {□, △}
3 {4, 16, 36}
4 a {(Dwayne, Fred), (Scott, Fred), (Scott, Dwayne)},
   b {Dwayne, Scott}, {Fred, Dwayne}
5 a {10°, 150°, 45°, 175°}, {acute, obtuse}
   b {t, s}, {t, u, w}

Exercise 6c   page 91

1 a

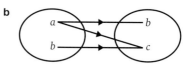

b

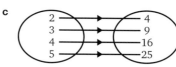

c

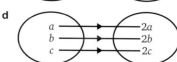

d

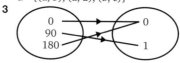

2 a {(1, 4), (3, 8), (5, 14)}
   b {(1, 2), (2, 2), (3, 2), (4, 5)}
   c {(a, b), (a, c), (b, c)}
   d {(a, b), (a, d), (b, c)}

3

Exercise 6d   page 94

1 a $1:1$ **b** $n:n$ **c** $1:1$ **d** $1:1$
2 a $1:1$ **b** $n:1$ **c** $n:n$ **d** $1:n$
3 $n:1$

Exercise 6e   page 94

1 a

x	1	2	3	4
y	2	4	6	8

b

x	2	4	6	9
y	1	2	3	4.5

c

x	10	7	5	0
y	0	3	5	10

d

x	0	1	2	3	4
y	0	4	6	8	6

2 a $1:1$ **b** $1:1$ **c** $1:1$ **d** $n:1$
3 $1:n$, one value of x maps to different values of y
4 a $1:n$, one value of x maps to different values of y
   b $n:n$, two values of x map to one value of y and one value of x maps to two values of y
   c $1:1$, one value of x maps to one value of y

Exercise 6f   page 96

1 missing values: 3, 9
2 missing values: 3, 11
3 missing values: 8, 4, 2
4 missing values: 10, 8, 0
5 missing values: 2, 5, 17
6 missing values: 1, 7, 31
7 missing values: 2, 4, 8
8 a missing values: 0, 6, 12
   b {1, 2, 3, 4}, {0, 2, 6, 12}

c
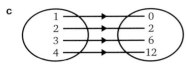

d 1 : 1

9 a missing values: 5, $6\frac{1}{2}$

b $\{1, 1\frac{1}{2}, 2\}, \{3\frac{1}{2}, 5, 6\frac{1}{2}\}$

c
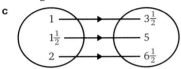

d 1 : 1

10 a missing values: 2, 2
b {1,2,3,4}, {0,2}
c
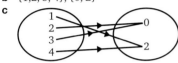

d $n : 1$

11 a missing values: 0, 6, 0
b {0, 2, 3, 5}, {0, 6}
c
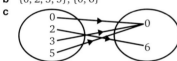

d $n : 1$

Exercise 6g   page 98

1	A	**3**	B	**5**	D	**7**	D	**9**	B
2	C	**4**	D	**6**	C	**8**	B	**10**	C

REVIEW TEST 1   page 101

1	A	**5**	C	**9**	B
2	B	**6**	C	**10**	C
3	A	**7**	A		
4	B	**8**	B		

11 a 2.432×10^2
  b 5.73×10^4
  c 4.26×10^5
12 a a^2 **b** a^8
13 a 40 000   **b** 4 300 000
14 a $\frac{11}{20}$ **b** 0.55
15 336
16 a 102_5 **b** 19_{10}
17 a 303_4 **b** 12_5 **c** 124_5
18 a 4   **b** $2\frac{1}{2}$
19 a $3x + 1$ **b** $20x - 26$
20 a i ⟶○
           -2
   b $2 < x < 10$
   ii ○⟶
         2

21 a 26, 8, 7

b
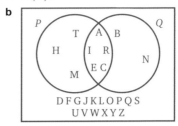

22 $A = \{2, 4, 6, 8, 10, 12\}$
   $B = \{2, 3, 5, 7, 11\}$
   $C = \{3, 6, 9, 12\}$, yes
23 a domain {1, 2, 4, 10}
       range {4, 5, 7, 13}
b
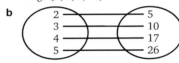

    1 : 1
24 missing values are 9, 17, 21
25 a missing values are 4, 1, 0, 1, 4, 9
   b domain $\{-2, -1, 0, 1, 2, 3\}$ range {0, 1, 4, 9}
   c
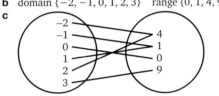

d $n : 1$

CHAPTER 7

Exercise 7a   page 106

1	A(2, 2)	B(5, 2)	C(7, 6)	D(4, 5)
	E(7, 0)	F(9, 4)	G(0, 8)	H(5, 8)

4 square   **10** (7, 1)
5 isosceles triangle   **11** (4, 1)
6 rectangle   **12** (5, 4)
7 square   **13** (3, 7)
8 isosceles triangle   **14** (2, 3)
9 (2, 5)

Exercise 7b   page 109

1 2, 3, 6, 1, -5, -3, 5, -3, -5, 5, 0
2 2, -2, 5, -4, 2, 5, -5, 0
5 square   **18** (1, 0)
6 isosceles triangle   **19** (4, 2)
7 rectangle   **20** (2, -1)
8 right-angled   **21** $(-\frac{7}{2}, 3)$
9 $(-1, 1)$
10 $(1, -2)$ **22** $(-3, -1)$
11 $(-1, 3)$ **23** $(-5, -2)$
12 $(-6, -1)$
13 $(-5, 1)$ **24** $(4, \frac{3}{2})$
14 $(0, -1)$
15 $(3, 2)$ **25** $(-1, 3)$
16 $(-1, 2)$ **26** $(-1, 0)$
17 $(-1, 3)$ **27** $(0, 0)$
       28 $(-1, 0)$

Answers

Exercise 7c   **page 111**

1 a

x	1	2	3	4
y	2	4	6	8

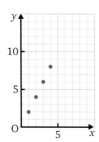

b

x	2	4	6	9
y	1	2	3	4.5

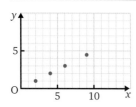

c

x	10	7	5	0
y	0	3	5	10

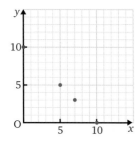

d

x	0	1	2	3	4
y	0	4	6	8	6

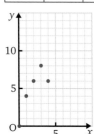

2

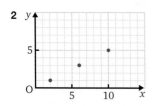

3 a

x	1	4	7	10	13
y	12	10	7	6	4

b $\{(1, 12), (4, 10), (7, 7), (10, 6), (13, 4)\}$
c $1 : 1$

4 a

x	0	2	4	6	10
y	1	2	3	4	6

b $\frac{1}{2}(x\text{-coordinate}) + 1$

c 5

d $3\frac{1}{2}, 9, \frac{1}{2}a + 1$

5 a

x	0	2	4	7	8
y	7	6	5	3.5	3

b $7 - \frac{1}{2}(x\text{-coordinate})$ **c** 4.5

d $6\frac{1}{2}, 1, 7 - \frac{1}{2}a$

6 a parallelogram   **d** both
c no   **e** no
7 a square   **d** both
c yes   **e** yes
8 a trapezium   **d** neither
c no   **e** no
9 a rhombus   **d** both
c no   **e** yes
10 a rectangle   **d** both
c yes   **e** no
11 rectangle, square
12 rhombus, square
13 parallelogram, rectangle, rhombus, square

Exercise 7d   **page 115**

1 a 2   **b** 3   **c** 7   **d** 12
2 a -1 **b** -6 **c** -8 **d** -20
3 a $-3\frac{1}{2}$ **b** $4\frac{1}{2}$ **c** -6.1 **d** 8.3
4 a -7 **b** 2   **c** $-5\frac{1}{2}$ **d** 4.2
5 a 10   **b** -8 **c** 7   **d** -5.2
6 a -1 **b** 3   **c** -2 **d** $\frac{4}{3}$
7 a 3   **b** -6 **c** 1   **d** -16.4
8 a -2 **b** 4   **c** $-\frac{3}{2}$ **d** $\frac{3}{4}$
9 $a = -5, b = 3, c = -4$
10 $a = -2, b = 8, c = 18$

11 $y = 3x$ **13** $y = -\frac{1}{3}x$

12 $y = -2x$ **14** $y = \frac{2}{3}x$

15 $(-2, -4), (6, 12)$
16 $(-2, 6), (1, -3), (8, -24)$
17 a above: $(2, 2), (-2, 1), (-4.2, -2)$
b below: $(3, 0)$

Exercise 7e   page 117
1–6

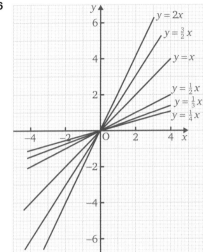

7–12

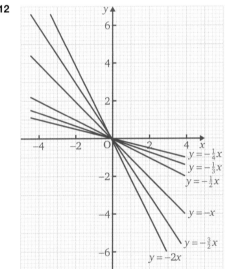

Exercise 7f   page 118
1 a 2   **b** 2   **c** 2
2 a −4   **b** −4   **c** −4
3 a 3   **b** 3   **c** 3
4 a −4   **b** −4   **c** −4
5 2.5
6 −0.5
7 a +   **c** +   **e** −
  b −   **d** −   **f** −

Exercise 7g   page 121
1 $y = 5x$

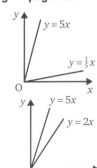

2 $y = 5x$

3 $y = \frac{1}{2}x$

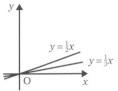

4 $y = -3x$

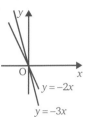

5 $y = 10x$

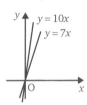

6 $y = -\frac{1}{2}x$

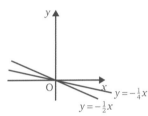

7 $y = -6x$

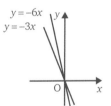

8 $y = 0.75x$

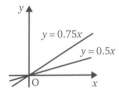

9 acute   **13** acute   **17** obtuse
10 obtuse   **14** acute   **18** obtuse
11 obtuse   **15** acute   **19** obtuse
12 acute   **16** acute   **20** obtuse

Exercise 7h   page 122
1 gradient 3, y-intercept 1, **a** −5 **b** 7
2 gradient −3, y-intercept 4, **a** 7 **b** −5
3 gradient $\frac{1}{2}$, y-intercept 4, **a** 3 **b** 4
4 gradient 1, y-intercept −3, **a** 7 **b** −2
5 gradient $\frac{3}{4}$, y-intercept 3, **a** 4 **b** 2
6 gradient 2, y-intercept −2
7 gradient −2, y-intercept 4
8 gradient 3, y-intercept −4

9 gradient $\frac{1}{2}$, *y*-intercept 3

10 gradient $-\frac{3}{2}$, *y*-intercept 3

11 gradient 2, *y*-intercept 5
12 gradient -2, *y*-intercept -7
13 gradient -3, *y*-intercept $+2$

Exercise 7i   page 124

1
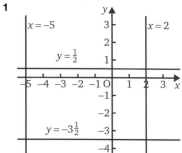

2
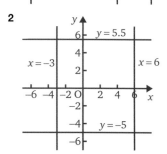

3
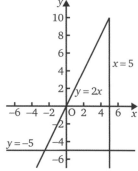

$(5, 10), (5, -5), (-2.5, -5)$
a right-angled triangle

4
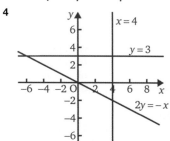

$(4, 3), (4, -2), (-6, 3)$
a right-angled triangle

5
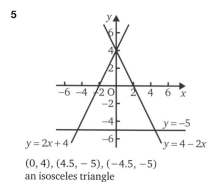

$(0, 4), (4.5, -5), (-4.5, -5)$
an isosceles triangle

Exercise 7j   page 127

1
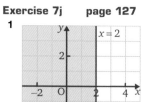

2
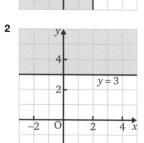

3
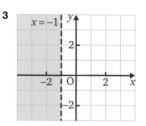

4
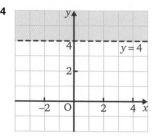

5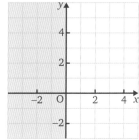

6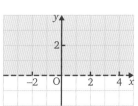

7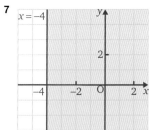

8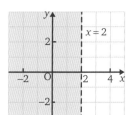

9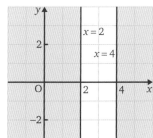

10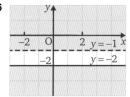

11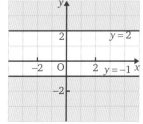

12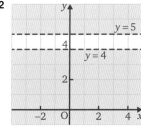

13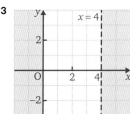

14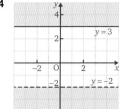

15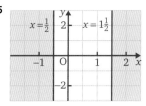

16

17

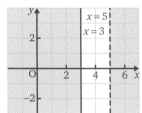

18 9: no   10: no   11: no
19 $x \leqslant 2$
20 $y < 3$
21 $x < -1$
22 $-2 \leqslant y \leqslant 2$
23 $-1 \leqslant x < 2$
24 $-\frac{1}{2} < y < 2\frac{1}{2}$
25 19: yes   20: yes   21: no   22: yes   23: no   24: no
26 $-3 \leqslant x \leqslant 1$
27 $-4 \leqslant y \leqslant -1$
28 $2 \leqslant y < 3$
29 $3 \leqslant x \leqslant 6$
30 26: yes   27: no   28: yes   29: no

Exercise 7k   page 130

1

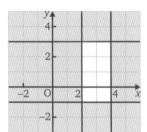

2

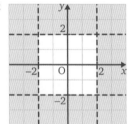

3

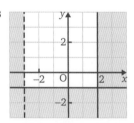

4

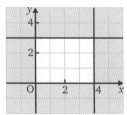

5

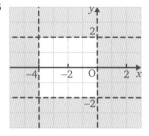

6

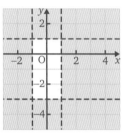

7

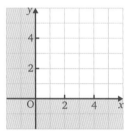

8

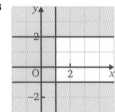

9 $-2 \leqslant x \leqslant 3, -1 \leqslant y \leqslant 2$
10 $-2 < x \leqslant 2, -2 \leqslant y \leqslant 1$
11 9: yes   10: no
12 $-2 \leqslant x \leqslant 1, y \geqslant -1$
13 $x < 0, y > 0$
14 $-2 < x < 2, -2 < y < 2$
15 $1 < x < 3,   1 < y < 3$
16 $-2 < x < 1$

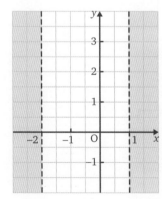

17 $1 \leqslant y \leqslant 2$

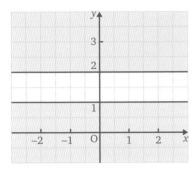

18 $-2 \leqslant x < 3$

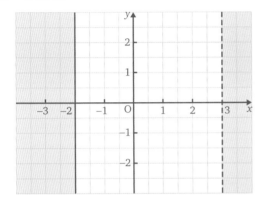

19

20

Exercise 7I   page 132

1	C	**4**	A	**7**	C	**10**	C	**13**	A
2	D	**5**	C	**8**	D	**11**	D	**14**	B
3	C	**6**	B	**9**	A	**12**	B	**15**	C

CHAPTER 8

Exercise 8a   page 138

1 A, B and C

2

3

4

5

6

7

Exercise 8b   page 139

1

2

3
none

4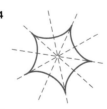

5

6

7

8

9

10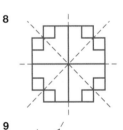

11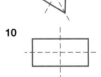

12
none

13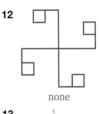

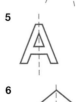
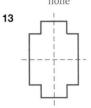

14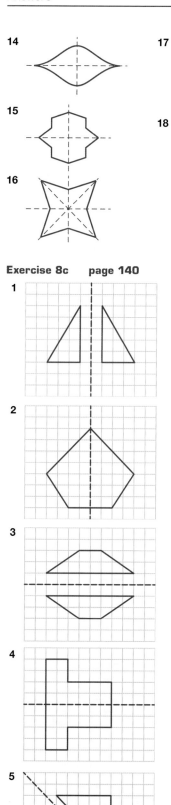

15

16

Exercise 8c   page 140

1

2

3

4

5

17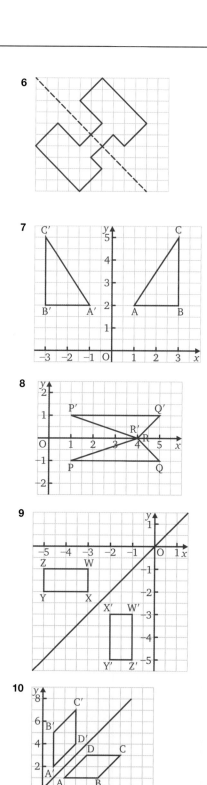

18

6

7

8

9

10

11

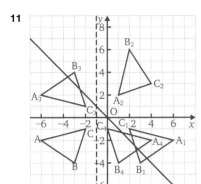

Exercise 8d   page 142

1

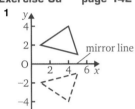

2

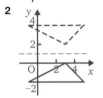

3

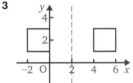

4

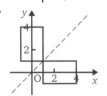

5

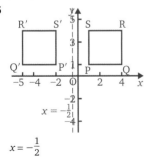

$x = -\frac{1}{2}$

6

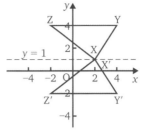

X, X′ are invariant points

7

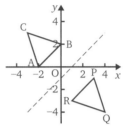

R is the image of A. There are no invariant points.

8

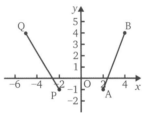

If there is a mirror line it has to be the perpendicular bisector of AP. But this line does not pass through the midpoint of QB, so PQ is not the reflection of AB.

9

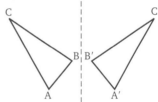

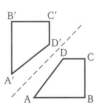

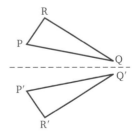

10

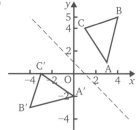

11

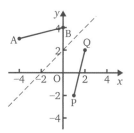

12

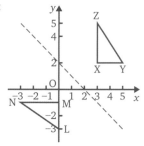

Exercise 8e   page 144

1 yes

2

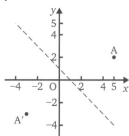

3

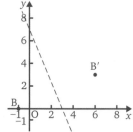

Exercise 8f   page 145

1 scalar   **3** scalar   **5** vector
2 vector   **4** scalar

Exercise 8g   page 146

1 $\begin{pmatrix} 3 \\ 2 \end{pmatrix}$ **3** $\begin{pmatrix} 4 \\ 0 \end{pmatrix}$ **5** $\begin{pmatrix} 3 \\ -4 \end{pmatrix}$

2 $\begin{pmatrix} 4 \\ 1 \end{pmatrix}$ **4** $\begin{pmatrix} -2 \\ 2 \end{pmatrix}$ **6** $\begin{pmatrix} -5 \\ -3 \end{pmatrix}$

7 $g = \begin{pmatrix} 5 \\ 0 \end{pmatrix}$ $j = \begin{pmatrix} -6 \\ 7 \end{pmatrix}$ $m = \begin{pmatrix} 0 \\ -4 \end{pmatrix}$

$h = \begin{pmatrix} -4 \\ 0 \end{pmatrix}$ $k = \begin{pmatrix} -6 \\ -2 \end{pmatrix}$ $n = \begin{pmatrix} 4 \\ 2 \end{pmatrix}$

$i = \begin{pmatrix} 6 \\ 2 \end{pmatrix}$ $l = \begin{pmatrix} 3 \\ -1 \end{pmatrix}$

17 Both pairs are parallel.

Exercise 8h   page 148

1 (7, 4)   **12** (−7, −3)
2 (1, −2)   **13** (−6, −1)
3 (−3, 7)   **14** {−2, −3}
4 (1, −5)   **15** (3, −2)
5 (8, 1)   **16** (−2, −3)
6 (8, 0)   **17** (1, −3)
7 (−1, 0)   **18** (1, 5)
8 (−9, −8)   **19** (−7, 4)
9 (2, 0)   **20** (−1, −10)
10 (7, −4)   **21** (−6, −6)
11 (−9, −1)   **22** (−1, 10)

Exercise 8i   page 150

1 $\begin{pmatrix} 6 \\ 2 \end{pmatrix}$ **5** $\begin{pmatrix} -5 \\ -6 \end{pmatrix}$ **9** $\begin{pmatrix} 0 \\ -12 \end{pmatrix}$

2 $\begin{pmatrix} 5 \\ -1 \end{pmatrix}$ **6** $\begin{pmatrix} 2 \\ -2 \end{pmatrix}$ **10** $\begin{pmatrix} 2 \\ 8 \end{pmatrix}$

3 $\begin{pmatrix} -6 \\ -1 \end{pmatrix}$ **7** $\begin{pmatrix} -2 \\ -2 \end{pmatrix}$

4 $\begin{pmatrix} 6 \\ 5 \end{pmatrix}$ **8** $\begin{pmatrix} -4 \\ -5 \end{pmatrix}$

Exercise 8j   page 151

1 (7, 3)
2 (6, 9)   **11** $\begin{pmatrix} 4 \\ 1 \end{pmatrix}$ **15** $\begin{pmatrix} -2 \\ -2 \end{pmatrix}$
3 (2, 7)
4 (1, 5)
5 (1, 3)   **12** $\begin{pmatrix} -1 \\ 1 \end{pmatrix}$ **16** $\begin{pmatrix} 1 \\ 1 \end{pmatrix}$
6 (6, −7)
7 (−2, −2)   **17** (5, 6)
8 (−4, −2)   **13** $\begin{pmatrix} 4 \\ 3 \end{pmatrix}$ **18** (−2, 3)
9 (9, −6)   **19** (−4, −5)
10 (2, 0)   **14** $\begin{pmatrix} 4 \\ 0 \end{pmatrix}$

Exercise 8k   page 153

1 $\overrightarrow{AA'} = \begin{pmatrix} -5 \\ 1 \end{pmatrix}$, $\overrightarrow{BB'} = \begin{pmatrix} -5 \\ 1 \end{pmatrix}$, $\overrightarrow{CC'} = \begin{pmatrix} -5 \\ 1 \end{pmatrix}$

yes, yes

2 $\overrightarrow{LL'} = \begin{pmatrix} 4 \\ 2 \end{pmatrix}$, $\overrightarrow{MM'} = \begin{pmatrix} 4 \\ 2 \end{pmatrix}$, $\overrightarrow{NN'} = \begin{pmatrix} 4 \\ 3 \end{pmatrix}$,

yes, yes

3 $\begin{pmatrix} 6 \\ 3 \end{pmatrix}$

4 a $\begin{pmatrix} -5 \\ 4 \end{pmatrix}$ **b** $\begin{pmatrix} 5 \\ -4 \end{pmatrix}$

5 a $\begin{pmatrix} 0 \\ -4 \end{pmatrix}$ **b** $\begin{pmatrix} -6 \\ 0 \end{pmatrix}$ **c** $\begin{pmatrix} 5 \\ 5 \end{pmatrix}$ **d** $\begin{pmatrix} 0 \\ 0 \end{pmatrix}$

6

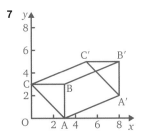

a $\begin{pmatrix} -1 \\ -4 \end{pmatrix}$ **c** $\begin{pmatrix} -4 \\ 3 \end{pmatrix}$

b $\begin{pmatrix} 1 \\ 4 \end{pmatrix}$ **d** $\begin{pmatrix} 0 \\ 0 \end{pmatrix}$

7

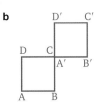

yes, $\begin{pmatrix} 5 \\ 2 \end{pmatrix}$, parallelogram − the opposite sides are parallel.

AA'C'C, BB'C'C

8 a

b

9

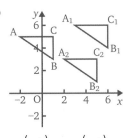

a $\begin{pmatrix} 4 \\ -2 \end{pmatrix}$ **b** $\begin{pmatrix} -4 \\ 2 \end{pmatrix}$ **c** $\begin{pmatrix} 1 \\ 3 \end{pmatrix}$

Exercise 8I **page 155**

1	B	**3**	A	**5**	A	**7**	C	**9**	B
2	D	**4**	D	**6**	A	**8**	C	**10**	C

CHAPTER 9

Exercise 9a **page 161**

1 50 mm
2 3 cm
3 500 m
4 3 m
5 150 cm
6 34.5 cm
7 540 mm
8 5 km
9 0.56 m

10 1.35 m
11 24 in
12 6 ft
13 4 ft
14 4 yd
15 2640 yd
16 15 cm
17 8 in

18 $37\frac{1}{2}$ miles
19 80 km
20 30 cm
21 200 in
22 180 cm
23 18 in
24 5 ft
25 540 m

Exercise 9b **page 163**

1 6000 g
2 2 kg
3 500 kg
4 500 g
5 1500 kg
6 3.4 t
7 0.3 kg
8 2 lb
9 224 lb
10 40 cwt
11 $3\frac{1}{2}$ cwt

12 24 oz
13 6.6 lb
14 3.6 1b
15 1.1 lb
16 2 tons
17 60 cwt
18 27.3 kg
19 2 lb 8 oz, 1 kg 170 g
20 3 kg 200 g, 7 lb 1 oz
21 500 g, 1 lb 2 oz
22 22 g

Exercise 9c **page 165**

1 a 36 °C **b** 78 °C **c** 77 °F **d** 176 °F
2 a EC\$432 **b** EC\$891 **c** US\$163 **d** US\$363
3 constant speed
  a 12 km **c** 1 hour 40 minutes
  b 21 km **d** $3\frac{1}{2}$ hours

4 a 54%, 77% **b** $32\frac{1}{2}$, 52

5 a \$43.75 **c** \$117.25 **e** \$251.43
  b \$84 **d** \$114.30

6 a 34 mpg **b** 22 km/litre
7 a 39 m/s **c** 65 km/h
  b 166 km/h **d** 49 m/s (to nearest unit)
8 a 9.5 cm **c** 6.5 cm
  b 5.8 cm **d** 9.2 cm

Exercise 9d **page 167**

1	D	**3**	B	**5**	D	**7**	C	**9**	C
2	B	**4**	C	**6**	C	**8**	B	**10**	A

CHAPTER 10

Exercise 10a **page 171**

1 12 cm
2 10 m
3 30 mm

4 7 cm
5 2 km
6 9.2 cm

Exercise 10b **page 172**

1 14.5 m
2 28.9 cm

3 18.2 cm
4 333 mm

5 54.7 m
6 1570 mm

7 226 cm
8 30.2 m
9 11.3 m
10 0.0880 km
11 44.0 cm
12 176 mm

13 8.80 m
14 220 mm
15 35.2 cm
16 970 mm
17 88 cm
18 24 m

19 1300 mm
20 220 cm
21 1600 mm
22 2000 cm
23 29 m

Exercise 10c   page 174

1 10.3 cm
2 10.7 cm
3 18.3 cm
4 20.5 cm
5 27.9 cm

6 33.6 cm
7 94.2 cm
8 62.8 mm
9 20.6 cm
10 45.1 cm

11 30.8 cm
12 41.7 cm
13 229.2 cm
14 67.2 cm

Exercise 10d   page 176

1 78.5 mm
2 62.8 mm, 88.0 mm
3 4.4
4 194 cm
5 176 cm
6 176 cm, 200
7 12.6 cm
8 94.2 cm

9 62.8 m
10 6.28 s, 9.55 revolutions
11 3140 cm
12 12.6 m
13 70.7
14 94.2 m

Exercise 10e   page 178

1 7.00 cm
2 19.3 mm
3 87.5 m
4 43.8 cm
5 73.5 mm
6 132 cm
7 5.76 mm

8 62.2 m
9 92.6 cm
10 13.9 m
11 16.6 m
12 59.8 m
13 31.8 cm
14 20.0 m

15 4.93 cm
16 9.55 cm each
17 3.82 cm, 45.8 cm
18 37.7 cm
19 4.77 cm
20 9.55 cm
21 9.55 cm, 29.1 cm

Exercise 10f   page 181

1 50.3 cm²
2 201 m²
3 78.5 m²
4 78.5 mm²
5 38.5 cm²
6 11 300 cm²
7 45.4 m²
8 9.62 km²
9 20 100 m²
10 25.1 cm²
11 51.3 m²
12 58.9 cm²
13 118 mm²
14 451 mm²

15 374 cm²
16 457 cm²
17 714 m²
18 942 cm²
19 3540 cm²
20 193 cm²
21 828 cm² (3 s.f.)
22 214 cm²
23 74.1 cm²
24 42.5 cm²
25 93.7 cm²
26 31.4 cm²
27 42.9 m²

Exercise 10g   page 183

1
707 cm²

2
236 cm²

3 491 mm²

4
26.2 cm²

5 no
6 21.5 cm²
7 8, 110 cm²
8 11 700 cm²
9 2

Exercise 10h   page 185

1 17.6 mm
2 9.55 m
3 37.7 cm
4 26.4 m²

5 491 cm²
6 28.6 mm
7 7.95 cm²

Exercise 10i   page 186

1 62.8 m
2 452 cm²
3 57.3 cm
4 50.3 m²

5 89.1 mn
6 40.9 cm
7 87.5 cm²

Exercise 10j   page 186

1 12.6 km²
2 308 mm
3 14 m

4 154 cm²
5 32.2 cm²
6 18.1 m²

Exercise 10k   page 187

1 C
2 B
3 B
4 A
5 A
6 C
7 D
8 B
9 A
10 A

CHAPTER 11

Exercise 11a   page 191

1 48 cm³
2 1600 mm³
3 5400 mm³
4 16 mm³
5 31.72 m³
6 10.5 cm³
7 24 m³
8 160 m³
9 12 cm³
10 7.2 cm³
11 4.32 m³
12 0.756 m³

13 64 cm³
14 125 cm³
15 8 m³
16 $\frac{1}{8}$ cm³
17 15.625 cm³
18 27 km³
19 512 km³
20 $3\frac{3}{8}$ km³
21 39.304 m³

Exercise 11b   page 192

1 8
2 6

3 8
4 12

Exercise 11c   page 193

1 a m³   **b** mm³   **c** cm³
2 8000 mm³
3 14 000 mm³
4 6200 mm³
5 430 mm³
6 92 000 000 mm³
7 40 mm³

8 3 000 000 cm³
9 2 500 000 cm³
10 420 000 cm³
11 6300 cm³
12 0.022 cm³
13 0.731 cm³

Exercise 11d   page 194

1 2500 cm³
2 1760 cm³
3 540 cm³
4 7.5 cm³
5 35 000 cm³
6 28 cm³
7 7 litres

8 4 litres
9 24 litres
10 0.6 litres
11 5000 litres
12 12 000 litre
13 4600 litres
14 67 litres

Exercise 11e   page 195

2   a   i 2   **ii** 2   **iii** 4 cm × 3 cm

b

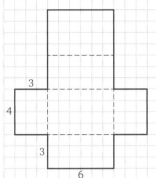

3   a   6

b

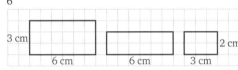

c

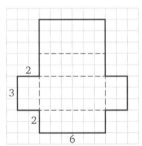

4   b   prism   **c**   triangular
5   b   no   **c**   pyramid
6   b   prism
      c   paralellogram
      d   22 cm
7   a

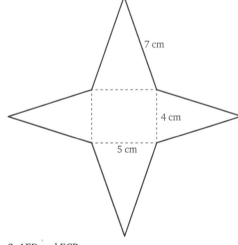

   b   2, AED and ECB
   c   2, ECD and EAB
8   a

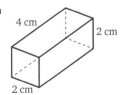

   b   IJ   **c**   G, K

9

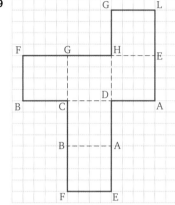

10   a   There are 35 arrangements altogether.
      b   11 will make a cube

Exercise 11f   page 199

1	30 cm³	**6**	40 000 cm³
2	2 m³	**7**	28 cm³
3	800 cm³	**8**	8 m³
4	600 cm³	**9**	17.5 cm³
5	5760 mm³	**10**	180 cm³

Exercise 11g   page 200

2	60 m³	**7**	300 m³; 300 000
3	7776 cm³	**8**	60
4	6480 m³	**9**	9000
5	125	**10**	64
6	48	**11**	1600

Exercise 11h   page 203

1	720 cm³	**11**	315 cm³
2	2160 cm³	**12**	450 cm³
3	1120 cm³	**13**	690 cm³
4	720 cm³	**14**	624 cm³
5	1242 cm³	**15**	864 cm³
6	128 cm³	**16**	720 cm³
7	660 cm³	**17**	5.184 m³
8	192 cm³	**18**	1344 cm³
9	2400 cm³	**19**	624 m³
10	2880 cm³	**20**	540 cm³
21 a	parallelogram	**b**	28 cm², 280 cm³
22 a	12 cm	**c**	90 cm²
b	parallelogram	**d**	540 cm³

Exercise 11i   page 207

1	126 cm³	**11**	322 cm³
2	113 cm³	**12**	407 cm³
3	314 cm³	**13**	330 cm³
4	59.4 cm³	**14**	651 cm³
5	3.14 cm³	**15**	70 800 cm³
6	15.1 m³	**16**	28.0 cm³
7	37.7 cm³	**17**	941 mm³
8	50.9 cm³	**18**	824 cm³
9	4520 cm³	**19**	1.60 m³
10	1390 cm³	**20**	44.0 cm³

Exercise 11j   page 208

1	1010 cm³	**4**	204 cm³
2	402 cm³	**5**	628 cm³
3	34.5 cm³	**6**	2160 cm³

Exercise 11k   page 209

1 **a** 3 200 000 cm³   **b** 3 200 000 000 mm³
2 1600 cm³   **5** 13 500 mm³
3 64 cm³   **6** 504 cm³
4 50 000 cm³

Exercise 11l   page 210

1 **a** 8000 mm³   **b** 0.000 008 m³
2 3.5 litres   **5** 120 000 cm³
3 300 cm³   **6** 1200 cm³
4 0.512 cm³

Exercise 11m   page 210

1 **a** 9000 cm³   **b** 9 000 000 mm³
2 440 cm³   **5** 2400 litres
3 216 cm³   **6** 78.5 cm³
4 288 cm³

Exercise 11n   page 211

1 0.0009 m³   **4** 8 cm³
2 10.8 litres   **5** 1.2 m³
3 75 litres   **6** 0.424 m³ (3 s.f.)

Exercise 11p   page 211

1	C	4	C	7	B	10	C
2	C	5	C	8	C	11	D
3	D	6	C	9	C	12	B

REVIEW TEST 2 page 214

1	C	4	C	7	D
2	D	5	D	8	B
3	C	6	B	9	B

10 **a** **i** 3558 mm   **ii** 5380 mm
     b 13.035 kg
     c 5.525 g
     d **i** 0.734 km   **ii** 9
11 $a = -6, b = 9, c = 2$
12 **a** $-4 \leqslant y < 3$ **b** no
13 **a**

x	11	9	5	1
y	2	3	5	7

     b $y = \frac{1}{2}(15 - x)$ **c** 6   **d** 7

14 **a** $(7, 1)$ **b** $(4\frac{1}{2}, 2\frac{1}{2})$ **c** $(4\frac{1}{2}, 2\frac{1}{2})$
15

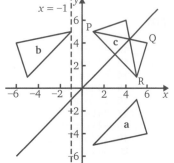

     a $(1, -5), (6, -4), (5, -1)$
     b $(-1, 5), (-6, 4), (-5, 1)$
     c $(5, 1), (4, 6), (1, 5)$

16

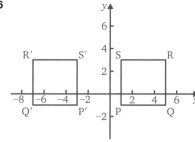

17 73.3 cm²
18 **a** 9.55 cm
     b 4.77 cm
     c 71.62 cm²
19 **a** 0.08 m³
     b 7 litres
     c 600 000 mm³
20 **a** 113 cm²
     b 30.9 cm²
     c 82.2 cm²
21 **a**

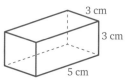

     b **i** HI   **ii** JK
     c I and C

CHAPTER 12

Exercise 12a   page 219

1	4 : 5	11	2 : 3 : 5
2	5 : 4	12	3 : 4 : 6
3	2 : 3	13	1 : 5 : 10
4	1 : 4	14	3 : 4 : 5
5	1 : 3	15	5 : 6 : 8
6	9 : 200	16	1 : 8 : 7
7	16 : 3	17	3 : 4 : 7
8	1 : 6	18	1 : 8 : 4
9	16 : 17	19	12 : 1 : 2
10	1 : 1000	20	14 : 9 : 2

Exercise 12b   page 220

1	15 : 1	11	8 : 5 : 3
2	8 : 1	12	2 : 3
3	3 : 2	13	40 : 9
4	3 : 1	14	2 : 15
5	4 : 9	15	15 : 19
6	7 : 10	16	5 : 4
7	35 : 24	17	1 : 2 : 3
8	9 : 4	18	4 : 3
9	16 : 7	19	4 : 3 : 2
10	10 : 7	20	3 : 4 : 6

Exercise 12c   page 221

1 5 : 7   **6** $10 : 24 = \frac{5}{9} : \frac{4}{3}$
2 13 : 8
3 5 : 8   **7** $8 : 64 = \frac{1}{16} : \frac{1}{2}$
4 7 : 10
5 $6 : 8 = 24 : 32 = \frac{3}{4} : 1$ **8** $\frac{2}{3} : 3 = 4 : 18$

Exercise 12d   page 222

1 $3:2, 2:5$ **3** $2:5, 8:3$ **5** $2:1$
2 $3:4, 9:16$ **4** $3:2, 2:3$
6 a $3:2$ **b** $9:5$ **c** $18:13$ **d** $1:1$
7 $8:12:9$ **8** $3:7$
9 a $12:3:5$ **b** $2:3$ **c** $5:3$

Exercise 12e   page 223

1 10   **5** 8   **9** 9
2 4   **6** 12   **10** 12
3 7   **7** 6
4 2   **8** 6

Exercise 12f   page 223

1 $22\frac{1}{2}$ c   **4** $10\frac{2}{3}$ cm   **7** 30 cm
                                           8 12 m
2 18 cm   **5** 10.5 cm
3 98 cm   **6** 27 cm

Exercise 12g   page 224

1 48 c, 32 c   **5** 30 c, 45 c
2 12 cm, 20 cm   **6** 16
3 $20, $25   **7** $2.50, $17.50
4 Dick 15, Tom 25
8 a 252 m^2 **b** 105 m^2
9 12
10 a 264 cm   **b** 110 cm,
11 a 210 g   **b** 126 g
12 Education $2730 000, Social Services $2184 000
13 Misha $350, John $250
14 $5:3$
15 $8, $10, $8
16 6 cm, 8 cm, 10 cm
17 $42 \text{ m}^2, 14 \text{ m}^2, 7 \text{ m}^2$

Exercise 12h   page 227

1 $1:50 000$ **7** 3 km
2 $1:500 000$ **8** 70 m
3 $1:100 000$ **9** 200 m
4 $1:500 000$ **10** 2 000 000 cm, 10 cm
5 $1:100 000$ **11** 1.8 cm
6 $1:2 000 000$

Exercise 12i   page 229

1 12m   **7** 9 hours
2 72   **8** $61.20
3 18 cm^2, 72   **9** $18 000
4 3.6 cm
5 105   **10** $56\frac{1}{4}$ minutes, $5\frac{1}{3}$ km
6 2 hours   **11** 54 minutes
12 $50 (must buy complete lengths)
13 hardly any! (no room to work)
14 $4\frac{1}{2}$ teaspoons

Exercise 12j   page 231

1 a 800 km   **b** 1100 km
2 a 48 km   **b** 84 km   **c** 54 km
3 a 1200 miles   **b** 1650 miles
4 a 90 km   **b** 135 km
5 a 9 miles   **b** 15 miles
6 a 52.5 m   **b** 89.25 m
7 a 32 miles   **b** 38 miles

8 a 4 km   **b** $2\frac{2}{3}$ km   **c** 10 km
9 a 37 miles   **b** 185 miles
10 a 500 m   **b** 850 m
11 a 1755 miles   **b** 4185 miles
12 a 30   **b** 72

Exercise 12k   page 233

1 a 2 hours   **b** 3 hours
2 a 5 hours   **b** $3\frac{1}{4}$ hours
3 a $\frac{1}{2}$ hour   **b** $1\frac{1}{4}$ hours
4 a $2\frac{1}{2}$ hours   **b** $5\frac{1}{3}$ hours
5 a $1\frac{1}{2}$ hours   **b** 5 hours
6 a $1\frac{1}{2}$ hours   **b** $4\frac{1}{2}$ hours
7 a 25 seconds   **b** 200 seconds
8 a 24 minutes   **b** 54 minutes
9 a 216 hours = 9 days   **b** $5\frac{1}{4}$ days
10 a $1\frac{1}{4}$ hours   **b** $2\frac{3}{4}$ hours
11 a $2\frac{1}{2}$ hours   **b** 5 hours 20 minutes
12 a $\frac{3}{4}$ hour   **b** $3\frac{1}{4}$ hours

Exercise 12l   page 234

1 80 km/h   **17** 12 km/h
2 60 km/h   **18** 8 km/h
3 60 mph   **19** 18 km/h
4 120 mph   **20** 18 km/h
5 20 m/s   **21** 54 mph
6 45 m/s   **22** 54 mph
7 50 km/h   **23** 60 mph
8 65 km/h   **24** 105 mph
9 35 mph   **25** 74.33 km/h
10 8 mph   **26** 138.5 km/h
11 36 m/s   **27** 693.3 km/h
12 17 m/s   **28** 482 km/h
13 80 km/h   **29** 162.86 km/h
14 90 km/h   **30** 253.62 km/h
15 64 km/h   **31** 102.97 km/h
16 120 km/h

Exercise 12m   page 237

1 9 km/h   **5** 75 km/h
2 10 mph   **6** 200 km/h
3 7 mph   **7** 3 knots
4 7 mph

Exercise 12n   page 238

1 a 90 km   **b** 2 hours   **c** 45 km
2 a 30 km   **b** 3 hours   **c** 10 km
3 a 107 km   **b** 3.2 hours   **c** 33.4 km
4 a 50 miles   **b** 2 hours   **c** 25 miles

Exercise 12p   page 240

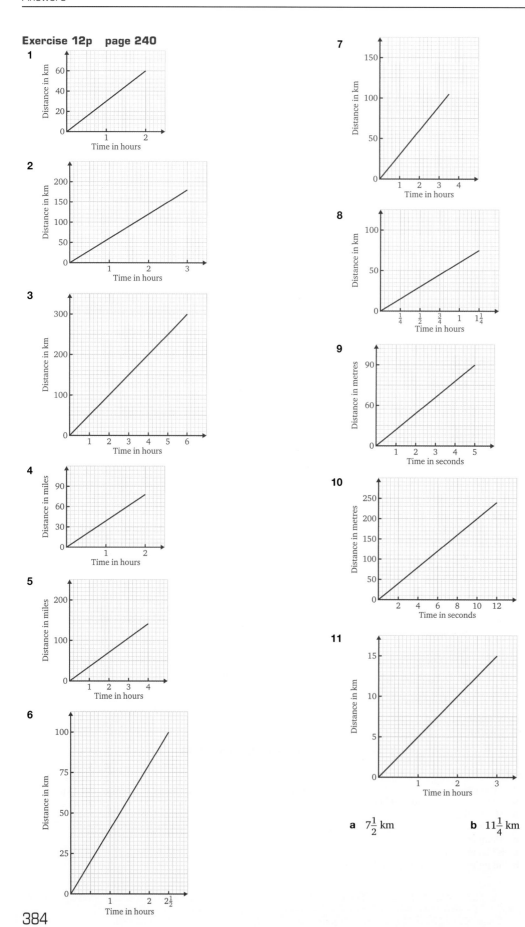

1

2

3

4

5

6

7

8

9

10

11

a $7\frac{1}{2}$ km   b $11\frac{1}{4}$ km

12

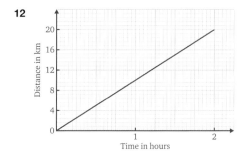

a $7\frac{1}{2}$ km **b** $12\frac{1}{2}$ km

13

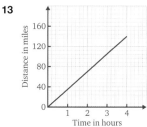

a 105 miles **b** 44 miles

14

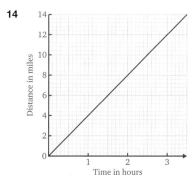

a 2 miles **b** 14 miles

Exercise 12q page 241

1 a i 1215 **ii** 1348 **iii** 1445

  b $2\frac{1}{2}$ hours

  c i $1\frac{1}{4}$ hours **ii** $1\frac{1}{4}$ hours

  d 64 km/h
2 a i 80 km **ii** 50 km
  b 2 hr 36 min **c** 30.8 km/h **d** 50 km
  e i 76 km **ii** 4 km
3 a i B **ii** B
  b i 80 km/h **ii** 64 km/h

  c $\frac{1}{2}$ hour **d** $2\frac{3}{4}$ hour

  e 58.2 km/h (counting the stop)

Exercise 12r page 244

1 1:10	**4** 9:7	**7** $12, $6, $8
2 7:6	**5** 1:500 000	**8** 510
3 2:5	**6** $5\frac{1}{4}$	

9 a 14 km/h
  b i 18 min **ii** 27 min
10 a 1950 miles **b** 5 hours **c** 390 mph

Exercise 12s page 244

1 $\frac{4}{9}$	**5** $8\frac{1}{4}$
2 5:8	**6** 100 m
3 $40:$52:$8	**7** 1:1
4 a 2:3 **b** 8:27	**8** $65.63

9 a 6.25 m/s
  b i 18 min **ii** 1 hour 36 min
10 60 mph

Exercise 12t page 245

1 257:144	**4** 33 m	**7** 91:20
2 32:24	**5** 6:3:1	**8** $770
3 10 kg	**6** 3.2 km	

9 a $5\frac{1}{2}$ hours **b i** 1 km **ii** $2\frac{2}{5}$ km

10 $16\frac{4}{5}$ mph

11 Mr Khan $220, Mr Newton $264

Exercise 12u page 245

1 A	**4** D	**7** C	**10** B
2 C	**5** B	**8** C	**11** A
3 B	**6** D	**9** A	**12** C

CHAPTER 13

Exercise 13a page 249

1 150%	**18** 75%	**33** 140
2 125%	**19** 30%	**34** 370
3 120%	**20** 15%	**35** 493
4 160%	**21** 65%	**36** 748
5 175%	**22** 58%	**37** 2768
6 135%	**23** 96%	**38** 849.3
7 148%	**24** 34%	**39** 104
8 400%	**25** $37\frac{1}{2}$%	**40** 185
9 275%		**41** 319
10 112.5%	**26** $66\frac{2}{3}$%	**42** 2415
11 157%		**43** 70
12 115%	**27** 47%	**44** 170
13 $\frac{130}{100}$	**28** 90%	**45** 189
	29 $\frac{60}{100}$	**46** 652.5
14 $\frac{180}{100}$		**47** 2448
	30 $\frac{25}{100}$	**48** 3312
15 $\frac{165}{100}$		**49** 62
	31 $\frac{66}{100}$	**50** 91
16 $\frac{230}{100}$		**51** 26
17 50%	**32** $\frac{88}{100}$	**52** 155

Exercise 13b   page 251

1 63.25 kg
2 $691.20
3 84
4 180 cm
5 33
6 $29 900
7 $42
15 a $36
16 63
17 94.3 kg
18 a $32 640
19 $5832
20 27 mpg
21 a $2.24   b 616 litres   c $20.16 less

8 $73.60
9 $756
10 $63 011, $630
11 $1500
12 198 kg
13 414
14 $660
  b $76.50

  b $27 744

Exercise 13c   page 253

1 a 0.85   b $\frac{17}{20}$
2 20%
3 42 m²
4 125%
5 $\frac{145}{100}$
6 a 98 cm   b 960 sheep
7 $87

Exercise 13d   page 253

1 $1488
2 $3024
3 $8928
4 $10 652
5 $9312
6 $39 930
7 $5980
8 $89 946
16 a $648
17 $2040
18 $5078, 20.7%
19 $819.50
20 Option 1 by $8580
21 $36 480, 32%
22 $6060
23 a $532.62   b $684.80   c 8%
24 $1249.60
25 $514.40
26 $1574
27 HP buy $17 178, rent $20 088, HP buy by $2910
28 a $553.50   b $4882.50

9 $75 082
10 $78 770
11 $888
12 $1372
13 $468
14 $50 800
15 $426
  b 25.7%

Exercise 13e   page 258

1 $400
2 $385
3 $431.20
6 a 7 h 40 min   b 38 h 20 min   c $357.27
7 $43\frac{3}{4}$ h, $458.50
8 a $7\frac{3}{4}$ b $38\frac{3}{4}$ c $350.30
9 a $235.60   b $328.60   c $347.20
10 $201.88
11 $314.50
12 $306.52

4 $475.20
5 $584.60

13 $468.72
14 $376.74
15 $267.88

16

16 a $7\frac{1}{2}$ h   c $213   e $225.78
  b $37\frac{1}{2}$ d $1\frac{1}{2}$ h

Exercise 13f   page 260

1 $1080
2 $736
3 $422
4 $1048
9 a 1125   b 500   c 625   d $962.50
10

5 $784
6 $1000
7 $805
8 $581.60

	a	bi	bii	c
Ms Arnold	186	100	86	$422.20
Mr Beynon	158	80	78	$362.60
Miss Capstick	194	100	94	$443.80
Mr Davis	225	100	125	$527.50
Mr Edmunds	191	100	91	$435.70

  d Thursday

Exercise 13g   page 262

1 $5850
2 $709.50
3 £304
4 $137.80
5 a $131.58   b $132
6 a $172.50   b $173
7 a $42.82   b $43
8 a $250   b $250
9 a $844.74   b $845
10 a $358.14   b $358
11 a $7.69   b $8
12 a $324.21   b $324
13 a $594   b $594
14 a $128.36   b $128
15 $526.32
16 £50387.60
17 $1140
18 $4.23
19 $128 973
20 £63.52

Exercise 13h   page 265

1 $65.50
2 $84.32
3 $105.80
4 $133.99
5 $168.77
6 $100.75
7 $152.33

8 $116.40
9 $90.20
10 $345.65
11 $2688
12 $4470, no, $4776
13 Amy by $191
14 $130

Exercise 13i   page 266

1 3
2 $\frac{1}{10}$
3 $1\frac{1}{2}$
4 1.2
5 0.06
6 0.02
7 8
8 2

15 16
16 1
17 12
18 3
19 1.8
20 0.144
21 0.56
22 0.84

23 4 hours
24 $\frac{1}{2}$ hour
25 10 hours
26 $2\frac{7}{9}$ hours
27 3 c
28 12 c
29 3.024 c
30 $1\frac{1}{2}$ c

Exercise 13j   page 268
1 $45
2 $54
3 $125
4 $118
5 $126.69
6 $111.24
7 $101.37
8 $145
9 $108
10 $113

Exercise 13k   page 270
1 **a** 338   **b** 105.06
2 58%
3 0.82 or $\frac{41}{50}$
4 **a** 94.5 m   **b** 8.8 miles
5 **a** $87.30   **b** $442.80

Exercise 13l   page 270
1 **a** $7144   **b** $2344
2 $574.59
3 **a** £262.50   **b** $1815
4 $159.75
5 $250

Exercise 13m   page 271
1 $2096
2 **a** $1620   **b** $67.50   **c** $337.50
   d $2295
3 **a** TT$1360   **b** US$ 80.88
4 $2438.60
5 $46.40

Exercise 13n   page 271
1 B   3 D   5 C   7 B   9 C
2 C   4 B   6 D   8 D   10 B

CHAPTER 14

Exercise 14b   page 276
1 g   3 d   5 f   7 d
2 e   4 e   6 f   8 g

Exercise 14d   page 279
1 60°   4 60°   7 110°   10 130°
2 110°   5 60°   8 120°   11 130°
3 75°   6 80°   9 30°

Exercise 14e   page 280
1 50°, 50°
2 130°, 130°, 50°
3 60°, 60° 60°, 120°, 60°
4 50°, 80°, 50°
5 70°, 80°, 30°
6 115°, 115°
7 140°, 40°, 40°
8 70°, 110°, 70°, 70°
9 50°, 45° 50°
10 55°, 125°, 55°
11 110°, 70°, 130°, 130°
12 40°, 100°
13 80°
14 90°, 90°, 50°
15 120°
16 40°
17 70°
18 60°
19 135°
20 55°
21 55°
22 120°
23 120°
24 45°

Exercise 14f   page 283
1 e   4 d   7 g
2 e   5 d   8 e
3 d   6 g   9 d

Exercise 14g   page 284
1 50°, 130°
2 130°, 50°
3 50°, 70°
4 260°, 40°, 60°
5 70°, 70°, 70°
6 45°, 90°
7 55°, 65°
8 60°
9 45°
10 30°
11 90°

Exercise 14h   page 286
1 e, g
2 e, d
3 e, g
4 e, d
5 h, f
6 d, g
7 70°, 110°, 180°
8 130°, 50°, 180°
9 140°, 40°, 80°
10 120°, 60°, 180°

Exercise 14i   page 288
1 120°
2 130°, 50°
3 85°
4 40°, 100°, 60°
5 55°, 125°
6 40°
7 80°, 80°
8 130°, 130°, 50°
9 80°, 100°, 80°, 100°
10 70°, 110°

Exercise 14j   page 289
1 $a = 107°$
2 $b = 90°$
3 $g = 50°, h = 140°$
4 $i = 75°, j = 39°$
5 $c = 45°, d = 97°$
6 $e = 143°, f = 48°$
7 $k = 116°, l = 64°$
8 $m = 50°, n = 130°, p = 38°, q = 142°, r = 88°, s = 92°$

Exercise 14k   page 291
1 yes
2 no, sides not equal
3 no, $\begin{cases} \text{sides not equal} \\ \text{angles not equal} \end{cases}$
4 no, $\begin{cases} \text{sides not equal} \\ \text{angles not equal} \end{cases}$
5 no, $\begin{cases} \text{sides not equal} \\ \text{angles not equal} \end{cases}$
6 yes
7 no, not bounded by straight lines

Exercise 14l   page 293
1 180°
2 360°
3 **a** $p = 100°, r = 135°, x = 55°, q = 125°$
   b 360°
4 **a** $w = 120°, x = 60°, y = 120°, z = 60°$
   b 360°
5 **a** 180°   **b** 540°   **c** 180°   **d** 360°
6 360°
7 **a** equilateral   **c** 120°   **e** 360°
   b 60°   **d** 60°

Exercise 14m   page 294
1 60°
2 90°
3 50°
4 50°
5 60°
6 90°
7 95°
8 55°
9 30°
10 125°
11 $x = 50°$
12 $x = 30°$
13 $x = 24°$
14 **a** 5   **b** 8

Exercise 14n   page 297

1	65°	5	70°
2	140°	6	70°
3	55°	7	45°
4	110°	8	parallel

Exercise 14p   page 297

1	80°	3	110°	5	50°	7	40°
2	60°	4	40°	6	40°		

Exercise 14q   page 298

1	D	4	C	7	B	10	B
2	C	5	C	8	C	11	D
3	B	6	C	9	A	12	B

CHAPTER 15

Exercise 15a   page 303

1	60°	5	$d = 60°, e = 120°$
2	75°	6	70°
3	100°	7	$p = 130°, q = 50°$
4	130°	8	$s = 70°, r = 110°$

9 $l = 60°, m = 100°, n = 20°$
10 $d = 30°, e = 75°, f = 105°$

Exercise 15c   page 307

11 90°
12 45°
14 They are parallel.

Exercise 15d   page 311

6 $\angle A = 53°, \angle B = 90°, \angle C = 37°$; 180°
7 8.6
8 $\angle YPQ = 90°, \angle PXZ = 43°, \angle XZP = 47°$
  so $\angle YPQ = \angle PXZ + \angle XZP$
9 The perpendicular bisector of LM passes through N.
10 The perpendicular bisector of PR does not pass through Q.
11 The perpendicular bisector of the chord AB which passes through the centre C.

CHAPTER 16

Exercise 16a   page 316

1 96°, 132°, 60°, 42°, 30°
2 128°, 152°, 48°, 24°, 8°
3 303°, 3°, 30°, 24°
4 84°, 204°, 48°, 24°
5 144°, 48°, 80°, 88°
6 96°, 120°, 36°, 72°, 36°
7 108°, 180°, 40°, 18°, 14°
8 72°, 13.5°, 85.5°, 94.5°, 54°, 40.5°

Exercise 16b   page 319

1 a business and professional

   b i $\frac{1}{12}$ ii $\frac{7}{36}$

2 a air conditioning

   b a little less

3 a i $\frac{1}{6}$ ii $\frac{1}{4}$

   b 20−39 and 40−59; under 10 and 60−79

Exercise 16c   page 321

	Mean	Mode	Median
1	4.43	2	4
2	14.1	12, 13 and 14	13.5
3	1.84	1.6	1.65
4	1.54	1.3 and 1.8	1.5

5 mean 119.2   median 124
   The median; one very low mark brings down the mean.
6 mean $7150   mode $5000   median $5000
   The mean. This suggests workers are paid a lot more than they are.
7 mean $180   mode $200   median $175
   The median because it is the lowest.
8 mean $21.22   median $18.10

Exercise 16d   page 323

1 2.00 (to 3 s.f)
2 3.8

3	a 4.28	b	5
4	a 3.64	b	6
5	a 1.57	b	1

Exercise 16e   page 325

1 2
2 1
3 3.5

4	a 3.5	b 3	c	3.48
5	a 2	b 1	c	2.2

Exercise 16f   page 327

1 a 39°, 12 noon c   36.3°
   b 36.6°   d 7 hours
   e no, readings between each hour not recorded
2 a i November   ii May
   b maybe for May to December
   c yes
   d e.g. Xmas cards
3 a 250 c
   b

Time after privatisation (years)	Value of share (cents)
1	300
2	350
3	430
4	520
5	530
6	560
7	590

   c the fourth year
   d an upward trend
4 a about 620 c
   b The share price is unlikely to maintain a steady 30 c rise for two years in a row.
5 a No; half-monthly sales figures would be about half the monthly sales, but sales can fluctuate a lot from week to week.
   b The overall sales for July were down on June; if sales increased in the first half of July, they must have slumped badly during the second half to give this downward trend for the month as a whole.

Exercise 16g   page 331

1 nominal
2 ordinal
3 interval
4 ratio
5 interval
6 nominal
7 ratio

Exercise 16i   page 335

1 **a** 68
   b 170
   c 30
   d 7 is a better estimate: 14 students took between 1 and 3 hours and some of these are likely to have spent 2 hours or longer
   e no; only 32 out of the 170 students took between 5 and 7 hours

2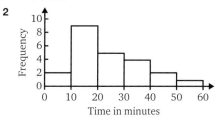

3 **a** 45
   b They were rounded up to the nearest half centimetre, or corrected to the nearest centimetre.
   c 28
   d the second group
   e We cannot know the height of the shortest student; his height lies between 150.5 cm and 155.5 cm.
   f 10; 6 students are at least 170.5 cm tall; 9 other students are between 165.5 cm and 170.5 cm tall and less than half of these (about 4) are likely to be taller than 168 cm.
   g About 10 students are in this range.
   h no

4 **a**

| Frequency | 7 | 13 | 7 |

   b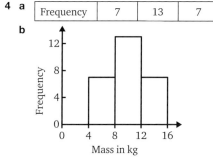

6 **a** Sally worked in units of 10 kg, from $50 < m \leqslant 60$ to $70 < m \leqslant 80$
   b Tom worked in units of 5 kg, from $50 < m \leqslant 55$ to $75 < m \leqslant 80$
   c Sally's chart is quicker to construct, but gives less detailed information.
   d Tom's chart takes longer to draw up, but gives more information.

7 **a** The second set gives a more even distribution of times; the average time taken on the second set was less.
   b Jenny was right; they discussed the problems they encountered on the first test before attempting the second. The second test may have been easier.
   c Yes; no one took as long as 13 minutes on the second test.

   d Nothing; we can only be sure that Sukei took no more than 12 minutes.
   e **i** This chart clearly separates and displays the two sets of data but it is not easy to compare them with one another.
       ii This one enables the heights of corresponding bars to be compared, but the second set cannot be easily pictured because the bars are displaced.

Exercise 16j   page 339

1 D   5 D   9 A   13 C
2 B   6 D   10 A   14 D
3 B   7 A   11 B
4 C   8 B   12 A

REVIEW TEST 3 page 342

1 C   4 B   7 A
2 C   5 D   8 C
3 C   6 D   9 D
10 **a** 12 : 7   **c** $144, $336
   b $\frac{7}{12}$ **d** 1 : 50 000
11 **a** 63 min   **b** 20 km
12 **a** 130%   **b** 75%   **c** 225   **d** 244
13 $\frac{1}{2}$ litre
14 **a** $73.60   **b** 308
15 **a** $182 020   **b** $54 020
16 **a** 40   **b** $496
17 $1892
18 **a** 10   **b** 20   **c** 4c
19 **a** $x = 50°, y = 130°, z = 70°$ **b** 6 cm, 60°
20 $a = 82°, b = 98°, c = 82°$
21 40.8 m³
22 $a = 80°, b = 75°, c = 25° \; d = 75°, e = 105°, f = 100°$
23 AC = 7.3 cm, BC = 5.2 cm, CD = 3.7 cm
24 **a**

Mass (kg)	Number
$40.5 \leqslant x < 45.5$	1
$45.5 \leqslant x < 50.5$	3
$50.5 \leqslant x < 55.5$	11
$55.5 \leqslant x < 60.5$	9
$60.5 \leqslant x < 65.5$	4
$65.5 \leqslant x < 70.5$	3

25 **a** 12.7 to 1 d.p.   **b** 15   **c** 13.5

REVIEW TEST 4 page 346

1 C   11 B   21 C   31 A
2 A   12 D   22 A   32 C
3 C   13 B   23 B   33 B
4 C   14 C   24 B   34 A
5 B   15 D   25 C   35 C
6 B   16 A   26 C   36 D
7 B   17 D   27 D   37 A
8 A   18 C   28 B   38 B
9 C   19 C   29 D   39 A
10 C   20 A   30 C   40 A

Index